Fund-Raising Fundamentals
A Guide to Annual Giving for Professionals and Volunteers

Fund-Raising Fundamentals

A Guide to Annual Giving for Professionals and Volunteers

JAMES M. GREENFIELD

John Wiley & Sons, Inc.

New York • Chichester • Brisbane • Toronto • Singapore

Credits: Exhibit 1.1, American Association of Fund-Raising Counsel, *Giving USA* (New York: AAFRC Trust for Philanthropy, 1993), 10–11.

Exhibit 1.3, Joseph R. Mixer, *Principles of Professional Fundraising* (San Francisco: Jossey Bass Publishers, Inc., 1993), 14. Reprinted with permission.

Exhibit 5.6 and 5.10, reprinted by permission of Prentice-Hall from *Nonprofit Organization Handbook* by Patricia and Daniel Gaby, copyright © 1979.

Exhibit 7.8, reprinted with permission from "Guidelines for Sponsorship Involving Charities and Companies," from *The Chronicle of Philanthropy,* June 1, 1993, 29.

Pages 240–241, reprinted from *The Ultimate Benefit Book: How to Raise $50,000-Plus for Your Organization,* copyright © 1987 by Marilyn E. Breutlinger and Judith M. Weiss. With special permission from Octavia Press, Cleveland, Ohio.

Exhibit 9.1, reprinted with permission of *The Chronicle of Philanthropy.*

The list on pp. 332–333 is reprinted with permission of *Fund Raising Management,* June 1993, 39.

This text is printed on acid-free paper.

This publication is designed to provide accurate and authoritative information in regard to the subject matter covered. It is sold with the understanding that the publisher is not engaged in rendering legal, accounting, or other professional services. If legal advice or other expert assistance is required, the services of a competent professional person should be sought. *From a Declaration of Principles jointly adopted by a Committee of the American Bar Association and a Committee of Publishers.*

Library of Congress Cataloging-in-Publication Data:

Greenfield, James M., 1936-
    Fund-raising fundamentals : a guide to annual giving for professionals and volunteers / James M. Greenfield.
       p.   cm. — (Nonprofit law, finance, and management series)
    Includes bibliographical references and index.
    ISBN 0-471-59535-7 (cloth : alk. paper). — ISBN 0-471-59534-9 (pbk. : alk. paper)
    1. Fund raising. 2. Nonprofit organizations—Finance. I. Title. II. Series.
HG177.G763   1994
658.15'224—dc20   93-35983

Printed in the United States of America

10 9 8 7 6 5 4 3 2 1

To all those who choose fund-raising as their profession and those who volunteer their time, talent, and treasure, year after year, to fulfill the vision and mission of their nonprofit organizations

Preface

To help finance their annual operating budgets, nonprofit organizations must raise money every year. It is fair to state that *annual giving* is the fund-raising method that acts as a fuel source; without it, nonprofit organizations would not be able to provide their programs and services to the public. Annual giving contributions are equally valuable because they are available for capital improvements, equipment, education, research, and a variety of other forms of quality improvement. Only a few organizations are financially independent, although many strive toward that goal. Organizations that have alternative revenue sources, and those that can draw on endowment earnings raised years before, may be less dependent on annual giving revenue for the substance of their operating budgets, but even these well-funded organizations will want to raise money every year to maintain the quality of their programs and to expand the services they provide for public benefit.

This book will concentrate on the methods and techniques of annual giving, one of the three areas of fund development practice. The other two areas—soliciting major gifts and offering planned giving programs—depend on a comprehensive annual giving program to prepare the volunteers, donors, and prospects they will need to succeed. Most nonprofit organizations use annual giving methods to raise the money they can spend immediately and to give donors the satisfaction of knowing that their money was used right away for the good works promised in the solicitation.

Annual giving is not an investment opportunity; there are no stockholders or venture capitalists investing gift dollars in hopes of making a profit in 12 months. Instead, volunteers and donors are investing their time, talent, and treasure by giving these personal resources away. They give them to the mission, purposes, goals, and objectives of each nonprofit organization they serve, because they believe their sacrifice will make a difference in the lives of others.

Do nonprofit organizations always seem to be asking for money? That is what an annual giving program is supposed to do. Many programs ask for a single gift each year; some ask more often but offer a variety of options for giving. Others, mostly churches, ask every·week. (Churches raise *half* the money given away each year in America.) Asking for money is only one part of what annual giving is all about. A comprehensive annual giving program is endlessly engaged in finding new donors, involving them as friends of the organization, and building a relationship that may eventually expand the level of their giving. Annual giving is the best way to initiate this kind of relationship. Fund-raising executives are the temporary custodians of the exchange between their organization and the people who invest in it; if the executives' efforts are successful, the number of friends and donors will increase each year as will their commitment to a mutually beneficial partnership. Annual giving programs possess these other benefits:

- Offer an active means for the organization to market its mission, purposes, goals, and objectives to a wide audience;
- Promote programs and services (and their benefits) to the public;
- Build respect, confidence, and trust through interaction with the community;
- Invite active public participation in accomplishing recognizable worthwhile goals.

This book is an in-depth presentation of the various methods and techniques of annual giving carried out by organizations that raise friends and build lasting relationships. Annual giving is the process that finds the many friends every nonprofit organization needs. Annual giving campaigns solicit gifts and then renew them year after year. Annual giving is *one of the most reliable sources* of revenue available to nonprofit organizations; major gifts and planned giving activities are the *sources of the most money.* The annual giving area requires hard work but it delivers high satisfaction. Managing an annual giving program is a complex and difficult skill because it is both art and science; yet, every fund-raising executive must learn how to succeed at it. Annual giving involves large numbers of people as donors; it also asks people for their time and energy while offering only a thank-you and good feelings in return. Most donors make several gifts each year, usually to six or eight nonprofit organizations plus their church or congregation. Annual giving is expensive to conduct but it is also profitable. Nonprofit organizations tend to underutilize annual giving because boards of directors and management too often see only its ability to deliver money.

All of these issues and perceptions are dealt with in conjunction with fulfilling the purposes of this book:

1. To explain the six principal methods used in annual giving and to describe how each of them functions (Chapters Two through Eight);
2. To explain how each method builds on the others to raise money, make friends, and build relationships with donors;
3. To explain other ways to raise money every year and demonstrate how they add to (but do not replace) the six principal methods;
4. To describe how to manage a comprehensive annual giving program for maximum success.

The sequence of chapters will direct the reader through all the necessary steps, from beginning an annual giving program (by testing lists) to managing a comprehensive enterprise that uses multiple methods every year and is carried out at maximum efficiency and effectiveness. The principles discussed in Chapters Two through Eight are illustrated with exhibits for the use in everyday practice. Sample letters, gift reports, and other documents show how each of these methods is put into action.

The Campaign to Clean Up America (CCUA) is a fictitious organization invented by Bruce R. Hopkins to illustrate the principles presented in his book, *A Legal Guide to Starting and Managing a Nonprofit Organization*, Second Edition (John Wiley & Sons, 1993). With his permission, I have created a Clean Up Cleveland Chapter of the CCUA and have focused on the decisions, actions, program implementations, and record-keeping methods of the Cleveland Chapter in relation to the topics covered in each chapter. The CCUA device links this book to the Hopkins classic as a companion book directed toward newer organizations. A short cast of characters has been created for the CCUA's Cleveland Chapter. These are the "people" who will bring these annual giving examples to life and will give the letters and reports emanating from Cleveland added reality:

The Campaign to Clean Up America—Clean Up Cleveland Chapter

National Chairman	Michael M. Activist

Cleveland Chapter Board of Directors

Chair of the Board	I. Harvey Clout
Vice Chair	Mary M. Moneybanks
Treasurer	Sidney M. Secure, CPA
Secretary	Theodosius "Ted" Worthy
Assistant Secretary	Titus Brown, APR

Members-at-Large	Steven Generous
	Iris B. Radiant
	Trafalgar "Telly" Temple

Board Committees	
Fund Development	Harold H. Connected
Gala Benefit Evening	Mary M. Moneybanks
	Trafalgar "Telly" Temple
	Iris B. Radiant

Fund Development Office	
Director	Karen I. Anderson
Executive Assistant	Alice B. Nice

A wealth of information is now available on the methods of annual giving described in this book. Chapter notes will identify the major resources where additional details are available. My advice to readers is: Search out and trust these experts; their wisdom is based on years of experience in doing exactly what you may be attempting to do for the first time. Additional resources and recommended readings are listed by topic, in the book's Selected References section. The volume of these materials is a sign that fund development has an evolving body of knowledge—a necessary step toward becoming a recognized profession. My hope is that those who use this book will find it helpful in building a reliable base of faithful friends whose annual gift support will move their nonprofit organizations forward.

The six keys to success in annual giving are easy to memorize:

1. Vision is mission.
2. Leadership is key.
3. Volunteers are golden.
4. Asking is required.
5. Giving is voluntary.
6. Donors must be recognized.

From this book, you will understand their meaning and their importance to successful annual giving efforts.

JAMES M. GREENFIELD

Newport Beach, California
November, 1993

Acknowledgments

Annual giving may be the most challenging area in all of fund-raising because it demands constant creativity, enthusiasm, and energy, and immediate results. After 32 years in this profession and 32 annual giving campaigns, I can state with confidence that no two campaigns are alike. Most of what I have learned about annual giving methods and techniques has come from (a) the experience of directing them, (b) evaluation of their performance and application of the lessons learned, and (c) the thoughtful suggestions of many volunteers and donors.

Eight nonprofit organizations have been my schoolhouses; thousands of board members, volunteers, and donors have been my teachers. Friends and colleagues in professional associations have been my coaches and mentors, as have several of my office colleagues. We have learned together, through conferences and workshops, articles and books, informal meetings and networking. One of the true pleasures of this profession is the sharing nature of all its members; we benefit our organizations and ourselves by learning from one another. For this reason, I have dedicated this book to all those who practice annual giving every day.

The National Society of Fund Raising Executives (NSFRE) Library proved a valuable resource for many of the references cited in this book; I am indebted to Cathlene Williams and Jeff Arnold for their consistent helpfulness and rapid response to my many inquiries for service.

A special thank you to my friend, Susan Golden, President of The Golden Group in Cleveland, Ohio. With her unfailing good humor and special knowledge of her hometown, she verified that all names, addresses, and telephone numbers in the Clean Up Cleveland feature were indeed fictitious! For this and all your helpful suggestions, Susan, I thank you.

I remain indebted to the team at John Wiley & Sons for all their support, especially to Marla Bobowick, Acquisitions Editor, for her encouragement in writing a second book and her many helpful suggestions for its improvement. Special thanks are also due to Maryan Malone of Publications Development Company of Texas, a superb manuscript editor whose ability to grasp any new subject gives quality to this effort. Their support of this book from start to finish is appreciated.

J.M.G.

Contents

List of Exhibits

CHAPTER ONE

Developing Annual Gift Support by Raising Friends and Building Relationships

For all of philanthropic practice, there are two overarching questions:

1. Why do we exist?
2. What's the money for?

These questions deserve great answers; in fact, many great answers will be needed. The purposes of annual giving go beyond merely raising money; that alone is an inadequate and insufficient answer to why we exist. The true objective is to find and build a constituency of friends who are willing to join a cause. During the period of their friendship, they will be encouraged to expand their relationship to active involvement that may last a lifetime. To build such friendships and life-long relationships between people and causes, charitable organizations must send these encouraging messages every year, communicating them through the medium of annual giving. Effective communication through annual giving programs will require careful thought, extensive preparation, and an efficient and effective delivery system.

A nonprofit organization begins by identifying the values that characterize it and by studying its "vision" of itself—what it has done and is doing now, and what its plans are for the future. This vision contains the fundamental values incorporated into the mission statement. They explain why the organization was formed, what its continuing goals are, what benefits it intends to provide to others, and why its functions are of value and should continue. Henry Rosso [1] writes that the mission statement "expresses more than justification for existence and more than just a definition of goals and objectives. It defines the value system that will guide program strategies. The mission is the magnet that will attract and hold the interests of trustees, volunteers, staff, and contributors." The mission statement should use clear language to describe the programs and services to be offered and to explain how the vision will be carried out and how the results will be achieved. Charitable organizations use several philanthropic practices—stewardship, volunteerism, a charitable purpose, and public advocacy, among others—to enable them to achieve their vision and fulfill their mission. "People helping people" is both the method and the model; helping, which implies action, is something everyone can do. Philanthropy, or what Robert Payton [2] calls "voluntary action for the public good," connotes association with others in the community and is the chief means to carry out the mission.

Once the mission is understood and the programs to fulfill it are in place, an organization must study its charitable purpose, an attribute that denotes altruism and enlightened self-interest. Donors give time or money to a charitable purpose that will help other people because they appreciate the implied mutuality of dependence that people have for one another. A charitable act is a social exchange that occurs each time a gift is made. The decision to make a gift comes after being asked by someone else, someone who is trusted by the donor. A gift implies a considerable amount of confidence and trust in both the solicitor and the charitable organization's ability (and faithfulness) to "do the right thing" with the money or, at the very least, to do no harm. Charitable behavior is a personal virtue advocated in every religious tradition; every citizen has the freedom to practice charity. To help another person or a cause can be practiced alone, between two people, or among millions acting together. Over centuries, the concept of charitable action has evolved into the practice of philanthropy today. Philanthropy requires a generosity of spirit that can be practiced anywhere and everywhere, at any time; it can accomplish any "charitable" purpose, and often will be accompanied by public recognition. Philanthropy has flowered in America, partly because of the protection it has enjoyed from the federal government since the ten amendments known as the Bill of Rights were added to the Constitution of the United States. The First Amendment states:

1. Congress shall make no laws respecting an establishment of religion, or prohibiting the free exercise thereof; or abridging the freedom of speech, or of the press; or the right of the people peaceably to assemble, and to petition the government for a redress of grievances.

Government has joined in philanthropic practice by legitimizing its reason to exist. Government also advocates that its citizens engage in charitable acts because these acts improve the common good. In most nations, government is responsible for a wide spectrum of public services. By contrast, whole areas of American enterprise, from the arts to education, from social welfare to healthcare, from religion to civic causes, are often carried out by citizens, acting alone or together. The consensus in America is that government cannot and should not be involved in many of these areas. There is also agreement that some areas of public activity can be better served when government, business, and philanthropy act together. This agreement is one of the most sacred privileges in the people's possession, a personal freedom that encourages them to practice philanthropy. Brian O'Connell [3] has given this perspective on the freedoms of the First Amendment:

> It is important to be reminded of the basic values of American society; the freedom, worth, and dignity of the individual; equal opportunity; justice; and mutual responsibility. Our largest vehicles for preserving and enhancing those basic values are:
> Representative government starting with one person/one vote;
> The freedoms of speech and assembly
> The free press
> A system of justice beginning with due process and presumption
>   of innocence
> University public education.

Philanthropic practice, or people acting together through charitable organizations, begins when active participation and financial support are requested from individuals, business, and the government itself. To be able to respond, the charitable organization must embody its vision and mission into a structure and an action plan. First, it must qualify as a charitable organization by being incorporated as a nonprofit, public benefit corporation in one of the 50 states. Second, it must be granted tax-exempt status by the federal government by qualifying as a pure public charity. The organization is then granted several privileges in exchange for its agreed-on obligation to perform one or more charitable activities, as described by Bruce Hopkins [4]:

> The federal tax definition of a charitable organization contains at least 15 different ways for a nonprofit entity to be charitable. These characteristics, found in the income tax regulations, IRS rulings, and federal and state court opinions, include: relieving the poor and distressed or the underprivileged; advancing religion, education, or science; lessening the burdens of government; beautifying and maintaining a community; preserving natural beauty;

promoting health, social welfare, environmental conservancy, arts, or patrio-
tism; caring for orphans or animals; promoting, advancing, and sponsoring
amateur sports; and maintaining public confidence in the legal system.

Over 20 subgroups or types of charitable organizations qualify under Section 501(c) of the Internal Revenue Code (IRC). Charitable organizations that demonstrate "charitable purposes" enjoy tax exemption
privileges on income, sales, and property, plus a charitable contribution
deduction for donors who make gifts. Organizations that qualify as
"501(c)(3) organizations" (Section 501(c), subsection (3) of the IRC) are
also permitted to engage in tax-exempt bond financing, to claim school
tax exemptions, to enjoy reduced postal rates, and to be relieved of federal unemployment taxes and corporate net income taxes, except where
they may qualify for unrelated business income tax (UBIT).

This impressive array of privileges is enhanced by the public benefits
and "good works" performed by each charitable organization. In all of
this activity, it is not organizations that act; it is the people within them
and the people who act through them on behalf of others. People exercise
a mutual obligation to care for one another through their voluntary association. In so doing, they take on themselves certain duties and responsibilities as owners of charitable organizations and stewards of the public's
trust. Their efforts succeed in building a new community, one that will
be held together by their commitment to carry out a charitable purpose.
This new community adds to its membership volunteers and staff,
friends and donors, clients and their families, and others who share in
the responsibility of doing their best to improve the human condition by
fulfilling the mission of the charitable organization.

Philanthropy holds a mirror to society's pluralism where the acts of
others fulfill the needs of all of its members. Hopkins [5], describing a
truly democratic state, warns that "the power to influence and cause
changes cannot be concentrated in one sector of that state or society.
There must be a 'pluralization of institutions' in society, a fancy way of
saying that the ability to bring about changes and the accumulation of
power cannot belong to just one sector—inevitably, the government."
Those who become active as members of a charitable organization become directly responsible for its welfare, whether they are board members, management, employees, or clients; all are bonded to the vision
and mission and become advocates of the organization's reason to exist.
Other memberships are filled by government, business, nonclients (or
not-yet clients), volunteers, and donors, who also join and become partners to the mission. John Gardner [6], founder of Common Cause,
has summarized the status of nonprofits in the United States: "In the
realm of good works this nation boasts a unique blending of private

and governmental effort. There is almost no area of educational, scientific, charitable, or religious activity in which we have not built an effective network of private institutions." With everything in order, and having been sanctioned with legal form by the government, charitable organizations go forth to fulfill their mission to benefit others. The philanthropic process has begun.

THE PHILANTHROPIC PROCESS

The philanthropic process has many parts. We have touched briefly on only the most essential ingredients: the vision and mission; rights of assembly, association, and community; charitable purposes and public benefits; and legal form. Legal form may be complex but it is necessary to all that follows. A charitable organization established by citizens must be constituted correctly as a nonprofit, public benefit corporation. Each such entity is a substantial enterprise and, as the chrysalis becomes the fragile but beautiful butterfly, it will require vigilant attention by all its members to preserve its life and to enhance its beauty. Volunteers who serve on its board of directors assume the stewardship of the public's trust on their collective shoulders; it is their duty to demand that everything be completely legal. To lose the government's endorsement is to cause the association to forfeit its benefits and privileges, cease to provide its public benefits, divide its property, and "wind up" its existence. Worst of all, it will lose public trustworthiness, a failure in its purpose for existence. Without legal form and public trust, no matter how lofty the vision or how humane the mission, they will go unfulfilled. Gardner [7] evaluated the importance of the independent sector in this ringing tribute:

> If it were to disappear from our national life, we would be less distinctly American. The [independent] sector enhances our creativity, enlivens our communities, nurtures individual responsibility, stirs life at the grassroots, and reminds us that we were born free. Its vitality is rooted in good soil—civic pride, compassion, a philanthropic tradition, a strong problem-solving impulse, a sense of individual responsibility and, despite what cynics may say, an irrepressible commitment to the great shared task of improving our life together.

To live up to these ideals, the members of each charitable organization must be active participants in the philanthropic process. They must recruit community residents and business executives to serve as board members, ask others to volunteer their time and talents, and invite the public to share in the organization's financial support. The domain of philanthropy has remarkable diversity, substantial numbers, economic power, and enormous public impact, all of which should be represented in the board, volunteers, and donor membership. Collectively, America's charitable organizations or independent sector are referred to as the third sector, after business and government, out of respect for their accepted value to the nation. When the domain of philanthropy joins in partnership with business and government, philanthropy shines as the uniquely American example of a democratic triumph.

John D. Rockefeller 3rd [8], long associated with highly visible philanthropic achievements, once commented:

> A healthy third sector keeps government honest, provides alternative ways to solve problems, helps maintain institutions that should *not* be taken over by government, and provides opportunities for the initiative and sense of caring that are the indispensable bedrock of a thriving democracy. . . . There is, however, a common thread that runs through the third sector; a belief in being of service to one's community and other people, without relying on government and without any expectation of personal profit. At the heart of the third sector is individual initiative and a sense of caring. . . . This means that the oldest form of support, philanthropic giving, is still the most important. It provides the crucial margin that gives third-sector institutions their most precious asset—independence.

The sections that follow will discuss philanthropic practice, the independent sector and the nature of charitable organizations, and the fund development process, all in preparation for study of the comprehensive annual giving program.

PHILANTHROPIC PRACTICE

The vision and mission of a nonprofit organization will answer the first of the two overarching questions: Why do we exist? The second question, What's the money for?, is far easier to answer when the vision and mission are known; without them, the message is only about money. In the vision and mission statements, dreams take shape and form, practical applications become visible through actual programs and services delivered, and defined purposes, goals, and objectives measure the results. All of these goals are brought to life through philanthropic practice. Philanthropic practice is volunteerism in action, and, says Payton [9], "[I]t might be argued that philanthropy is an essential defining characteristic of civilized society." It is expressed by people in several forms, from leadership and governance to public solicitation and giving. Hours of time and energy are given freely by people every year; they also share their personal talents, their assets, and other human and material resources. Why do they do it? A trio of leading analysts has offered these reasons [10]:

> People benefit from serving others. The most important benefits are satisfactions: spiritual, moral, and psychological. We accept the psychological evidence that voluntary service in behalf of others enhances self-esteem and self-worth. The secret seems to lie in the liberation of the self from its own preoccupations by sympathy for and empathy with others. . . . Voluntary acts of compassion and acts of community are always needed, in all societies, and always will be.

None of these valued attributes should be taken for granted; they must be developed with care and attention by charitable organizations.

Leadership is essential to success in any enterprise, including the charitable organization; volunteerism is second only to leadership in its importance to philanthropic practice. Leadership and volunteerism encourage others to make the effort to join in. Everyone is not a leader, and all leaders cannot serve at the same time. Nonprofit organizations are no more alike than are the types of business or the levels of government, and they do not act alike. Despite their high motives and good intentions, some people may not have the knowledge and skill needed to govern others nor the experience required to manage charitable organizations with effectiveness and efficiency. Their place may be as volunteers and there is much to be done by volunteers, including asking others for their annual gift once a year.

Philanthropic practice includes this asking for gifts. Few gifts are made without a request first being delivered in some way. Solicitation is believed by some people to be confrontational, a one-way conversation. Saying "no" is seen as a far easier thing to do than asking. For some people, asking for gifts is another form of sales, and, like sales everywhere, it is assertive, even aggressive at times. They are uncomfortable with this assignment. What is most important to the solicitation is that making gifts is a *voluntary act* each and every time. Giving is the result of an invitation; a reply is requested. Asking for money for charitable purposes is not begging. Gift appeals by charitable organizations, says Harold Seymour [11], "should aim high, provide prospective, arouse a sense of history and continuity, convey a feeling of importance, relevance, and urgency, and have whatever stuff is needed to warm the heart and stir the mind." Philanthropic practice is carried out by sharing valid needs with selected audiences who are invited to lend their support. The act of giving is the servant to philanthropic practice and is carried out whenever money or time is given. Not everyone is willing to ask friends for money; those who prefer not to ask can give their energy and talents to other areas. What is valuable in all of these actions is the volunteerism itself. Every citizen has this opportunity. More should try it; they might like it. For philanthropic practice to succeed, gifts of money are required. Everyone who asks others to give should make his or her own personal gift each year. Those who are asked should consider the invitation seriously; many do, and they make a contribution. In fact, most of the people who decide to give will make more than one gift to a charitable organization each year. Despite this generosity, raising money is not the end to be achieved; it is only the means to the end. Fund-raising follows leadership, volunteerism, and public generosity toward fulfillment of the vision and mission. Of all the acts of philanthropic practice, the privilege and freedom of voluntary giving may be the least understood and the least appreciated.

THE INDEPENDENT SECTOR AND THE NATURE OF CHARITABLE ORGANIZATIONS

After many years of acting alone or in groupings by type of organization or service provided (the arts, colleges, museums, and so on), the great variety of charitable organizations active in America began to come together, drawn by common needs for advocacy, communications, research studies, and threats of governmental regulation. The Tax Reform Act of 1969, which imposed operating regulations and excise taxes on private foundations, may have served as the catalyst for this awakening. The 1975 report of "the Filer Commission" [12] included a specific recommendation "that a permanent national commission on the nonprofit sector be established by Congress." True to the American tradition, private citizens began the organization instead, and Independent Sector was founded in 1980 under the leadership of John Gardner and Brian O'Connell. Within its mission was the responsibility to serve as the collective spokesperson and rallying point for the variety of nonprofit organizations that exist in America. The sheer size and diversity of the independent sector may come as a surprise to many readers. Harvey Dale [13] described these dimensions in 1991:

> It is estimated to comprise more than 1.3 million organizations, of which more than two-thirds are charities or social-welfare entities (which together make up the so-called independent sector). Nearly 10 percent of the U.S. labor force works in that sector. The net value of assets held by charities alone is probably in excess of $300 billion today. Charitable giving in this country has exceeded $100 billion annually for the past few years. Even that

large number has accounted for less than 30 percent of the receipts of the independent sector; *total* annual receipts—which also included dues, fees, charges, investment income, and government payments—exceeded $325 billion in 1987 and must be greater now. By any measure, the independent sector in our country is very substantial.

The Internal Revenue Service (IRS) reported in 1993 that the number of 501(c)(3) charitable organizations stood at 546,100 (excluding churches, integrated auxiliaries, and subordinate units) out of a total of 1,140,388 tax-exempt organizations registered with the IRS [14]. Total giving in America for 1992 was $124.31 billion, a 6.4 percent increase over 1991 (see Exhibit 1.1).

The authority to guide each of these charitable organizations rests with the board of directors. The directors are men and women who act on behalf of their organization's self-interest; they guide their enterprise toward fulfillment of its vision and mission, its reason to exist. "Mission is entrusted to the governing board, and governance entails stewardship" [15]. The directors accept with equal duty their

| | Billions | | | Percent |
	1991	1992	Percent	Change
Sources of Contributions:				
Individuals	$ 95.32	$101.83	81.9%	+6.8%
Bequests	7.78	8.15	6.6	+4.8
Foundations	7.72	8.33	6.7	+7.9
Corporations	6.00	6.00	4.8	+0.0
Totals	$116.82	$124.31	100.0%	+6.4%
Uses of Contributions:				
Religion	$ 53.92	$ 56.71	45.6%	+5.2%
Education	13.45	14.02	11.3%	+4.2
Human Services	11.11	11.57	9.3	+4.2
Health/Hospitals	9.68	10.24	8.2	+5.8
Arts/Culture	8.81	9.32	7.5	+5.9
Advocacy/Public Policy	4.93	5.05	4.1	+2.4
Environment/Wildlife	2.93	3.12	2.5	+6.5
International/Foreign	1.75	1.71	1.4	−2.3
Undesignated	10.25	12.56	10.1	n.a.
Totals	$116.82	$124.31	100.0%	+6.4%

Exhibit 1.1   *Giving USA's* National Annual Giving Data: Total Philanthropy in America

accountability to the public for the actions of the organization, its employees and staff, its clients, and its financial affairs, and for all of its assets. It is not an overstatement that the ultimate responsibility for the existence and welfare of the organization rests with the board of directors. It is also fair to propose, although each board has its well-defined duties, that board members serve as a collective example to everyone else within the entire independent sector, not just one organization. Given such levels of responsibility, the members of the board of directors are well-advised to study the following standards [16]:

First, the nonprofit board has and uses a systematic process for assessing the strengths and weaknesses of the composition of the current board. Strengths and weaknesses are usually assessed in terms of demographic characteristics, expertise, and skills, and the result is a board profile.

Second, the board profile is used to identify the personal characteristics and expertise/skills desired in new recruits to the board.

Third, recruitment of potential board members is systematic and rigorous in that potential members are thoroughly informed as to the mission and goals of the organization; its financial condition; and the time, effort, level of contributions, and fund-raising activities expected of them. Potential members are interviewed by a board committee (and perhaps the full board) as to their motives and interests in volunteering for board service.

Fourth, new board members receive additional, thorough training and orientation beyond that provided during recruitment and selection.

Fifth, board members commit significant time to board duties, not only attending board and committee meetings but also preparing for meetings and undertaking other assignments, perhaps including fund-raising activities.

Sixth, board meetings are characterized by a process through which all are encouraged to participate and disagreement is welcomed, while relationships are collegial and consensual. The board works as a team.

Seventh, the board uses processes of assessing the performance of the board as a whole and the performance of individual members. The board has and follows standards of removing members who do not perform.

Eighth, the board's chief tasks are to (a) select, evaluate, and, if necessary, dismiss the chief executive; (b) define and periodically reevaluate the organization's mission and major goals, develop a strategic plan, and approve budgets and policy statements consistent with the plan; and (c) ensure that the organization obtains the resources necessary to meet the plan.

THE ROLE OF FUND DEVELOPMENT

Vision and mission can lift the spirit; leadership and volunteerism provide the example others are to follow. What are others asked to do?

How can the public be involved in the mission and in the programs and services that carry it out? Great answers will again be required. The fund development department has the major responsibility for financial support but also has many duties other than raising money. Fund development is often where the public's invitation to participate is centered, where communications begin and continue, and where opportunities for a lifetime of involvement can be fulfilled. Fund development performs a variety of essential services for nonprofit organizations because its methodology demands planning, marketing, promotion, and community relations. Some may choose to believe that these services are the result of fund development activities, but it is important to understand that they must be carried out before fund development can succeed. Lastly, fund development is the area with primary responsibility for raising friends and building relationships for nonprofit organizations. These uses for fund development in philanthropic practice have been defined in many ways; one of the best was provided by Seymour [17]: "Development is the planned promotion of understanding, participation, and support." Fund development is how and where the public is invited to join the cause, to give of their time, talent, and treasure, and to become an active part of a solution to meet human needs. The several methods and techniques of fund-raising are the tools used for (not the purpose of) fund development. The grand design for their use can be illustrated as a pyramid that has three levels of fund-raising activity: (1) annual giving, (2) major giving, and (3) estate or planned giving (see Exhibit 1.2). Volunteers and donors are invited to begin their relationship by accepting information about the organization. Building the relationship will take time and will involve repeated opportunities for giving. In this way, their interest and personal involvement will increase to a level where investment decisions will be made. To spearhead the attainment of these levels of continuing relationships, fund development will be asked to play several roles. Among them are the following:

Building community.

Responding, not directing.

Being a catalyst to facilitate action.

Finding opportunities for investment in humanity.

Being dynamic because the mission and cause are dynamic.

Seeking a design to accomplish objectives, not merely to give money away.

Viewing solicitations as a "contact sport," not a duty or chore.

Offering a means for donors to fulfill their aspirations.

Using social exchange to achieve higher purposes.

Working always, *always* in the future.

Being more artist that scientist.

Fund-raising is a "'responsibility system,' ethical at its base and tied to a larger complex of authority, control, and responsibility. Honesty, openness, and accountability are therefore essential to the integrity and credibility of fund-raisers. The professional fund-raiser is ethical and virtuous as well; wholehearted, persistent, and impartial" [18]. The purpose of fund-raising is more than marketing, more than promotion,

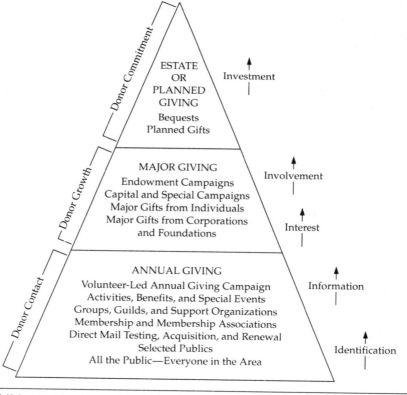

Exhibit 1.2   The Pyramid of Giving

more than the money raised. Its value is in the results accomplished by the organization's use of the money. Fund development is the process where mission and purposes are matched with the public's desire to help; "people helping people" is carried out through fund development activities. Peter F. Drucker [19] has described its evolution:

> [A] non-profit institution that becomes a prisoner of money-raising is in serious trouble and in a serious identity crisis. The purpose of a strategy for raising money is precisely to enable the non-profit institution to carry out its mission without subordinating that mission to fund-raising. This is why non-profit people have now changed the term they use from "fund-raising" to "fund development." Fund-raising is going around with a begging bowl, asking for money because the *need* is so great. Fund development is creating a constituency which supports the organization because it *deserves* it. It means developing what I call a membership that participates through giving.

The stars of fund development are donors. They are the best friends a nonprofit organization can hope to have; retaining their friendship and expanding their relationship are the primary duties of the fund development program. The value of donors and of what they give enables charitable purposes to be carried out and aids realization of the vision and mission. The objectives may be clear, but donors' motives for giving are complex. They are a mixture of feelings, values, fond wishes, and a sincere desire to make a difference—all of which can be nurtured with praise and public recognition. Donors possess considerable influence within this relationship. They can be offended and upset by errors and mistakes and, in the next instant, can be consumed with satisfaction about the good they have made happen. Many donors begin giving with a glow of enlightened self-interest. In time, these same donors grow to appreciate that what they can do with their money is less important than what philanthropic practices can do with their money for others. Among donors' motives for making gifts are:

1. To be charitable and to help others.
2. To enjoy ego satisfaction.
3. To gain public recognition.
4. To achieve public respect.
5. To observe religious guidelines (and rewards).
6. To participate in a worthy cause.
7. To join with others in a common purpose.
8. Because the organization has a good public image.

9. Because they have confidence in the organization and they trust it to use their money well.

10. Because the organization has good people in leadership positions.

11. Because the organization is fiscally sound and operationally well-managed.

12. Because they were asked to give.

Many more factors are at work in each gift decision. Some donors may give on impulse, others because of a genuine interest, and a few according to an integrated giving plan [20]. Everyone may possess any number of complex (even competing) motives that occur with each gift decision. The objective of fund development is not to manipulate donor motives but, by understanding them better, to be able to assist each donor to fulfill his or her aspirations through gift support. Donor behavior is much more than a single gift decision or one episode of giving, and it may be triggered by internal motivations and external influences (see Exhibit 1.3). Donors achieve personal values from giving—beyond the tax deduction, if they choose to claim it. The spirit of altruism, of "people helping people," is an act of charity at the highest level. Such gifts are made without expectation of anything in return other than the courtesy of a "thank-you" letter or a receipt. "Philanthropy is misunderstood when it is reduced to any one of its elements; therefore, fund-raising is not the whole of philanthropy and is about more than money, being inextricably tied to philanthropic values, purposes, and methods" [21]. All donors may not be satisfied with the mere exchange of money; some may want to participate in philanthropic practice. For this type of donor, volunteerism is the answer most of the time. Donors will benefit from actions taken on behalf of others, even if they perform no action and receive no material rewards for their efforts. The fund development process must acknowledge that donors are deserving of appropriate recognition for their good works. Donor relations affirms the quality of action taken more than the amount given. Every gift is worthy of justifiable praise and should be acknowledged by the nonprofit organization. Those who are able to give more in a single donation may indeed receive more attention, but their accolades should be the same as those for every other donor whose cumulative giving eventually achieves the same level of support. Nonprofit organizations must be alert to the danger of selling recognition in exchange for the promise of rewards, no matter how a donor has indicated a desire to receive them. Among the ethics of philanthropic

Internal Motivations	External Influences
Personal or "I" Factors	*Rewards*
Acceptance of self or self-esteem	Recognition
Achievement	Personal
Cognitive interest	Social
Growth	
Guilt reduction or avoidance	*Stimulations*
Meaning or purpose of life	Human needs
Personal gain or benefit	Personal request
Spirituality	Vision
Immortality	Private initiative
Survival	Efficiency and effectiveness
	Tax deductions
Social or "We" Factors	*Situations*
Status	Personal involvement
Affiliation	Planning and decision making
Group endeavor	Peer pressure
Interdependence	Networks
Altruism	Family involvement
Family and progeny	Culture
Power	Tradition
	Role identity
	Disposable income
Negative or "They" Factors	
Frustration	
Unknown situations	
Insecurity	
Fear and anxiety	
Complexity	

Exhibit 1.3 Framework for Determining Why People Give. Reprinted with permission from *Principles of Professional Fundraising* by Joseph R. Mixer (San Francisco: Jossey Bass Publishers, 1993), 14.

practice are fairness and equality to all who give and to whom appropriate recognition can be offered.

Ethical fund raising is the prod, the enabler, the activator to gift making. It must also be the conscience to the process. Fund raising is at its best when it strives to match the needs of the not-for-profit organization with the contributor's need and desire to give. The practice of gift seeking is justified when it exalts the contributor, not the gift seeker. It is justified when it is used as a responsible invitation, guiding contributors to make the kind of gift that will meet their own special needs and add greater meaning to their lives [22].

THE ROLE OF ANNUAL GIVING

Annual giving programs, the front lines of fund development, are where most people become involved with nonprofit organizations, where most of the gift exchange takes place, and where the greatest variety of fund-raising methods and techniques is found. Annual giving may be the entire fund-raising program of nonprofit organizations that depend on the income from their annual giving appeals to cover their annual operating expenses. Annual giving combines identifying and recruiting new donors with renewing and upgrading previous donors. Annual giving is also a means to expand the involvement and participation of current donors at all levels through membership associations or induction into donor clubs, guilds, and support organizations. Annual giving offers a great variety of opportunities for donors to become active as volunteers and to exercise leadership, especially in the popular areas of activities, benefits, and special events. Identification and recruitment of new donors and continuation of the commitment of prior donors remain constant through all of these annual giving methods. These techniques offer a rich multitude of opportunities for taking philanthropic practice beyond just asking for money. Friend-raising and relationship-building should be at their peak when all these opportunities are available!

WHAT TO USE IN MAKING ANNUAL GIFTS

Does every gift qualify as being tax-deductible? No; tax deductibility depends on what is given, to whom it is given, and the amounts of other charitable deductions in the same year. What then can people use to make a gift each year? People can give cash and currency, pledges, gifts of securities, gifts of personal property, gifts-in-kind, and donated services.

Cash and Currency

Cash, checks, and money orders are the most common forms of giving. Credit card charges are also available with most nonprofit organizations. Depending on the card used, a small service fee (up to 3 percent) may be assessed. The amount charged is received by the organization right away as a full-value donation. The IRS rules permit a total charitable contribution deduction of up to 50 percent of a donor's adjusted gross income for the year of the gift, with a five-year carryover of any excess deduction value. However, only a donor who files an itemized ("long form") return will be able to claim the deduction. (Nonitemizers lost their deduction for gifts to charity under the 1986 Tax Reform Act.)

Pledges

The use of pledges for annual gifts is less common than cash and currency and incurs administrative costs for record-keeping, billing, and collections. Because of the general nature of annual giving, cash is preferred: the organization will use the money as soon as it is received. Pledges are necessary when solicitation is performed over the telephone or on radio or television, or if payment is arranged via payroll deductions by the employer. (United Way has pioneered this simple but effective payment plan.) Because most annual giving programs are tied to the calendar or tax year, the pledge period normally ends on December 31. Alternatively, it may end on the fiscal year-end date of the organization. Pledges have the potential for some amount of nonpayment, depending on the solicitation method used and the time period allowed. Pledges may disappear in light of recent Financial Accounting Standards Board (FASB) recommendations that they be counted as revenue for their full value when received, and then treated as assets [23]. If unpaid, the organization has the obligation to pursue payment, including legal redress—a set of conditions not likely to be viewed as conducive to donors' making formal pledges in the future.

Gifts of Securities

Stocks and bonds are valuable assets, but they have changing market value. Donors may choose to act when stock values are up, or a securities gift decision can be deferred until market conditions are favorable. Most annual gifts involving securities are modest in size (under $5,000 in value) and will occur before the tax year ends. Donors expect the stock to be sold so that the proceeds can be used toward annual giving priorities. If securities are sold by a donor and the proceeds are delivered as a gift to charity, the donor will be assessed a capital gains tax on the sale. Donors should be advised to give the securities to the charity instead of proceeds from their sale. Using this method, capital gains are deductible at full market value, subject to the deduction limit of 30 percent of the donor's adjusted gross income in the year of the gift, with a five-year carryover. The tax law changed in mid-1993 regarding gifts of appreciated property. Qualified gifts were removed from the alternative minimum tax (AMT) calculation—good news for generous donors and their favorite nonprofit organizations. Calculation of the charitable contribution value for gifts of securities requires three steps, in keeping with IRS regulations:

1. Establish the value for gifts of securities by calculating the mean average price of the stock on the date when ownership was transferred to the charity.
2. Verify the calculation (a) with a broker and (b) in the next business day's edition of a newspaper that carries the stock exchange listing (*The Wall Street Journal* or *The New York Times,* for example).
3. Confirm the gift value in writing to the donor.

Gifts of Personal Property

This category includes anything other than cash, securities, and real estate, and has two subcategories: intangible personal property and tangible personal property. The method to complete the transfer of a gift of intangible personal property (stocks and bonds, patents, copyrights) is the same as for gifts of securities. Transfer of tangible personal property is more complex and requires extreme care. Examples of tangible personal property include art works, antiques, collectibles, cars, boats, computers, china, silverware, and similar valuables. The IRS rules are clear but not widely understood. Nonprofit organizations are advised to observe IRS procedures with exactitude in order to protect their donors. If a donor created the donated item, this donor may deduct only his or her cost of materials. If the donor purchased the item, the donor may claim full appreciated value if the donee organization's use of the item is related to its exempt purpose. If the item is for unrelated use, the donor may claim only the cost of acquiring the item. If the value of any item is $5,000 or more, the claim for deductibility must be authenticated in writing by a certified professional appraiser, at the donor's expense. Further, a copy of the appraisal must be signed by the donor and the nonprofit organization and attached to IRS Form 8283, which accompanies the donor's annual tax return. If the organization sells the item within two years after its receipt, it must report the amount of the sale to the IRS on Form 8282. The IRS will compare the appraisal value with the sale value and may challenge the donor's claim if there is a noticeable difference between these two figures.

Gifts-in-Kind

Some donors are in a position to give goods and services that can be used for charitable purposes in lieu of cash, securities, or personal property. Called gifts-in-kind, these are donations that can be valuable when they are directly usable for the organization's charitable purposes or in direct support of an activity, benefit, or special event. Examples are free or reduced-price printing of invitations, programs, or tickets by a professional printer; decorations and flowers from a florist; food from a caterer or wholesaler; table favors from local merchants; wine and similar items from appropriate sources. Gifts-in-kind can help to reduce the direct costs of staging an event and allow greater net proceeds to the nonprofit organization. As with gifts of personal property, tax deductibility rules are precise and the same validation procedures must be followed each time.

Donated Services

People's time has value and the time and talent they give to nonprofit organizations is no less valuable, but the IRS does not allow any charitable deduction for contributions of personal time and talent. Deductions are allowed for unreimbursed expenses connected with a donation of services, mileage, tools, and parking (or the cost of transportation to and from the site where the services were provided). The FASB has allowed contributions of services to be recognized at the fair value of services received (but not recognized as revenue). The qualifications include whether "the services received (a) create or enhance nonfinancial assets or (b) require specialized skills, are provided by individuals possessing those skills, and would typically need to be purchased if not provided by donation" [24].

This book will present the entire panorama of annual giving programs, illustrating how the various methods and techniques are used to invite people to become donors, and how to build an initial gift relationship into long-term active participation by the donor in the life of the organization. The relationship begins with list selection and testing by mail and, through a series of expanding steps, it progresses into a comprehensive annual giving program. The testing determines who should receive the invitations and how to explain the vision and mission. "Roll out" invitations are part of the direct mail program, and a renewal cycle follows quickly afterward. Membership adds "belonging"—being part of a group of other donors—and other forms of association such as donor clubs, guilds, and support organizations offer further enhancement. With structured groups and volunteer leadership in place, the annual giving program gains advantages from inviting the public to join in its activities, benefits, and special events. All of these resources help the organization to build a base of continuing donors that is broad enough to support volunteer-led personal solicitation. Using an "annual campaign" model, the organization can give these most faithful donors the personal attention they require. Along the way, there will be multiple opportunities to experiment with one or more of the "other ways to raise money every year" (see Chapter Nine). The scope and magnitude of this entire effort, which can be implemented within a period of three to five years, require professional management and direction by fund development staff from the beginning.

The methods and techniques used in annual giving are not the most efficient forms of fund-raising. Each can and should be managed with efficiency and productivity on its own merits, but that is all that can be expected. The methods' greater value is in their collective ability to generate enthusiasm and a broad base of faithful followers. By tracking the results, using the formats shown in Exhibits 1.4, 1.5, and 1.6, progress can be monitored in three areas of activity respectively: (1) sources of giving, (2) purposes and uses of funds raised, and (3) results of each annual giving method. Monitoring of the sources of gifts will disclose where increases and decreases in the number of donors occur as well as their level of support and average gift size. The report on purposes and uses of funds raised reveals the degree to which the public has accepted the priority of needs request with funds in the areas needed. Each fund-raising method used in annual giving will perform differently and each method used should be reported. The number of gifts each is able to provide, the gift income, and the average gift size are valuable performance measurements.

Throughout the book, there will be references to several basic principles. As already stated, the first purpose of annual giving is to raise friends and build relationships for the organization. Money follows

Sources of Annual Gifts	Number of Gifts	Gift Income	Average Gift Size
Trustees/Directors		$	$
Professional staff			
Employees			
New donors (acquisition)			
Prior donors (renewal)			
Membership associations			
Groups, guilds, and support organizations			
Activities, benefits, and special events			
Volunteer-led, personal solicitation campaigns			
Other annual giving programs in use			
Unsolicited gifts	_____	_____	_____
Totals		$	$

Exhibit 1.4   Report on Sources of Annual Gifts

Purposes or Uses of Annual Funds	Number of Gifts	Gift Income	Average Gift Size
Unrestricted cash		$	$
Capital and equipment funds			
Gifts restricted for:			
Programs			
Research			
Education			
Staff/Students			
Loan funds			
Unrestricted endowment			
Restricted endowment			
Other restricted purposes	————	————	————
Totals		$	$

Exhibit 1.5 Report on Purposes or Uses of Annual Funds

people; if enough people join in the cause, if the organization serves the cause well, and if a comprehensive annual giving program is in place, the money will follow. Annual giving programs must also possess flexibility. The roster of priority needs will be constantly changing as the nonprofit organization carries out its programs and services year after year. The unique challenge to annual giving is to be able to plan and execute as much activity as possible within 12 months, and to continue those plans and activities with the same enthusiasm, energy, and success in the next year, and the year after that. After three to five years, the results should begin to be reliable enough to forecast performance from year to year. Some advice, from experience: Go back and review the results of each method used. Review again the reasons why selected fund-raising programs were chosen. Measure how well they are doing today. When guidance is called for, turn to Tom Broce's "nine cardinal principles" of fund raising [25]:

I. Institutional or organizational objectives must be established first.

II. Development objectives must be established to meet institutional goals.

III. The kinds of support needed determine the kinds of fund-raising programs.

IV. The institution must start with natural prospects.

V. The case for the program must reflect the importance of the institution.

VI. Involvement is the key to leadership and support.

Annual Giving Programs	_Number of Gifts_	_Gift Income_	_Average Gift Size_
Direct mail tests		$	$
*1.			
2.			
Direct mail acquisition			
1.			
2.			
3.			
4.			
Direct mail renewal			
1.			
2.			
3.			
4.			
Membership associations			
1.			
2.			
Groups, guilds, and support organizations			
1.			
2.			
Activities, benefits, and special events			
1.			
2.			
3.			
4.			
Volunteer-led, personal solicitation campaigns			
1.			
2.			
Other annual giving programs in use			
1.			
2.			
Totals		$	$

* Number of programs in each category will vary.

Exhibit 1.6 Report on Results of Annual Giving Programs

VII. Prospect research must be thorough and realistic.

VIII. Cultivation is the key to successful solicitation.

IX.   Solicitation is successful only if Cardinal Principles I through VIII have been followed.

Within the 365 days in each year, there is just enough time to stop and reflect on what is in operation and how well it is performing. Repetitious activities are slightly at risk of becoming fixed because everyone accepts how well they are working. Measurement and evaluation make people nervous; they are afraid something may be discovered to be wrong. The opposite result is more likely: improvements may be found and may make even better performances possible. If assessments are not made, improvements will not be found. Perhaps more important to leaders and volunteers is the fact that studies of current activities may yield ideas that can keep annual giving programs fresh and exciting. Here are five basic rules that annual giving can live by [26]:

1. An annual fund drive is annual. Don't skip a year for any reason.
2. Select the best possible people you can find to serve in the leadership positions of the campaign.
3. Develop your case for support.
4. Involve as many volunteers as possible. The more people who ask for money, the more money you will receive.
5. Work closely with each volunteer and provide every tool needed to get the job done. Be absolutely certain to give recognition when the campaign is over.

Annual giving can bring great satisfaction to all who are involved in its practice. It has pace and excitement and is hardly ever dull. It calls for creativity and experimentation and gets instantaneous results. It involves the best of people working for the best of causes: helping others. It has influence in the community and importance to the organization. The friends it finds and develops into committed donors will remain thankful for the opportunity. The money it raises is put to work immediately, and all can see the results. Nonprofit organizations that have comprehensive annual giving programs working on their behalf can depend on their reliable performance, year after year, and can continue with confidence to pursue the fulfillment of their vision and mission.

CHAPTER TWO

Asking for Money: Begin with Testing by Mail

Asking for money goes on all the time, among friends and neighbors, men and women, parents and children, and even among children, their siblings, and their classmates. Everyone does it; some people do it many times a day. And, sometimes, it works! For example, a person may approach a prospect and say: "Can you please help me? I need money for food." The prospect will decide instantly and will either reach into a pocket or reply: "No; I'm sorry." If "No," the asker moves on to the next prospect and tries again with the same approach. Whether it is called begging, panhandling, "mooching," or soliciting, asking for money is much the same every time.

What separates fund-raising from begging? Is it the request for money for someone else or something else, such as a nonprofit organization and not for oneself? If the same prospect described above was approached by a volunteer solicitor, the opening line might be the same as a beggar's: "Can you please help me?" But the volunteer solicitor might then say: "I'm a volunteer with The Campaign to Clean Up America; we need money to help clean up our city streets." The prospect is likely to decide right away, yes or no. If the reply is: "No; I'm sorry," the volunteer moves on to the next prospect and tries again.

How is asking for money for a cause different from asking for money for oneself? The words used are not all that different. Was either asker described above uncomfortable when asking a stranger for money? Did both feel like beggars? Why is asking for money so difficult for so many people? There are people for whom asking for a charitable cause lifts the request to a higher plane, adding morality, humility, honor, and dignity to both the giving and the receiving. But most askers are afraid to be turned down, do not want to be embarrassed, or are fearful of the confrontation required in asking for money.

The mission of every nonprofit organization is to fulfill a charitable purpose by helping others—providing public benefits, advancing the community, improving the world's condition in some large or small way. Commitment, dedication, hard work, and leadership are all necessary. So is money; money is needed every day to make these good deeds possible. To get the job done, people must be willing to ask their friends for money throughout the year. Volunteer solicitors are more essential than people to be asked. Prospects already surround us; the challenge is to find good askers! Finding good askers requires time and attention. It begins with the first efforts to recruit people who are willing to ask their friends for money, which happens to be one of the more difficult first-time assignments people are likely to encounter. Once they have tried this task and succeeded, watch their enthusiasm grow!

ACQUISITION: THE EVERLASTING SEARCH

Asking people for money can be done in a variety of ways. Each technique is quite different and, as this book will illustrate, several tested and proven fund-raising methods can be used with success. There are just three basic ways to ask:

1. In writing (impersonal);
2. By voice or video (at a distance);
3. In person (face-to-face).

In-person solicitation is more effective than telephone contact (voice or video); telephoning is more effective than direct mail letters. Despite this confirmed performance difference, most nonprofit organizations conduct the majority of their annual giving solicitations by mail. Why? Perhaps because it's easier, the organizations do not have to recruit and train volunteers, and no one has to actually "confront" a donor or prospect and ask for a gift.

Several decisions are needed before asking can begin. After deciding who will be recruited, persuading them to help, and training them in how to solicit, the final step is selecting who will be asked. Two rules apply:

1. Concentrate on those who are most likely to respond positively.
2. Consider what else the people being asked might be able to do besides being donors. Might they volunteer for other tasks?

Nonprofit organizations need all the help they can get if they are to succeed in areas other than fund-raising. The entire process is one of "friend-raising" and "relationship-building." Making new friends for a nonprofit organization is the most significant contribution that can be achieved. Friendships and relationships built with care over time become enormously beneficial to an organization. Two axioms should be kept in mind throughout this book:

1. Friend-raising precedes fund-raising.
2. Money follows people.

The more new and old friends a nonprofit organization has, the more giving can be achieved. Friends bring with them their time, talents, and energy as well as their money. All four are equally valuable to a nonprofit organization. These multiple goals should be highlighted constantly, beginning with the first time a new volunteer is asked to help out. A future relationship with each of these potential new friends is possible. Can they help with community relations and legislative activities? Become active leaders in annual giving, major giving, and estate planning programs? Each of their talents will benefit the nonprofit organization for many years, but it will never know how until it asks.

Not everyone who is asked will be interested in being a volunteer or in giving money. Not everyone will want to become a friend to the organization or to develop a "relationship" with it. But some will, and these few valuable people must be found. Acquiring a few new friends who are able to volunteer *and* give money is well worth the effort, which is why such activity is an everlasting search. Nonprofit organizations must continuously recruit new friends, new volunteers, and new donors. There are never enough new people who are trained, experienced, and ready to replace those who are already active but then move on to new tasks, higher levels of assignment, or new locales. Where to begin? How to begin? Who should be recruited first, prospects or volunteers? Will those asked to participate become donors too?

In the warmup area just behind the starting gate are the prospect selection criteria: knowing the organization well enough to understand its areas of possible public appeal, and knowing the targeted community well enough to understand its preferences, style of volunteerism, giving potential, current concerns, economic conditions, and general demographics. These criteria will provide insight into whom to approach and how best to communicate with possible volunteers. The first means available for contact with them will be either first-class personal letters or third-class, bulk-rate letters. With either choice, the objectives are to identify and then select those within the community who are considered the best "suspects." Suspects are better candidates than prospects (unknown names on a mailing list) because they are judged to be more likely to respond to mailed invitations. These questions should be answerable for each name on the mailing list: Why has this person been selected? What will this person be invited to contribute—time, talent, energy, advice, counsel, and/or money? If the letter is an invitation to work in some capacity, will this person's capabilities match the "job description" for the work that needs to be done? Mailed invitations should recruit the best talent available to fill these jobs. If the invitation is just to give money, does the letter provide adequate information about the projects that need money, the uses that the organization has planned for the funds received, the numbers of people who will be served, the quality and value of what they will receive, and the benefits that will be rendered to the community? All these messages can be woven into direct mail letters. But the first (and most challenging) task is to locate exactly the people who should receive the letters.

Why is this first task so important? If enough willing people cannot be found, the nonprofit organization will not meet its mission to conduct charitable purposes and to provide public benefits. The mission explains why the organization wants and needs more than their money. True, their first and second gifts will be essential as operating cash; but each new donor will be done a great disservice if offered only a single-minded, mercenary goal. Nonprofit organizations that are successful year after year—and even decade after decade—begin by carefully selecting those who are invited to be their friends. From among the prospects and suspects available to them, these organizations find those people who have the potential to become personally involved and will commit to be supportive in multiple ways for many years. Seven criteria are recommended for this initial selection process. Each is discussed in the sections that follow.

1. Identification;
2. Qualification;
3. Influences;
4. Education and training;
5. Participation;
6. Leadership;
7. Recognition.

Identification

Everyone who is invited will not agree to serve in some capacity, so it is important to be selective right from the start. The people contacted and what they are asked to do are the primary search criteria. Any search for prospects and suspects must begin with people who are available— within reach and interested. If possible, the invitation letter should have data to which they are likely to reply favorably. The people most qualified to be volunteers should be asked to come to work. Those most qualified to give should be asked to consider a contribution at a level well within their financial range. It helps when people recognize the name of a nonprofit organization or know about its charitable purposes when they first receive an invitation, but a proper invitation form matters most of all. Inviting people to consider helping a good and worthy cause is not offensive. If something that coincides with the interests and concerns of those being invited can be included in the message, they may more readily accept. Some people may not have the time or money right now, or care that much about the cause, or even know enough about it to make an informed decision. Asking will stimulate their thinking. Some people will reply that they are fully subscribed to other organizations at this time. Raising friends is a continuous process, and education begins with the first contact. If the interests of those invited are known to be similar or favorable, they will not resent being asked to help, especially where a recognized problem is presented and they are being asked to be part of the solution. The invitation message should also explain why they were selected and be clear about what they are being asked to do to help.

Selection criteria define who will be invited and measure the probability of their acceptance. The next step is to sort them according to the purposes or tasks they are being asked to do. Some guidelines are: If only asking for money, verify financial ability; if asking for voluntary service, verify other volunteer experience and performance matched to the job descriptions. Some people are asked over and over again because they have already proved they are interested and willing to help, and they enjoy charitable work. They have also decided how and where they will give their time and their money to philanthropic activities. From experience, most will have narrowed their choices and will reply only to causes they prefer and have verified to be sound. These are the best candidates to ask. The first request may not succeed unless a current, urgent reason that makes sense is offered, such as sympathy for the cause or need, respect for the person asking (a peer or a high-level and respected volunteer), and trust that their energy and talents plus the time they have to serve will be put to good use. If all these criteria are in order, their commitment and their money are sure to follow.

Surveys by Independent Sector have shown that households that gave 2 percent or more of their income and were active volunteers gave three and a half times as much money as those households that gave less than 2 percent [1]. Beyond the time and dollars involved, every nonprofit organization has a variety of job opportunities that need volunteer help. The area or task that needs help can be defined in terms of time, or money, or both. As with any other job description, it is essential to recruit people who are matched to the work to be done. If they enjoy what they do, believe it is helpful, and see it as an assignment they can perform successfully, they will come back and work again. These are the volunteers who are so vital to any organization. Some will move on to higher levels of responsibility. Their financial support, growing alongside their involvement, will become a firm commitment to serve the present and future needs of "their" organization.

People generally do not have a lot of experience with well-defined volunteer work. They may be a bit hesitant or suspicious when asked about taking on a new assignment area, or when recruited to a new cause or organization—and for good reason. There are many unknowns to be mastered yet again. Also, others may have abused their good intentions or failed to utilize their skills or their time well. People are also a bit suspicious of requests for their money that are actually asking for their time and skills as a ruse to try to get more of their money. Again, well-defined selection criteria matched to specific duties that point with clarity to the value of the work to be performed are the important ingredients in successful invitations.

Finding people with a capacity to become volunteers, donors, *and* leaders is hard work but they are exactly the "triple threat" candidates needed. Finding people who have only one attribute can also be worthwhile. With a little time and effort, all three attributes might be realized. People bring their own potential for expanding their interests, enthusiasm, and commitment. They also bring access to a larger circle of family, friends, club members, business associates, and contacts, and may share these resources later. Finding such valuable individuals within the community and asking them to become an active part of an organization is worthy of the best hours of the day. The steps involved are: spend time identifying as many qualified people as possible, designate solid assignments for them, prepare to train them to do the work needed, and formulate a plan to supervise, evaluate, and reward them for all they do. Every nonprofit organization can meet its most urgent needs for today and for its future with just a few "triple-threat" stars on its team.

Qualification

Assuming that people who have similar interests, prior experience, and some financial ability have been identified, what should they be asked to do? The exact tasks assigned will depend on how what is known about them matches the work that needs to be done. People who are available to nonprofit organizations as volunteers bring with them a variety of usable skills as well as wide experience and infectious enthusiasm. Matching their interests with individual tasks related to the mission, purpose, goals, and objectives of the organization will take time and effort, but the results will be enormous, for each of them and for the future of the organization.

Some people are available only to give money. Their chief qualification will be a track record of a generous habit of giving, usually with some public notice. They are quite likely to reply to invitations because they seek involvement, visibility, and public recognition. They want to make a difference, to become a respected member of the community. Each organization needs to recruit these proven donors, not because they have given to others, but because of their potential to give repeatedly to each organization they choose. Donors who will give often are needed more than people who will give only one gift. The time and effort (not to mention the cost) required to recruit a single gift are reason enough to seek out donors who have a proven potential for repetitive giving.

Identifying qualified present and future leaders for nonprofit organizations is the most difficult task of all. Other nonprofit organizations will not train their leaders and then give them away. The best leaders are developed within each organization. They are a product of extensive knowledge, proven ability, demonstrated commitment, and a history of faithful gift support. Such preparation takes a lot of time and should follow a carefully prepared program that has leadership as its objective. Leadership positions will not be immediately available to everyone, but recruitment of potential leaders should never be off the organization's agenda.

Perhaps the most important criterion when identifying leaders from early lists of potential donors and volunteers is whether their abilities will have the opportunity to flower within an organization, allowing them to rise to its highest levels of leadership. First invitations sent to selected prospects may be received by future leaders. What plans are in place for their training and development?

The list of tasks available for volunteer work should be matched with abilities and talents that can be put to good and efficient use. Some people look for a chance to volunteer in order to do something new and different, or to learn new skills. The only qualifications needed may be prior experience in nonprofit voluntary work, rapport with the cause or mission, time to give, reliability, a willing spirit to work within the structure or system offered, and some financial ability. Strong personalities who prefer (or demand) their own way of doing things are not always a happy match, even if they are quite successful on their own. They know how to get things done, but their domineering style may drive others away—a bad outcome for nonprofit organizations. If they cannot fit into a committee system, they may be productive with a task that is not managed in a group or by a committee, or with a one-on-one manager–volunteer arrangement. This kind of arrangement should be reserved only for people who have a high potential to help.

Influence

Recruiting people of influence will be essential to the future of each nonprofit organization. Some individuals can be selected for invitations because they are known to influence others and can bring their influence to benefit the nonprofit organization's cause. Boards of directors are often composed of individuals chosen because their influential affiliation adds prestige to the cause. Influence can be applied through access to others, which is most important for success in fund-raising. Influence is a means to get things done—usually the types of things that managers and staff, and even other volunteers, cannot accomplish on their own. Influential leaders who accept leadership assignments inspire people to follow them. They also attract others like themselves into supportive roles.

Education and Training

Each organization must provide fairly complete information to those invited to serve. Assimilating new information takes time. Training can be met only partially with printed materials; people need a translator to interpret details in person. An orientation program can explain operating procedures and provide details on the mission, purposes, goals, and objectives of the organization. When a newcomer accepts an invitation to serve, a planned program of education and training will keep excitement and enthusiasm at a high level. Much more information is required for new board members than for new volunteers or new donors, because of the degree of obligation involved. However, all newcomers need information that will build their confidence, commitment, interests, and involvement and enable them to continue their intended level of support.

The information given at the time of first contact can be limited, but it must be adequate for the invitee to make an informed Yes decision. Once the relationship begins, there is more time to add details, expand knowledge, and lay the foundation for a long-lasting relationship. A plan for continuing education should aim to systematically bring everyone to (1) a level of understanding about the organization and (2) an appreciation of the value of time donated by volunteers to help fulfill the mission and purposes that are being advanced.

Participation

An organization that plans how everyone who volunteers can be a part of the organization is more likely to channel qualified people into positions where they will be most effective. High levels of personal involvement are important to leaders among the volunteers. One of the reasons they choose to become associated with nonprofit organizations is the access it gives them to others who share in their commitment for community service. They join because they enjoy being part of something larger than themselves; they stay if they are given some *active* role to play. Without it, they will soon lose interest and move on to another organization that is better prepared for their active involvement. Other volunteers will be satisfied with a more distant relationship and will rely on communications to maintain their interest and to continue their support.

Every organization that plans and uses its volunteers well will receive added benefits from their commitment. Personal involvement counts highly with volunteers. Those who participate feel more closely attached to the organization and will remain close for many years—some, for the balance of their lifetimes. Out of this pool of talent and commitment come the people who will help the organization realize its future. Some will serve at the highest levels of leadership, others will donate the largest gifts. Communications such as thank-you letters, newsletters, invitations, informative reports, brochures, and annual reports maintain their interest and provide them with all the information necessary for their success in this relationship.

Leadership

The most effective nonprofit organizations are those blessed with people who can lead others. Volunteer leaders aid in the direction and management of internal and external activities at several levels. Their example of stewardship responsibility is a stimulant for action. Leaders within nonprofit organizations can be carefully prepared for this level of duty through on-the-job experience. They may be assigned several jobs with several organizations over time. They benefit from careful orientation for each new assignment and from some form of performance evaluation. Each nonprofit organization has its own style of management, its "corporate culture" or behavior patterns, its policies and procedures, rules of operation, and internal politics. Leaders want to be successful in their assignment (some will not accept a position until they are assured of that success), but they also want to help the organization realize its present and future plans. They bring their talents and experience and they offer advice, counsel, and hard work. Every idea will not be useful at every moment, but their energy and enthusiasm are invaluable and must be cultivated at all times.

Recognition

This criterion is last on the list, but preparations to thank, recognize, and reward volunteers should be made at the beginning of planning, when job descriptions are written. People who give of their energy and skills want to know that their efforts are helpful. The best way to acknowledge their good work and to encourage them to do more is to thank them properly. There are ways to express this appreciation again and again. Recognition can include reporting their names and accomplishments to others and presenting them with token forms of appreciation (certificates, paperweights, plaques, and other mementos). These tokens of appreciation will be graciously accepted and acknowledged in the spirit of gratitude in which they are given. The object itself is not as important as the sincerity behind it. The presentation should be made with honesty, at the right time, in the right setting, and with the right people present. It represents grateful feelings of true appreciation for what they have done to advance the organization's mission.

These selection criteria will be revisited throughout this book because they are so essential to every part of fund-raising. Volunteers are the arms and legs as well as the eyes and ears of nonprofit organizations. They represent the community and its willingness to support the mission and purposes of the organization. These leaders, volunteers, and donors are ambassadors who are willing to speak to others with knowledge and positive praise about the organization. Such dedication sets an example others will want to follow.

FINDING LIKELY FIRST-TIME DONORS

When asked what is the most important investment they will make, small business owners are likely to cite the amount of effort and cost they believe must be put into finding new customers. A multinational corporation, asked the same question, is likely to deliver a crash course on advanced applications of modern marketing and advertising techniques.

Both entities invest heavily in finding first-time customers because their business (and their profits) depend on being successful at both finding and retaining customers to buy their products. Are nonprofit organizations any different? The selection criteria and techniques used to acquire first-time donors are much the same as those used by small businesses and multinationals to acquire customers. The limiting difference may be the amount of money available to be spent.

Most nonprofit organizations have to reach out widely to identify likely first-time donors. Some nonprofit organizations, because of their mission, have no natural constituency to begin with. Some are unpopular or unknown. For many organizations, the people who use their services and participate in their programs are their first source of prospective donors. Most nonprofit organizations are small in size, locally based, and comparatively unknown. Fewer than 100,000 out of more than 1 million nonprofit organizations in America are large enough to be widely known; these are America's colleges and universities, and its prominent hospitals and museums, which have achieved a positive image and reputation with the public. Smaller, local, unknown organizations find it difficult to compete with these established organizations because the public begins with comparisons. Another factor is that the better known organizations have already captured much of the time and money available in the community. One of the compelling reasons in founding United Way was to help the smaller, weaker, lesser known organizations to gain the attention, respect, and support of a wider public. Competition is a harsh reality. Thoughtful effort will be required to recruit new volunteers and first-time donors for nonprofit organizations. No one should expect that every organization can become an instant celebrity and use that brief moment of fleeting fame to gain enough public attention to attract all the necessary donors and leaders.

The best way to find and recruit new donors is to use tested and proven techniques:

Start with people whom those in the organization know.

Ask these people to expand the list of candidates by selecting among their friends, relatives, neighbors, business colleagues, club members, and social contacts.

Expand beyond this new circle of friends and contacts, reaching out to *their* friends and contacts.

This ripple-effect or "circles of influence" process is an effective way to begin, but it has limits, takes a lot of time, and loses its selectivity in finding well-qualified prospects fairly soon.

Multinational corporations learned long ago that using only one method to recruit new customers was inadequate. Several avenues must be explored, and each of these invitations must be coordinated to reinforce and be reinforced by the others wherever possible. Today, an advertising campaign to introduce a new product is test-marketed in several communities across the country at the same time. A combination of local newspaper, radio, and television advertising is matched with visible promotions in outlet stores—all reinforced with direct mail distribution of product samples to the homes of selected customer groups. The message is almost impossible to miss! A telephone and mail market research study is conducted in each community prior to the campaign, to establish base-line buyer attitudes toward the new product. A second survey, after the testing campaign, measures changes in public attitude. All these data are added to sales results and all input is used to refine the strategy. Only the methods of communication that work best will be used when the new product is offered to other, equally select audiences of customers in the next test.

Nonprofit organizations can utilize strategic marketing to establish their public image, the value of their cause, their mission, and their charitable purpose. Modern communications methods are necessary to tell their story widely, to influence public attitudes about the quality of their programs and services, and to persuade people to become active supporters. Most nonprofit organizations do not use for-profit marketing and advertising tactics because they endorse a conservative attitude, or they lack the marketing expertise and money for such a campaign. Competition may bring change in their approach in the future. A few nonprofit organizations have begun to use multimedia techniques with the same skill and success shown by for-profit corporations; however, most do not as yet. Until they do, their leadership and management are likely to endorse only the most modest and cost-effective promotions, even when executives on the board are using more modern methods for their own businesses. The results can be predicted to be modest and of low impact. When fund-raising communications are the only means used for marketing and promotion, they too will yield a poor response.

Everyone has to start finding prospects somewhere, even if at modest levels. There are several ways to get started. Who lives nearby? Who is using the services offered, attending the programs, learning what services the organization is providing? Whom is the organization trying to serve? How is it getting its message to those it wants to serve, those who are supposed to hear about its programs? These people are natural candidates for a request to support the organization. Why not start by making a list of them? Exhibit 2.1 identifies two groups of likely candidates to become first-time donors. Some choices will have to be made; these

Suspects	People living nearby.
	People who have been served.
	People to whom service is directed.
	People who work for suppliers.
	People who respond to invitations.
	People who respond to media messages.
	People who respond to similar causes.
	People identified by selection criteria.
Prospects	All the above suspects.
	People who participate in similar causes.
	People who currently participate in the organization.
	People identified by others who are involved.
	People buying tickets to activities.
	People of influence.
	People with proven leadership skills.
	People who were donors in prior years.

Exhibit 2.1   Likely Candidates as First-Time Donors

available audiences can often be interrelated. A list of natural candidates is likely to include some of the same people. The nonprofit organization should make an effort to coordinate its mailing lists, the messages being sent, their means of delivery, and the type of response(s) being requested. Only then can it begin to measure the results.

Before beginning to reach out and stimulate constituents to become new volunteers and donors, a review of the objectives and advantages of the use of direct mail as the chief means of communication and solicitation will be helpful. Direct mail is the most thoroughly tested and proven method to find prospects and to recruit their first gift and their repeated gifts. Robert Torre and Mary Anne Bendixen [2] believe that mail communications have several other uses that support fund-raising:

> Direct mail can and should be used in annual, capital, and planned giving campaigns. Few development professionals now feel that direct mail should be used only to solicit "smaller" gifts from prospects, former donors, and current donors. Direct mail, telemarketing, and personal calls are equally powerful ways to approach our constituencies.

These researchers have identified 14 objectives and advantages for the use of direct mail [3]:

1. A direct mail program should raise funds cost-effectively.
2. Direct mail can dramatically increase the number of donors to an organization.

3. A direct mail program can broaden an organization's visibility and make it more recognizable.

4. A direct mail program can identify more substantial prospects for capital or planned giving campaigns.

5. A direct mail program can identify new volunteers/workers for the organization.

6. Direct mail will reach the great majority of those you wish to contact in the way that you want to contact them.

7. Direct mail can take advantage of current events because it can be formulated and implemented in a very short time period.

8. A direct mail program gives more control to the development office.

9. A direct mail program provides instant gratification.

10. A direct mail program requires less staff time to implement than a phonathon or in-person calls.

11. A direct mail program gives the organization a full opportunity to tell the complete story.

12. A direct mail program can be individualized/personalized and segmented to a specific audience.

13. A direct mail program should be looked upon as a continuing program in the upgrading of donors.

14. A direct mail program provides an easy "follow-through" advantage in solicitation.

TESTING, TESTING, TESTING

Before any invitation, solicitation, or other form of mass communication is mailed, it is essential to test the package, message (copy), offer, timing, and, most important of all, the mailing lists that will be used. Testing proves what will work best for this organization today, not someone else's a year ago. Substitution of guessing for testing is a highly visible and expensive way to prove that an organization is out of touch with its constituency. Failure to test also can cause unemployment for fund-raising executives! In one of my personal experiences, we prepared for our first venture into mass direct mail solicitation for a large, well-respected nonprofit organization by testing 45 separate lists within a six-state area. The results were quite promising in every respect save one; we neglected to pay a bit extra for a merge-purge—a computer technique that searches for similar names and addresses and reduces them to a single mailing label. The chairman of the board (naturally!) received 40 copies of the test package! He was forever convinced that direct mail was not worth the powder to blow it up, no matter how many donors were acquired or how much money was raised. He also concluded that we did not know what we were doing, and professional help was brought in.

Testing requires professional help for every part of the mailing process, beginning with the lists to be used and the size of the test for each list. Costs for rental, lease, or purchase of lists start at $35 per 1,000 names; testing is an added expense. Professional direct mail consultants make their living by *being successful* in mail solicitation. To prevent disaster and ensure success, they all recommend testing prior to mailing ("roll out") to the entire mailing list. Besides, testing works!

There is much wisdom in the advice of professionals like Mal Warwick [4]: "The most important factor to test at the outset is whether or not direct mail acquisition is even feasible for your organization. Direct mail fundraising won't work for every organization—but you've got to try to find out for sure." Direct mail solicitation is a complex method of fund-raising. Before any venture into either mass mailings or testing, a quick review of the following seven rules, issued by Kay Lautman and Henry Goldstein [5], should be done:

1. All tests should have as their goal a measurable increased percent of return and/or average gift. . . .
2. To be accurate, test only one thing at a time. (This rule excludes lists, which you are *always* testing.)
3. Mail test packages within the same week.
4. Mail test packages at the same postal rate, unless it is postage you are testing.
5. Mail test packages to the same lists and split your list for testing on an nth (or random sample) select. . . .
6. Any test conducted using fewer than five lists of 2,500 names each is rarely valid. Ten lists of 5,000 names each is preferable.
7. After test results are in, test the same thing once again.

Exhibit 2.2 provides a list of the basic elements in a mail package, all of which can be tested with several variations. A few elements will have the biggest impact on the results; all the rest will have only moderate to low impact. Those high-impact elements are the ones that will demonstrate the mail program's potential for success, according to Warwick [6]:

In other words, if anything's going to give your mailing program a big lift, it's probably one or the other of the following . . . items:
- LISTS!
- Higher or lower minimum suggested gift
- Telephone follow-up

- Offering a product to those who give
- Involvement device
- New package
- Outer envelope design and copy
- Sweepstakes offer

But, be very cautious if you elect to acquire donors using a sweepstakes offer or offering a product in exchange for an initial gift. Your response rate may, indeed, be higher. But respondents to sweepstakes or premium offers may lack interest in your cause or organization, and their value over the long

Basic Components	Options
Mailing lists	Prior donors Members and volunteers Prospects and suspects Clients and neighbors Rented/leased/purchased lists
Outer envelope	Addressee information Complete return address "Address Correction Requested" Indicia/stamp/metered postage Special "teaser" message
Appeal letter	Official stationery Personalized salutation Personal message style Persuasive wording Request for a gift amount Typed/printed/computer-output text "P.S." message
Enclosure	Brochure, card, or giveaway Photograph and message Reprinted news article or ad
Response form	Donor's name, address, phone number Gift amount options Gift club option Information for inquiries (on wills, bequests, special gifts)
Reply envelope	Preprinted and preaddressed Space for return address Postage (blank/metered/stamped) Combination response form/envelope (business reply envelope)

Exhibit 2.2 Components and Options in the Direct Mail Package

haul may be substantially less than that of donors or members acquired without such inducements to greed.

Once the mail program is a success, later tests can experiment with other elements. Subtle changes can help to improve results already achieved. Here are some of the possible options:

Postage (use of stamps/meter/indicia);

Endorsement by celebrity/recognized community leader/executive director;

Computer-personalized/"Dear Friend" printed letter;

Envelope design (name and address in a window envelope/on a label/ personally printed);

One-page/four-page letters;

Front-end/back-end premiums;

Enclosures (brochure/card/photo/nothing);

Reply envelope (postage paid/envelope needing a stamp);

Survey form;

Timing (seasonal/year-round).

To be as fair as possible and to realize truly valid results, new elements should be tested only against one another, not against prior experience with other mailings or against disparate elements.

There are accounting rules that must be followed regarding joint costs of information materials included in any mailings, even test mailings. Joint costs arise when the solicitation package includes an information brochure that was not prepared for use in fund-raising. Rather, it is a document that accurately informs or promotes the programs and services of the organization. The accounting profession will then permit a portion of the mailing cost to be allocated to the programs and services budget, thus reducing fund-raising cost calculations [7]. For full details on allocating joint costs of mailings, organizations should consult their professional auditors.

Analysis of the results of test mailings requires some level of experience and—usually—professional help. A reasonable guide for whether a list has been successful in a test mailing uses three measurements:

1. A minimum of 1 percent response rate (at least 30 responses for each list tested);
2. An average gift size of $20 or more;
3. A direct cost of $1.25 to $1.50 per dollar raised.

As it gains more experience with testing lists and measuring their success, an organization may adopt more sophisticated methods of evaluation:

1. Number of replies received;
2. Percent of respondents who send money (minimum of 30 responses for any test list);
3. Number and percent of mail pieces returned as undeliverable (accuracy of the list);
4. Average gift size;
5. Gross revenue received;
6. Total direct costs for the mailing;
7. Net revenue received;
8. Cost per dollar raised (for each mailing).

Applying these eight quantitative measures to each list's performance will show whether the list is valid for the message sent. These same eight factors can be used to compare the performance of one list against another. Which list had the highest number of respondents? the highest gross revenue? the lowest cost per dollar raised? Other information that may be beneficial to subsequent fund-raising programs can be culled from the lists: demographic data on age of respondents, home value, length of ownership, income level, and similar facts. ZIP codes are a key to geographic areas or zones (ZIP + four digits) with higher response rates. Like a giant puzzle, all these pieces of information fit together to deliver a clear picture that points the way for future testing and better results. The marketing, planning, and public relations staff in the organization can use all these data for enhancement of public image and awareness, choice of product line, strategic marketing, market penetration, and related activities. These staff members' interpretation of the tests can add unique insight that will help in the preparation of the package, message, contents, and lists for the next mailing.

Use of the three basic measurements mentioned earlier will indicate whether there is sufficient evidence to justify continued testing, whether a full "roll out" (mailing) to the entire list is validated, or what segments of the list have met or exceeded the desired minimums. Direct mail fund-raising is a way to find the donors needed for an organization; it reveals more than just how much money might be received or how soon it can be delivered. Direct mail can find those people who will respond again to future requests and those who will contribute their time as talent as part of their response. These select people will help to fund the future needs of the organization and will become its faithful volunteers and leaders. Remember: Friend-raising precedes fund-raising, and building lasting relationships is one of the primary goals of every annual giving program.

Because cost usually is *the* controlling factor, successful direct mail packages are simple and direct in design and message, and are mailed with the lowest postage allowed (third class, presort, bulk rate). Responsiveness is being tested first: What elements will stimulate both the numbers of respondents and their average gift size? Cost–benefit analysis (1) correctly places limits on all the variables that do not affect responsiveness and (2) provides the data that help guide decisions on which lists (or pieces of lists) to use again, what message works best, and what giving levels to suggest. United States Postal Service regulations control a few parts of every direct mail package—size, weight, and cost. Money and creativity should be invested in lists, packages, and messages that can be proven to yield the best results. The primary indicators of how direct mail will continue to succeed in acquiring new friends, new donors, and new dollars are results based on tested responses.

The first test mailing initiates the solicitation program. Replies with money will arrive quickly, so systems for gift processing, donor records, and acknowledgment should all be in place. Each test response form should be coded so that accurate results can be tabulated. Test mailings produce the organization's first group of new friends and new donors. They become the control group and the model; their performance sets the standard all the other mailings will have to meet or exceed.

Testing should be conducted often, at least once every other year. Future testing will reveal how a little variety in the package or message can help improve the results. Lautman and Goldstein [8] advise:

Following are elements that usually can remain the same:

- Length of letter;
- Size and format;
- Colors;
- Postage;
- Premiums or other special offer;
- Size of gift requested;
- Mail date;
- Lists.

Future testing must be focused on one or more of those key elements; they can make a real difference in replies when everything else remains the same.

The decision to "roll out" a major mailing to a full list selected from results analysis can now begin with high confidence. The final variables are beyond the organization's control: rapid political and economic change, natural disasters, fiscal realities, and national crises can work for or against any mailing. Knowledge of the fixed details (lists, message, envelope, contents, postage) that have been proven to work in multiple tests is the best prevention available against unpredictable variables.

There are two remaining variables: (1) timing, which is a matter of judgment that can be enhanced by being observant and by having good counsel, and (2) letter texts, which require a writing skill that hits the bull's eye of people's awareness of and sensitivity to the cause and stimulates them to action.

LETTER TEXTS: WRITE LOVE LETTERS!

Much has been written and said about how to write successful annual appeal direct mail letters. Their mission is simple: to inspire people to action. Who writes these letters? What is the key to their success? Arthur Frantzreb [9] provided one great answer: Write love letters! He was suggesting that the direct mail letter writers think about the last love letters they wrote: their preparation time, their careful choice of words, all the emotions the letters contained, even the letters' length (more than one page, no doubt). Much was at stake with each love letter. What were the essential ingredients that inspired a reply of equal enthusiasm? Or, where or why did the message fail? The answer to either of these questions will ensure success with direct mail letters! When given equal time and attention, writing letters for friend-raising purposes is not all that different from writing love letters.

Most appeal letters written for nonprofit organizations are drafted by professional staff in the fund development office. They have written them before; their letters have received lots of replies with money enclosed. Other organizations invite professional letter writers and direct mail consultants to help them. Two of the better books of instruction on how to write direct mail letters are Jerry Huntsinger's *Fund Raising Letters*, a series of study guides [10], and *Dear Friend*, written by Kay Lautman and Hank Goldstein [11]. As an example of the wisdom shared in these texts, here are Huntsinger's four basic marketing principles for fund-raising letters [12]:

Principle 1. The techniques you employ to create your letter and package must be determined by the nature of the audience receiving the package.

Principle 2. Any direct mail package that is not personalized is compromised.

Principle 3. The only certain method of discovering exactly what works best for your audience is to engage in extensive and ongoing testing.

Principle 4. You must learn the basic principles, but you must break the principles to be successful.

The primary purposes of a direct mail appeal letter, especially the first one sent to carefully selected suspects and prospects, are: to be read and to be acted on. How can a few simple words perform such magic when the mission or cause of a nonprofit organization cannot be contained in one letter? The intent when writing direct mail appeal letters is *not* to tell the whole story all at once. Instead, another part of the story is told in each letter. The writer adds interesting facts, expands on what people have heard about or read before, tells about the people served, introduces the people who provided this service, educates readers about the cause and its direct relationship to their lives, and even tries to influence the readers' thinking. Can anyone hope to do all this in *just one letter?* No; but the organization intends to write more than once. How many times can it write? As often as it gets enough replies! How long should a letter be—one page, two pages, four, six? Will anyone read a six-page letter today? Lautman and Goldstein have declared [13]: "Of course you would—*if* the information was presented in a lively, interesting manner that aroused your curiosity, convinced you the author knew his or her subject, and taught you something. And that is exactly what a good appeal letter should do—arouse curiosity, stimulate interest, instill conviction, and one more thing: inspire action: *a contribution to your cause!*" All this from a first letter, whether it is on one page or six. Lautman and Goldstein recommend attention to four key ingredients in any direct mail letter text: style, format, credibility, and appearance [14]. They also have compiled this list of 13 basic rules for effective direct mail copy [15]:

1. Don't typeset the letter. Reproduce it from perfectly typewritten copy. (When was the last time you sent a typeset personal letter?)

2. Don't have the copy photographically reduced to cram a long letter into a short format. Remember, most of your donors are likely to be over 40 and may have difficulty reading small type. (We do!)

3. Don't omit the ("Dear Friend") salutation, and do try to include a dateline if possible. They are part of the real letter look.

4. Long paragraphs are admittedly hard to read, but don't overreact with a letter composed of a series of short paragraphs identical in length. They are equally difficult to read.

5. Don't overdo the underlining. Call attention to pertinent phrases or paragraphs through indented copy blocks, check marks, bullets, giant

quotation marks, color, and photographs. The longer the letter, the more important this is.

6. Pretend you are writing to one person. Indeed, you are.

7. Rework the opening and closing paragraphs until they "sing."

8. Don't wait until the last page to mention money. It's okay to ask on page one.

9. Don't try to be funny. Your cause is serious and so is charitable giving. We've tried humor. It doesn't work.

10. Don't bore the reader with the merits of your organization. Rather, write about the people it serves. Give the people names—real people and real names if possible.

11. Write with emotion and back it up with facts, not vice versa. People don't give because your organization needs the money. They give because they are touched or angry or saddened and want to do something to help!

12. Use your P.S. wisely because it will be read. Too many postscripts just take up space.

13. Don't use big words or jargon.

My best recommendation about writing letter texts is to get professional help from the fund development staff and from an outside adviser or counsel. This book focuses on annual giving as a program that will work effectively year after year to build relationships with new and old donors and volunteers. In the pyramid of giving shown in Exhibit 1.2, direct mail is one of the elements in the base that supports the entire fund development process. The burden laid on direct mail letters is a large responsibility indeed! The letters are crucial to the many successes that will need to follow; an exceptional beginning is not always a guarantee of continuing effectiveness. Solicitation begins with careful list selection and testing. The final ingredient for success is letters that inspire people to reply. When the addressees have been carefully selected and the lists, message, and package have been tested, everything else rides on the letter text.

Letters arrive in an outer jacket that sometimes has extra enclosures (a response form, a reply envelope, maybe an eye-catching throw-in). What is most important about the letter itself? Personalization! Readers can do some firsthand research here, among the solicitation letters recently received:

Were the letters personally addressed (did your name appear) on the outer envelope *and* at the start of the letter?

Did the letters begin "Dear Friend" even though your name was on the outer envelope?

Have you ever begun a love letter (or any letter to someone you knew well and/or wanted to know better) with "Dear Friend"?

If you received a love letter that began with "Dear Friend," would you characterize it as open, direct, and seeking closer ties, or as a bit stiff, less appealing, or perhaps defining new parameters for the relationship?

Personalization costs extra but it provides the best results.

The advent of computers has enabled the segregation of mailing lists by census data, demographics, ZIP codes, and other factors. Computers and their faithful servants, ink-jet printers, now produce personal letters that appear to have been individually typed to the person whose full name, full address, and salutation (by name) appear in their proper places at the top of the page. With refinements, added bits of personal information—a reference to the city of residence (contained in the address above), or the exact amount of the donor's last gift (from the donors' gift record file)—can be inserted at other places in the text. Computerized, personalized direct mail is the minimum standard today. The Arthritis Foundation has mastered the use of personalization in mass mailings at the lowest possible cost. The Foundation's tidy envelope with windows reveals the complete mailing address. When the packet is opened, the name and address appear at the beginning of a personal message. And, representing the ultimate in one-page letters, the entire message is presented in full on one side of a 3" × 5" piece of paper! The reverse side describes the Foundation's use of funds raised and offers several available giving levels, which prospects are invited to consider. Should every nonprofit organization be using this same package design? No; every organization is not as well known as the Arthritis Foundation and will not send out over 100 million pieces of mail a year. Economies of scale are working in the Foundation's favor because of instant name recognition and a modest gift request (a minimum donation of $5).

Literally hundreds of details are associated with direct mail appeal letters. The Direct Mail Marketing Association's annual conferences are attended by hundreds of professional direct mail experts who discuss and debate the merits of every facet of "direct response advertising." There are differences in response rates, gift sizes, and costs required, depending on the choice of such details. All these elements are important for each user to consider because mailings are often in the thousands or even millions of pieces. When reviewing options and possibilities regarding the design of a direct mail package and the all-important letters, some basics should be kept in mind. Huntsinger [16] recommends including these six "vital elements" to create the "look" of a real letter:

1. Date Line;
2. Name and Address;
3. Dear Somebody;
4. Body Copy;
5. Signature;
6. Postscript.

To have a letter "look right" and serve its primary purpose of stimulating action, Huntsinger provides seven layout suggestions [17]:

1. Make everything easy to read, use short paragraphs, indent the first line of every paragraph.
2. Use underlining to capture the eye.
3. Avoid all caps. CAPITAL LETTERS ARE DIFFICULT TO READ, AND GIVE THE FEELING THAT YOU ARE SHOUTING. But when you underline your words, the effect is stronger.
4. Keep your lines short, don't discourage the eye with long lines and skimpy white space. Wide margins increase readership.
5. Use dashes instead of commas—at times—to break up the routine look.
6. Be sure and put one eye grabber on each page.
7. Use large typefaces. Only 1% of the population has perfect eyesight.

A nonprofit organization can rely on direct mail appeal letters to stimulate large numbers of new friends who will join in the cause. The appeal letters will cultivate, educate, and inspire these newfound friends and donors to continue their faithful support year after year. The letters serve as invitations to encourage participation in other ways, such as to volunteer, or to attend events and activities and bring their friends with them. All this is a heavy burden for any letter to bear, whether one page or six pages long. These fragile messengers will often need some help. They can be part of a larger message linked to other annual giving activities. In the continuing example in this book, the activities of the Clean Up Cleveland Chapter are linked to the vision and mission of the fictional national organization called The Campaign to Clean Up America (CCUA) [18]. The CCUA's cause is larger than just one person or one organization. The workings of the Cleveland chapter of this national campaign are a microcosm of the events, decisions, documents, personnel, and problems that form both the challenges and the routines when relationships are built through annual giving campaigns. At the end of each chapter, the topics covered will be illustrated in a focus on the CCUA Clean Up Cleveland Chapter.

Focus: CCUA Clean Up Cleveland Chapter

The Campaign to Clean Up America (CCUA) is a newly formed, national nonprofit organization dedicated to improving the environment and public health through wide public participation in helping to clean up America's cities and using all this trash to generate electricity for public use. The national board of directors, headed by Michael M. Activist, a prominent conservationist, is headquartered in New York City. Members of the board of directors were selected by Activist from among his personal friends in the environmental and conservation movement. I. Harvey Clout, Chairman of the Cleveland Cast Iron Works, has been invited to head the CCUA Clean Up Cleveland Chapter.

Clout has recruited a few other volunteers from the greater Cleveland area to serve on the board of directors of the Clean Up Cleveland Chapter. The new organization is housed at Clout's accounting firm, which is headed by Sidney M. Secure, CPA. Clout and the board have begun to recruit a director of development. Clout and Secure will pay salaries and operating costs out of their own pockets until local funds become available.

At the May meeting of the national board of The Campaign to Clean Up America, held in New York, each chapter chairperson was given a notebook with detailed instructions on initiating a combined marketing, public relations, and fund-raising program in each of several major American cities. The notebook calls for a test mailing to at least six separate lists in the area. The objective of this first mailing is to begin a combined public awareness and fund-raising campaign. A sample first-appeal letter was provided in the notebook, along with other details. Clout returned to Cleveland and recruited two volunteers, Mary M. Moneybanks and Theodosius Worthy, to join the local chapter's board. The board members, plus Titus Brown, President of The Brown Agency, and advertising and public relations counsel to Harvey Clout and the Cleveland Cast Iron Works, have begun to develop six mailing lists to be used for the first test mailing. Each list is to have at least 2,500 separate names following merge-purge or duplicate-elimination processing. The notebook provided a sample letter for test mailing purposes (Letter B). Titus Brown and Harvey Clout believe they should also test a letter written earlier by Clout (Letter A), to see which one receives better response. Both test packages are to be mailed on July 10. The six test lists defined for the Cleveland area will be evenly split for Letter A and Letter B:

List	Definition
1	5,000 Cleveland Heights residents
2	5,000 East Cleveland residents (Chagrin Falls, Gates Mills, Mentor, and Solon)

3	NE Ohio members, National Audubon Society
4	NE Ohio members, National Conservancy
5	Subscribers (Browns/Cavaliers/Indians)
6	Subscribers (Cleveland Orchestra/Cleveland Play House)

The texts of Letter A and Letter B are presented in Exhibits 2.3 and 2.4. The test results are in Exhibit 2.5.

Analysis of the results suggests the following findings and directions:

1. Through the letters, 348 new donors were acquired!

2. Funds raised did not cover the cost of mailing, but that result was expected in the test program.

3. The cost of testing is high, but will be reduced by one-half when the full mailing is prepared (unit costs for envelopes, bumper stickers, letter preparation, and data processing will be cut).

4. Clout's Letter A did not appeal very well to any audience except Cleveland Heights residents and Audubon Society members (more than .01 percent response). The most cost-efficient gifts came from Audubon Society members (at $0.84 to raise $1.00).

5. Letter B clearly outperformed Letter A, suggesting this style of message will get the best results.

6. Poor response to Letter B by affluent communities and sports subscribers suggests testing them again later; all other lists look quite promising and should perform well in a mailing to the full list, scheduled to be received by October 30.

Letter A

The Campaign to Clean Up America
Clean Up Cleveland Chapter

July 10, 199X

Dear Fed Up with Trash:

I don't know about you, but I'm fed up with all the trash on our city's streets.

Cleveland boasts of its "emerald necklace," its theatres and museums, but we are the butt-end of jokes as the city whose river caught on fire and whose lake died.

Well, we cleaned up the Cuyahoga River and restored Lake Erie, didn't we? Now it's time to clean up our streets. How about it; do you want to help me do it? Great. Here's how we can get it done together.

The Campaign to Clean Up America is at work in every big city right now. But there's more to it than picking up trash. Our goal is to recycle our trash into new, clean energy we can all use. You might say we've found the way to cut our electric bills, right under our feet.

We estimate about 100,000 tons of trash is lying in our streets right now that can be converted into 32,000 megawatts of electricity to meet the needs of 18,000 homes for a year, plus reduce *everyone's* electric bills by *$12 a month* and *$124 a year.*

Here's what you and I can do to help make this happen.

First, stop being a "trasher." Pick up after yourself.

Second, bag all the trash you find around your house, garage, and yard, and put it out with your garbage next week.

Third, join with me in our Clean Up Cleveland Chapter. Your gift of $12 is what you will save on electric bills each month from our new energy plant.

Fourth, spread the word. Talk about what we are doing; tell your neighbors and the people you work with. Ask them to get involved and join in cleaning up Cleveland. Put your bumper sticker on your car or truck (it's magnetic). Let everyone see that you support a cleaner Cleveland.

As the saying goes, "Every litter bit helps." Your bit of cleaning up and giving will help out a lot. The money we raise is divided equally between our public awareness and education efforts, and construction of our new energy plant.

The energy conversion plant has been approved by the City Council. Land for the plant has been given to the city by Centurion Energy Corp., who will operate this new plant the same as the one already in operation near Perry, Ohio. Estimated cost is $3.5 million, two-thirds of which will be provided by federal and state matching funds. All we need to do is raise $1,250,000 from the people who live and work in Cleveland.

It's all up to us now. Let me see those bumper stickers and let me hear from you real soon.

Many thanks, friend.

Sincerely,

I. Harvey Clout
Chair of the Board
Cleveland Cast Iron Works

P.S. Last week, my son and I picked up three bags full of paper, cans, and bottles around our plant during lunch time in less than 30 minutes. On Friday, 35 managers will go all over this plant to pick up all the trash they can find in 30 minutes. Their goal is to match our three bags full. We have begun!

Exhibit 2.3   First-Time Acquisition Direct Mail: Test of Letter A versus Letter B

Letter B

The Campaign to Clean Up America
Clean Up Cleveland Chapter

July 10, 199X

Dear Friend for a Trash-Free Cleveland:

Every day when I drive to and from work I see a lot of paper and other trash on our streets, along with cans and bottles, boxes and plastic bags.

We all know the City has cut back on trash collecting and street sweeping because of the recession, but they are not keeping up with the trash, not at all. And, our city is not the only city that has this problem.

When I was invited to New York last month to hear about The Campaign to Clean Up America, I wanted to go for two reasons. First, this is a serious plan to do something about all the trash that is polluting our country. Second, they've got a great idea. Build a new energy conversion plant that uses trash to make electricity and cuts our energy bills at the same time!

We estimate there are 100,000 tons of trash lying in our streets and around our buildings right now. With energy conversion in a new plant, this trash can become 32,000 megawatts of electricity to meet the needs of 18,000 homes for one year. And, this plant will *reduce* everyone's electric bills by *$12 a month* and *$124 a year*. This great idea got my attention and I volunteered to chair this program for Cleveland. We all will benefit from this effort. We need your help to do it. Each one of us can participate quite easily. Here's what we would like you to do.

First, stop being a "trasher." Pick up after yourself.

Second, bag all the trash you find around your house, garage, and yard, and put it out with your garbage next week.

Third, join with me in our Clean Up Cleveland Chapter of The Campaign to Clean Up America. Your gift of $12 stays in Cleveland. It also is what you can expect to save on electric bills each month from our new power plant.

Fourth, spread the word. Talk about what we are doing; tell your neighbors and the people you work with. Ask them to get involved and join in cleaning up Cleveland. Put your bumper sticker on your car or truck (it's magnetic). Let everyone see that you support a cleaner Cleveland.

You know the saying, "Every litter bit helps." Each of us can help to make our city a lot cleaner. Your contribution of $12 will help too.

Contributions will be divided between our public awareness and education programs and the cost of construction of our new energy plant.

As you may know, the new energy conversion plant has been approved by the City Council and the land for the plant has been given to the city by Centurion Energy Corp., who will manage this new plant the same as their plant now in operation near Perry, Ohio. Estimated total cost is $3.5 million. Two-thirds of this cost will be met by federal and state matching funds. What we need to do is raise $1,250,000 in private contributions from the people who live and work in Cleveland.

I hope you can join with me and others who are working for a cleaner Cleveland. Let me hear from you soon.

Sincerely yours,

I. Harvey Clout
Chair of the Board
Cleveland Cast Iron Works

P.S. Last week, my son and I picked up three bags full of paper, cans, and bottles around our plant during lunch time in less than 30 minutes. On Friday, 35 managers will go all over this plant to pick up all the trash they can find in 30 minutes. Their goal is to match our three bags full. We have begun!

Exhibit 2.4   First-Time Acquisition Direct Mail: Test of Letter A versus Letter B

List No.	Number Mailed	Replies Number	Replies Percent	Gift Income	Average Gift	Cost per Dollar Raised
Letter A:						
1	2,500	26	0.0104%	$ 512	$20	$1.98
2	2,500	18	0.0074	216	12	4.69
3	2,500	48	0.0192	1,200	25	0.84
4	2,500	24	0.0096	600	25	1.68
5	2,500	18	0.0072	360	20	2.81
6	2,500	22	0.0088	480	22	2.11
Total/Avg.	15,000	156	0.0104%	$3,368	$22	$1.82
Letter B:						
1	2,500	38	0.0152%	$ 895	$24	$1.13
2	2,500	12	0.0046	124	12	8.17
3	2,500	52	0.0208	1,800	28	0.56
4	2,500	44	0.0176	900	20	1.13
5	2,500	18	0.0072	480	27	2.11
6	2,500	28	0.0112	960	29	1.06
Total/Avg.	15,000	192	0.0128%	$5,159	$27	$1.19
Grand Total/Avg.	30,000	348	0.116 %	$8,527	$24.50	$1.74

Expenses: Costs for each mailing are identical:

Unit (Individual Letter)	Cost per Unit
List (@ $35/1,000 names)	$0.035
Outer envelope	0.080
Reply envelope	0.050
Bumper sticker	0.080
Letter/reply form	0.060
Data processing	0.080
Mail preparation	0.020
Postage	0.090
Total	$0.495
	× 2,500 units per list
	$1,237.50 per list

Total cost ($0.495 × 30,000 mailed) = $14,850

Exhibit 2.5   Test Results: Acquisition Letter A and Acquisition Letter B

CHAPTER THREE

Direct Mail Acquisition: Constituency Building

B efore beginning an annual giving program, it's worth-while to take a moment to think about why asking for annual gifts is so important. What can the asking do? What ought it to do? How can it help a nonprofit organization? The one-word answer is: Money. Asking can raise money quickly. The main reason for conducting annual giving programs is to build a con-stituency of faithful friends and generous supporters. Annual giving has the following characteristics, which yield a multitude of added benefits:

1. Raises money, usually for operating purposes;
2. Lasts 12 months each year and is designed to be repeated every year after that, with increased results each time;
3. Allows for multiple solicitations to occur within each 12-month period;
4. Communicates with more people than any other means available to a nonprofit organization;
5. Is a reliable source of annual revenue to meet current priorities of need;
6. Finds and recruits new donors each year;
7. Relies heavily on prior donors to repeat their gifts;
8. Offers opportunities for volunteer recruitment, training, and participation, and for leadership development;
9. Complements the marketing and community relations programs because of its high visibility;
10. Is a well-planned, highly coordinated, and well-executed activity.

These characteristics must be used to full advantage, channeled and coordinated for positive effect. From 30 years' experience, I am convinced that *planning* is the most important ingredient for success in any annual giving program.

Planning a successful annual solicitation campaign requires close coordination among management staff, volunteers, and leaders, sometimes facilitated by professional fund-raising staff, consultants, and vendors. Together, they define why public support is needed (the case), how the funds will be used (the priority), how much is required (the goal), when the money is needed (the deadline), and how much it will cost to succeed (the budget). These decisions are based on an assessment of the organization's public image (through market research), the prior performance of volunteers (their training), solicitation methods and fund-raising staff (the results), and an analysis of productivity (a.k.a. efficiency). In short, a plan for success is based on measurable performance, not on speculation or wishful thinking.

Acquisition is also the base, the necessary foundation for the entire fund-raising program of every nonprofit organization. To be successful with the full range of annual giving program options demands serious time and attention to finding and keeping scores of donors. Much more is possible when new donors are being recruited in a steady stream. This type of effort is a commitment to build the future constituency of the organization. In time, maximizing the performance of each annual giving program helps the organization meet its priorities of need. Coordination of these programs year after year requires attention to every detail of annual giving activity prior to, during, and after each solicitation effort. To many individuals, especially fund-raising office staff and management staff, the routine of annual giving can be boring; the activities have to be repeated year after year. By developing annual giving to its maximum potential and by preserving enthusiasm for it, a nonprofit organization will be guaranteed that it can recruit all the new friends and funds it needs, market its programs and services, and raise money to fulfill its mission within the targeted 12-month cycle. Reliable financial support is a wonderful asset for any nonprofit organization; annual giving programs that deliver plenty of dollars with reliability are gold mines and should be treasured.

As proof of the value of annual giving, this entire book has been created as a comprehensive guide to that one facet of fund-raising/friend-raising/constituency building. Once in place and blended with ongoing marketing and communications activities and with donor relations techniques, annual giving will yield a multitude of benefits. Edith Falk [1] has summarized them as follows:

Establishing an annual program is the first step for any organization dependent on outside support for its operating budget. In addition to generating critical, immediate dollars, the complete annual giving program:

Develops public awareness and understanding of the organization. A successful annual campaign demands effective communication with donors and potential donors. Organizations whose annual giving program includes—at the very least—an end-of-the-year mailing are generally better known in their communities than those that do little or no fund-raising.

Stimulates unrestricted support. Unrestricted gifts are essential to an organization because they can be applied where they are needed the most. Many annual programs include opportunities for both restricted and unrestricted giving.

Identifies new prospects for giving and upgrades current donors. Securing broad-based philanthropic support is one of the primary goals of annual giving programs. A growing core of loyal donors—rather than a series of one-time givers—is essential to maintain a stable, creative organization.

Cultivates essential volunteer and donor involvement. Annual giving programs are ideal for the identification and training of new volunteer leaders. They provide an important opportunity for donors to become active in special events and other fund-raising and public relations activities.

Identifies future capital and planned gift prospects. Annual giving is the bottom rung of the donor acquisition ladder. A strong annual support program can provide leverage in persuading prospective donors to make major gifts and grants, help attract gifts of property or deferred gifts, and build a strong base for a successful capital campaign.

There are numerous opportunities for variety and creativity in the design of annual giving programs. Most of the successful solicitation methods—those used by thousands of organizations and proven after repeated applications in every city and town in America and most parts of the world—are presented in this book. This text will help anyone to design and get started with a program for success. Improvements can always be made to what each organization is doing now. One benefit that comes from inviting new people to join in the annual fund-raising activities is that their new ideas are encouraged and can be tested against what is being done now. Perhaps they can add some sparkle (or just sparks) to a tired program and reignite the enthusiasm of volunteers and donors. Society changes rapidly. So do individuals and their perceptions about urgent community (and personal) needs. Nonprofit organizations must be flexible and able to respond to the changing needs of their communities. Newcomers bring energy and creativity; they breed excitement and increase the potential to maintain continuous improvements in annual giving activities. New fund-raising ideas, however, must be evaluated on their own merits first, and then compared with the known performance of existing programs to assess their short-term and future potential. Can they help to find new donors? Can they inspire prior donors to give again? Can they improve the organization's image? Do they complement the overall fund-raising program's design? Before committing volunteers, staff, and resources to any new idea, testing is required to find out what the idea will bring to the total solicitation program. A note of caution: Just because a nifty fund-raising idea worked for someone else yesterday does not always mean it will work for any other organization, today or any day.

MEETING CHANGING NEEDS

Nonprofit organizations must conduct their own analysis of their solicitations each year in order to resolve how ideas for change or improvement can affect their ability to achieve multiple benefits. These annual evaluations guide the selection of the activities that will stimulate the greatest public response and produce the most cash. As with any investment, organizations must commit sufficient time and financial backing to each annual solicitation method that they believe can help to meet their needs. Each fund-raising method must be given the opportunity to grow to its own level of maturity, and to demonstrate the numbers of donors it can acquire and retain and the amounts of reliable annual support these donors can give in the future. It takes usually a minimum of three years for annual giving programs to begin to "pay off" with a dual return (numbers of participants and amounts of gifts) on the initial investment. Adherence to those activities that work well becomes a reliable plan, especially if it proves it can enhance the relationship of new donors to the organization. The objective is not just the money they will give; their *commitment* to the mission, purposes, goals, and objectives of the nonprofit organization causes their annual gift to become reliable. These reliable and faithful friends are destined to become the foundation on which secure financial development for the future will be built. To make a first-time gift is the beginning of a relationship that can last a lifetime. The grand design is for an overall fund-raising program, one that becomes a constant and reliable source of new volunteers and leaders and, in time, major gift donors, as well as annual contributions. Each individual donor must be encouraged to develop a strong commitment to assist in meeting the current and future needs of the organization. Through a variety of programs, multiple benefits beyond cash can be gained from the broadest amount of participation by the widest segment of local residents. It must be understood from the beginning that another objective of a complete fund-raising program of annual giving is to find the people who may become potential clients for programs and services at some future time.

Most annual giving programs succeed because of attention to two separate sets of criteria: (1) overall design ingredients and (2) individual performance yardsticks. Both are used for each fund-raising method. Design and results work in combination; they complement one another. Performance measurement of each annual giving method is essential, to assess not only the method's results but also its effect on each of the other programs being offered within the same year. The audiences available for participation in several annual solicitation techniques throughout any one year are often the same people; consideration must be given to the number of requests made of them, the constant message each receives, the timing of all the requests, and their ability to continue to respond as often as possible.

Among the great variety of solicitation options used in annual giving programs, seven critical elements are required for individual and collective success [2]:

1. A well-defined purpose;
2. Extensive planning;
3. An efficient organization;
4. A realistic timetable;
5. Meaningful fare;
6. Realistic assignments;
7. Logical order.

Each of these elements should be incorporated into the design of the total annual giving plan prior to beginning each year's program. Their performance should be measured after the campaign, to understand their effect on the overall effort as well as their individual results.

A unique value of each annual giving method is its brevity. Only its ability to produce immediate results (cash) is more valuable. Nearly every annual fund-raising activity can be carried out quickly, start to finish. Mailings take a few weeks to prepare, but most replies arrive within four to six weeks of mailing. Benefit events, usually held only once a year, are planned and promoted over three to six months and are over in one evening or one weekend. Membership drives are promoted for a month or two, held within a 30- to 60-day period, and concluded by a well-published deadline. Evaluations can be held immediately after all the results are in, and corrections can be implemented in time to help improve the next mailing or event or drive. The cycle continues endlessly as does the expectation to do better each time.

THE "CASE" FOR ANNUAL GIFT SUPPORT: GOALS AND POTENTIAL

The "case" for annual gift support is a written statement that lists the reasons why certain identified funds and projects are needed by the nonprofit organization. The case is a story that explains how the funds raised will be used to achieve beneficial purposes—usually, the conducting of charitable and public benefit programs and services to fulfill the nonprofit organization's mission. The case statement is a summary of essential details arranged to encourage understanding of a need and to spark a positive response. The case statement may be one paragraph or an entire letter, or it may be printed in a brochure or proposal. Most case statements for annual giving are based on the nonprofit organization's carefully developed, long-range strategic plan. It explains this year's design, reports progress made in the past year, and enlists support to continue making progress. By telling this story in yearly chapters, annual case statements form a record of the organization's progress and describe the most urgent current priorities that must be met in order to continue to move forward. The intended result is to be able to inform the public, several times throughout each year, how the organization is progressing, where it is going, how public support has helped and will be needed again if the organization is to continue to benefit the community it serves.

A case statement will translate the specific areas of need identified each year into uncomplicated stories that can be appreciated as opportunities for public participation. The case simultaneously describes and advocates programs and services that are of value. The story may offer specific details about equipment, construction and personnel costs, operating expenses, and similar items, to explain how these areas of expense will improve the organization's ability to provide existing programs that serve people or causes. Exhibit 3.1 lists the ten basic elements of a case statement. The causes that need attention are stressed, as are areas that are publicly recognized as unmet needs crying out for action. The role of the "case" is to communicate how the funds needed will be spent, what results will be achieved, and how the community will benefit. Projected results have public appeal; performance that fulfills the projections seals the relationship. Achieving promised positive results merits the time and attention of all those invited to join as volunteers and as donors.

1. The case must reflect the mission of the nonprofit organization.
2. The case must demonstrate fulfillment of a charitable purpose.
3. The case must reflect the validity, relevance, and public benefits to be gained from the programs and services being offered.
4. The case must enunciate the goals, objectives, and long-range plans of the organization.
5. The case must be measured against the competence of the organization to provide these services.
6. The case must demonstrate the organization's competent leadership and sound financial management.
7. The case should advance arguments in favor of monetary support for its cause with truthfulness and confidence.
8. The case should demonstrate how the gift support received will be used and to whom these benefits that make a difference will be provided.
9. The case should explain the community benefits to be gained by successful completion of this work or a solution to this problem.
10. The case should explain the benefits gained by all who join in to provide support to this effort—volunteers and donors alike.

Exhibit 3.1   Essential Features of a Case Statement

After issuance of the case statement, with its definition of public benefits, the financial details are revealed. How much will this program or service cost to provide? Was there a process of investigation to search out various solutions? Is the solution picked as most likely to succeed also the one that is most cost-effective? In short, can the financial details withstand public scrutiny? Are they reasonable figures? Operating budgets have dual roles as internal guides for management of every area of activity and as "shopping lists" where the public can see the valid use of donated funds. A high degree of trust is implied in every gift; the organization must spend donors' money carefully and wisely.

Once the case statement and financial projections are complete, those responsible for fund-raising must match the stated goals and objectives, including the amount of funds needed, against the ability and potential of annual solicitation methods to raise the funds needed to operate such well-defined programs and services. An accurate matchup requires an understanding of how each annual giving solicitation method described in this book actually raises money. There is an equal need to appreciate the importance of designing and directing each solicitation method to achieve its maximum capability for raising some or all of the money needed. There are limits, even in the best circumstances, to how much performance each fund-raising method can achieve within one year. Accurate estimates are complicated because performance is so often dependent on such factors as leadership, the number of volunteers involved, the availability of support materials, competent staff support, and similar factors. Many of the methods of annual solicitation can be used only once a year; others offer multiple opportunities within each annual cycle. For example, direct mail letters can be used several times within 12 months, but a major golf tournament or a black-tie ball may be held only once a year. All three methods will require most of the year to plan, prepare, and execute. Each technique's potential for results is composed of a mixture of elements that can point to future success. Results are a function of four key features:

1. Access to qualified prospects;
2. The relevance and urgency of the need or cause;
3. The ability of volunteers and their leaders to perform well;
4. Adequate staff and budget.

When a fund-raising activity is already in place and ready to be used again, its potential can be measured for the ability to maintain and increase its own prior-year performance. An activity's potential depends on an ability to fit volunteers, donors, and prospects into the area or project that needs funds *this year.* Priority projects will change from year to year, and, despite a past level of popularity, each must be sold all over again, with conviction, to all the volunteers, donors, and prospects. Each method of solicitation must measure its ability to attract and retain volunteers, donors, and prospects when their willingness to participate must be redirected to the changing, and not always popular, needs of the organization. Because every fund-raising method has a finite potential in numbers of donors and amount of dollars, realistic goals should be estimated for each solicitation activity and predictions should reflect actual results realized when everyone works together each year. After three or more years of operation, predictions become easier and more reliable. Solid estimates of performance become increasingly valuable to managers as the nonprofit organization attempts to plan the programs and services supported by the cash received in the annual giving campaign. With each method, efforts to improve performance and achieve full capacity in subsequent years will continue.

Each of the several fund-raising methods used for annual giving solicitation has different performance levels for effectiveness and efficiency, and each is exposed to a multitude of uncertain facts that affect performance. Among them are:

1. The nonprofit organization's image and reputation;
2. The public's understanding and acceptance of the urgency of the need (the appeal of the "case");
3. Perceived public benefits to be achieved;
4. Local economic and demographic conditions;
5. Public acceptance of the method of solicitation used;
6. Time of year when the solicitation occurs.

Analysis of these factors helps to estimate how each solicitation method will compete for public attention. Add to this analysis the length of time each solicitation method has been in use, the competence of its volunteers and leaders, continued access to new prospects and donors, and confidence in the fund-raising program plan, and the forecast of performance begins to take on confidence and insight. All of these realities will affect results fairly quickly; an economic downturn or a local fund-raising scandal can defeat, overnight, the best case story ever written. These elements do not have an identical effect when different nonprofit organizations use them in their annual giving programs. Using the same fund-raising methods year after year does not guarantee the same performance either. Fund-raising, like every other human endeavor, does not perform at the same level every time it is in operation. Year after year, each organization must define its own annual giving program plan, evaluate the individual results of each fund-raising method it uses, and measure the levels of performance achieved. This process will demonstrate which methods work best and why they will continue to perform well. Those methods to which the public responds best should be selected for continued use, provided they are capable of producing the same level or a continued growth of donors and dollars each year *and* are cost-effective in their operation.

GOAL SETTING FOR ANNUAL GIVING SOLICITATION

Goal setting for each fund-raising activity is a challenging exercise; setting goals for a group of solicitation activities to be conducted within the same year is considerably more complex. (See Exhibit 3.2.) Goals are, at best, informed estimates of program behavior based on prior results and proposed improvements. Goals cannot be based only on how much money the nonprofit organization wants or needs. The need for money may be valid, but the ability of any one solicitation method—or any combination of methods—to meet an income goal may be unrealistic this year. Other fund-raising options and other revenue

1. *The Project*
   - Select a project or program that will have immediate public recognition as being valuable or an unmet need.
   - Identify the number of community residents who can and will benefit from this project or program.
   - Summarize the credentials the organization has for providing this service with competence, based on past experience.
   - Evaluate how gifts will expand the numbers served, the quality of service, and the expected benefits to the community.

2. *The Audience*
   - Evaluate how many local people are qualified to receive this service and how they will have access to it.
   - Identify potential numbers of available prospects and donors who would be interested in supporting this effort, including whether they might also need or use this program or service at some time.
   - Evaluate the financial value this program may have to the community; calculate the per-person cost of providing it.

3. *Gift Size*
   - Define gift options linked to the per-person cost (above) to deliver this service.
   - Ask for a number of gifts that is linked to the projected number of people who will receive service from each dollar received.

4. *Goal Setting*
   - Estimate the total dollars required this year to fully fund this program; express the costs in amounts or units of service to be provided.
   - Estimate each annual giving program's potential to produce funds to support this program; set goals.
   - Secure all approvals for the fund-raising plans and budget required, based on the estimated net proceeds to be raised.
   - Establish a master solicitation schedule for meeting the goals on schedule.

Exhibit 3.2   The Goal-Setting Process for Annual Giving

sources will be necessary. When the money needed is raised by using annual giving solicitations year after year, that success illustrates how each method chosen has been highly coordinated with all of the organization's other annual fund-raising activities. Each method can be prepared, according to its own multiyear program plan, for budget support, revenue estimates, and assessments of various benefits from broad public participation. By bringing all these critical factors to light, goal-setting exercises assist with realistic preparations and selection of reasonable goals. As with any investment program, some level of continuing commitment is necessary to achieve the full flowering of potential. A single fund-raising program or its one-year use as a solicitation activity is only its beginning; it is not the culmination of that program's capacity nor the apex of its achievement. Because each method of fund-raising does not perform the same as others, each will return a different yield from its investment from year to year. It is recommended that individual goals be set for each activity as a sound management practice.

Annual giving achieves the highest levels of success when managed as a combination of programs that strongly support one another. Careful planning involves thoughtful use of a variety of annual solicitation methods, awareness of their timing, and knowledge of their relationship to audiences recently solicited. Factors to be considered include external conditions (such as the local economy), competition from other nonprofit organizations, leadership and volunteer commitment, and even a bit of luck. A constant evaluation of the performance of each method in use is necessary for informed decisions on what to offer next, when, and to whom. Great flexibility is needed to design a plan that can continue to be productive throughout the year and will enhance the potential for repeated use next year. As an example, five mail donors gave $500 each in response to a letter appeal program last year. In the next campaign, these five donors will be solicited by the volunteer-led personal solicitation committee (whose goal also will increase by their potential to deliver another $2,500). This strategy ensures that a volunteer will talk with each of these five donors about continuing their gifts at $500 or perhaps giving more. It works; three give $500 again and two increase their gift to $1,000. Personal solicitation has been effective in renewing all five gifts; the organization has received $3,500, which is $1,000 above the $2,500 given in annual support last year. However, the direct mail renewal program, which brought in these five gifts last year, has now been challenged to find new donors or to upgrade others within the donor pool in order to replace the gift amount of $2,500. To meet this goal, the direct mail program personnel will have to work harder, expand the lists and the number of solicitations, and spend more budget. A likely result may be 25 new donors at $100 each, or 250 new donors at $10 each, or some combination. If the organization is to receive added funds each year from each technique of annual solicitation, each program must complement the others and receive adequate support for its own separate objectives.

THESE ARE DONORS, NOT NUMBERS

Annual giving goals must be based on expectations of how each method of solicitation will be used and its relationship to the other methods being used. If the overall annual goal is $250,000, the solicitation plan might well include four mailings, three benefit events, two personal solicitation campaigns, and one membership drive. To illustrate the flexibility needed, let us assume the largest annual donation is from a local businessman who gave $25,000 in each of the past three years, but who has just been promoted and has moved to another state. The organization is likely to lose this gift; and chances of replacing the businessman with another single donor are slim. However, active solicitation of five other businessmen who are major gift prospects has begun; each has a $25,000 gift potential. Unfortunately, none of the five can give the full amount of $25,000 this year. The back-up plan is to ask all five to consider a gift of $5,000 each. Their prior best gifts were between $1,000 and $2,500 each. Business is poor, and they cannot increase their present level at all this year. It is not reasonable to expect each donor to increase his giving by a factor of five, just because the campaign needs to replace one donor at $25,000.

What other facts are in this year's case statement that, along with its package of priority needs, provide quality motives for giving? For solution of its $25,000 shortfall, the organization is likely to have to turn to other fund-raising activities. How flexible are the other annual giving programs? Can they increase their performance by $25,000? The solution will depend on existing donors; no new donor is likely to make such a large first-time gift. One or more of the other fund-raising programs might agree to ask 25 of its donors for an extra $1,000 each, or 100 donors for an extra $500 each, or 250 donors for an extra $100 each to achieve this goal. What effect will this extra pressure for performance have on these donors? Will they reduce other gifts to the organization, normally given at other times in the year? How will they respond to next year's appeals? Some caution must be exercised in the "solution" being considered, beginning with a respect for donor preferences of amounts, timing, and purposes of their current gifts. The bottom line reads: Anticipate that every donor (major or not) will stop giving some day. Time and attention must be given *now* to the identification, cultivation, and preparation of replacement donors and prospects who will pick up where others have left off. There is more to annual giving than just asking last year's donors for money again.

Fund-raising does not perform "by the numbers" despite good intentions and hard work by volunteers and staff. Without an urgent, compelling reason, people cannot be pushed or pressured into higher levels; they will not give more frequently just because the extra money is needed. They can be asked and asked well, but these extra solicitations may appear "greedy" and could sour their continued relationship. The decision of how often to ask requires sensitive and considerate evaluation. The value of multiple annual solicitation programs is twofold:

1. Some methods may be able to exceed their goals, making up part or all of the difference when others fall short.
2. Other methods may appeal to the same group of donors; they will not object to being asked to participate in different ways more than once a year.

A well-balanced array of activities is desirable for other reasons, besides greater reliability in meeting dollar goals. Prior donors may not have the ability to increase their gift each year, even when well asked; in fact, solid work may be required just to renew their gifts at the same level year after year. But they may be able to be more generous in future years.

The potential to increase the amount of money raised from the same constituency is dependent on two factors: (1) the number of loyal and committed donors who are matched with energetic and well-trained volunteers, and (2) a continuous effort to recruit new donors. Whatever each donor will give at any one time in response to any one request will be valuable. If the amount falls short of a desired goal, donors must still be told that their efforts did make a difference and are deeply appreciated. With this approach, they will be more inclined to give again next year. Managing donors' enthusiasm and confidence year after year is as valuable a goal as realizing the targeted dollar amount.

Analyses of prior-year results and of current external conditions are essential to realistic goal setting. What activities and individuals worked well or did not work well? What amount of true costs was required and how were the results produced? (Results can and should be measured on several levels when setting new goals. It is essential to understand, to the degree possible, *exactly* how these results occurred.) How many donors responded? What percentage of those who were solicited replied? What was their average gift size? What was the number of volunteer solicitors who helped, and what was their performance level? There is a lot of good data to study. The budget required to support solicitation activities can be measured against results as a way of understanding efficiency and gathering information for next year's budget requirements. Exhibit 3.3 provides several internal and external evaluation areas that can be helpful when results must be measured or when an income amount, if these activities are repeated in the next solicitation sequence, must be predicted.

Realistic goal setting can be performed for each of the annual giving activities in use. Measurement of prior performance should begin with a

1. Accuracy and Usefulness of the List
   • Complete mailing addresses
   • Correct name spelling and ZIP code
   • No duplications or "salting" of names
   • Number of incorrect address pieces returned
   • Number of address correction requests returned

2. United States Postal Service
   • Technical advice on successful preparation
   • Handling time at drop site location
   • Average delivery time (14 days or less for third class, bulk rate letters)
   • "Address Correction Requested" service

3. Printing Services
   • Realistic bids for services
   • Art work and package design
   • Established and met deadlines
   • Quality of finished product

4. Test Mailing Procedures
   • Random selection of names to test
   • Quality control on test package
   • Tabulation and analysis of test results

5. Mail House Services
   • List processing and consolidation
   • Duplicate-elimination procedures
   • Package assembly and accuracy in preparation
   • Advance deposit to postal account
   • Correct preparations for U.S. Postal Service acceptance
   • Address correction procedures

6. Mail Solicitation Response (by List)
   • Percentage rate of return
   • Average gift size
   • Average cost per gift
   • Individual list cost-effectiveness
   • Overall cost-effectiveness
   • Overall performance analysis (each mailing)

Exhibit 3.3   Assessment Criteria for Acquisitions Mailings

review of the organization's priority of needs and the public's acceptance of the priority list. Next, the organization should review the timing of solicitations, the training and performance of volunteers, the budget available to support each effort, the competence of staff members who supervise these activities, and much more. Among the external conditions to be considered are: fund-raising competition, economic and political conditions, demographic and diverse cultural influences, and media and other communications influences. Society changes rapidly today, and it is immensely complex. Consultants and vendors will enhance a general understanding of external factors. Unforeseen events can also have an immediate effect on the best of plans. Examples are: natural disasters and their immediate fund-raising responses, which can claim priority over other needs; major elections, which spawn extensive political fund-raising activities; an unexpected change in the organization's leadership; a fund-raising scandal widely covered by the media; or the inroads of a nearby, competing organization whose multimillion-dollar capital campaign has been in full swing for several months.

Sometimes, unforeseen events can provide an opportunity to bring an organization's needs to the attention of the public. Awareness of external events and conditions is important; anything that receives high visibility within the area of service may either help or hurt an organization's solicitation activities. Positive effects might be: easier recruiting of leaders and volunteers, greater public confidence in the organization because of its thoughtful response, and more motivation for people to participate in service efforts that have proven to be successful.

Achieving annual goals can be a success story that gives pride and confidence to volunteers and adds credibility to the entire goal-setting process for next year. Failure to meet goals, on the other hand, can be quite damaging to the entire annual giving program even after those involved are provided with full details to help them understand the failure. If, for example, volunteers were excluded from the goal-setting discussions, they can lose confidence in those who set them along with a sense of their ability to meet these demands in the future. Perhaps goals should be called "targets," with the inner circle to be aimed at and the bull's eye to be hit whenever possible. Failure will not motivate people to donate their time and their money.

THE ANNUAL FUND—MASTER SCHEDULE

Each nonprofit organization has exactly 12 months in which to schedule its annual solicitation activities. The first step is to review the calendar and keep each fund-raising activity unopposed and unduplicated in the time slot that is assigned. A savvy approach to scheduling will permit the best efforts of volunteers and donors to have a clear run to their goal. A master schedule may be possible but it must take into account the plans of all concerned and the value of each fund-raising method in case overlap occurs. With such a schedule in place, annual giving solicitations can be taking place all year long. Competing organizations will be actively soliciting as the same time, no matter when a program is in progress, and community and seasonal events may erode interest for brief periods.

Among the positive features of a master schedule are: (1) reinforcement of public attention to and support of the needs of the organization and those whom it serves, and (2) the ability to compete effectively with other organizations. By setting a schedule (being mindful of other organizations, where direct conflict may be unwise), a claim to certain times of the year is established, and the others must decide how to compete with the strength of the announced activity. The quality of an organization's performance is its strongest asset. It will gain respect from others while it reinforces the confidence of volunteers and donors. Everyone believes too much mail arrives and too many telephone calls are received, all asking for money. Fund-raising has become pervasive. To avoid an immediate negative response to an appeal directed toward select donors and prospects, an organization must plan each of its appeals and all of its other communications on a master schedule that best meets its needs, has the competition in mind, and allows each of its activities the best hope of success.

Several factors should be considered when making a master schedule for annual giving solicitations:

1. When was the solicitation conducted last year and the year before?
2. Was the calendar year-end used (for tax motives)?
3. Was there any conflict with known dates of others?
4. Did people reply at the same time as in prior years?
5. How did people reply? Did they give more or less?
6. Did volunteers follow the schedules in fulfilling their asking assignments?
7. Did any other requests influence this effort?
8. Which programs met their goals and why?
9. Which programs fell short of their goals and why?
10. What back-up plans had to be used and why?
11. Did the back-up plans help to meet the goal?
12. How will all these factors affect next year's goals?

There are many pieces to the scheduling puzzle. Two of the most important factors involve determining, from everything available, (1) what is the best time for the organization to ask for money and (2) what amount of time (and budget) will be needed to plan, organize, and conduct each solicitation activity at the performance level that is necessary to achieve the annual giving goal. Both factors lead back to the need for planning.

MAKING AND FOLLOWING PLANS:
THE FREQUENCY OF APPEALS

There are traditional calendar periods when most nonprofit organizations actively solicit annual gifts. The months of October through December are considered to be the best because of the favorable combination of traditional holiday spirit and the end of the tax year (an unbeatable combination). The second best period extends from March through June; for many organizations, the fiscal year ends on June 30. That leaves the third best period as January to March (publishers often renew subscriptions at this time). The least productive period is the summer months, when vacations consume most discretionary income. Even with good coordination among ongoing solicitation activities, there will be months, usually October through December, when more than one solicitation activity will be in progress at the same time. Some programs, such as direct mail and personal solicitation, can complement one another because they can work in sequence (a letter is followed by a phone call or appointment) and they use common lists of donors and prospects. Other solicitations may be in direct conflict: one letter may be asking for an annual gift, another for a special campaign gift, and a third for attendance at an event. What is needed is a plan that prevents confusion and reduces the appearance of uncoordinated and excessive overlapping solicitation. It is acceptable to deliver, with a solicitation, an invitation to a popular benefit event that is six to eight weeks away. Donors usually have to make choices when more than one appeal arrives from the same organization (hopefully not on the same day!), but loyal donors may spread their giving decisions among several options. Those who have to make a choice most of the time will still be choosing one of the organization's activities. They are unlikely to respond with separate gifts to each appeal and may ignore the third one entirely, but the message that important needs exist and that their help is vital has been delivered.

The point of sensitivity must be stressed here. Appeals can be too aggressive, no matter how noble the cause or how desperate the need. Stirring the ire of the public is never wise. At times, management and volunteers stress the need for action over the need for sensitivity. It's a tough call; jobs may be on the line. Writing to current donors about an emergency that has developed (which may include failure to meet a goal) will be more acceptable than writing to nondonors who know little about the organization and its goals. What schedule of contacts and what messages have already been sent to both groups? What is the potential for their conclusion that the appeals are ill-timed and inconsistent, appear to use pressure, and may even border on harassment? It is impossible to predict how each person will respond to repeated solicitation, except to know that more people will become upset as appeals become more aggressive and repetitive. Nonprofit organizations do not have the right to bombard the public with relentless appeals. There are limits to the amount of free speech the U.S. Constitution protects. First and foremost, this is a friend-raising business; second, it is a fundraising business. Each appeal must be financially successful in order for an organization to raise the money it needs; it cannot act with financial irresponsibility and expect to receive public support.

After a few years of supporting an organization, its constituency will become more comfortable with multiple solicitations *if they make sense* and do not border on abusive practices. The donors will have learned that several annual giving solicitation programs coincide and that they will be regularly invited to participate in more than one. When they receive a letter appeal for an annual gift, a second letter about a special campaign, and an invitation to a benefit, they may become more willing to at least consider a response to each request, depending on the extent of their interest in (and enthusiasm for) the organization and its needs. Consistency in the annual case statements can help here. Recipients will be less upset when multiple requests arrive if they have been informed, via the case statements, of the full spectrum of targeted needs. An organization must remain sensitive to the frequency with which appeals are sent to its existing donors, and the master schedule acts as a control sheet for communications to every audience.

At times, other organizations may have to revise their schedules to avoid the risk of directly competing with an organization that has well-established patterns of solicitation. A highly respected annual benefit event sponsored by a leading organization in a charitable fund-raising field is likely to be supported and attended by representatives of other organizations in the same field. For example, during National Heart Month (February), donors to the American Heart Association and hospitals with specialized cardiac facilities can be expected to interchange appearances at annual giving activities and benefit events. The focus moves from individual organizations' goals to the overriding goal of emphasizing the successes of cardiac research and treatment and the need to contribute toward their continuation and growth.

The time needed to organize annual solicitation programs varies. The cheerful estimate, "As long as is needed for good results," denies the need for an organization to plan thoroughly, measure the results, and then improve the plan if necessary. Estimates of the time to be invested in each fund-raising program may be general, but they must be made. Usually, planning and organizing an annual volunteer-led, volunteer-staffed, personal solicitation program scheduled for, say, the month of October, will require intense effort in the entire 11 months between appeals. An annual benefit can take three to six months to prepare but the effort disbands for six to nine months after the event is held. Direct mail programs, often a fund-raising staff activity that requires only limited volunteer participation, can be prepared and executed in 60 days [2]. No single calendar period is magically successful; careful planning and realistic measuring of results will indicate whether the date or time period was well chosen or should be rescheduled in the following year.

PLAN TO BE FLEXIBLE

Murphy's law—"If something can go wrong, it will"—can creep into the best of plans and schedules. Flexibility is a virtue in any plan, but Murphy's law seems to apply less often when solid planning is implemented and flexibility is reserved for "just in case" situations. Well-made plans are good protection against the unexpected; for some activities, they may even be able to push performance beyond the goals because they allow volunteers, donors, and prospects to concentrate on the urgency of the nonprofit organization's need for funds. Solicitation activities are sensitive to timing, and schedules must be carefully planned to facilitate success and to avoid inordinate pressure on volunteers and donors. Good planning can prevent annual giving programs from turning into last-minute panics in which everyone abandons carefully designed plans, just to achieve a dollar goal. When returns are lower than anticipated, some people may question their own ability to meet defined goals. Others will question the merits of the plan. It is important for board members, managers, volunteers, and staff to appreciate that the willingness of the public to respond with personal gifts cannot be controlled with an on–off switch. Giving is voluntary. Reliable public support is built slowly and carefully. It is based on confidence and trust in the organization and the proven solicitation methods used, and it works best when following highly coordinated annual solicitation plans.

Emergencies do occur. When they are not caused by lapses in stewardship and are well-communicated, they do not lessen the public's confidence and trust in the organization's judgment. Conditions can change. When the changes are understood, they can become enlightening footnotes to the story already being told in the case statements. If public confidence and trust are lost, however, even the best of plans or the strongest case statement cannot help. Broad consensus on annual giving methods and adherence to fund-raising plans are the best protection against unwise just-get-the-money pressure. Every "quick buck," "quick fix," or "easy money" idea I ever heard about had the same major flaw: It showed that the organization was not well-managed, did not plan well, was unable to anticipate common emergencies, and was willing to sacrifice sound business practices for the sake of money. Quick fixes can do irreparable harm to public confidence and can lead to less than professional conduct or even to unethical practices that promise easy money. Great damage is done to all charitable organizations when a scandal in one of them becomes a major news story. The entire telemarketing industry has become suspect because of a few widely publicized abusive practices. When a highly visible negative event occurs, wise nonprofit organizations will review their own activities for any improprieties and then reassure their public, perhaps in a special letter or advertisement, of the soundness of their administrative practices and the checkpoints established to foil any misuse of funds. Constant accountability, including open and full disclosure before and after any questionable incidents, is the best policy. Without it, the years and dollars invested in building positive relationships with volunteers, donors, and prospects are placed at risk or wiped out. These consequences are a hundred times worse than a failure to meet an arbitrary dollar goal.

The final component for success with goals and objectives is measurement of performance or results. Goals should be announced early and made clear to volunteers, donors, and prospects. What were the results from last year's campaign? How was the money used? Did the expected public benefit occur? How many people were served or helped? What difference did it make in their lives? First proposed in the case statement, these are the details that need to be verified before any further solicitation is conducted. What were the fund-raising results? Was the scheduling workable for each solicitation activity? What were the results of each method of fund-raising? How were budgeted dollars spent? How did actual performance compare to the anticipated goals? Is a report on these results available to everyone involved—staff, volunteers, and donors? These answers should be on hand for communication to the public.

Communications about success are important motivators for volunteers and donors. Volunteers who responded to expectations should be asked to help again, in the context of a compliment and a thank-you. Donors should receive a "big picture" report that highlights contributions within the perspective of the organization's overall goals. Everyone should be informed how the performance of each of the solicitation activities is monitored. The public benefits achieved through gift support of the organization's programs and services should be stressed. Future direct mail letters can brag about the effectiveness of the group effort that made good things possible. Several of the criteria listed in Exhibit 3.3 can be adapted for use in public reports. If people are told what is being done with their money and how valuable their gifts are, they will be more comfortable with the messages in the case statement and with multiple annual solicitation activities.

WHERE PLEDGES FIT IN ANNUAL GIVING

Many nonprofit organizations encourage pledging as an active feature of their annual giving programs. Pledges encourage lasting relationships with the organizations because pledges are, in effect, long-term commitments that involve frequent contacts (installment payments are spread throughout the year). For some organizations, pledging has become the traditional form of annual giving; for others, it may not work at all. Pledges are especially well-liked by donors, but they place increased burdens on nonprofit organizations. The positive features of using pledges are (1) early commitment and (2) convenience for donors. The negative features are: (1) delayed revenue, (2) record-keeping costs, (3) defaults by pledgers, and (4) extra administrative costs. Nonprofit organizations should investigate their potential for both the positive and negative features before deciding whether to offer pledges as an option in direct mail and other annual giving programs. Once begun, a pledge program is difficult to terminate.

Pledging can be used positively in several situations. One type of pledge—a payroll deduction to aid United Way campaigns—has become successful nationwide because of the degree of reliability in collections. Each type of pledge has its merits; each enhances and improves annual giving results. Do the funds actually get collected? Loyalty ranges from low to high, depending on how well the nature of the pledge is matched to the annual giving method (see Exhibit 3.4). The value of a pledge can be evaluated for each fund-raising method. The pledge option should be explained in the first direct mail acquisition letter of the campaign, and reminders should be inserted in future mailings.

One Gift a Year

When donors make annual pledges, they are invited to select, early in the year, the total amount of their contribution. Quarterly or monthly installment payments are common, but, as a convenience, they may be allowed to arrange another payment schedule better suited to their resources. This type of pledge should be reserved for an important level of gift support ($500, $1,000, or more). The positive features are: early commitment, and recognition as a major participant. On the negative side, a Yes response to a pledge is easy because the payments are put off until later. There is some potential for nonpayment and delinquencies.

Pledge Selected	Collectibility Score
One Gift a Year (Direct mail annual pledge with full payment due by 12/31/— or end of fiscal year)	Low/Medium/High
Membership Dues (Scheduled amount due by deadline to retain membership privileges)	Low/Medium/High
Tithing (Fixed total amount with regular payment amounts)	Low/Medium/High
Payroll Deduction (Employee-authorized direct payments out of regular paycheck)	Low/Medium/High
Matching Gifts (Employer agrees to match employee gift amount)	Low/Medium/High
Upgrade Option (Donor to increase pledged amount to qualify for higher recognition and extra benefits/privileges)	Low/Medium/High
Introductory Offer (Donor commits to a get-acquainted discounted entry into a gift category, with full payment due by a future date)	Low/Medium/High
Pledge by Phone (Donor replies with verbal intent to make a gift)	Low/Medium/High
Multiyear Payment Plan (Donor signs pledge form and is allowed more than one year to complete full payment)	Low/Medium/High

Exhibit 3.4 Scorecard for Types of Annual Gift Pledges

Record-keeping, mail-back payment forms for periodic billing, and re-minder letters to delinquent donors will be required. In addition, when donors make a once-a-year gift decision, there is less chance they will agree to any additional gifts during the same year.

Membership Dues

The key feature in any membership program is a fixed dues amount as-sessed on all members. Payment entitles the member to all of the orga-nization's rights and privileges for a defined period. The payment schedule may have an extended deadline (calendar or fiscal year-end) and may allow quarterly or monthly payments. Use of a firm deadline establishes an anniversary date for annual membership (which sim-plifies renewal requests) and limits operating costs to the period of the membership drive rather than having them spread throughout an entire year. Retention of status as a member in good standing, entitled to certain benefits and privileges, hinges on payment of dues by the renewal date (or within a reasonable grace period). Chapter Five will describe membership programs and all their uses and benefits.

Tithing

Possibly the oldest and best known type of pledge used for annual giving purposes, tithing combines the once-a-year gift decision with membership status and gives the donor satisfaction at having fulfilled an important obligation. Tithing has been used most often by religious organizations as testimony of their followers' commitment to a level of annual financial support (sometimes expressed as a percentage of personal income). Tithing's biggest advantage is its reliability of full payments received on schedule. Among its hazards are: (1) the tithe stays a fixed amount year in, year out, and (2) the organization may assume faithful payment and spend accordingly, only to find that some tithers have abandoned their financial commitment partway through the year.

Payroll Deductions

In this widespread practice, donors ask their employers to provide a service by taking a portion of their salaries and sending it to a nonprofit organization as payment for a personal gift pledge. The employees stipulate a fixed amount (or percentage) to be taken out, the schedule for withdrawals/payments, and the total amount to be paid for the year. Payroll deduction is an employer's decision and it implies some solicitation activity in the workplace, usually performed by employees, not outsiders.

Matching Gifts

Payroll deduction can also be used by employees who want to make gifts to several nonprofit organizations where their company will match all or a part of their donation. A corporate matching gift program may be available as a separate plan or as a payroll deduction privilege, to encourage employees to be active in their community and to demonstrate civic participation. The amount matched will vary in each company and will usually have a cap on percentage of contribution or dollar amount. Most companies issue a list of generic or specific nonprofit organizations qualified to receive matching funds. The nonprofit organizations selected then receive two annual gifts as long as the employee stays a loyal donor.

Upgrade Option

A scale of increasing annual gift amounts, each offering expanded benefits and privileges, may encourage donors to be progressively more generous. Each larger gift decision achieves greater rewards. Upgrade options can be used in almost every annual giving program described in this chapter; they are most effective when promoted in the solicitation renewal cycle.

Introductory Offer

A pledge option is often successful in encouraging a prospect or donor to make a first gift. The offer may allow a discount price (for the initial year only) for access to the benefits and privileges usually reserved for donors who pledge a higher amount. The key is to ask for partial payment up front, with the balance to be paid by a future deadline. This plan requires accurate record-keeping and other administrative support because overhead costs are incurred. There is some potential for resentment among donors who gave the full amount in their first year of membership but, in the spirit of the organization's purposes, it may be evident only in heavier assignments being given to the newcomers. A membership program can often make the best use of an introductory offer; it may not be as useful to the other annual giving applications. The introductory offer should not be renewable for any donors.

Pledge by Phone

Telephone solicitation relies on a verbal pledge to secure a gift decision. Telemarketing is pervasive in our society and is used in every type of commercial sales and nonprofit solicitation. The public is becoming increasingly irritated with and even distrustful of telephone requests. Despite the advantage of a two-way dialogue, use of the telephone for fund-raising must be studied carefully. Preparations must include solid training and rehearsing for callers, and rapid follow-up to confirm the pledge and ask for payment. Payments spread over several months are not recommended for telephone pledges because of the collections problem. The nonpayment rate is higher for the pledge by phone approach than for other pledge methods.

Multiyear Payment Plan

An occasion may arise where a multiyear pledge may be appropriate, but it is not a typical plan. It could be an incentive to achieve a higher level of membership dues or tithing, or as an upgrade option where a two- or three-year payment period would be allowed to achieve the higher donor levels. Multiyear payments are typically reserved for capital campaign gifts from individuals, corporations, and foundations.

Pledges Cost Money

Nonprofit organizations should recognize that their decision to use any type of pledging in support of their annual giving program will be accompanied by extra internal expenses for record-keeping, billing, collections, and related support activities. The costs to mount a broad-based annual giving program, especially for a new nonprofit organization or one that is introducing new fund-raising methods, are already high because of up-front acquisition costs. The addition of internal costs to support pledges counteracts the efficiency and cost-effectiveness of overall annual giving performance. For example, a membership program should be added to overall annual solicitation activities only when it will increase the potential for retaining annual donors. Members will expect fulfillment of member services, modest membership perks, a members' directory, and possibly an annual meeting for election of officers. They are usually unaware and unconcerned that these operating expenses must be paid out of membership dues revenue. Allowing a pledge payment option for membership dues will spread revenue receipts over several months and further increase record-keeping and mailing costs. Overall net proceeds to the nonprofit organization may be diminished dramatically.

Pledges can conflict with good fund-raising practice. Pressure to meet a goal, a volunteer quota, or a "fair-share" average gift may be offensive. When a solicitation program concentrates too much on reporting how much money was raised, or when volunteers become too enthusiastic about making their assigned goal of gifts achieved, there is a potential for negative effect. Donors may feel an obligation to respond positively to a friend and say Yes to a pledge, but remain uncommitted to make payment. Some donors have decided that one way to handle a persistent caller (short of hanging up) is to agree to a pledge they never intend to fulfill. Such practices lead to misleading reports, inaccurate expectancies, and displeased donors. There is also potential for deceptive practices; an aggressive volunteer or employee may secure a pledge by offering benefits that cannot be fulfilled. As additions to routine annual giving programs, pledges can be a mixed blessing.

Fund-Raising Costs

Expenses occur throughout the acquisition cycle. The costs to acquire first-time donors are the highest of all fund-raising expenses. Reasonable cost estimates to acquire a first-time donor can range from $1.00 to $1.50 for each dollar raised; there should be at least a 1 percent response rate among those invited to give. This level of performance is an acceptable standard and can be used as a guideline for acquisition direct mail efforts. As is illustrated in the book's ongoing example of the CCUA Clean Up Cleveland Chapter, all the costs are tracked carefully and measured against the results. It is important to include *everything* involved in finding, motivating, and servicing a donor's first gift. These data are invaluable in making decisions that will continue to build a constituency of faithful, committed donors who can be depended on for generous annual gifts. Analysis of performance will identify, for the nonprofit organization's management and fund-raising team, the acquisition mailing lists and messages that have produced the best results.

ACQUISITION THROUGH MAIL APPEALS

Annual giving means finding new donors each and every year and soliciting all the previous donors again. New nonprofit organizations have no prior donors; they must begin their solicitation activities by communicating their valid needs to lists of unknown prospects and suspects. The most effective way to acquire a large number of first-time donors is to reach out broadly, soliciting their interest and support by mail. Any nonprofit organization can begin its fund-raising program by mailing a few thousand solicitation letters. However, to have a successful mailing the first time, the fifth time, or the fiftieth time requires strict attention to proven concepts and to details. Using the mail *successfully* is not easy, despite the quantities of appeals that arrive through the mail. The sheer volume of requests is amazing. The reason? Mail solicitation works!

A new organization must start with mailing lists—names and addresses of prospects and suspects. Lists can be compiled from among board members and volunteers; they can also be bought, leased, or rented. Whatever their source, all the entries must be collected together, studied carefully, and made available in some common and usable form. Along with the case statement and the mail package, lists should always be tested (see Chapter Two). The story in the case statement must be converted into letter form. Envelopes, response forms, and any added materials must be designed and their costs estimated; receipt and reply procedures, including thank-you letters, must be firmly in place. Financial controls for handling each gift and depositing the money, record-keeping of all donors' data and individual gifts, and reports that summarize the results are essential business requirements. Estimated costs for all the printing, computer time, postage, and handling costs of outgoing, incoming, and acknowledgment mail must be reliably tallied. Only after total costs are understood can the final decisions be made about how many letters must be mailed to achieve the anticipated results.

Tom Broce [3], in his excellent summary of annual giving preparations, lists these as the essential preparation details: A well-defined purpose, extensive planning, an efficient organization, a realistic timetable, meaningful benchmarks, realistic assignments, and logical order. Broce continues:

> Several other factors are considered "givens" in fund-raising programs. Remember that the annual program requires
>
> (1) a well-researched prospect pool;
> (2) well-kept records and well-planned solicitors' materials, including brochures and pledge cards;
> (3) an adequate professional and clerical staff to help the volunteers;
> (4) an adequate support budget;
> (5) institutional leadership, including that of the chief executive officer; and
> (6) appropriate gift-acknowledgment and report systems.
>
> The lack of any of these elements may be reason to delay or reevaluate the organization's ability or preparedness to conduct a fund-raising program.

These details all must be resolved before committing the funds necessary to prepare the letters to be taken to the post office. Roger Craven [4] explains why:

> Direct mail has been deprecated as a fund-raising tool because the gifts it produces are relatively small, costs are relatively high, and, as a rule, the technical and professional skills required to manage a professional mail program are not available on many fund-raising staffs. However, the organization that asserts itself in learning the real purpose and proper use of the medium will reap significant rewards, discover new special-gift and major-gift prospects, educate its constituency, and reach its peripheral constituencies, thus making them more active contributors.

Advice abounds on how to succeed with mail solicitation, whether for commercial or charitable purposes. Expert professional help is necessary to achieve success. "Direct response advertising" is a well-established form of mass communication that is widely used because it gets results—it works! Will it work for everyone? Probably, if used properly. Fund-raising by mail alone, however, is not likely to meet all the needs of a nonprofit organization. In the base of the giving pyramid (Exhibit 1.2) mail solicitation has a most important place, but it is not alone. Modern, computerized direct mail solicitation is a complex activity. It can work equally well for smaller and for larger nonprofit organizations. Professional counsel is available to help maximize the potential uses of direct mail, but, by following some basic rules and recognizing that investments of both time and money are required, most organizations can make their programs profitable. Ed Mayer [5], an early direct mail artist, craftsman, and teacher, created the following seven cardinal rules for success when using the mail:

1. Start with the objective of your program.
2. Reach the right person on the right list.
3. Present the case in terms of benefits to the reader.
4. Use appropriate copy and layout.
5. Make it easy for the prospect to take action.
6. Tell your story over and over again.
7. Research your direct mail efforts.

Direct mail is a primary medium for mass communication; it happens to work well for fund-raising. "The direct mail program must clearly and effectively communicate the institution's needs to potential donors" [6]. Those who read the letters (1) will be introduced to the cause and the needs it describes, (2) will learn something about community problems and proposed solutions, and (3) will find out about nonprofit organizations that are committed to providing needed services. These are critical objectives, and none of them mentions money.

Where do the financial results fit in, alongside these answers?

	True	False
As many as 90 percent of all appeal letters are discarded unopened.	✓	___
Only 10 percent of those who open appeal letters will reply with money.	✓	___

Why bother with direct mail if it is so obviously uneconomical, such a waste of time and money? The answer lies in understanding the multiple values that communication by mail can and does have for nonprofit organizations. Letters offer the opportunity for:

1. Exchanging information;
2. Continuing education;

3. Building an image;
4. Forming respect and trust;
5. Encouraging involvement and commitment;
6. Making new friends;
7. Raising dollars for charitable purposes.

Cost-effectiveness is another measure of positive performance, but an organization needs some history before it can determine whether its patience and attention to detail have yielded efficiency. Renewal is where profit lies. Most nonprofit organizations are here to stay; through the mail, they can tell their story to a wide audience and then invite any persons who are interested to be part of the solution to problems.

WHY USE THE MAIL?

The chief purpose of any appeal letter—the first, the fifth, or the fiftieth—is to stimulate a reply. Letters are used best as personal, people-to-people communications. When trying to recruit people to action, the steps are: (1) get their attention, (2) explain a need that exists and the organization's competence to provide answers, and (3) invite them to be a part of the solution. The actual letter text is crucial to success, but it must first be delivered to individuals who will open and read it. Selective mailing lists represent the means to find those individuals who will be interested in reading the letter and are likely to reply. By finding and writing to people who have a potential interest, the organization will be using an effective and efficient method for locating those who will respond to the call for action. Those who do not reply are not necessarily wasted potential resources; they may reply to a second appeal. Repeated mailings are valid so long as enough replies with donations enclosed are received. Periodic mailings may convince potential donors that the organization is dynamic, that its need is real and urgent, and that resolution is attainable. They can still help if they choose, and the amount requested is not unreasonable. When acquiring new donors, the organization is making new friends; effort, persistence, and understanding are all needed. Professional mail consultants recommend sending repeated invitations to qualified donors who have not yet responded. People have to be encouraged to take action just as they have to be persuaded that their action will make a difference.

A nonprofit organization can never assume that because it needs money, interested people will respond with a donation. Fund-raising is not that simple. Realistic answers to these four essential questions are in order:

1. Does the mail package work (is it raising money and friends)? If so, is it because of the validity of the need or because of the organization's good image and reputation?
2. What success can be expected right now, based on analysis of the results of the last appeal, the local competition, the time of year, and the economy?
3. How much money will the current mailing bring in?
4. Is investment in another acquisition mailing the best use of a limited budget?

To find its own answers, an organization needs a detailed self-analysis. The following test, prepared by direct mail experts Kay Partney Lautman and Henry Goldstein [7], has helped many of their clients decide whether to use direct mail for fund-raising purposes:

1. Does your organization or cause have broad name recognition?
   (a) in the local community?
   (b) in the state?
   (c) nationally?
2. Does it deal with specific issues rather than broad or abstract ideas?
3. Does it serve or help specific constituencies—for example, minorities, the ill, the elderly, children, handicapped, the poor or disadvantaged, or animals?
4. Are there other organizations performing the same or similar services? If so, how is your organization unique?
5. Does your organization have a demonstrable track record?
6. If your organization is new, does it expect to respond to a critical issue in a dynamic way?
7. Is there a threat to the organization, those it serves, or to traditional funding sources? In other words, is there an issue, a crisis, or an emergency to be dramatized?
8. If yours is a membership organization, are tangible membership benefits offered? If yours is a cause-oriented organization, can you show the donor how his or her gift will make a difference?
9. Would your organization be financially able to survive a loss of 40 percent or more of its investment should the test mailing fail to recoup costs?
10. Do you have the patience (and the investment money) to wait between two and four years before realizing so-called spendable net income?

If you answered "yes" to half these questions, direct mail may be appropriate for your cause and a test mailing can be made a low risk. However, if you answered "no" to questions 9 and 10, think twice. Newcomers to direct mail must not view it as a fix for immediate financial problems, but as a calculated investment in the organization's future.

Readers who have evaluated all these answers and decided, with the blessing of their organization's leadership, to proceed, should reread Chapter Two's discussion of how to test a mailing plan. Testing is how and where direct mail acquisition must begin. Testing is essential; it protects against errors and waste of money. Only after completing an evaluation of its test results should an organization prepare for a full "roll out" of a direct mail solicitation program. Sound testing results promise considerable success in this year and for several to come.

MULTIPLE ACQUISITION METHODS

Preparations should target multiple mailings, not just a single letter. Testing shows which lists, messages, and package elements have the greatest appeal. Beyond money-raising, a successful mail acquisition will yield an understanding of the quality of the lists used and will indicate the investment required to satisfy valid needs and desired community benefits. The plan should project a three-year, multimailing program, a minimum of five to six mailings each year, and a total of between 15 and 18 letter packages to be sent to substantially the same people. From this entire effort, the organization will be able to measure several objectives, including its ability to:

1. Acquire new donors whose future gifts will serve as the foundation for reliable annual income for the future;
2. Advance the image and reputation of the organization and its mission;
3. Raise the money needed to fund immediate programs and services of public benefit;
4. Report the outcomes of their work to donors and prospects alike, to reinforce their decision to support the organization again.

After three years, the organization should have a favorable public image. By then, hundreds and perhaps thousands of donors should be committed to support of its mission. A continuing obligation to each of them is *communication*, to preserve their interest and maintain their active support for as long as possible.

The next step is a "roll-out," a commitment to mail to the full list or to as many names as prudence and the budget allow. This decision is expensive because all the costs are up-front. The boards and managers of nonprofit organizations are not gamblers; they hate risks of any sort. Test results should give them confidence in the expected rate of returns and may even prove to them that most, if not all, of the funds invested will come back as gifts within 30 to 60 days. If early tests did *not* prove that enough money will come back, another test should seek the lists (or list segments) and the message that will achieve at least a break-even financial return. (The segment of the CCUA Clean Up Cleveland Chapter story that appears at the end of this chapter provides an example.)

MULTIPLE MAILINGS

Any schedule of mailings is a sequence; for every first appeal, a follow-up letter is sent within 30 to 45 days. The results of each mailing should be measured before tallying the joint results. To make the sequence work as a single appeal:

Use the results of each mailing as a basis for decisions about the next mailing;

Study the replies from each segment of the mailing list used, sifting and sorting the individual responses for each time mailed;

Count the number of replies received from each list and note the average gift size and total gift revenue;

Read any comments or letters sent with the replies.

The percentage of response shows the receptiveness to the appeal. Average gift size shows ability and motivation to give. If the gifts received average only $8.00 per person, the list liked the appeal but does not have much money to give or does not think more than a token gift is merited. Total gift revenue should be compared with total preparation and mailing costs to measure efficiency and cost-effectiveness. If each mailing produces a 1 percent rate of return, an average gift of $25 and a cost of less than $1.50 for each dollar received:

Mail the appeal again to everyone who has not yet replied;

Keep mailing to the same list, and, after each mailing, cull those list segments that are not producing at least half the results above, or better;

Use the same list until it no longer meets good performance and profitability standards;

Retire the list and begin the same procedure with others.

WHEN TO MAIL AND HOW OFTEN

The timing for each mailing deserves careful study. For first-time donor acquisition mailings to lists never before used, the timing is critical. Traditional mailing periods are those times when the competition can be expected to be active as well. As identified earlier in this chapter, the preferred times, in order of preference, are: October to December, March to June, January to March, and July to September. Each organization must settle on the schedule it believes will work best for the people on its lists. One period may work as well as any other, depending on local conditions and many other unique factors. There is enough time in each of these periods for two letters—and possibly for three, if the returns are especially strong. Each of these primary mailing periods can be used to set up the next sequence, prepare to build on the messages already delivered, and add some details about how many other people have replied. Keeping track of what was written to each list in each mailing sequence is an important precaution. People always get the message about being asked for money. If the letters inform them of new facts about the organization, they are more likely to read the text—and, possibly, to respond.

Each nonprofit organization chooses its own mass mailing timetable. The schedule becomes a guide for the frequency and timing of not only its solicitation letters, but all of its other fund-raising solicitation activities and all of its other public communications needed during the year. There are limits to what people receiving all this mail can endure. There is also a limit on how much money the organization can afford to spend on all its mail communications. Because results provide guidance for all subsequent mailings, it is essential to measure the results of each mailing by asking:

1. Is it as efficient as possible, especially as measured by its public?
2. How many new donors and how much money has each appeal brought in?

Mailings are most successful when designed as a coordinated effort. The messages should complement one another to reinforce the validity and urgency of the appeal. A lot of work is involved but, because of the amount of money invested in these mailings, they must prove they can achieve reasonable performance expectations. Each nonprofit organization's overall marketing, promotion, and mass communications plans should be highly coordinated. After all, the audiences are the same.

The true test of performance for appeal letters and their messages is the length of their run, not how many weeks pass between mailings or how many mailings are planned within a year. Jerry Huntsinger [8], a current "dean" of direct mail fund-raising and one of the most talented and prolific mail experts around, has defined the following critical elements for analysis and future decision making, against which each separate mailing should be measured:

1. Number of pieces mailed
2. Cost of the mailing
3. Total income generated
4. Number of responses received
5. Percentage of response
6. Average gift
7. Net income
8. Cost to raise a dollar.

As long as the list is producing acceptable results (usually, a 1 percent rate of response with an average gift of $25), these good people can be asked for their help, on a schedule that works best within the organization. I once kept writing to a start-up list of 200,000 names for 11 mailings over a three-year period. The list shrank each time; some people moved away, others requested to be taken off the list. I kept mailing to this original group because each appeal yielded more than a 1 percent rate of return and maintained an average gift of $50 or more each time it was used. After 11 mail appeals, both the percentage and gift size fell and it was time to put the original list aside and begin using others.

Careful study of the returns must be performed after every mailing. What geographic areas within each list are doing better than others? (ZIP codes are the link, especially those with nine digits.) Average gift size is a measure of enthusiasm for the message sent and confirms where the quality of the list may be concentrated. If other data are available regarding the list, such as home value, income level, age, occupation, and so on, a more detailed analysis will add clues that can increase performance in future mailings. These studies can also point out lists, or areas within lists, that did not perform well. Any list or segment of a list that does not perform as well as others probably should be discarded or set aside for use only in a final year-end appeal. People are not likely to change their convictions about a cause or a need within a few weeks' time, on the basis of letters alone. The science of direct mail allows each user to establish individual performance guidelines to aid in achieving targeted performance goals. Usually, these are: not to waste money needlessly and not to harass the people on the lists. Letters are intended to create friends for the nonprofit organization; to educate the public about the organization's mission, purposes, goals, and objectives; to build respect for the organization and its methods; and to raise the money it needs. The mail should be used to make friends whenever possible; no one needs enemies who will complain to others about the endless mail they receive from the organization or cite it as an example of wasteful management practices.

After the mailing has been "dropped," three additional options may encourage results and may help to preserve the value of the investment in the lists used and in the production costs:

1. Consider adding the words "Address Correction Requested" to the outer envelope. Some of the letters will be returned as undeliverable; people move, others die, and mailing lists have errors. The Postal Services will charge $0.35 for each piece of mail that is returned, but it will come back with a correct mailing address to which future appeals can be directed.

2. Evaluate results from the first mailing within three to four weeks, to allow for a few last-minute changes to the next mailing. The materials and letter text are already finished at this point and cannot easily be changed without delaying the next mailing. But there is time to cut back on any list or segment of a list that is obviously failing, or to expand from a segment to the full list if results were outstanding.

3. Prepare to process all the gifts received by sending a "thank-you" letter or an appropriate message of gratitude on the preprinted gift receipt form. Be ready to write to people who answer the appeal but do not send money; they may need more details before deciding to give. If they request to be taken off the mailing list, honor the request right away.

There will be adequate time between major mail sequences for more detailed evaluation (which parts of the package are in need of revision or can be dropped; what lists or segments of lists should be used again) and for response to anything that received wide public attention during the mailing. Perhaps materials for the next message will be revealed during these catch-up activities.

IMPROVED RESULTS WITH MULTIMEDIA APPEALS

Other communications scheduled to appear within the same time period may help some mailings to succeed. This "multimedia" technique is defined by Huntsinger [9] as follows: "The term "multimedia" refers to the combination of one or more media to sell a product or promote an organization. . . . So when you venture into multimedia, you venture into an area that has potential for fantastic failure or fantastic success." To illustrate, a notice about an annual giving appeal might appear in reports, newsletters, marketing materials, and other promotions. The widespread coverage keeps the appeal in the public eye. News releases that report on the people helped through the organization's programs and services further reinforce the message. Public service announcements (PSAs) on radio (and, possibly, on cable television) enhance the appeal messages by adding sight and sound. PSAs are inexpensive; by comparison, paid advertising will inflate fundraising costs. The value of these extra messages is in their repetition of the organization's name; the mail recipients will recognize the appeal when it arrives. "Direct marketing is an interactive system of marketing which uses one or more advertising media to effect a measurable response and/or transaction at any location" [10]. "Direct response advertising" has become a major means of communication. The sheer volume of mail appeals has created fierce competition for public attention—and considerable public resistance to the medium. The dominant users are for-profit corporations that use the mail to sell their products. The common nickname for direct mail mass communications is "junk mail." People joke about sorting their unopened and unread mail over the trash basket. In this decisive time span (estimated at five seconds or less), name recognition can be critical. The purpose of multimedia efforts is to save unread appeal letters from immediately becoming recyclable trash.

Nonprofit organizations cannot compete with the large advertising and multimedia communications budgets of for-profit corporations. Maximal results for nonprofit organizations will come from careful use of their limited communications budgets and from coordinated and cooperative multimedia message combinations. The marketing, public relations, and fund development staff should work together to keep the messages in their communications consistent and to place them for multiple and maximum effect. Because the audiences chosen for each of these communications are often the same people—community residents—better results will come from coordinating the joint use of shared mailing lists. Working together is efficient, effective, and smart; unfortunately, it is not often attempted. Each department has separate goals and its performance is measured by different results. Even a small effort—such as reference to a current appeal in a regular newsletter, magazine, or report, or in a separate "piggy-back" message that can be inserted in a mailing package for the same postage cost—can improve results.

Change is hard for some people; so are new ideas. Not everyone possesses a cooperative spirit. Some people hold on to textbook theorems about "pure" message delivery or have been warned against the potential for audience confusion from multiple messages. Some have even told me that fund-raising appeals might "poison" the audience against their message. Given the precious few dollars available for communications, perhaps it is time for management-level decisions calling for coordination and cooperation among staff, to eliminate arbitrary barriers or insecurities that handicap the potential for optimum results. Taken from a strategic marketing standpoint, what might be the result of attempting a joint communications effort in the most heavily used mail communications period of October to December? Isn't it worth a test to find out?

OTHER OPTIONS FOR ACQUISITION MAILINGS

Highly coordinated multimedia communications will continue to be a most effective strategy for nonprofit organizations. There may also be other opportunities where these communications can be used to effect the acquisition of new, first-time donors. To continue the speculation just above, referring to the October–December period, what might result from the unexpected, or from a Murphy's law scenario? Suppose a large local retailer proposes a cause-related marketing promotion that will advertise a special sale offer during November and December, the highest sales months in the year. The retailer's offer is 10 percent of all sales proceeds as a gift, in exchange for use of the organization's name and the name of its priority appeal project as benefactor of all funds raised by the arrangement. The marketing strategy is to conduct a blitz of advertising in November, just ahead of the holiday shopping period, using local radio, television, and newspapers, plus posters, bus-back and billboard advertising, and similar spaces. Each advertisement will feature the organization's priority fund-raising appeal; the retailer's schedule fits perfectly with the organization's year-end annual giving direct mail solicitation schedule. The expected level of visibility from such a campaign far exceeds what the organization could even hope to afford or accomplish on its own. But how flexible are its marketing, public relations, and fund-raising plans? Will everyone (or just the fund-raising office) adjust to this unusual opportunity? If the project proves financially successful to the retailer and nets an important gift to the organization, would both be likely to seek a joint promotion again next fall, or perhaps even in the spring of next year?

Other opportunities to enhance a first-time acquisition effort may not be as dramatic as this example but there are many possibilities: news stories about the project during the mailing period; publicized major gifts ($1,000 or more) received from a local corporation or foundation; a human interest story about a family who benefited directly from the service area of the appeal; progress reports announced with proper fanfare at public events. Ideas generate other ideas. The challenge is in making them happen.

Focus: CCUA Clean Up Cleveland Chapter

Harvey Clout continued with his efforts to form the Cleveland Chapter. In a workbook he had received from the national office were step-by-step instructions on how to start his program. The workbook suggested recruiting a chapter board of directors, hiring a full-time director of development to manage fund-raising and communications, and completing plans for the first full year of solicitation and communication activities. Each of these tasks was to be completed before sending out any more appeal mailings.

Chapter Board of Directors

Appointing a local board was easy for Clout. He was already serving on six nonprofit boards, two of which were just concluding successful major capital campaigns. He had also helped Mrs. Clout organize a new board for the Downtown Art Center, and, from his service on the executive committee of the Greater Cleveland United Way, he knew many corporate executives who were actively involved in several other nonprofit organizations. He had already invited a few friends and business associates to help him get the chapter started. These included Sidney Secure, his auditor; Mary Moneybanks and "Ted" Worthy, personal friends; and Titus Brown, his advertising and public relations counsel. A board of 21 members was recommended by the national office. Clout recruited the first 12 board members and gave nearly all of them specific assignments. Two other members, Steve Generous and "Telly" Temple, were added because of their positions as board chairpersons for the Cleveland Orchestra and Cleveland Play House, respectively. Here is how the chapter's initial board of directors looked after these appointments:

Board of Directors, CCUA Clean Up Cleveland Chapter

Officers

Chair of the Board	I. Harvey Clout
Vice Chair	Mary M. Moneybanks
Treasurer	Sidney M. Secure, CPA
Secretary	Theodosius ("Ted") Worthy
Assistant Secretary	Titus Brown, APR

Board Members and Committee Assignments

Development Committee Chair	Harold R. Connected
Board Members-at-Large	Steven Generous
	Iris B. Radiant
	Trafalgar ("Telly") Temple

Fund-Raising Executive

Earlier, Harvey Clout had asked Titus Brown to help him conduct a search for a director of development. Within four weeks, Brown presented three final candidates to Clout, all of whom had been successful at raising money for other organizations in the city. Interviews were arranged to allow new officers of the board to meet all three candidates. Karen I. Anderson, the assistant director in the National Audubon Society's local office, was chosen, accepted, and reported for work two weeks later. Within two weeks, Anderson had hired Alice B. Nice as her executive assistant. They remained in Clout's corporate offices, and Clout continued to meet all the daily operating costs for supplies, telephone, and mail services.

First Year's Solicitation and Communications

Karen Anderson studied the results of the initial test mailings (Exhibit 2.5). She began to plan for a follow-up "roll out" mailing to a larger segment of the overall Cleveland population. A few changes were needed, based on her analysis of test results. Anderson chose Letter B (Exhibit 2.4) over Letter A (Exhibit 2.3) and decided to drop List 2 and List 5 (eastern suburbs and sports teams' season ticket holders) for now; the tests showed these two groups were not likely to perform well enough to cover the costs of mailing and production. The four remaining mailing lists, after duplicate-elimination procedures, contained 80,595 names, made up as follows:

List	Definition	Names
1	Shaker Heights residents	28,565
3	Northeast Ohio members, National Audubon Society	17,615
4	Northeast Ohio members, The Nature Conservancy	12,637
6	Subscribers to the Cleveland Orchestra and	
	Cleveland Play House	21,778
	Total names	80,595

Karen Anderson estimated that slightly better than a 1 percent rate of return from these four lists was possible, which would provide 800 new donors. Assuming an average gift of $25, the mailing would yield income of $20,000. She also estimated the cost, based on the test mailing, at $.405 per letter. For 80,595 letters, "roll out" expenses would be $32,640.98. Given an income projection of $20,000, this first mailing would suffer a loss of over $12,000, which was not acceptable and could be a major setback to the entire chapter start-up. Anderson knew she had to find a way to increase the number of responses *and* the average gift size in order to achieve a break-even or better response on this first major mailing. Her proposal to Clout was to create a "Circle of Champions," an introductory donor club offer that conferred charter membership for a first-year reduced membership fee of $100. To try to catch the attention of the people who were on the remaining four lists, she proposed an extra benefit to go with the introductory offer—a free pass to some special event or performance by the Cleveland Orchestra or at the Cleveland Play House. She estimated the Circle of Champions idea would close the gap and make this first mailing profitable. Her calculations were as follows: If 5 percent of those who reply to the mailing become charter members at the reduced fee of $100, this will add $4,000 in net income to the bottom line; if 10 percent of those who reply join, $8,000 will be added. Because neither amount would be enough to offset the $12,000 shortfall, she estimated two additional possibilities:

1. Ask Clout to solicit the new board for at least $250 each, which would add $3,500;

2. Offer a variety of giving options, at levels of $100, $250, $500, and $1,000, to the Circle of Champions program, with special benefits for each level.

To reflect all these features and the early commitment from the new board members at $250 each, the text of Letter B and the response form were modified to add charter membership in the Circle of Champions, gift options, and the special event invitation from the Cleveland Orchestra or Cleveland Play House. Draft thank-you letters, for regular donors and for Circle of Champion charter members, also were prepared. The entire package was presented to Clout for the final decision to proceed with the mailing.

The First Full Mailing is Resolved

Harvey Clout loved the idea of the Circle of Champions. He called Steven Generous, board chair of the Cleveland Orchestra, and "Telly" Temple, board chair of the Cleveland Play House, and asked each if they could arrange a special offer for the charter members, such as an invitation to attend one of their programs. Clout told them that no more than 100 people would be involved. They both reported back in a few days to confirm the offer. Any donor of $100 or more would be invited to a special performance during the coming year. Both asked Clout for $10 from each gift as their share, but Clout convinced them that the CCUA Clean Up Cleveland Chapter needed all the money it could raise during this first year to get the chapter up-and-running successfully, and then to begin collecting funds for building the new energy plant. Generous and Temple agreed, and Anderson completed the "roll-out" package illustrated in Exhibits 3.5 through 3.9.

Results Analysis

Anderson's analysis of the results is shown below. The figures suggested that a few more modifications would be needed for the spring mailing campaign:

1. A total of 1,156 new donors was acquired.
2. A total of $35,758 was received.
3. An average gift of $30.93 was achieved.
4. Total cost per dollar raised was $0.91.
5. The number of charter members in the Circle of Champions was 118; they gave a total of $12,403, or an average gift of $105.
6. All the other donors (1,038) gave a total of $23,355, or an average gift of $22.50.
7. Net proceeds were $3,117.02.
8. The Circle of Champions made the difference.

The combined performance from the original six-list test mailings (348 donors and $8,527) and the "roll-out" to the surviving four lists came to a total of 1,504 donors and $44,285, at a cost of $44,890. Given the national average for a first-time acquisition mailing ($1.25 to $1.50 to raise a dollar), the CCUA Clean Up Cleveland Chapter was off to a solid start. The next step was to plan a second acquisition mailing in the spring, and, equally important, to prepare to renew the gifts of these first 1,504 donors.

Letter B (Revised)

The Campaign to Clean Up America
Clean Up Cleveland Chapter

October 15, 199X

Dear Friend for a Trash-Free Cleveland:

Every day as I drive back and forth to work I see a lot of paper littering our streets, along with cans and bottles, boxes, plastic bags, and more.

We all know the City has cut back on trash collections and street sweeping because of the recession, but they are not keeping up with the trash, not at all. And, our city is not the only city in America with this problem.

Earlier this year, I was invited to New York to hear about The Campaign to Clean Up America. I wanted to go for two reasons. First, this is a serious plan to do something about pollution in our country. Second, they've got a great idea. Build a new energy conversion plant and use all the trash to make electricity and cut our energy bills at the same time!

I estimate about 100,000 tons of trash is lying in our city streets and around our buildings and homes right now. With energy conversion in a new plant, this same trash can become 32,000 megawatts of electricity and meet the needs of 18,000 homes in our city for a full year. Further, this plant will reduce all of our electric bills by $12 a month and $124 a year.

Each of us will benefit from this project. That's why I need your help. Here's what I want you to do to support this City-wide effort:

First, stop being a "trasher." Pick up after yourself.

Second, bag all the trash you can find around your house, garage, and yard, and put it out with your garbage next week.

Third, join me as a member of our Clean Up Cleveland Chapter of The Campaign to Clean Up America. Your minimum gift of $12 stays in Cleveland. And $12 is the amount you will get back each month in savings on your electric bill from our new power plant.

Fourth, give $25 if you can. The sooner we raise the money and build the new energy plant, the sooner our new electric bills will go down and our city will be clean.

Fifth, join me in the "Circle of Champions," if you can. Your extra generosity at $100 entitles you to a charter membership in this new group of community leaders. Please note too that each charter member will be receiving an invitation to a special event next year to be offered by both the Cleveland Orchestra and Cleveland Play House.

Sixth, spread the word. Talk about what we are doing. Tell your neighbors and the people with whom you work. Ask them to get involved. Ask them to join you in the Clean Up Cleveland campaign. Put your bumper sticker on your vehicle (it's magnetic, not adhesive) and let everyone see you are a supporter of a cleaner Cleveland.

You've heard the old saying, "Every litter bit helps." Each of us can help a bit to make our city a better place to live. Your contribution of $12 or more is what is needed. All contributions will be divided, with 25 percent going to our public awareness and education programs and 75 percent going to help pay for the construction of our new energy plant.

Our proposal for the new energy plant has been approved by the Cleveland City Council. The site has been selected near Perry, Ohio, and the land has been donated by Centurion Energy Corp., who will also operate the new plant. The estimated total cost is $3.5 million. Two-thirds of this cost will be met by federal and Ohio matching funds. What we have to do is raise $1,250,000 in private contributions from the people who live and work in Cleveland.

I hope you will join me and commit yourself to help clean up Cleveland. Your bumper sticker is enclosed along with a response form to be returned with your gift. Let me hear from you soon.

Sincerely yours,

I. Harvey Clout
Chair of the Board
Cleveland Cast Iron Works

P.S. Last week, my son and I picked up three bags full of paper, cans, and bottles around our plant during lunch time, in less than 30 minutes. This coming Friday, our 15 managers will go around this plant, inside and out, and pick up all the trash they can find during their lunch break. The goal is for each of them to match our three bags full. Send me your ideas of what you are doing to help clean up our city.

Exhibit 3.5 Letter B: Final Text with "Circle of Champions" Added

The Campaign to Clean Up America
Clean Up Cleveland Chapter

[ ] YES! Count me in the campaign to Clean Up Cleveland. Attached is my gift to help:

   [ ] $12   [ ] $25   [ ] $50   [ ] $_____.

[ ] Yes! I would like to become a Charter Member of the "Circle of Champions" donor club. Attached is my membership gift of:

   [ ] $100   [ ] $150   [ ] $200   [ ] $_____.

[ ] Sorry. I cannot send a gift at this time. I do support your effort and will use the bumper sticker to help in this campaign.

THANK YOU FOR YOUR SUPPORT!

Name _____

Address _____

City _____ State _____ ZIP: _____-____

Exhibit 3.6 Sample Response Form

Letter B Results

List Name	Letters Mailed	Replies Number	Replies Percent	Gift Income	Average Gift	Cost per Dollar Raised
Cleveland Heights Residents	28,565	414	1.45%	$18,321	$44.25	$0.63
Audubon Society Members (NE Ohio)	17,615	372	2.11	8,916	23.96	0.80
Nature Conservancy Members (NE Ohio)	12,637	158	1.25	3,476	22.00	1.47
Orchestra & Play House Subscribers	21,778	212	0.97	5,045	23.80	1.75
Totals	80,575	1,156	1.43%	$35,758	$30.93	$0.91

Cost of mailing ($0.405 × 80,595) = $32,640.98.

Summary: Among the 1,156 donors, 118 joined the Circle of Champions and gave $12,403, for an average gift of $105.00.

Exhibit 3.7 Results of Letter B: "Roll Out" Mailing with "Circle of Champions" Offer

The Campaign to Clean Up America
Clean Up Cleveland Chapter

December, 199X

Mr. and Mrs. Robert Smith
16210 Shaker Boulevard
Shaker Heights, OH 44120

Dear Mr. and Mrs. Smith:

Thank you for your gift of $25.00 in support of a trash-free Cleveland.
Your level of support is most important to this effort and we appreciate
your extra generosity at this time.

Welcome to the Clean Up Cleveland Chapter of The Campaign to Clean
Up America. I am delighted with the response from our friends and
neighbors in this community who want to help.

Your gift stays in Cleveland; no part of it goes to the national effort.
Our City has a bright future, thanks to you. And, with your extra help,
the new energy conversion plant soon will deliver electricity to you at a
lower cost.

I have begun to see our magnetic bumper stickers on cars and trucks
all over town. Please be sure to use yours right away and help to spread
the word.

Again, thank you for your generous gift and your commitment to
support our efforts for a cleaner city and reasonable rates for
electricity.

Sincerely yours,

I. Harvey Clout
Chair of the Board
Cleveland Cast Iron Works

Exhibit 3.8   Standard "Thank-You" Text for First Gift

The Campaign to Clean Up America
Clean Up Cleveland Chapter

December, 199X

Mr. and Mrs. Phil Anthropy
23350 South Woodland Road
Shaker Heights, OH 44122

Dear Mary and Phil;

Thank you for your gift of $100.00 to support a trash-free Cleveland. I am deeply grateful to you for your commitment to join our Clean Up Cleveland effort. I value your personal support very much.

Welcome to Charter Membership in our new "Circle of Champions" donor club. With your extra help, we will get our City back in shape and build the energy conversion plant all that much sooner.

You will be hearing from the Cleveland Orchestra and Cleveland Play House with your invitation to their special event coming early next year.

I have begun to see our magnetic bumper stickers on cars and trucks all over town. Please be sure to use yours right away to help spread the word. If you would like extra bumper stickers, please give my office a call.

Again, thank you for your generous gift and your commitment to support our efforts for a cleaner city and reasonable rates for electricity.

Sincerely yours,

I. Harvey Clout
Chair of the Board
Cleveland Cast Iron Works

Exhibit 3.9   Charter Membership "Thank-You" Letter

CHAPTER FOUR

Donor Renewal: A Communications Art

After a first gift is acquired, the new donor should be told about the organization and about how the donated money was used. A pathway is then marked for asking the donor to give again. A first gift begins a relationship between a donor and his or her choice of nonprofit organization; the extra effort to build the relationship must come from the party seeking association and friendship. One of several reasons for expanding the relationship is to achieve a return on the initial investment—a renewal of the new donor's first gift. Nonprofit organizations should *not* look on fund-raising as only a once-a-year cash exchange. If they do, they will fail to receive the full return that is possible on their investment—getting to know their donors, educating them about the good works being performed, and helping to motivate them to give again and again. New donors are like new friends or new customers. If treated properly, they can be part of a lasting friendship and good customer relations. Once a relationship is built, the money will follow. Among the added benefits that will result from the combination of donor relations, communications, and renewal solicitations are:

1. Prior donors are the best prospects for other gifts as well as renewal gifts;
2. At least 50 percent of prior donors will repeat their gifts in the same amount;
3. As many as 15 percent of prior donors will increase (upgrade) their gifts, if asked to do so;
4. After the second renewal (third gift), a donor is likely to remain faithful for seven more years;

5. Renewal donors will give from five to eight times more money than new, first-time donors;

6. After five years, renewal donors will provide 80 percent of the money raised each year.

Donor renewal is the means to true success in fund development. Communications with donors between gifts, and invitations to volunteer and to make other gifts, will enhance the annual gift and form a foundation for the desired mutual friendship and respect. Such a friendship can last a lifetime; its value expands over time. The focus must always remain on building the relationship, and the building begins with the first gift. How well it grows and its ultimate return on investment are in the hands of the nonprofit organization. As fundraising competition increases, the strength of the bond between donors and their favored nonprofit organizations will make the difference in retention of donors. Long-term success in fund-raising depends on developing positive relationships with the largest possible number of faithful donors. If their confidence and trust are maintained through constant communications, donors can be expected to continue their faithful support for many years, possibly even over their lifetimes.

For any nonprofit organization, its most critical decision in fundraising involves the quality communications, renewal opportunities, and recognition programs that constitute its donor relations. By fostering and preserving friendships with donors, the organization gains benefits far in excess of the costs to secure the first gifts, regardless of their size. Mature fund development programs (in place five years or more, with broad-based annual giving activities) can expect that 80 percent or more of their annual cash will come from their prior donors. Why? Because these nonprofit organizations have continued to invest in building their relationships with their prior donors. They have also established a firm pattern of multiple and repeat giving. Board members and management staff of nonprofit organizations often place too much emphasis on how much money is being raised. They should concentrate on who is giving, on the amount of effort needed to maintain their gifts, and on expanding communications and attention to current donors.

The strength of any annual giving program is its ability to expand and renew gifts from its faithful prior donors throughout the year. If motivated to give year after year and to give to many different programs within each year, donors will accumulate a grant total far above what they might have imagined possible. Their potential for support makes it imperative to recognize their continued contributions.

Annual giving is a plan designed to foster the constant renewal of a donor's interest and enthusiasm as well as to encourage and facilitate his or her continuous support. It is the responsibility of nonprofit organizations to guide their donors along this path of multiple giving opportunities, thereby fulfilling their aspirations to do the best they can for the cause they have chosen to support. This guidance is best achieved through (1) communications opportunities, (2) involvement opportunities, and (3) donor renewal, revival, and reward. As with any lifelong friendship, constant effort must be given to building as well as to retaining the relationship. Lacking attention, it will weaken and can quickly be lost. If a nonprofit organization is interested only in the money given and not in the donor as a person who has needs, wants, and desires, the friendship is not likely to last beyond the first gift.

COMMUNICATIONS OPPORTUNITIES

Renewal of donor gifts has the potential to achieve, at a minimum, from five to eight times the original gift value. It is important therefore, to begin communications with donors immediately after their first gift, using these guidelines:

Educate them about the organization—its mission, purposes, goals, and objectives;

Concentrate on the people served or the cause, the quality and effectiveness of the work being done, and the specific benefits it delivers;

Tell how their money will be used, how their funds make a difference by helping other people, whole communities, or the environment;

Be creative in selecting the means and methods for communication;

Be sensitive to the frequency and appearance of the messages.

The following should be decided *before* the communications plan is begun:

Message—its purpose(s) and content;

Medium to be used (mail, telephone, newspaper, television, videocassette, or combinations of media);

Appearance of the piece (color, size, length);

Frequency planned for each piece;

Overall objectives (to inform, invite, involve, stimulate to act);

Estimate of all the costs involved;

Measurement to evaluate results.

Donors expect their gift dollars will be used for charitable purposes. They will not react well if they receive expensive and glossy reports, newsletters that arrive too frequently, and other unnecessary (and unwanted) "give backs." Striking the right balance in appearance, content, and length has first priority; choices in frequency and message medium follow closely after. Written communications sent to 200 or more individuals can be mailed at third-class and bulk-mail rates, which save money. The message is still delivered, although its arrival may take anywhere from a few days to a few weeks. Most nonprofit organizations have room for improvement in the amount of coordination between staff members who manage public communications and the people assigned or contracted to design and write them. A balance between professional appearance and cost-effectiveness is the goal, and correct English is a must. If the piece looks "too slick," if the several components of a mailing do not look like they were sent from the same organization, if the messages are unconnected, or if the reply requests ask donors for too much too often, the results are confusion and criticism. Coordination on timing alone will help reduce the negative reactions that come from showing up too often in donors' mail boxes.

In today's message-overloaded world, the communications challenge lies in being seen and heard by the people the message is supposed to reach. Mailing list management must select precisely who is to receive each specific message, what each audience is to be sent each year, and ways of making the communications personal and efficient. Broadcast mailings sent to every resident are usually inefficient; they will not communicate effectively with those who should hear the organization's story. Each nonprofit organization has to find its own way to speak directly to its donors. Personalized communications—those that look as though they have been individually prepared—are best. Personal mail ("high touch") is recommended as the best way to achieve success in donor communications because it enhances personal giving in return.

Coordinating Messages to Audiences

Nonprofit organizations that achieve the highest level of coordination and cooperation among their marketing, public relations, community relations, and fund development professionals are most likely to be effective and efficient in all their communications. The master mailing lists prepared by these departments for their separate communications can be brought together with the objective of creating one current and viable master list for the organization. Each department would be encouraged to use only a segment of the master mailing list at any one time. Occasionally, there may be a message that the entire list needs to receive. With planning, a well-defined sequence of messages can be accomplished, and the content of each piece can build on the others to transmit the desired information or stimulate the action requested. When donor communications are well-coordinated, responses improve. The most effective messages focus on relevant topics and priorities, are personalized, arrive at regular intervals, and are clearly sent from the same organization. Achieving such coordination among all the staff departments involved may sound like an obvious and simple goal, but it has proven difficult to achieve within many organizations. Each unit must prepare separate goals and strategies for its communications, with performance evaluations based on achieving defined results. Each unit can also participate in setting joint goals and can be measured for its contribution toward achieving multipurpose goals.

There are several good reasons for making the extra effort to define a coordinated communications plan among all the departments that send out messages to the public. Once the plan is established, there will be opportunities to "piggyback" more than one message in a single package, which can achieve cost savings. "Multimessaging" (two or more messages in the same mail package) can provide a variety of interesting materials that are of potential use to donors, friends, and customers. Multimedia packages (more than one message medium is employed) are becoming common. Examples are major public awareness campaigns that include billboard and bus-back announcements, radio and newspaper advertisements, and two or more direct mail packages delivered to select residents—all timed for maximum impact in a two- to four-week period. Newsletters and magazines, while less frequent, can report on the same activities described in the earlier communications. Each message reinforces those before it.

Many nonprofit organizations now advertise special services, timely offers, and the programs and services they make available to the public. They also include helpful details on their program and service activities in their newsletters and magazines, and list phone numbers for further information. Telephone and mail fulfillment services must be prepared to reply promptly to each request, whether for information, service, or professional advice. Donors may seek information on how to buy a ticket to a coming benefit event, or may wonder about the tax-deductibility of their next gift. A common practice is to insert or bind gift reply envelopes into the organization's newsletter or magazine, to suggest another gift. The cost of this insert seldom pays for itself in dollars received; its true merit is its subtle message that gifts are always welcome. The envelopes are convenient reminders; some donors will remove them (especially if the postage is paid) and save them for use another day. The envelopes' effectiveness can be tested by printing a code on them, separating them when they are returned, and tallying the number received and their total receipts.

Avoiding Treating Donors as Objects

The primary objective of continuous communications with donors is to educate and inform them about the organization. Every contact need not solicit another gift nor should it always ask for a reply. Some fund-raising executives believe donors need to be rehearsed to reply positively to each offer; they seek to "train" donors to continually say Yes to each request. I am extremely cautious about using any form of psychology with prospects and donors. Charitable contributions should be willingly made after deliberation; they should not be regarded as a pre-conditioned or (worse yet) unmotivated response "triggered," like Pavlov's dog, by reflex autosuggestion. This is no way to treat friends! Donors should have the opportunity, each time they are asked for their support, to study the request, ask questions and request details, and, only then, decide freely whether to reply or to send money. Open channels of communication are best; it is always wise to avoid appearing to be "too slick" in fund-raising.

There is real potential that too frequent solicitations will "turn off" a donor when the next request arrives. People resent being "hit on" too often. The timing of each communication must be given careful thought. What message preceded this contact and when was it sent? Were any comments or written responses received? Were there any negative reactions that need to be corrected? Support pieces mailed on a regular basis, such as newsletters, invitations, and other materials mailed by other departments of the organization, should be reviewed frequently to avoid repeating the same message over and over without adding new facts or a new twist to the story.

How can all these elements be made to fit together? Which pieces should be sent at the same time solicitations are in progress, and which ones before, during, and after the gift is made? How can the stage be set prior to asking, to create the need and establish its urgency? Each mailing piece that follows should add something to the story—how the funds raised are being used; photographs of people receiving service or attending programs; a brief story about a successful client or patient. Pieces mailed after the gift occurs can report on fund-raising results (people like to hear that others joined them in giving) as well as changes in quantity and quality of programs delivered. If messages are carefully planned, donors can benefit in some way from each one. Each mailing piece must be able to stand on its own, be informative and interesting, and retain reader interest. The volume of messages received daily via mail, audio, and visual media will only increase; everyone is competing for attention. Being creative is only part of the answer; better coordination and cooperation within the organization and use of strategic techniques and modern technology constitute the communications plan that will probably yield the best results.

What to Say after Receiving the First Gift

When a nonprofit organization receives its first gift from a new donor, it has already achieved several major breakthroughs:

1. It has found an interested person;
2. The message caught that person's attention;
3. The person was stimulated to action;
4. The person acted to send money.

The organization's reply, to be sent back within 48 hours, must report that the money was received safely, express thanks for the gift, and promise to use it to benefit others as described in the appeal. If the gift was large ($1,000 or more), a second, more focused thank-you letter should be sent, or a volunteer leader should call the donor. A donor at this level deserves some extra attention.

The *next* letter, after the thank-you letter, is possibly the most crucial communication in this new relationship. Before starting to write the message, it helps to imagine the questions within the mind of a donor who has just made a first gift of $50: "What does the appeal propose to do with my money? Why did I send the gift? What response can I expect to receive? Am I supposed to know more about the organization's progress? I wonder, did others give? How much? What was the total received?"

Providing specific answers will take some time and effort, which is why a plan for communications is so necessary. One way to begin is to prepare a one- or two-page narrative in letter form over the signature of the CEO, and mail it third-class, bulk-mail rate every 60 days to everyone who gave $50 or more in the prior two months. Organizations can write about their own programs and services with ease; they achieve results every day. These stories can be told every other month or so. Not much time or money will be required to circulate them, but their value will be significant. After another 60 days, the regularly scheduled communications can continue this contact. A new donor can be overwhelmed with too much information and too many communications received too quickly.

Exhibit 4.1 shows a 12-month activity schedule for donor communications. The cycle begins after the donor's first gift is received in response to the annual giving campaign. Because this schedule takes advantage of

Activity	Timing
1. Acquisition solicitation	1 per year
(-) (First gift received)	(within 1–6 weeks)
2. Thank-you letter	Within 48 hours
3. Bimonthly activity report	6 per year
4. Newsletter	3–4 per year
5. Invitation to public event	1–2 per year
6. Special report	1–2 per year
7. Basic information brochure	1 per year (within 30 days after gift)
8. Extra appeal/special campaign	1 per year
9. Invitation to benefit event	1–2 per year
10. Invitation to annual meeting	1 per year
11. Annual report	1 per year
12. Annual gift renewal solicitation	3–4 per year
Total:	20 to 26 mail pieces per year possible

Exhibit 4.1   Communications Opportunities in Donor Annual Activity Cycle

existing materials and ongoing activities, a donor could receive between 20 and 26 separate items within the first year! Only one message (the last in the series) is the formal request to renew the annual gift. Some decisions are needed to select what messages to send, which medium to use (newsletter, report, invitation, or letter), and when to send them. The best procedure is to decide what must be said to each donor group and then plan the message, medium, and schedule. The objective is to have donors receive the information when it best meets *their* needs, not the organization's.

Newsletters and Annual Reports

Most of the regular communication from nonprofit organizations is carried in their newsletters. These publications report briefly on a wide variety of activities and (hopefully) will match one or more interest areas of nearly everyone on the mailing list. Newsletters allow a nonprofit organization to talk about its priorities, directions, current programs, new services, and plans, as a way of continuing to inform prior clients, donors, and others. Newsletters can feature leaders, volunteers, and donors by name and can reproduce photographs showing their interactions with professional and management staff; they can also promote coming activities and events and encourage all supporters to join in. Newsletters are effective when they are brief (4 to 16 pages), are short on text, include a host of donors' and volunteers' names and pictures, and arrive infrequently (quarterly) but reliably. Nonprofit newsletter editors and writers should appreciate how their audiences (the same people who receive commercial newspapers and magazines) are accustomed to succinct messages delivered in easy-to-read style and enhanced with charts, graphs, and photos that aid their quick understanding of the messages.

Annual reports are more formal documents. They have space for articles that require more than a casual scanning; readers must find the time necessary to concentrate on their content. Annual reports from for-profit corporations have escalated in design, quality, appearance, and expense to the point where they are nearly coffee-table keepsakes. This expensive presentation is not one that nonprofit organizations should imitate. Their annual reports are intended to be read because they report on accomplishments, illustrate financial status, and show how gift dollars were used to achieve some of the organization's most outstanding results. Some nonprofit organizations believe their annual reports must compete favorably with for-profit and commercial products for the sake of image, not substance. Others have a goal that includes competing for awards. The true objective in preparing annual reports is to communicate effectively with the community served, including volunteers, donors, and prospects. Image impressions and award competitions have their place, but the annual report should concentrate on the substance of the message. Donors are not motivated to make gifts based on receiving prize-winning newsletters or glitzy annual reports. They are more likely to be motivated to give again when they receive a modest presentation that conveys information they can understand about the good works performed by organizations they support. A communication's effectiveness can be measured by counting the number and amount of renewed gifts it stimulates.

Invitations

Invitations are quite different communication tools: they ask for a reply to a specific request for information, for access to a service, for attendance at an event or activity, or for some favor. People do not object to being invited to attend a lecture, public event, or party, even if an admission fee is required. What they appreciate first is being remembered with the invitation, even when they cannot attend. If the topic, people involved, and event are of interest, they will consider attending. Nonprofit organizations build their relationship with donors each time a reply is stimulated, because another instance of personal involvement and participation has been created. Involvement stimulates increased participation, which is followed by enthusiasm and commitment. Because donors are the backbone of an organization's support, invitations to attend lectures, tours, and open-house days are ideal opportunities for drawing attention to the programs and services of the organization. Lectures and tours open an organization, its professional staff, and its work to the public. Arranging for the professional staff (resident experts) to be guest speakers increases public knowledge of the organization and conveys information. Invitations have the additional advantage of being personal forms of communication, a feature unmatched by newsletters and annual reports.

Invitations also offer donors and prospects privileged access to the organization's programs and services, a way to expand their awareness of the mission, purposes, goals, and objectives. Colleges invite the public to use their campus facilities for lectures, cultural events, and athletic activities, and to return for continuing education classes. These visitors to the campus will help the college to make its "case" for public support and to communicate its needs when it asks this same public for money. Museums and other cultural organizations exist so that visitors can come to their facilities all the time. Their mission is to encourage people to view their collections, listen to their music, watch their performances. Attendance increases people's understanding of the value of preserving art and history and their appreciation of where their money is being spent, why it was needed, and how they can help again when asked. Hospitals and national health agencies advocate wellness and promote disease prevention and personal responsibility for self-health. Their invitations encourage people to take action on their own, to follow good health practices (exercise, stop smoking, eat wisely) in order to prevent costly health intervention later on. Healthcare facilities are open to visitors of patients, but people are not invited to tour hospitals to look at sick people or to watch surgery. Many other types of nonprofit organizations, especially those involved in direct public services such as feeding the homeless, often invite the public to come and help them to deliver their programs for serving others. The public expects any activity or event to be worth their time, to present what was advertised, to have other people present, to start and finish on time, to have had advance planning, to provide a memorable experience, and to be carried out with an appropriate level of quality and style. In other words, people want the experience to prove worth the time invested in it. If it does not, they may not attend again. There are more than enough opportunities here for the kind of errors at which people take offense. Given the precarious nature of donor relationships, inviting people to attend activities and events and to visit the organization's facilities can create a minefield of delicate interpersonal relations. Wherever and whenever possible, however, inviting the public to visit the facilities is always good for communications.

Gift Invitations

Gift invitations also seek replies from donors. Those who choose to respond may designate the program or service or other cause within the organization that is to receive their gift. When they make such a designation, the organization has an obligation to fulfill their request in detail. The fact that the gift was invited adds an extra dimension to the solicitation. Each person who replies has moved to a new level of donorship, out of personal interest; he or she has a willingness to give something of themselves to benefit others, a wish to act as a good neighbor and be a good citizen. The recipient organization is obliged to use the funds only for the specified purpose or for the benefit of others. If that stipulation is observed, the donors may be inclined to give again when asked—up to a point. Each gift invitation also is an opportunity for donors to come closer, to become more informed, more involved, more committed and enthusiastic, more actively a part of their favorite organizations. Fulfilling each special gift's requirements to the satisfaction of its sponsor remains the obligation of the nonprofit organization, and this duty must be taken seriously. People have high expectations about being treated correctly, especially when they make the decision to send a large amount of money. Exhibit 4.2 traces the pathway and the people involved when a gift arrives from a donor. The numerous tasks listed are elements in the organization's accountability.

Personal Letters

After donors receive a few newsletters, an annual report, and some event invitations, the next avenue of communication is personal letters. Only telephone calls and face-to-face meetings are more effective forms of personal communication. Because all three approaches are personal in appearance and style, they have a decided advantage over every other mass communications option. Personal letters can be sent more often (and more cheaply) than invitations, newsletters, and annual reports. They require some writing skill when copies of one letter will be sent to an entire mailing list.

Personal letters, discussing the latest information, can be sent between event invitations and newsletters. They should be brief, personally addressed, and signed by someone whom the recipient may have met or may respect. These letters are likely to be read and appreciated. Nonprofit organizations should keep track of the known interest areas of their major

1. The donor makes a gift by mail, in person, or by phone (charging a credit card); or sponsors or underwrites an event or gift; or purchases a special-event ticket.

2. Processing begins with the data processing staff's tasks:
   Data entry
   Update of donor records and donor files
   Journal preparation
   Batch processing
   Transmittal Sheets

3. The accounting or business office takes responsibility for:
   Deposit slip
   Deposit of money into the bank
   Revenue entry on the organization's books

4. The bank, upon receipt of the money and thereafter:
   Records the deposit
   Records expenses
   Processes checks
   Pays on account
   Prepares a bank statement

5. The accounting or business office of the organization:
   Receives bank statements
   Reconciles revenue and withdrawals
   Prepares an accounting statement

6. The fund development office:
   Reconciles income and expenses
   Prepares gift reports
   Sends gift reports to the board for review/approval

7. The auditor:
   Reviews all financial activity
   Prepares the annual audit statement
   Sends the audit to the board for review/approval

Exhibit 4.2   Steps in Processing, Recording, and Reporting Gifts

donors and make an effort to send them notes, clippings, progress reports, and other details that are relevant to those areas. Personal letters are made easier by personal computers, word processing software, and laser printers. Used effectively, personal letters can carry a major share of the task of retaining donors' personal interest in the organization.

Plan for Donor Communications

Annual giving programs provide a variety of communication opportunities that can be brought to the attention of donors throughout the year. Within reasonable budgetary constraints, a nonprofit organization can be in contact with its donors every 60 to 90 days. Each communication should include, if possible, information about programs that are working, services being performed, people being helped, causes being advanced, and coming events. Most donors are unaware of routine activities going on inside a nonprofit organization; they are usually outside, looking in. People who may have visited the facilities or used one or more programs or services in the past will have a personal experience on which to base their views. Otherwise, most people have limited knowledge about the work done, its value to others, and the results it achieves. Communications are essential because they give nonprofit organizations several opportunities, at minimal cost, to share information with those who are "outside the walls" and are known to be interested. Well-informed and enthusiastic investors (donors) who tell friends and neighbors about "my nonprofit" organization are valuable ambassadors-at-large.

A special advantage donors enjoy is access—being "in the know," receiving direct reports, being invited to public and social events, being a part of something of value, perhaps being asked for advice. Donors enjoy knowing about—even bragging about—how their funds are being spent and the results their dollars are achieving. The challenge to each nonprofit organization is in finding ways to encourage such interest by sending donors useful information. Donors do not expect or want their contribution to be spent on brochures, newsletters, and reports sent back to them. They are reassured when they hear, from time to time, about the programs and services they are supporting. Some of the best communications methods are inexpensive, which suggests there are no serious barriers to communicating with donors.

INVOLVEMENT OPPORTUNITIES

Donors should have opportunities to participate with a nonprofit organization in ways other than giving money. The key opportunity or request is service as a volunteer—giving time, energy, and talents. Most nonprofit organizations should be able to draw benefit to themselves from their volunteers' time and skills (see Exhibit 4.3). Volunteering to help with fund-raising is one of several options. Some donors prefer to be involved directly with the actual programs and services provided by the nonprofit organization. A volunteer also can be a spokesperson in the community, help with identification and recruitment of others as donors and volunteers, and help to identify those in need who might benefit from the programs and services offered. Volunteers may be asked, where appropriate, to share their professional and vocational

1. Help to provide service to others;
2. Help to staff programs offered to the public;
3. Identify those who need the programs or services;
4. Share their skills and talents;
5. Join a committee;
6. Bring a friend or neighbor to a function;
7. Provide access to others—open doors;
8. Be an advocate;
9. Identify others who are likely donors;
10. Solicit others for their support;
11. Make more gifts;
12. Become a leader.

Exhibit 4.3   What Volunteers Can Do

skills in management and operations areas (a major opportunity for cost savings to the nonprofit organization). The more time they give, the more they become personally involved; the more they know and experience first-hand, the more committed and dedicated they will become. Donors, like investors, appreciate knowing about future plans as well as current priorities, because this kind of information reinforces their personal commitment to continue their financial support. When donors who are also volunteers are asked to make an additional special-need gift during the year, they are likely to be well-informed about the need and motivated to contribute their financial support. It should come as no great surprise that the best donors are volunteers; they are the people most directly involved in "my nonprofit" organization. Most have a good time as well, which is important. Nonprofit organizations benefit from a ripple effect of volunteer participation. Knowledge and experiences are shared with family and friends, business and social acquaintances, and others in the community. They in turn may want to share in the same worthwhile efforts; enthusiastic volunteers will encourage others to become involved too. Their friends and acquaintances may become equally active as informed spokespersons, recruiters of new clients, or volunteers who give time, energy, and skills. These new volunteers will be a source of gifts as well, when asked.

Multiple Solicitations

Annual giving programs are designed to encourage multiple gifts within each 12-month period. Donors and nonprofit organizations have multiple needs that cannot be met with a single gift per person per year. Many people still think one gift is all that is needed or required of them. Donors may choose to give only once, or they can participate in several annual giving activities, such as those described in this book, within each year. Donors can choose to use some of these activities at any time. For example, commemorative giving can be used as a birthday, anniversary, or holiday present to honor a friend or someone the donor respects or wishes to memorialize. In a relationship with a nonprofit organization that offers commemorative or tribute giving, donors can make several of these thoughtful gifts each year to express various messages. Over the years, donors can continue to honor the memory of a family member, business colleague, or personal friend who has passed away. A new gift is made each time. The amounts are usually modest, but they are gestures of praise or remembrance, or thoughtful expressions of sympathy that are of value to the donor and to the family or person honored. The nonprofit organization is responsible for reporting each gift to the honoree or his or her family, and can use the contact letter to describe some uses of the donated funds. Gifts of this kind are quite visible and are perceived as valuable and thoughtful by everyone involved.

Donors expect to receive more than one invitation to special and benefit events during the year. These are other forms of requests for additional gifts. Most nonprofit organizations arrange more than one such annual event, usually of a social or sporting nature. The objective is to encourage personal participation from among the universe of the organization's friends and donors. From each volunteer or donor who participates, additional funds are gained. When they are asked to volunteer a few hours to help plan an event or function in some capacity during its duration, donors can choose to give something other than money. Their participation maintains their involvement and their interest. Donors and prospects should be invited to activities and events throughout the year. If they say No, it means they cannot join in right now; it does not mean they resent being invited.

A corporate matching gift program is another area in which multiple solicitation is possible. Employers offer this program to encourage their employees (and often their retirees) to be active in civic and community service. The company agrees to match their personal contributions with a company gift of an equal or prorated amount to the same nonprofit organization. The donor benefits by causing two gifts to be made to the designated organization. The corporation benefits (1) by fulfilling a corporate objective of encouraging good citizenship among employees, and (2) by placing corporate funds in public support of charitable enterprises in the community. The nonprofit organization benefits most of all because it receives two gifts. Many companies allow their employees to participate in other gift decisions of the company. Employees who are actively involved with nonprofit organizations as donors or as volunteers are eligible to recommend that additional gifts be given to the organization in which they are active.

When donors are offered a variety of giving opportunities each year, their interest and commitment are more easily maintained. Repeated gifts often reveal preferred areas of interest. When these same programs have extra needs or require major support, the nonprofit organization should turn first to these donors to ask for help. From their personal involvement and from regular communications, they may already be well aware of these extra needs. When asked to help, they can probably be counted on to do whatever they can.

Inviting Donors to Be Volunteers

Donors should not be asked, in every communication they receive, to give money. They should be invited to share their professional and vocational skills too. If they agree to serve by doing rather than by giving, they can save the nonprofit organization the cost of hiring part-time employees to perform the same work. The value of volunteerism is significant when donated services are expressed in financial terms. Apart from counting the hours donated or calculating how much a hired person would have to be paid for the same amount of time, volunteerism is an enormous resource that can take many forms. Within each organization are a host of projects that need attention, not in high-skill areas or in applications that require great preparation or training. They just need someone with the will to see them through. Volunteers bring several motives with them, including a work ethic that can influence the performance of others. Areas that are directed outside the organization, such as advocacy or legislative support on local, statewide, or national issues, are in constant need of help via letters, petitions, and attendance (or speaking) at public hearings. Gifts of personal property, as simply as donations of food and clothing in special drives to aid the homeless and the indigent, are in widespread short supply. Products and merchandise may be available from a donor's employer, at a discount or free, if requested. However personal participation is expressed, it can be beneficial to a nonprofit organization. Among the added benefits is the fact that these services are most often performed in the same community where donors work and live. Volunteerism "feels good," and the good deeds and acts of charity will be seen by others. Some recently expanded activities include tutoring elementary and secondary school students, and teaching English to newly arrived immigrants. Either activity may take only two to four hours a week, but the level of satisfaction gained is a high multiple of the numbers of hours given.

Nonprofit organizations should be prepared to offer each person who wishes to volunteer a well-defined and organized form of service, a task with value. Nonprofit organizations thrive because of their volunteers, and the volunteers thrive because of their service. As noted in Chapter Two, satisfied volunteers who have spent time in worthwhile work are more than three times as likely as nonvolunteers to become and to remain donors. Volunteering is one of the active ways in which people can draw as close to an organization as they choose. Organizations that plan well for public participation will be well-rewarded. These actions complement one another and, in time, the association produces increased reliability in volunteer duties, a higher level of performance, and faithful annual gifts.

Planning for Donor Recognition

Donors have needs too. Their generosity must receive the proper response, not just "politically correct" routine thanks. It is important to treat donors with respect at all times. Here are some actions that might be taken on their behalf:

1. Thank donors for each gift they make;
2. Keep track of each gift and its purpose;
3. Write a different personal message in each thank-you letter (this requires some thought and effort);
4. Establish a written policy guide so that everyone in the organization knows how to manage relations with donors;
5. Plan and monitor the valued relationships being built with donors;
6. Ensure that every donor is treated equitably and fairly;
7. Send occasional reports to donors on how their funds were used and on the progress their nonprofit organization is making in meeting community needs with their help.

Donors have a great interest in the results of their contributions. Their gifts represent being part of something valuable and making a difference. Volunteerism helps to satisfy their need to be involved, even as they implement the funds they have donated. Invitations to public events and activities encourage donors to be active within the organization. Newsletters, reports, and other communications keep them informed. What else can be done? What else do donors want? Attention, respect, and access. Those who give large amounts and those whose faithful giving builds a cumulative gift history over a period of years want to be recognized proportionately. A properly structured donor recognition program takes these differences into account.

Donors who claim their gifts as charitable contribution deductions on their annual income tax returns require supporting documentation for each gift transaction. The Internal Revenue Service (IRS) will accept canceled checks as routine evidence for each smaller gift, but a confirmation letter that states details of the amount and date of the gift, any restrictions on its use, when it was received, and so on, must now be supplied by nonprofit organizations to donors of gifts of $250 or more. Nonprofit organizations that fail to provide donors with these basic services in a timely manner may lose them to other organizations that will. No extra costs are added when full details are presented in the basic thank-you letter.

A record should be kept of every gift; donor recognition can begin immediately after acquisition of the first gift. A well-defined donor recognition program makes itself visible and well known to the public. Such a program can become written policy approved by the board of directors (see discussion and exhibits in Chapter Six). Extra benefits and privileges are offered to donors who make larger gifts and whose cumulative or historic giving total merits special attention and/or public notice. Forms and materials used (plaques, portraits, memorabilia) should not be confused with direct purchases in exchange for gifts. The intent of donor recognition is to convey a sincere expression of appreciation for faithfulness in giving as much as for the total amount given. One approach is to invite all donors of $500 or more (or whatever base amount is appropriate for the range of gifts received) during the past year to be guests at a special reception. The invitation can describe the reception as an expression of appreciation and an opportunity to tour the facility and see the results of the gift support. Among this event's added value is the chance to meet others who share the same degree of interest and financial support. New friendships and business contacts may develop from the meeting.

The use of premiums or "give backs" are a visible form of direct exchange for gifts. Premiums, if used, should be selected carefully. They should not cost too much and they must not trigger a reduced deduction on the value of the original gift claimed by the donor for tax purposes. The IRS requires nonprofit organizations to inform donors when the value of benefits and privileges given back *exceeds* "the 2 percent test" (the cost of the item given the donor should not be worth more than 2 percent of the original gift amount or $25, whichever is greater). Possible premiums should be studied carefully *before* they are offered, to ensure that these "give backs" will not adversely affect donors' tax claims and possibly negate their next gift decision.

METHODS OF DONOR RENEWAL, REVIVAL, AND REWARD

When asking donors for their next gift, the methods of solicitation are often the same as those used to acquire their first or their previous gift. The purposes of donor communications during the past year were: to increase donor awareness of the value of their support and to explain any benefits and privileges donors received. Everything presented and proposed in the interim comes together when it is time to renew the gift. Refinements to the request are worth considering. A small, select group of people is being approached, and the following improvements may help to retain a maximum number of donors and at least a repeated amount of gift dollars:

Previous Annual Gift	*Improved Request*
1. Form letter	1. Personal letter
2. Personal letter	2. Personal letter plus phone call
3. Personal letter and phone call	3. Phone call to request an appointment
4. Appointment	4. Personal tour

By improving the form and style of the renewal request, the organization shows that attention to the donor is a priority and that his or her continued support is valued. It will help to know: What information was received during the prior year's contacts and activities? What programs, activities, or events did the donor reply to? What other gifts did the donor make? This information will profile the donor's degree of interest and enthusiasm and will point the way to the preferred areas of association with the organization. The donor's replies during the year are a road map for how to maintain present interest while inviting greater participation in the preferred activities.

The primary objective in renewal solicitation is to achieve gifts from as many prior donors as possible. Some will have given to other programs in the organization since their last gift; others will make only one gift, usually at about the same time each year. Some will not give again right now; others will never give again. The second objective in renewal is to persuade donors to give at least the same amount of money as before. Their pattern of giving becomes more valuable at each repetition. Upgrading (donating a larger gift) should be proposed as a way to allow the organization to achieve more of its good work.

Retention performance should recapture at least 50 percent of the prior donors each year. If that percentage cannot be repeated, the organization may never achieve a secure financial base of public support because (1) replacing the funds realized from prior donors is enormously difficult; (2) more costs, in time, multiple requests, and general expenses, are required because the same amount of money must be found among nondonors through acquisition; and (3) the relationship with prior donors may be lost. It is important to try to understand why the donations were not repeated. A review of the communications and activities of the past year may yield clues. If the prior donors were unresponsive to all appeals and then did not renew their annual gift, it may be fair to assume that their first gift was less of a commitment than an experiment to see how the organization performed. Most of the time, a donor who is unresponsive to the organization's other invitations can be assumed to be uninterested in further giving.

Resolicitation messages should remind donors that their benefits and privileges will expire unless a renewal gift is received. A printer's deadline for the annual report, which will contain the names of all donors who renew their gifts, should be announced early and often. It remains important to stress the value of the support and good works made possible by prior gifts, but human nature is such that retaining privileges and remaining on a published list are strong motivating factors. Every nonprofit organization would like to be able to rely on a core of proven donors whose faithful annual support meets all its current and future monetary needs. Board members, management staff, and employees work hard throughout the year to fulfill their part of the gift exchange bargain; renewal is the donors' part. The renewal request might mention this partnership in a message that enumerates the areas of need that depend on continued giving. People have to *want* to give; there is no requirement that they must do so. All any nonprofit organization can do is put its performance on the line and be sure to ask as well as it can.

Not everyone will give faithfully, year after year. Some attrition should be expected, but it can and should be contained as much as possible. A 50 percent retention rate is recommended as a guide. Donor communications, involvement, and recognition are all pointed toward achieving this goal. Resolicitation has the potential to perform five to eight times more profitably than acquisition of the same number of equally generous first-time donors. Donors are always better prospects than those who have never given. What may tip the scale is whether donors have heard from the organization more than once since their last gift and how they reacted to the interim communications.

Asking: How Many Times?

When asking prior donors to give again, there comes a point where reasonable propriety blows a whistle. Bombarding people with repeated requests (once a month for six months) can become offensive. Wise fund-raisers will review all the other communications, especially requests of any type, that were sent to donors within the past 90 days. (Exhibit 4.1 will help.) To continue solicitation endlessly is likely to be fruitless, can breed criticism, and should be discontinued, at least temporarily, when it becomes financially unprofitable. Donor records will report what other gifts these donors have been making during the year, when their last gifts were made, and details about their preferences, timing, and gift amounts. Delinquent donors should not be treated as a group; each has had individual reasons for discontinuing support. When should the effort stop? The results of prior renewal solicitations will help to indicate when others from the same community felt an appeal had run its course of efficiency and cost-effectiveness. Because prior donors remain from five to eight times more likely to give than nondonors, other opportunities for the same list should be created later on. The final answer lies in good judgment and attention to performance data. The organization's first business is friend-raising.

There is an old theory in fund-raising that no name should be removed from a mailing list, no matter what it costs to maintain it there. The reasoning is: because donors are always better prospects than nondonors, they should be kept forever. This assumption is enhanced by the retelling of a tale of a one-time $25 donor who died a decade later and left the organization a large bequest. The organization had kept writing, year after year, without any reply, so the rationalization suggested is that the bequest was received because the donor's name was kept on the mailing list. Permanent mailing lists are hard to justify today, when accountability for fund-raising expenses (printing, postage, staff time, and so on) must be measured with efficiency and cost-effective results. Accountability, a hard taskmaster, is not sympathetic to possibilities of lost bequests. It is not profitable to continue to solicit every living donor of record on the off-chance that these messages protect an unseen future legacy. Instead, there may be good reason to introduce a planned giving program, given an adequate size and age of the donor pool. Details about planned giving and estate planning options can be communicated to all donors easily during the year.

Among the important reasons for keeping records of prior donors' gifts is the link between cumulative and historic giving and the donor recognition program. Each gift made—no matter when, for what purpose, or in what form—is added to the donor's permanent gift history. Over time, as the cumulative total begins to build, the donor qualifies for added benefits and privileges, as defined by the donor recognition policy (see Chapter Six). A cumulative history of all gifts has many purposes. It reveals areas of special interest favored by the donor, preferred solicitation methods, responses to event invitations

and campaign solicitations, routine levels of annual support, attendance records at benefits and public events, planned giving activity,
and much more. This same donor profile is a valuable guide to volunteers and staff in assessing key interest areas, gift amounts, and timing
for the next renewal solicitation. Should a donor be invited to consider
an increase in his or her annual gift, to qualify for a gift club? Is a faithful donor ready to undertake a major gift opportunity? Should a long-
term donor be approached about an estate planning interview? The
donor gift history may hint at the next level of recognition a donor is
ready to achieve. Visible recognition can be the extra incentive needed
for an increased next gift. Recognition levels can also be used as an incentive to join the next level in the donor club program.

PERFORMANCE ANALYSIS

Why is measurement of donors' renewal performance a must? To monitor how many donors continued, how much they gave, and how many
(and what funds) were lost. The following list of performance characteristics should be reviewed after each renewal solicitation:

1. The percentage of prior donors who renewed;
2. Their average gift size;
3. How many donors renewed;
4. How many donors increased, decreased, or maintained their annual gift (gain–loss report);
5. How many donors were asked to increase or "upgrade" their last
   gifts and what increased amount (if any) was received;
6. The total dollars received (all renewal efforts);
7. The detailed results of each renewal program;
8. What other gifts were stimulated (number and amount);
9. How many donors retained their donor club level, how many increased to a new level, and how many fell below their last level;
10. How many failed to renew, and the value of their last gifts;
11. How current results compare with last year's;
12. What changes are needed before the next renewal;
13. The total cost of each renewal solicitation and the cost–ratio
    comparison with revenue produced.

It is also important to review the giving performance of prior donors
throughout the year. Are they making more gifts this year compared to

last year? To which programs? For how much money? How does this year's total compare to those of prior years? These faithful donors and their multiple gift decisions speak eloquently of their personal estimation of the worth of the nonprofit organization's leaders, staff, programs, and services. Their history also illustrates the level of their commitment, their willingness to be involved, and their confidence and trust that the organization is using their money well. These donors are rare and precious jewels; they are the best friends. How should they be shown appreciation?

Upgrading Annual Gifts

One of the least understood renewal techniques is "upgrading." Experience has proven that from 10 to 15 percent of prior donors will increase their gift when asked to do so. However, a more telling statistic is that the *other 85 to 90 percent* are more likely to renew their gift *at the same amount.* An upgrade request should be a regular part of every renewal invitation because of its value to preserve donors' level of giving. The 15 percent who give more are worth extra attention too—membership status or induction into a donor club—especially if they are making other gifts to the organization during the year.

Lybunts, Pybunts or Sybunts, and Locusts

Lapsed donors are individuals who did not make any gifts within the past year. William Grasty and Kenneth Sheinkopf [1] divide them into these categories:

Lybunts	Last year but unfortunately not this year
Pybunts	Prior year but unfortunately not this year
Sybunts	Some year but unfortunately not this year
Locusts	People who give every seven years.

All of these people are prior donors and will remain better prospects than nondonors. How should they be resolicited? Segregation and personal treatment might work. For example, assume that, if asked, they will respond again, at a rate better than nondonors' rate. The guideline for nondonors is response from 1 percent of the list. When lapsed donors' replies fall to that level, the list may be used up. Another measurement is gift amount. The longer the span between the last gift and the most recent resolicitation request, the more the gift will fall below prior levels. Experience will identify each organization's performance measurement guideline. It is not unreasonable to solicit all donors at least once a year, usually as part of the regular year-end appeal. Eventually, the organization will maximize whatever retention is possible, and can retire (throw away) the list.

It is always difficult to know whether to retire a list of "old" prior donors. Costs are always involved, and advocates of keeping them need to make some effort to contact them during each year, even if only through newsletters, reports, and similar media. An inexpensive piece might be sent to them a week or two before resolicitation, especially in the first and second year after their last gift. All donors should continue to be informed about the organization and its current priorities; it may be possible to restimulate their desire to help. Or, given recent economic conditions, the desire to help may have been constant but the means may not. No suggestion that they have been resistant or stubborn should be allowed entry into thinking or communications. Special handling just might restart their gifts, and it allows room for good reasons for not giving. They may need to be treated differently than before, perhaps welcomed warmly on a lower level of giving. Did they reply to any other invitations or requests? If so, does the amount solicited give any clue to what they can afford now? Some assumptions can be made about why they may have declined to give, but the focus should be on their concerns and on reporting how the organization has improved. All who do respond again, no matter what the gift size compared with prior history, should be welcomed back with a special thank-you letter. There is every prospect now that, with care and sensitive attention, they may remain faithful donors for many years to come.

There are exceptions to the general rule about keeping people on a mailing list. Those who ask to be removed from the list should be deleted immediately. They should not have to repeat the instruction. If they continue to receive appeals, they will become irritated by the insensitivity to and lack of respect for their request. A former friend will become an outspoken enemy. The deleted names should be transferred to a "Do Not Mail" list or a "flush file," against which all future mailings can be cross-checked.

Performance Review

Fund development staff should analyze their own results and confer together about their messages, materials, schedules, and achievements. Some of the specific areas to review are:

1. What were the results of each solicitation activity?
2. How well was each message received?
3. Were any trends seen in the responses?

4. How did the message and performance of each program affect the response to each of the others?
5. Were there any generic or unusual problem areas?
6. What recommendations would be suitable for the next sequence of solicitations?

Staff discussions should include an evaluation of the amount of coordination achieved in areas such as the use of mailing lists, the schedule for special appeals, the underwriting and sponsorship of coming events, the mailing schedule for invitations to benefits and special events, the authorship and distribution of newsletters and annual reports, and the approaches used in mailings, telephone campaigns, or telemarketing activities addressed to donors. Objective analysis of each program's performance will encourage interrelated effort, higher levels of efficiency, and greater cost-effectiveness. The progress of the overall fund development program is linked to the success of each activity and of the total effort to welcome new friends, renew old friendships, and raise more dollars.

Fund development staff should also confer with their colleagues at nearby nonprofit organizations. They should share data to compare their performance with similar fund-raising methods. Attendance figures at activities and events are among the solid data available for comparison. Staff participation in fund-raising conferences and workshops encourages learning from the experience of others, helps to interpret the implications of results, and invites other suggestions that may improve response. Methods of fund-raising vary in success among nonprofit organizations, but the impact of traditional annual giving methods and techniques in common practice elsewhere, especially locally, can be instructive. Differences in performance are most often traceable to subjective factors such as geography, access to wealth, volunteer training, and length of time each solicitation program has been in operation. Observation of the results of others helps to detect changes in public responsiveness to techniques and to appeal messages. Incoming direct mail is a good barometer of public attitudes. Staff can monitor the following factors and ask about results in data comparison surveys:

1. Direct mail packages they receive at home;
2. Current literature on direct mail;
3. Subtle details such as "teaser" messages on the outer envelope, colors used, signature style, and number of pieces per package;
4. Use of one-, two-, or four-page letter texts;

5. Use of postage-paid return envelopes;
6. Donor club programs, gift levels, and benefits;
7. Premiums and "give backs" and their link to various gift amounts.

Evaluation of mail samples used by other, established annual giving programs, especially those with experience in the same community, can suggest new options and guide future decisions. Comparisons of the mail packages of both commercial and nonprofit mailers can point to what is working best with local audiences. Commercial mailers are good illustrators of "what's hot" in the direct response advertising business. Their methods may not work for nonprofit organizations (even if they could afford their higher costs), but they remain a solid barometer of public responsiveness. Monitoring of other mail users will open up some possibilities and may justify changes in the appeal message's length, design, and content; donor clubs; premium offers; timing; and similar characteristics of the package.

Fund development staff should also confer often with their colleagues in the planning, marketing, community relations, publications, public relations, and volunteer departments. These internal groups are in frequent communication with the organization's constituency (community residents). Their objectives and their messages have the same origins, even if what they promote or request may be different. Frequently, their goal is to establish a positive image or to stimulate the public's use of the organization's programs and services. A high degree of coordination, cooperation, and communication among staff departments can only improve on the success each will have individually in meeting annual goals and objectives. Critical to fund development in particular is the realization that, if these staff partners and their communications programs are effective, they help the entire fund-raising performance. If their efforts are not effective, fund-raising success will be hindered. Collaboration should also include sharing the results of everyone's separate measurements and analyses of results. All these data are useful to the entire team's involvement in public communications.

Another internal group to talk with are those on the "front line"—the professional and support staff who provide programs and services directly to the public. Their daily contact gives them a unique sense of what people need and want and what is known and thought about the organization. They hear firsthand how it is perceived, what are judged to be its strengths and weaknesses, and how it is rated "on the street." Professional and support staff have a critical role in advancing the organization's goodwill and positive image: they interact directly with the public at the point of service. They hear about the mistakes made, the criticisms aimed at appeals received at home, and the rumors and incorrect information their clients may hear and repeat. Direct public contacts are critical input for professional and support staff. An employee can enhance or harm the good image of an organization, multiplying or undoing all the goodwill that countless mailings, messages, and activities have established over many years. Donors and volunteers can offend someone, or become offended enough to speak against the organization. Volunteers and donors are "customers" too, and poor customer relations can hurt the entire organization more severely than good customer relations has the power to repair.

In the intensity of providing service every day, hard-working line and staff members can forget that those being served are possibly the same people who have supported their department with personal gifts. Fund development staff should ask to address groups of employees about the public they serve. Everyone within the organization must be aware of daily donor relations and good customer relations. Sensitivity to the reality that "the public" is, has been, could be, or will be donors, volunteers, and friends is essential, not optional, among staff members.

Professional Help Is Readily Available

Outside consultants and other professionals are available to assist in interpreting public responses and evaluating annual giving results. Their experience can help guide decisions to make changes that will improve results and bring variety into future plans. These professionals can help in all the areas of planning, marketing, publications, public relations, community relations, volunteering, and fund development, and usually at reasonable fees. Consultants provide an objective view of present programs and their performance; their experience allows them to interpret results correctly. Consultants often become working partners with staff and volunteers, monitoring results and guiding future decisions. They have firsthand knowledge of other organizations' performance, and, although professional standards of confidentiality limit the detail they can reveal about other clients, they can give beneficial insights. Because of their length of experience and their concentration on specific fund-raising methods (such as direct mail or special events), they can also provide detailed recommendations on mailing-list choices, list merchants and letter shops, skillful letter writing, package design, added inserts, and audience reactions. They prove their value when their suggestions reduce the cost of mail communications *and* improve net income in a subsequent year.

Other professionals whose knowledge and experience are outside the organization can also be of great use. Local market research firms constantly monitor public reactions, survey public attitudes, and perfect their demographic data. Creative design firms constantly test public responsiveness to the products each of their clients uses. Entry into the fields of telecommunications, television, video messaging, video conferences, and other new-age communications will soon become necessary in order to reach select constituents with reliability. Modern mass communications is an area that nonprofit organizations must learn how to use to their advantage. The days are long gone when highly motivated (and overworked) employees could approach these communication techniques to learn "just enough to achieve adequate results." Without professional guidance in the highly competitive arena of mass public communications, a nonprofit organization will more likely fail to be seen and heard, and will fail to find the donors who might have provided the money to fulfill its mission.

DONOR RELATIONS

Attention to annual donors through recognition and reward should be a proactive part of every nonprofit organization. The budget required to be nice to these best friends is small in comparison to the extent of their present and future generosity. Donors have invested in the organization and should be treated accordingly. Opportunities to be nice are readily available. Some suggestions are:

1. Send them special invitations to regular public events held at or by the organization;
2. Ask them to be guests at a VIP table at one of the benefit events;
3. Invite them to tour a new or renovated part of the facilities;
4. Mail their copy of the annual report with a brief personal cover note attached.

Because it makes good sense to pay attention to donors, it is reasonable to define a written policy that provides for consistent treatment to every donor, fairly and equitably, year after year (see Exhibit 4.4). It also makes good sense to establish donor clubs that give extra privileges and special attention to larger donors. Well-treated donors will continue to reward their favorite nonprofit organizations with additional gifts. It makes good sense to report regularly on the good results achieved with donors' funds and to speak out about the charitable purposes their funds have helped to provide. Prior donors will continue to give if they receive attention, respect, consideration, and warm, friendly treatment.

A. Donors whose cumulative *annual* contributions add to the following gift levels will be accorded full donor recognition privileges for the following year:

Amounts	*Donor Recognition Level*
$100 to $499	Circle of Champions Club
500 to 999	Ambassadors

B. Donors whose cumulative contributions add to $2,500 or more will be accorded permanent donor recognition privileges on the main Donor Wall as follows:

Amounts	*Donor Recognition Level*
$ 1,000 to $2,499	Friends
2,500 to 4,999	Sponsors
5,000 to 9,999	Patrons/Life Members
10,000 to 24,999	Benefactors
25,000 to 49,999	Meritorious Benefactors
50,000 to 99,999	Honored Benefactors
100,000 or more	Distinguished Benefactors

C. Donors of future interest, planned, and estate gifts, including irrevocable gifts in trust, life estates, and gift annuities, will be accorded full donor recognition privileges as members of the Heritage Society. The names of these individuals will be added to the Heritage Society section of the main Donor Wall.

Exhibit 4.4 Donor Recognition Programs

Focus: CCUA Clean Up Cleveland Chapter

The initial "roll out" letter campaign for the Clean Up Cleveland Chapter produced more than 1,500 donors from last fall's first acquisition mailing. Harvey Clout was disappointed that only 1,500 Cleveland residents had replied with money. Karen Anderson, Director of Development, after clarifying that only one letter had been mailed to 80,000 people, pointed out that a 1.8 percent response was quite good, especially for a new organization and without media coverage to help spread the word. She added that the letters had been effective in informing a select group of key residents first, an important step in this city. When she told Clout that people were talking about the chapter's bumper stickers, he confessed that he had received positive comments about them too, and had seen quite a few around town. He agreed that their message was beginning to be heard after all, and asked Anderson to develop suggestions about what they should do next.

"Roll Out" and First Renewal Mailing Plans

Anderson has studied the results of the test mailings to the six original lists and has compared them with the "roll out" letter campaign, which was mailed to four of these same test lists. She believes the mailing list should now be expanded to every fifth homeowner in the city of Cleveland and to the ten largest residential suburbs. She also believes she can justify, based on past performance, a mailing budget for a total of 200,000 names. She recommends (1) a two-part acquisition mailing for the spring (drop dates of March 15 and April 30) and (2) a first renewal request using a computer-personalized letter format to resolicit all 1,504 new donors (348 from the July test and 1,156 from the fall "roll out"). The chapter is now in a new tax year; prior gifts in reply to the test mailings were made between four and ten months ago. The renewal replies are projected to speed up cash flow and help pay for all the mailing costs incurred in the first half of this fiscal year. However, Anderson decides not to resolicit those names on the four test lists that did not respond well to the fall test mailings. In her opinion, after two solicitations within six months last year, they have been tapped out and should be reserved for next fall's mailing sequence. Some of these same residents might be on the new rental lists to be used in the spring "roll out" mailing, but that is not a problem. Anderson drafts a news story to be released March 15, the drop date of the next mailing. To get additional coverage, she will ask the board to make a few phone calls to local papers and radio stations in an effort to spread the word about the CCUA Clean Up Cleveland Chapter's campaign and to alert the public about the open invitation for them to join.

With all this planning completed, Anderson rents a list of every fifth homeowner in Cleveland and its ten major suburbs through Cleveland Mass Communications, a local mail house hired to prepare the 200,000-piece mailing using the chapter's new third-class, bulk-rate permit. She decides to continue to use the text of Letter B (see Exhibit 3.5, page 97) as her appeal letter. She also drafts Letter C (Exhibit 4.5), a follow-up solicitation text to be mailed 45 days after Letter B is dropped.

Her next project is Letter D (Exhibit 4.6), a renewal request to be sent to all 1,504 first-time donors in the fall campaign. This letter will be a combination renewal and upgrade solicitation appeal and will be mailed (first class) on March 14, one day ahead of the drop date for the 200,000 community invitation letters. Anderson then designs a new Circle of Champions information card (Exhibit 4.7), to be inserted into all the spring mail packages. The card will test the idea of a membership in the CCUA Clean Up Cleveland Chapter and will encourage larger gifts.

Anderson reviews all these proposals and draft texts with Harold Connected, whom the board has just appointed as chair of the development committee. Connected was a board member at the local Audubon Society

The Campaign to Clean Up America
Clean Up Cleveland Chapter

April 30, 199X

Dear Concerned Resident:

Last fall, we began our campaign in Cleveland by asking community residents to join with us in cleaning the streets of our city. We had over 1,500 positive replies.

On March 15, we mailed our second invitation and have already received over 2,000 replies. If you missed our letter, you may want to "check us out" this time around.

I'm sure you have seen the new Clean Up Cleveland bumper stickers around town. They are ours, and if you do not have one, call my office and we'll send you one, free.

All I ask in return is that you join us to help clean up our city streets and, if you can, send us a personal gift to help us in our campaign.

Pollution is a tough problem; I know because I operate a steel mill and we've invested millions to clean up the air. But, that's not enough.

The Clean Up Cleveland Chapter of The Campaign to Clean Up America aims to remove trash from our city streets and convert it into electricity we can all use. That's a great plan with a bonus. Here's how it will work.

We have to raise $1,250,000 to build the new energy conversion plant; the rest of the money will come from federal and Ohio matching funds. We'll be cleaning up our streets at the same time.

We will use 75% of your gift to help build the plant, which will reduce everyone's electric bills by $12 a month and $124 a year. The other 25% helps to pay for our public education campaign.

Your gift of $12 will come back to you. If you give us $25 or more, these plans will all happen sooner.

Join us now. Give what you can to help, and spread the word to Clean Up Cleveland.

Sincerely yours,

I. Harvey Clout
Chair of the Board
Cleveland Cast Iron Works

P.S. Charter membership in our Circle of Champions is still open. Please consider an entry gift of $100 or more if you can. Many thanks.

Exhibit 4.5 Letter C: Follow-Up Mailing to Every Fifth Household

The Campaign to Clean Up America
Clean Up Cleveland Chapter

March 14, 199X

Mr. and Mrs. Robert A. Smith
16210 Shaker Boulevard
Shaker Heights, OH 44120

Dear Mr. and Mrs. Smith:

Thank you again for your contribution last fall. Your gift helped to launch our campaign on its way to success.

I have three purposes in writing to you today.

First, I can report that more than 1,500 local residents like yourselves heard our call for action. Total contributions were $35,758, an average of just over $30 per person. Ours was a great beginning, thanks to you.

Our plans for use of these funds are that the first 75% is set aside to build the energy conversion plant, with the remaining 25% used to continue our Clean Up Cleveland public education campaign.

My second reason is to alert you that we are mailing tomorrow more than 200,000 invitations to selected local residents, asking them to join with you in this campaign.

If you have placed a Clean Up Cleveland bumper sticker on your car or truck, friends and neighbors may be asking you what it means. Enclosed is another bumper sticker. Tell our story and ask others to join now.

My third reason is to ask you to consider your next gift to our campaign, perhaps a larger gift this time. Our campaign is far from over and we need you to continue your support.

Our introductory offer to become a charter member of the Circle of Champions donor club with a gift of $100 or more is still open (see the enclosed card for full details). Charter members will be invited to a special event by both the Cleveland Orchestra and the Cleveland Play House.

Thank you again for your first gift last year. I hope you will continue to support our communitywide effort to Clean Up Cleveland. I look forward to hearing from you soon again.

Sincerely yours,

I. Harvey Clout
Chair of the Board
Cleveland Cast Iron Works

Encl. 2

Exhibit 4.6   Letter D: Renewal and Upgrade Solicitation

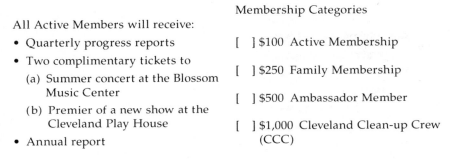

The Campaign to Clean Up America
Clean Up Cleveland Chapter

Circle of Champions

Charter Membership Offer (at $100)

Membership Categories

All Active Members will receive:

- Quarterly progress reports
- Two complimentary tickets to
  (a) Summer concert at the Blossom
      Music Center
  (b) Premier of a new show at the
      Cleveland Play House
- Annual report

[ ] $100 Active Membership

[ ] $250 Family Membership

[ ] $500 Ambassador Member

[ ] $1,000 Cleveland Clean-up Crew
         (CCC)

For more information, please call the
Clean Up Cleveland office at (216) CLEAN UP.

Exhibit 4.7   Circle of Champions Membership Information Card

chapter and knows of Anderson's success in managing its membership program by mail. He agrees to her plans and invites her to present them at the January board of directors meeting.

At the meeting, the board reviews the project in some detail and approves the entire program. A budget of $100,000 is authorized for the costs of mailing the pieces selected, for analysis of the results (Exhibits 4.8 and 4.9), for mailing of a thank-you letter (Exhibit 4.10), and for preparation and release of a news story in support of the spring mailing (Exhibit 4.11).

Results and Analysis

At the May board of directors meeting, Anderson reports on the results of the spring mail campaign. She begins with a review of the two-part acquisition mailing (Letters B and C) to every fifth household in Cleveland and ten residential suburbs:

1. A total of 3,653 new donors were acquired!

2. A total of $116,911 was received!

3. An average gift of $32 was achieved!

4. Mailing costs for Letters B and C were $99,000.

5. Net mailing proceeds were $17,911.

6. Cost per dollar raised was $0.85.

7. A total of 76 new donors who joined the Circle of Champions gave a total of $8,550, for an average gift of $112.50.

For Letter D, the combined renewal and upgrade solicitation text that was sent to the 1,504 first-time donors, the results were:

1. The number who renewed was 914 (60.77%)!

2. A total of $31,064 was received!

3. The average gift increased to $33.99!

4. A total of 94 members recruited to the Circle of Champions gave a total of $12,502, for an average gift of $133.

5. The cost of the renewal mailing was $1,827.

6. Net proceeds were $29,237.

7. Cost per dollar raised was $0.06.

Combining all mail results to date, including last July's test letters, Anderson reports that solicitation letters and bumper stickers have now been mailed to over 280,000 residents. A grand total of 5,257 donor-residents have replied with a total of $192,260 in contributions. With overall costs of $115,677, the net proceeds are $76,583. The success of the Circle of Champions membership introductory offer and the strength of the first renewal response have been encouraging. Overall results in this first year are well above the national standard of $1 to raise $1, using only direct mail. "The reason for our success," Anderson tells the board, "is increased public concern about pollution of the environment. I've talked with the development officers at several other chapters of The Campaign to Clean Up America; they are also reporting good results. It seems the public is ready to respond with action, if given a valid purpose." Anderson concludes her report to the board with two recommendations:

1. The fall mailing campaign should concentrate exclusively on membership in the CCUA Clean Up Cleveland Chapter.

2. Because of the strong community support shown to date, applications should be prepared for submission to local corporations and foundations for grants (a) to support the energy conversion plant as a major capital construction project, or (b) to expand the public education campaign throughout northeast Ohio.

Both recommendations are approved. Anderson is directed to proceed according to the plan she has outlined.

Destination	Letter Sent	Number Mailed	Replies Number	Replies Percent	Gift Income	Average Gift
Cleveland	B	100,000	650	0.65%	$16,601	$25.54
City Limits	C*	98,795	605	0.61	17,521	28.96
Cleveland	B	20,000	212	1.06	10,600	50.00
Heights	C	19,245	213	1.11	12,985	60.96
University Hts						
Lyndhurst	B	20,000	205	1.03	4,588	22.38
	C	18,985	190	1.00	4,096	21.56
Lakewood	B	15,000	192	1.28	6,365	33.15
	C	14,355	216	1.51	4,005	18.54
Lorain	B	15,000	172	1.15	5,136	29.86
	C	12,995	182	1.40	6,679	36.70
Parma	B	20,000	209	1.05	6,615	31.65
	C	18,887	229	1.21	7,607	33.22
Mentor and	B	12,000	191	1.59	7,031	36.81
Willoughby	C	11,205	187	1.67	7,082	37.87
Total/Average	B	202,000	1,831	0.91	$ 56,936	$31.10
	C	194,467	1,822	0.94	59,975	32.92
Total/Average (B + C)		396,467	3,653	0.92%	$116,911	$32.00

Costs:

List rental (@ $25/1,000 × 200,000)		$ 5,000
Printing costs (@ $.12 each × 400,000)		48,000
	Outer envelope	(.02)
	Reply envelope	(.02)
	Letters	(.06)
	"Circle" cards	(.02)
Bumper stickers (@ .01 each × 200,000)		2,000
Computer services/mail preparations		12,000
Postage (@ 0.08 each)		32,000
Total (@ 0.2475 each):		$99,000

* The Letter C list is smaller because of gifts received (donors' names are removed from the list, to prevent future solicitation for the same campaign), undelivered mail, and "Do not mail" replies from Letter B.

Exhibit 4.8 Results of "Roll Out," Letter B and Letter C

Donor Area	Donor Population	First Donor Gifts (Tests)			First Renewal Gifts		
		Number of Replies	Gift Income	Average Gift	Number of Replies	Gift Income	Average Size
Shaker Heights Residents	Test	64	$ 1,407	$21.98	38	$ 879	$23.15
	Full	414	18,321	44.25	308	14,440	46.88
	Total	478	19,727	41.27	338	15,319	45.32
NE Ohio Audubon Society	Test	100	3,000	30.00	58	1,880	32.41
	Full	372	8,916	23.96	197	4,950	25.13
	Total	472	11,916	25.25	255	6,830	26.78
NE Ohio Nature Conservancy	Test	68	1,500	22.06	36	885	24.58
	Full	158	3,476	22.00	82	1,950	23.78
	Total	226	4,976	22.02	118	2,835	24.03
Orchestra/Play House Subscribers	Test	50	1,440	28.80	27	950	35.19
	Full	212	5,045	23.80	135	3,450	25.56
	Total	262	6,485	24.75	162	4,500	27.77
Eastern Suburbs Homeowners	Test	30	340	11.33	22	1,200	54.55
Sports Tickets	Test	36	840	23.33	19	380	20.00
	Totals	1,504	$44,285	$29.45	914	$31,064	$33.99

Retention rate = 60.77%
Cost of mailing: = ($1.215 × 1,504) = $1,827.36
"Circle" renewals = Started with 118; retained 78
Upgraded 10; added 6 new = 94

Exhibit 4.9 Results of Letter D: First Renewal Request

The Campaign to Clean Up America
Clean Up Cleveland Chapter

April, 199X

Mr. and Mrs. Robert A. Smith
16210 Shaker Boulevard
Shaker Heights, OH 44120

Dear Mr. and Mrs. Smith:

Thank you for your wonderful gift of $100, and welcome to Charter Membership in our Circle of Champions donor club. I value your personal support very much.

With your extra help, we move closer to our goals of cleaning up our city streets and building the new energy conversion plant.

You will be hearing from the Cleveland Orchestra and Cleveland Play House in the next few weeks about your invitation to their entertainment event. Both are planning a special program for all our Charter Members.

By the way, our Clean up Cleveland bumper stickers are fast becoming a hot item around town. I'm enclosing two more for your use or to share with a neighbor. If you want more, just call my office at 565-9500.

Again, thank you for your generous gift and for your commitment to support our efforts to achieve a cleaner city and lower electric rates.

Sincerely yours,

I. Harvey Clout
Chair of the Board
Cleveland Cast Iron Works

Encl. 2

Exhibit 4.10 "Thank-You" Letter to New Circle of Champions Donor

---

FOR RELEASE AT 9:00 A.M., MARCH 18, 199X
CLEVELAND, OHIO.

Harvey Clout, head of Cleveland Cast Iron Works, has announced the
inauguration of the Clean Up Cleveland Chapter of America's newest
environmental advocacy group, The Campaign to Clean Up America.

The local Chapter is the eighth to be established in the past six months.
Others are in Atlanta, Detroit, Chicago, Los Angeles, Newark, New York, and
Pittsburgh.

Mr. Clout also announced a special project adopted by the Clean Up
Cleveland Chapter: To build an energy conversion plant that will turn trash
into electricity for local use. A local fund-raising campaign has begun to
provide $1,250,000, one-third of the funds required. The balance will come
from federal and state energy grants.

Several public awareness campaigns are in preparation to increase
awareness of every resident's duty to help keep city and neighborhood
streets clean. "A clean neighborhood is a safe neighborhood." stated Mr.
Clout. "Our environment is made up of more than clean air and clean water.
It also includes collecting and proper use of the trash that litters our streets."

"Clean Up Cleveland" bumper stickers are being mailed to local residents
to encourage public support of this new effort. The local chapter is also
inviting residents to join the new organization. Membership contributions
begin at $12. Charter memberships in the newly formed "Circle of
Champions" are available for a $100 annual contribution.

In addition to Mr. Clout, who is also serving as chair of the board,
members of the local board of directors include vice chair Mary Moneybanks
and treasurer Sidney Secure, CPA. The secretary and assistant secretary are
Theodosius "Ted" Worthy and Titus Brown, APR.

To request a bumper sticker or additional information, please call (216)
CLEAN UP.

Exhibit 4.11   Sample News Release in Support of an Early Mailing

CHAPTER FIVE

Membership and Membership Associations

T he effort to acquire and retain donors who will give again this year, next year, and the year after that, takes some creativity and requires personal attention to these individuals. Why not invite them to become part of the organization? Treat them like members of the family so that they are more likely to remain close to the organization. Nonprofit organizations can offer a variety of reasons why people might "join up." When they become members, they:

1. Become partners in fulfilling the mission;
2. Associate with others who have similar interests and share a common cause;
3. Join an organized and successful group;
4. Become involved in voluntary community, service, or civic work;
5. Give something back to the community;
6. Gain the respect of others.

The advantages and challenges in offering a formal membership program to donors should be weighed carefully. Obligations are required of members, and professional staff are necessary to manage the ongoing membership programs. The advantages are many, however. Exhibit 5.1 reproduces Constance Clark's [1] analysis of what membership is, what it does, and why it is important.

There are a variety of civic and service membership associations across America today. Not all are available everywhere. Some restrict their membership; others limit access on the basis of qualification. For example, membership in a college alumni association usually requires

Membership builds loyalty. It gives people a greater sense of ownership or participation in the organization's mission and activities.

Membership builds depth of commitment. People feel they are important beyond simply the amount of money they can give. Their volunteer help, opinions, and, sometimes, voting rights on policy and program matters are also important to the organization.

Membership includes participation as part of the organization's action network.

Members expect to be called on to take certain actions, such as participating in petition drives or writing to elected officials, especially as "hot" issues arise in the public arena.

Membership conceptually prepares people to continue their support through annual membership renewals. When a person becomes a *donor* to an organization, he or she does not necessarily expect to be asked to renew the gift; a *member* knows or assumes that membership renewal will be an annual event.

Membership programs solicit a higher-quality donor. Although it may be more difficult initially to solicit a membership dues gift rather than a one-time donation, supporters who do say "yes" to the membership option will usually stay with the organization longer. Members are also more likely to respond to appeals for larger gifts.

Exhibit 5.1　Qualities and Characteristics of Membership Programs [1]. Reprinted with permission.

a period of formal student status. Every membership association is prohibited by law from discrimination on the basis of sex, race, creed, physical handicap, or national origin. Most of the membership programs offered by nonprofit organizations are open to anyone who is willing to make an annual gift. Other qualifications may be an interest in joining, the annual payment of dues or a requested gift amount, and a willingness to support the mission, purposes, goals, and objectives of the organization.

LEGAL AND TAX-EXEMPT STATUS

There can be many forms of membership association. Among the several legal forms of tax-exempt nonprofit organization under the provisions of the Internal Revenue Code (IRC), some forms of membership association may qualify as charitable entities and be tax-exempt organizations. Bruce Hopkins [2] is the best source for an explanation:

The federal tax law uses the term *charitable* in two ways. The broader definition means all organizations that are eligible to receive deductible contributions. Used this way, charitable includes entities that are religious, educational, scientific, and the like, as well as certain fraternal, cemetery, and veterans' organizations. To get technical for just a moment, most of these organizations (not the fraternal, cemetery, and veterans' groups) are "501(c)(3) organizations"— they are governed by Section 501(c)(3), probably the most widely recognized provision of the Internal Revenue Code.

In the narrower definition, the term charitable organization is restricted to organizations that match the descriptions of that type of entity under the law.

Any type of nonprofit organization can offer a membership affiliation or operate a membership association. But, because every exempt organization cannot offer its members deductions for their charitable contributions, this threshold question should be resolved before memberships are offered to the public. Tax deductibility for annual dues contributions is an important member service in membership organizations that, on their own, fulfill Internal Revenue Service (IRS) requirements for being fully qualified as tax-exempt. Not all tax-exempt membership groups are able to offer their members a charitable contribution deduction for their dues payment. The public cannot be expected to know whether deductibility is allowed. Organizations that are qualified should say so; those that are not are required by law to disclose that gifts made to them are not deductible. Hopkins' description [3] of various nonprofit organizations is reproduced as Exhibit 5.2.

The range of fully tax-exempt nonprofit organizations that often feature membership affiliation includes churches, cultural alliances, libraries, museums, public radio and television stations, civic and community service groups, and many more. Some membership associations may take on the form of an autonomous or fully independent entity, completely self-sufficient from their parent or sponsoring nonprofit organization. Using the college alumni example again, the association may be separately incorporated, possess its own full tax-exempt status, elect its officers and board of directors from among its members, hire its own employees, and manage all its own financial affairs including the distribution of funds raised to its affiliated college or university. Such an association is guided by its own articles of incorporation and bylaws; its mission, defined in its mission statement, is to support the college or university. If the college had never existed, the alumni association would not exist either. But, should the college cease to function, the association could continue until all its members (former students) were deceased. All of the remaining funds would then have to be directed to a qualified successor college or university.

- *Advocacy organizations.* These groups attempt to influence the legislative process and/or the political process, or otherwise champion particular positions. They may call themselves "social welfare organizations" or perhaps "political action committees." Not all advocacy is lobbying and not all political activity is political campaign activity. Some of this type of program can be accomplished through a charitable organization, but that outcome is rare where advocacy is the organization's primary undertaking. In some instances, two nonprofit organizations are used, to have it both ways—a blend of charitable and advocacy activities.

- *Membership groups.* Some nonprofit organizations—associations, veterans' groups, and fraternal organizations—are structured as membership organizations. This is not to say that a charitable organization may not be structured as a membership entity; it can, but there are other categories of membership groups. Frequently, these are "business leagues."

- *Social or recreational organizations.* Nonprofit organizations may be organized as formal "social clubs" (like country clubs, and tennis and golf clubs), or hobby, garden, or sports tournament organizations. The key factor is their primary purpose; some social activity can be tolerated in charitable groups. There is some overlap with other categories, for example, a social organization can be structured as a membership entity.

- *Satellite organizations.* Some nonprofit organizations are deliberately organized as auxiliaries or subsidiaries of other organizations. Examples of these organizations include title-holding companies, the various types of cooperatives, and retirement and other employee benefit funds. The "parent" organization may be a for-profit entity, such as a business corporation with a related foundation.

- *Employee benefit funds.* The world of compensation is intricate, regardless of whether the employer is a for-profit corporation or nonprofit organization. Various current and deferred benefits for employees are provided, including retirement and profit-sharing programs. When properly organized and operated, these funds are tax-exempt entities.

Exhibit 5.2 Examples of Membership Organizations [2]. Reprinted with permission.

MEMBERSHIP OPTIONS

Membership associations may offer a variety of options for affiliation and for classes of membership. Dues or fees are usually personal gifts, are modest in amount, and are paid by each individual, although membership status in some organizations may also be extended to family members. Categories of membership may use terms such as active, associate, corporate, family, or life, based on the individuals' qualifications, the size of their gifts, or the sources of their membership dues. Membership also may be tied to a specific dues level ($100 for annual membership, $150 for associate or family membership, $500 for a business partner or corporate membership, $1,000 for contributing membership, and $10,000 for life membership). Each membership level often confers detailed privileges offered by the membership association. Members may be asked to serve in a variety of voluntary roles, such as committee member, chairperson, or board member. Normal terms of office are one to three years, with a possible reappointment to another term. Members may also be selected to be representatives to another association, such as a local chapter or district; delegates to the parent corporation; or representatives to a related national association or society.

The mission and purpose of a professional trade association is to recruit as broad a cross-section of individuals who represent the many qualified professionals in the field as is possible. Their related trade partners, affiliated consultants, and vendors are also qualified and invited to join. Although a trade association is partially tax-exempt under Section 501(c)(6) of the Internal Revenue Code and member dues are not deductible as charitable contributions, the trade association can establish a fully qualified "related organization" in the form of a subsidiary 501(c)(3) foundation to serve this purpose. Members' annual gifts (not dues) can be made to the related foundation for uses that further the purposes of the trade association. Professional memberships are often paid by an employer, firm, or business, to encourage employees to increase their knowledge of their profession or craft, to meet and talk with others holding similar positions, or to expand business contacts. Memberships also may be offered to employees as a "perk" for management or technical and skilled positions.

Nonprofit organizations can use membership associations as an effective way to invite their constituency to become more active in the organizations. Several forms of affiliation and association can be offered, and any new membership plan should be as flexible in its design as possible. The forms available should be well-structured so that people outside the organization will recognize and respect them. They should attract as wide a following as possible (without becoming unmanageable by the parent nonprofit organization) and should be open to both individuals and businesses. To continue with the example of college alumni associations, many grant memberships to all graduates automatically; dues promote a member to active standing. A university alumni association may divide its members into subgroups that reflect the level of their degrees and the fields in which they were awarded. Individual subgroups may be offered for graduates of the business, engineering, law, and medical schools. Memberships in individual subgroups may be formed for science, arts, and physical education alumni; for specialized graduate and professional school alumni—for example, in nursing, foreign languages, social sciences, or fine arts—or for Asian American, Black American, Native American, or Chicano alumni. Former students may be eligible for membership in more than one alumni group and are welcome to join any subgroup for which they qualify. Each subgroup remains affiliated with the parent alumni association but its operating independence may include election of its own board of directors, appointment of planning committees from among the membership, publication of its own newsletters and other communications, fund-raising for its priority projects, and scheduling of separate reunions, which may or may not coincide with parent alumni association or college events such as the annual homecoming or class anniversaries. Each subgroup offers former students a compatible interest group in which they can be active participants. The number and size of all alumni subgroups can become unwieldy and too expensive to manage and support centrally from the parent alumni association. Some institutions are indifferent to where their alumni associations focus their attention and funds, so long as they are active, self-supporting, and consistently gaining long-term members. Active membership is the primary goal to be promoted and retained, the goal that justifies a college's distributing its alumni budget as seed money to each of its alumni groups.

There can be problems. Subgroups may choose activities, goals, and priorities that are not consistent with college policy statements' and announced priorities. However, alumni remain a powerful resource to any college or university, and some accommodations and compromises are beneficial to both sides if any controversy arises. Everyone involved may need to be reminded that the primary mission of alumni relations is to support the college. Alumni membership groups can help to accomplish that mission by maintaining active contact and involvement with as many alumni as possible—usually a benefit to both groups. Alumni annual giving represents important and necessary funds coming to the college for annual operating support, scholarships and fellowships, and construction and renovation projects. Alumni activities also encourage and promote use of the library, attendance at athletic and artistic events, community liaison, and legislative and public relations support. Alumni often continue their formal education to receive advanced degrees and to utilize adult education classes in pursuit of personal interests and professional growth. On balance, the college gains through its promotion of nearly every form of alumni activity.

Cliff Underwood [4] has stated four key principles that will determine success in any membership program:

Principle 1   Produce more new members with a successful acquisition program;

Principle 2   Increase the renewal rate of existing members;

Principle 3   Persuade existing members to give more frequently by offering supplemental income and added gift appeals; and

Principle 4   Persuade existing members to upgrade their membership levels.

This chapter concentrates on how these four principles apply to memberships and membership associations in their support of the annual fund-raising programs of nonprofit organizations. All of the major forms of membership programs and membership associations that are engaged in fund-raising will be mentioned. Whatever their solicitation activities and membership programs, their operations must begin with a basic design, must include annual dues and gifts, and must provide benefits and privileges to the members.

BASIC DESIGN

One of the general purposes of a membership program or membership association is to manage a relationship with others who share a common cause. The mission statement defines the purposes to be followed, includes a commitment to public service, and describes the members' privileges. All of these work together toward fulfillment of the mission. Each nonprofit organization offers to its members, in exchange for their annual dues or contributions to the membership program, a variety of services not otherwise available to them. Some benefits and privileges may be reserved for more expensive levels of membership, but most members are eligible to fill a variety of voluntary roles, to serve on committees, and to be elected officers and directors.

Prior to starting a new membership program or new membership association, preliminary market research should be conducted to determine the likely receptivity to the proposal. The alternative, guessing the outcome, could be disastrous. The following series of questions, suggested by Clark [5], will provide the details necessary to resolve not only how and where to begin, but what results to expect:

1. How many *competitor* organizations exist? How large are their membership rolls? How are they different? Can a smaller niche be carved from a

larger organization by offering a more specialized group? Or can the organization serve as an umbrella, gathering members from several smaller groups?

2. How many individuals *share an interest* in the organization's mission? This cannot always be determined; however, figures available from a number of polls and surveys give an idea of how many Americans enjoy certain hobbies, like scuba diving or needlework, and how many are in various demographic categories (the number of parents with college-age children, for example).

3. How many names are available through *list rental or exchange?* A reputable list-brokerage firm can be consulted for information on mailing lists that have produced good direct-mail results for comparable organizations. Would colleague organizations be willing to exchange mailing lists, for purpose of membership solicitation?

To become a member often implies active service or a similar level of obligation on the part of the member. Active membership means acceptance of and allegiance to the organization's tenets of ethical conduct or code of professional standards. The group often acts as the voice of its members; it enunciates their views or advocates their position when calling for or taking action. For example, advocacy groups have been formed out of a common concern for the way things are now and the direction events are taking; they promote one group's views and attempt to persuade others to endorse those views. They use the celebrity of members' names and the force of their membership numbers when they speak out. Because their activities are usually highly visible, they are able to market their cause, recruit new members, and retain present members.

Annual membership dues or gifts paid represent the primary source of revenue for most membership associations. Annual operations use this income to provide member services (public education, social activities, newsletters, and so on) that keep the members involved with the group and validate the amount paid. To be successful, a membership association must serve its members, whether they choose to be active or passive supporters. Activities, meetings, newsletters, and reports are member services delivered, and these services are necessary for recruitment and for membership renewal. Member services are available only to members in good standing, a factor the association will use when soliciting renewal memberships. Gaining the commitment and loyalty of individual members is as much a goal as advancing the cause everyone shares. Thus, membership transfers the concept of raising the money needed for operations to the members themselves, and they choose to renew their dues in order to continue to receive benefits they value and to achieve the mission they support.

ANNUAL DUES AND GIFTS

Annual dues and gifts will vary for each membership program. Most members pay as individuals, through annual gifts; these gift levels are more modest than memberships paid by employers to professional or trade associations. Dues are often offered on a schedule matched to membership standing or position within the organization. Two examples will illustrate. The first is the Cleveland Zoological Society, whose membership grew from 1,784 in 1982 to 24,878 in 1992. Most of this growth occurred between 1990 and 1992, when an aggressive marketing and communications program was built around creative membership concepts. Annual dues begin at $25 for an individual adult. Family membership that includes two adults and their children or grandchildren 18 years and under is $40. Seven additional memberships range from $50 to $1,000. Senior citizen ($17) and senior couple ($30) levels are available for those 62 years and older. There are also six corporate membership groups ranging from $100 to $5,000. The total of 15 categories in all is not unusual for membership programs. What is striking about the Cleveland Zoological Society's approach? The creative names given to the larger gift categories and the comprehensive list of benefits and privileges granted to them (see Exhibit 5.3): The Orang Gang ($250), Chimp Champs ($500), and Gorilla Givers ($1,000). Each has its own brochure, decal, donor certificate, passes, and logo. All are irresistible.

The second example is the National Society of Fund Raising Executives (NSFRE), a 501(c)(6) professional trade association. NSFRE membership is open to individuals who are employed by nonprofit organizations and are responsible for managing fund-raising activities; to fund-raising consultants; and to closely related vendors. NSFRE's 14,000 members at the end of 1993 were linked together through 125 local chapters in communities across America and Canada. Management is directed through an Executive Committee composed of the elected officers and at-large members, plus a National Assembly composed of member delegates who represent the proportional size of local chapters' membership. Metro I Chapters (150 or more members) have three delegates; Metro II Chapters (50 to 150 members) have two delegates, and Metro III Chapters (under 50 members) have one delegate. As shown in Exhibit 5.4, membership classifications and dues are assessed on an individual (not institutional) basis, are paid annually, and include active status in both the local chapter and the national organization [6]. The application process requires completion of the membership invitation form, payment of the appropriate annual dues amount, and the signatures of two voting members of NSFRE. Each completed application is presented for review and approval by the local chapter's

Member Benefits	Membership Level						
	$25 Ind.	$40 Fam.	$50 Cont.	$100 Sustain.	$250 Orang Gang	$500 Chimp Champs	$1,000 Gorilla Givers
Free admission	X	X	X	X	X	X	X
Zoo News magazine	X	X	X	X	X	X	X
Discount at Zoo gift shop	X	X	X	X	X	X	X
Discount for Zoo education programs	X	X	X	X	X	X	X
Free special Zoo functions	X	X	X	X	X	X	X
Membership decal	X	X	X	X	X	X	X
Membership card	X	X	X	X	X	X	X
Discounts at The Rainforest	X	X	X	X	X	X	X
Guaranteed admission at The Rainforest	X	X	X	X	X	X	X
Poster					X	X	X
Donor certificate					X	X	X
Zoo Life magazine					X	X	X
Invitations to "category" events					X	X	X
Name on plaque on Zoo grounds					X	X	X
Name in Zoo News					X	X	X
Name in annual report					X	X	X

Exhibit 5.3   Cleveland Zoological Society Membership Benefits Program

board of directors. Following formal acceptance, the document is forwarded to the national service office.

BENEFITS AND PRIVILEGES

Not all classes of members will have voting rights or equal access to voluntary management of the organization. Such privileges may be reserved for special members ("Regular" and "Retired" members, in NSFRE) who are the only members eligible to hold office and to serve on the local or

---

The National Society of Fund Raising Executives

Member Categories   *Dues and Fees*

Regular Membership   **$215.00/year**

Open to those individuals who have had <u>at least one year</u> of development experience at the time of applications as fund-raising executives for philanthropic organizations or as a consultant to said organizations or as a member of consulting firms who are currently engaged in fund-raising management, and who subscribe to the Code of Ethics and Professional Practices of the Society and its Bylaws. All Regular Members enjoy full voting privileges.

Student Membership   **$119.00/year**

Open to those individuals who are <u>enrolled</u> as full-time Students in degree-granting programs, or who are serving fund-raising internships on stipend only. Applicants must reapply annually for Student Membership and are <u>non-voting</u> members.

Intern Membership   **$125.00/year**

Open to those individuals who have <u>less than one</u> year of experience, and who subscribe to the Code of Ethics and Professional Practices of the Society and its Bylaws. <u>Non-voting</u> members.

Retired Membership   **$140.00/year**

May be extended to individuals who have retired from the field and who subscribe to the Code of Ethics and Professional Practices of the Society and its Bylaws. Retired Members receive full voting privileges.

Affiliate Membership   **$215.00/year**

May be extended to individuals who work in fields related to fund-raising, or who have mutual interest with fund-raising individuals. Affiliate category <u>does not</u> permit voting privileges.

Exhibit 5.4 Example of Professional Association Membership Categories (NSFRE)

national board of directors. It is common practice to provide some public services to members at a reduced fee and to charge nonmembers more for access to the same activity, as an incentive to join. For example, members pay reduced registration fees when they attend annual meetings and conferences; they also receive discount prices for association products and services. Other benefits reserved for active status range from receipt of annual reports to discounts on car rentals, group travel, and health or life insurance plans. The discounts can be an attractive feature when membership renewal invitations arrive. James Brandt [7] warns that the offer of membership or renewal must give members benefits they desire or need. Among them are:

1. *Informational benefits* such as newsletters. These are especially good for advocacy-oriented groups whose members want to be kept up-to-date.
2. *Token benefits* such as thank you letters and membership cards. These are important for fundraising-oriented organizations, but they shouldn't be too extravagant.
3. *Prestige benefits* such as photos and certificates. These are effective only for celebrity-endorsed organizations and only when members truly believe that their memberships "entitle" them to be associated with the celebrity.
4. *Throw-away benefits.* Group insurance, car rental discounts and credit cards rarely increase response to marketing promotions, but they rarely hurt response either, if selected carefully and not overused. Exception: They can be effective if they relate to the organization's mission or if prospects don't believe they can get them anywhere else.

A similar variety of benefits and privileges can be used in a membership association operated by a nonprofit organization. A college alumni association may require only one qualification for membership—prior student status at the college or university—but may limit service on its board of directors to individuals with earned degrees, or to those who are paid-up active members. Privileges of alumni membership may include discount prices in the campus bookstore or theater, or advance opportunity to buy tickets for athletic and other events.

THE VALUE OF A GIFT MEMBERSHIP

Gift levels and membership standing are often combined because they work well as incentives to join an organization and to remain an active member. Annual giving activities can be enhanced through a gift membership program by offering membership to donors whose existing annual gift levels qualify them to join. Special privileges can be linked to a donation that repeats the prior gift amount, and added benefits can be tied to higher levels of giving. A gift membership plan is often accompanied by offers of perceived or material value described as services in the membership association. These privileges are designed to be incentives to anyone, whether a donor or a prospect, who gives the required amount.

The privilege of association then becomes added to the gift membership. To join and to remain a qualified member is a one-step process: continue to make annual gifts. In time, donors will learn about the other, higher gift levels and their associated benefits, and some will elect to give the amounts required to gain access to these desired levels. Donors are well aware that their gift decision will be seen by others, and some may be motivated on the basis of public image and respectability. Exhibit 5.5 illustrates a typical gift membership plan with escalating privileges for higher annual contributions.

Benefits and privileges are essential to a gift membership program. They act as marketing tools to recruit new members, to encourage member retention, and to increase the total of annual gift revenues received. The membership organization may also provide a variety of opportunities for members to become volunteers and active participants, and to join in one or more active projects the group has undertaken. Because of the great variety of membership associations and operating styles that exist, multiples of benefits and privileges can be defined, all designed to increase the attention and personal involvement of the membership. These options will concentrate on one or more of the following specific

Membership Amount	Title	Benefits and Privileges
$ 100	Active Member	Membership card Membership directory Newsletter Invitation to Annual Meeting
150	Associate Member or Family Member	Same as above

500	Business Partner
	Corporate Member
		Same as above *plus:*
		Separate listing in annual
		  Directory
		Two free tickets to Annual
		  Meeting

1,000	Contributing Member	Same as above *plus:*
		Name added to permanent
		  Donor Wall at *Friend* level
		Invitation to Annual Donor
		  Luncheon

5,000	Life Member	Same as above *plus:*
		Name added to permanent
		  Donor Wall at *Patron* level
		Permanent member card
		  for member and spouse

Exhibit 5.5 Annual Membership Levels with Benefits and Privileges

features: personalization, orientation of new members, mentoring, access, group projects, retention, record-keeping, and recognition.

Personalization

With a gift membership, a request for an annual gift to a nonprofit organization is converted into a personal invitation from a membership association to join a group of like-minded and public-spirited individuals. Personalization is quite important to the member candidate who has been nominated, to the current members who have nominated the member, and to the membership association. The invitation attempts to be sincere; a positive reply *will* be welcomed by comradeship. Many of the routine communications prepared and sent by nonprofit organizations to nearby community residents are, of necessity, impersonal and distant. A letter of invitation personally addressed to a prospective member at his or her home or business address is much more likely to be opened, read, and appreciated. This letter is a best effort to reflect a personal message to the invitee; it uses personal pronouns and is signed by someone whose name may be recognized by the recipient. The text of the letter outlines the uses planned for the gift membership and the mission of the membership association. It reports what the association and its members have accomplished as direct community support and defines the commitment to achieve additional public benefits. This letter also explains the specific projects the membership association has undertaken, describes the benefits and privileges of membership, and may include the roster of current officers, board members, and active members. An information card or small brochure may be included to explain the balance of its activities, programs, and services. This invitation is accompanied by the membership invitation, which is to be completed and returned to the sender. After the member candidate has replied affirmatively, a personal letter of welcome is sent back with a complete membership packet: a membership card, copies of the most recent newsletter, a schedule of coming events and activities, and other details.

Orientation of New Members

A new member may harbor several anxieties—not knowing many or any of the other members; not knowing the community, if a newcomer to the area; and not being current on the activities, meetings, or events. An orientation program will bring comfort as well as the necessary details and information, will convey a warm welcome, and will provide proper introductions. Newcomers should feel, as soon as possible, that they belong.

Exhibit 5.6 lists some activities suggested by Patricia and Daniel Gaby [8] to help newcomers get started toward becoming actively involved and valuable members.

Mentoring

A current member may be assigned to a newcomer to assist with introductions. This mentor will offer to escort the new member to the next meeting and arrange to introduce the others present. The mentor will explain current activities, encourage selection of a committee or participation in a work project, and convey an invitation to the next meeting or to an upcoming social event, again in the company of the mentor. Spouses and other guests can be included. This level of personal attention is crucial to newcomers; they immediately feel welcome and will have begun a more rapid integration into the group.

---

1. Make a special effort to introduce them to other members. You might put a red tab on their name cards and encourage older members to approach them with a special greeting.

2. New members often feel more comfortable if seated with other new members at their first meeting, at a special table perhaps, so that they can compare notes with other people as inexperienced as they. Some groups have a special "New Members Dinner" at which newcomers can be welcomed publicly.

3. Welcome them as well in your publication, including short biographies. Talk them up.

4. Give them something to do as soon as possible. This shouldn't be something too trivial, nor should it be an obvious piece of make-work—that could be perceived as an insult. But it shouldn't be too demanding either—that could be discouraging.

5. Some organizations have a new members' counselling program in which each new member is invited to come for an interview. The main objectives of the organization are explained to him; his interests and reasons for joining are discussed; and he can be taken on a tour and meet the staff.

6. A new member is a source of new ideas—show him you appreciate this potential in him. After he's been with you a short while, ask him his opinion of the group's structure and functions. Ask him if he's getting everything he had hoped for out of belonging.

Exhibit 5.6 Suggestions for New Member Orientation [8]. Reprinted with permission.

Access

Membership associations offer access to all their members for multiple purposes, particularly for business and personal use. Business contacts and networking are valid activities that add to the attractiveness of membership. The new friendships formed may lead to business and professional opportunities for both parties. If the new member is also new to the community, these new contacts can be valuable for personal references of a doctor or dentist, banker or accountant, nanny or baby-sitter, insurance or real estate agent, and for locations of shops and reliable service businesses. Access also includes the services of the nonprofit organization the members represent. Meetings may be held at the institution or agency where its programs and services are delivered and where its professional and management staff have their offices. Access to these additional programs and services, whether the organization is a museum, school, hospital, library, or other interest center, is included as a benefit of membership, and is often an important additional incentive to remain an active member.

Group Projects

The gift membership association may have a special focus of community service or be directed toward support of one or more nonprofit organizations. It may select specific areas for the use of its dues and other funds raised. These areas are often featured in membership recruitment and renewal communications, adding value to the membership gift amount by directing the funds raised toward specific charitable purposes. This focus helps the nonprofit organization to communicate its story about community needs and its capacity to satisfy them, thanks to the members' generosity. The members become associated with each worthwhile project and its success. They are kept informed about public education and awareness projects designed to aid their association in meeting its operating goals and objectives. The membership association can use these visible first-priority projects as effective marketing tools when it is actively seeking and renewing members.

Membership associations that adopt fund-raising goals for community benefit will enhance their image and gain the respect of the surrounding community. Their separate identity, reputation, and commitment will also enhance their membership activities. The association will stay highly visible as an active partner of the nonprofit organization it serves, and its successes will reinforce the organization's other annual giving activities. Membership associations can also accept multiyear projects, such as during a major capital campaign.

Retention

When personalization, orientation of new members, mentoring, access, and group projects are well-managed, recruiting and renewal of active members can be performed with greater effectiveness and efficiency. Annual programs planned and carried out by each membership association should include all the areas of focus in addition to a full schedule of member services. In combination with demonstrated competence, success, and professionalism, these programs achieve their own level of attractiveness for new and current members. When exciting and valuable activities are in full operation, new candidates will come forward and current members will want to continue their association with these enterprises. Current members also may be encouraged to consider increasing their annual level of gift support or contributing "something extra"—a kind of gratuity at the time of annual dues payment, to assist the association in meeting its financial goals and to express personal support of its priority commitments. Renewal should never be taken for granted. Successful retention of members requires a well-prepared plan for continued communication with new and prior donors after their gifts are made. Invitations to public and benefit events, newsletters, and opportunities for voluntary participation should be sent during the year, perhaps on an every-other-month basis. Richard Trenbeth [9] has pointed out: "A major problem all membership groups have in common is a normal but sometimes shockingly high drop-off rate of first-year members. This is especially true of persons who enroll in response to a premium or free gift offer. The chief reason is the new member's failure to take advantage of the benefits that would weld him or her to the organization."

Membership Records and Other Data

The membership association should retain data on its members and their activities. From its membership records, the association should be able to retrieve:

The names of current members who were active in asking new members to join, how many of those asked joined, and at what levels;

Who was assigned to each new member as a mentor and might approach that member at renewal time;

Which areas individual members chose as their focus for active voluntary support;

Which members attended meetings, social events, and so on.

Every member should be asked to help with the annual membership campaign by soliciting new members and asking current members to give again. Personalization continues as the most effective means to maintain a vibrant membership program.

Access to reasonably priced in-office personal computers with highly efficient (and equally inexpensive) software programs permits every fund development office to maintain complete records on all its donors. The decision to add computerization should not be based on when there are enough donors on file to justify the expense, but on how long the program can continue to perform without the efficiency and effectiveness that computer record-keeping provides. Trenbeth [10] acknowledged that several questions need to be assessed in order to resolve the decision on computerization of records:

- Can you afford the cost of complex data collection? Can you staff such a system? Is the right software available for the computer system you plan to use? Or would you have to create your own programs?
- Can your proposed computer system expand to accommodate larger and more complex database information?
- Will the system give you ready access to the information you need? How quickly can you get the segmentation you need for analysis and renewal? Can it generate the reports you need?
- Will the system let you produce mailing labels, dues statements, receipts, and other types of acknowledgments? Will it be able to personalize your communications to your members?
- If you intend to test large mailing lists, can the proposed computer system use a merge/purge program to eliminate duplicates?
- Is the proposed computer system compatible with word processing equipment you may already own?

Recognition

Most cakes can benefit from a little frosting. Adding a few donor recognition features to the list of existing member benefits and privileges will help to sustain member satisfaction and encourage faithful payment of dues. These extra benefits must be valid and consistent within each level of membership. Members must get the message that their friendship and support are important to the membership association and to the nonprofit organization that benefits from their funds. Recognition can be expanded with a "credit" system. For example, dues paid to the membership association can be credited again as annual gift income by the parent nonprofit organization, as part of its overall annual giving program. This linkage permits the parent organization to invite members to participate in its annual giving campaign and special-project fund-raising programs during the year. If the parent organization operates a donor recognition policy that keeps track of every contribution it receives, including membership dues, these annual gifts will quickly add up. If the organization then provides one or more visible forms of recognition to donors for their cumulative or lifetime giving, members will have an extra motive to continue their membership affiliation and annual gift support.

A listing in the annual membership directory offers several additional recognition opportunities: the membership level of each active member, the year the member joined, and the number of years of unbroken membership achieved so far. Special membership levels, such as Life Member or Sustaining Member, can be coded on the general list and featured on separate lists. Those who make a "something extra" gift each year might have an asterisk before their names or be gathered on a separate list. Each of these devices can be repeated in the newsletters and annual reports of the membership association and its parent nonprofit organization.

Active members can be invited to assist their association in several way:

Provide leadership to activities, events, and committees;

Join the board of directors;

Qualify as recruits for other services to the parent nonprofit organization;

Respond to support areas where their personal or professional expertise will be of value;

Join in an advocacy effort or legislative support activity.

Leadership and volunteerism are enormously valuable resources to any nonprofit organization that is alert enough to ask for help and to stimulate the interest and enthusiasm of all its affiliated members. Active members should be invited to attend the social activities and benefit events conducted by the nonprofit organization outside the community. Commemorative or tribute-giving programs should be offered to them at least annually, and they can be invited to support other annual, capital, and endowment fund-raising campaigns. Other responsibilities within the nonprofit organization's total fund-raising effort may appeal to them, such as leadership in other annual giving activities and committees. Each member should be provided uniform information about planned giving and estate-planning opportunities.

MANAGEMENT OF MEMBERSHIP ASSOCIATIONS

Member services, the major area of responsibility for most membership associations, may vary greatly among groups. They may be merely a response to competition, or may be tailored to fit the unique needs and desires of the members. Among the member services a membership association can offer are:

- Personal standing;
- Journals, newsletters, and library resources;
- Leadership on committees and on the board;
- Recognition;
- Local chapter or affiliate activities;
- Invitations to social activities and benefit events;
- Advocacy, letter writing, and lobbying opportunities;
- Discounts on services;
- Education and training (conferences, workshops, seminars);
- Regulatory activities and instructions;
- Research services, studies, and reports;
- Personal services (life, medical, dental, and disability insurance);
- Planned giving and estate-planning opportunities;
- Travel services.

Employee Qualifications and Experience

Nonprofit organizations should hire, as employees for membership associations, men and women who have done prior membership organization work, have fund-raising experience, have been trained to manage volunteers and volunteer-led associations, and have served as active volunteers themselves. These employees may be active members of a trade association, such as the Association for Healthcare Philanthropy (AHP), Council for Advancement and Support of Education (CASE), National Catholic Development Council (NCDC), National Society of Fund Raising Executives (NSFRE), Planned Giving Society of America (PGSA), or others. Their volunteer experience may have come from service in one or more United Way organizations, from a volunteer-intensive annual campaign, or from service to a variety of nonprofit associations or societies. Personal experience counts greatly in learning the internal and external operating details of membership organizations. Active membership offers exposure to on-the-job professional training that cannot be simulated elsewhere. These staff professionals must become expert in annual recruitment and renewal techniques and in the delivery of membership services in a satisfactory and cost-effective fashion.

The common management features shared by membership associations, whether they are service and civic clubs, trade associations, nonprofit organizations, or other types, include:

1. A mission statement (to support the parent organization);
2. Bylaws or operating rules and procedures;
3. Election procedures for service on the board of directors;
4. Well-defined committees and their duties;
5. Opportunities for leadership and volunteerism;
6. Operating budgets, accounting procedures, expense reports, and audits.

Role of the Board of Directors

Voluntary active service in membership associations is open to all the members, but leadership opportunities and positions may be limited to one or more categories of active members in good standing. The members-at-large elect the board of directors, who make long-range and strategic plans, set dues amounts, oversee their organization's financial affairs, and operate their annual activities and services in accordance with approved policies and procedures. The officers of the association are elected from among current board members; each serves a specified term and has assigned duties. The bylaws spell out all the areas where members can be involved—election procedures, terms of office, standing committees and their duties, required meetings, and financial obligations—plus other details for annual operations. Changes to these bylaws must be approved by the membership. In essence, the annual operations of a membership organization, social and civic club, or trade association are much like those of every other nonprofit institution or agency.

Prospective Members: Who Are They? Where Are They?

Each membership association has the potential to appeal to at least one segment of the population. Defining an organization's mission in terms that will match well with the concerns and motives of several population segments will contribute greatly to success in membership recruitment and retention. With proper preparations, say Gaby and Gaby [11], likely membership response can be evaluated from the following sources:

1. Published lists of contributors to drives and charitable efforts that are allied to your group's interest.

2. Membership lists of professional groups (social workers, teachers) in fields related to yours.

3. Lists of church and community groups.

4. Nonaffiliated people who have dealt with your group or used its services in the past.

5. Lists of subscribers to magazines dealing with your area of interest.

6. Finally, ask each of your members to search his brain for the names of three people he personally knows to be likely candidates for membership.

Collecting these names and their current mailing addresses is only the beginning. They must all be assembled in a master list, usually on a computer, so that letters, envelopes, mailing labels, and other details can be maintained accurately and used repeatedly during the coming year. Personal communications can now begin. Some prospects will respond to the first invitation, but the majority will not. Communications must continue to be sent to the entire list, and increased membership responses can be expected over time. These recruitment strategies and expected results are similar to those described for direct mail solicitation (see Chapters Three and Four), especially if membership appeals use only direct mail as their communications channel. Management will be required to keep each list current (as many as 20 percent of the entries on a list may have a change of address or of name each year). Once these lists are assembled, additional work will be required to learn something about who these people are: their professions, gift history, age, active association with the parent nonprofit organization, and other details. This information is helpful in getting to know these candidates and, consequently, in meeting their needs and desires. Their abilities can be a valuable addition to the talent pool.

Recruitment and Renewal of Memberships

Most of the day-to-day activities carried out by a membership association are designed to gain membership recruitment and renewal and to serve the parent nonprofit organization. Membership associations live and die according to how they find and keep members, a rather unique style of annual giving. Membership is a large part of the mission and purpose of the association, club, or society because dues revenue is so vital to financial operations. Considerable attention is given to membership recruitment strategies, which are often carried out at all times of the year. By contrast, membership renewal is often conducted at a specified time in the year, a period either tied to the anniversary date of membership or set aside for an annual renewal drive for all members. Membership goals for recruitment and renewal are set each year and are then linked to services to be provided from dues revenues. New-member recruitment must always be carried on to replace those who have retired, left the area, or dropped their active status. Renewal may account for between 75 and 85 percent of membership revenue in mature associations; new memberships complete the target goal. (These percentages will be reversed in a new group that is building up its membership base.) Membership recruitment and renewal are also the duty of each member. All members should be prepared and encouraged to act on membership opportunities at all times. Active voluntary participation and involvement is the chief reason most members cite for their own continued membership. Asking every member to be part of the membership committee and to be active in the annual "every member" campaign is vital to the continued success of the association.

Competition for member attention is always present. Creativity is required when asking people to join or to renew their memberships year after year. The needs and desires of a society can change rapidly; so can its interests in community service. Success in membership renewal activities is important because less time and effort are required than for first-time recruiting. Mature organizations can expect at least 75 percent of their membership to renew each year; this level of performance can increase over time, with extra year-round effort. One suggestion put forward by Gaby and Gaby [12] was to divide current members into two groups. The control group received the full set of regular renewal materials on the same schedule as prior years. The experiment group received a different mailing package that exhibited new ideas, making renewal more desirable, more vital, or just easier. Renewal percentage rates and net revenues increased for the experimental group. Some of these creative ideas were:

1. A new stuffer emphasizing the benefits of membership in a new way, or one announcing some new action or achievement by the organization.
2. A new invoice permitting payment of dues by credit card.
3. A business reply card offering the option of a new car decal or sticker.
4. A new membership card that says "Member since _____" and "Valid until _____" instead of "Expires on _____." Perhaps this could be made of plastic instead of paper (though plastic cards can run into money).
5. An insurance company reminder, if applicable in your case, that the holder's benefits will expire at midnight on the date shown on his old card.
6. A change in billing procedures, allowing more or less lead time.

7. A letter to dilatory members from the president, with a message on the left and a blank space on the right wherein the recipient is invited to write any comments or complaints he may have.

Any experiment requires some time to validate the testing methods used. Were there adequate numbers in the survey? Were there enough replies for the results to be statistically sound? The trial should be conducted alongside the regular program throughout the membership renewal cycle, and comparative measurements should be taken when the trial is concluded. Only one variable should be tried at any one time; two may confuse the results so that neither can demonstrate its extra effectiveness. If the evidence points to any one or more improvements that can be attributed to either renewal package or to its contents, further study may determine whether old ways should be abandoned in favor of the new, now proven changes. New ideas also tell members that a good-faith effort is being made on their behalf, which will help their good feelings about their own active standing.

Communications

One or more regular communication pieces are needed to keep the members informed about the association and all of its operations, and to fulfill the many member services. As is true with all other forms of annual giving communications, members (donors) need to hear, between solicitations, from the organizations they support. Meetings and newsletters, which are most often used to report on membership and association activities, can be supplemented with professional journals, special reports, legislative action bulletins, and constant promotions of the special programs and services that the association has promised to its members. Frequent communications give visibility to members who are active as volunteers and in leadership roles. Publishing the names of new members, of recipients of outside professional promotions and awards, and of others who have had notable life changes is well-received. Members need reminders on future social activities, annual meetings, conferences, and workshops they are invited to attend. Advertisements from local business and service enterprises will help to pay for communications costs. Discount prices can apply to members who wish to buy space for their business or professional promotions.

Members as Volunteers

The strength of any association is in members who are active, voluntary participants. Their time, energy, talents, and commitment are all provided free of charge and with the best of intentions. They offer their association an enormous reservoir of human resources. A business or corporation could never recruit a similar group of nonemployees who would volunteer and then work so hard for free. Managing members who volunteer is a skill area that comes from some training and long experience. Volunteers come in with varying degrees of enthusiasm and willingness to perform any task that needs doing. Not all volunteers can be helpful, despite their eagerness and willingness to try; the tasks that are within their capabilities need to be defined. There is always a mix of personalities to be managed. Without causing divisive responses, the manager must be able to identify leadership candidates and committee workers who can work well with others. A multitude of tasks can be accomplished when the members and their leaders are relaxed about who does each task, where it's done, when it gets done, or how well it is performed. The guidelines listed in Exhibit 5.7 represent advice from Arch McGhee [13] on how to effectively manage membership associations.

1. Select assignments that fit the talents and personality of the member. Members will do best those things which they like to do.

2. Make assignments definite. Whenever a member is given an assignment, he should know just what he is supposed to do. Sometimes this may mean consultation to determine the requirements and the limits of the job. Indefinite assignments put the member on the spot—he can feel neither quite sure of what he is to do nor when he is finished.

3. Set completion dates where specific projects are involved.

4. Do not be afraid to ask. A member is complimented, not insulted, by being asked to undertake an assignment. The very worst that can happen is a refusal.

5. Never ask for volunteers. This is usually an evasion of administrative responsibility—by asking the volunteer to select himself instead of being selected. Those who volunteer may not be those best suited for the project at hand.

6. Make sure that each assignment calls for a worthwhile contribution from the member. A member who is given a trivial assignment or is put on a committee with nothing definite to do will not be interested because of his participation—in fact, the contrary, disinterest, is apt to be the result.

7. Never divide responsibility between committee or members. What if everybody's job turns out to be nobody's job.

Exhibit 5.7 Guidelines for Management of Membership Associations [13]

Recognition (Again)

Recognition is the preferred way to thank each member and to show others (including nonmembers) how members are honored and respected for their decision to join and give faithful service. A variety of membership classes may be offered, and the annual membership fee that is linked to each class can point to the degree of recognition or standing in the association that each member may achieve. The privileges reserved for each class of membership expand with the higher fees; these are important opportunities for the organization to create meaningful benefits. Membership cards, mailing lists, certificates, and directories are available to all members, as are the opportunities to give voluntary service on committees, to gain leadership positions, and eventually to be nominated for election to the local or national board of directors. Recognition can also be offered in the form of invitations to speak at workshops or seminars, to act as a delegate to other organizations, or to perform similar special services. Extra honors should be reserved for those who have performed prior services or held elected office, or those whose cumulative giving has reached higher levels. Formal award programs conducted before a membership audience are excellent occasions to reward members annually for their achievements in several categories of service. Recognition by one's peers, one of the most valued ways to achieve respect, is an essential feature of opportunities for honors and rewards. Everything performed in the name of communications, voluntary service, and recognition continuously contributes to both membership recruitment and renewal.

ANNUAL GIVING OPPORTUNITIES FOR MEMBERS

In each membership year, there are several opportunities to ask for contributions beyond membership gifts. However, the members need some understanding and appreciation of the purpose or need for these extra gifts. Most members believe their once-a-year dues payment is all that is required of them. The dues maintain their membership standing in the association, but the nonprofit organization cannot sustain its public benefit programs and services based on dues revenue alone. It is to the association's advantage to be able to offer its members other options for their active participation. There should not be any barriers or hesitancy when the parent organization invites a premier group of its friends and donors to help when financial needs arise and additional support from volunteers and contributors must be requested. For its major capital campaigns, its community relations programs, and its advocacy, legislative, and lobbying agendas, the organization will turn again to these same association members. When estate planning and planned giving opportunities are offered to these members, the offers should be packaged as additional forms of membership services, to be used in conjunction with their own tax and retirement planning.

Supplemental Income Programs

Membership associations need to bring their own and their parent organization's long-range plans and strategic objectives to their members' attention. The focus on member services tends to tilt day-to-day operations toward fulfilling members' needs, but there are larger issues to which members owe some allegiance. Special needs do arise; priorities do change in response to external conditions or internal requirements; and members can benefit from knowing about these other opportunities. Supplemental income programs will attempt to stimulate (1) increased participation by the members and (2) increased income from new and established sources. Exhibit 5.8 offers several ideas that have proved beneficial for supplemental income programs.

---

1. Year-end and holiday appeals. Tax motives and holiday traditions are combined in the calendar year-end solicitation message.
2. Special gift clubs. Select privileges should be reserved for donors who make extra gifts to one or more gift clubs. These can be directed to children or seniors as special benefit offers.
3. "Something extra" gifts. Additional amounts can be given at the time of annual membership renewal, purely out of generosity and respect for the organization and the public benefit purposes it supports.
4. Special and benefit events. The members stage a social or sporting event for members and for the public. Net proceeds are added to the treasury.
5. Business and corporate memberships. This separate membership class offers unique programs designed to meet the needs of executives and managers.
6. Special campaigns. Occasional capital or equipment projects have select fund-raising objectives for members' participation; each project has its own goal and special recognition opportunities.
7. Life memberships. Priced at a value equivalent to 10 or 20 years' membership dues payments, this concept offers a dual convenience: a major, one-time cash payment, and revenue infusion to the operating budget.
8. Endowment funds. Permanent annual support can be achieved through larger gifts to an endowment fund; the advantage is long-term growth with increased annual earnings.

Exhibit 5.8 Supplemental Income Options for Membership Associations

Offering a variety of options to individual members is a means of increasing their ties to the association and encouraging better relationships. Satisfied customers, access to additional privileges, improved personal attention, strengthened commitments, and more secure financial support of the parent nonprofit organization—all of these are possible results.

Special offers can be provided within routine annual giving programs or conducted parallel to membership drives. Nonprofit organizations must be committed each year to building up the numbers of their friends and donors by every means available. Those whose donative spirit is greater, or to whom multiple gifts with added privileges are attractive, can consider accepting an invitation to make one or more special gifts, beyond membership dues. It never hurts to ask! The benefits to the member from such additional contributions must be well defined and should be adequately enticing. If not properly explained, these strategies can cause confusion and result in negative impressions among the membership. Each "second ask," which can quickly become as routine as the "second collection" in church, must be clarified and justified as a special priority or need of the association and as a request reserved for members only.

Various "invitations" to make additional gifts during the operating year are sent by the parent organization. These can include invitations to buy tickets to special and benefit events, or to attend lectures, dedications, receptions, annual meetings, and similar occasions. The membership association will be offering its own calendar of activities and events, for its own marketing and recruiting purposes. Options might include first nights at newly opened restaurants, gallery exhibits, or other public and private facilities—events that are primarily advertising vehicles for the host facilities. Members are invited to attend the "opening" for an added-on fee, and the proceeds (or a percentage of the sales) are delivered to the membership association for that year's fund-raising project. When the membership association undertakes a special project on behalf of its parent nonprofit organization, such as a multiyear pledge to assist in a major capital campaign, the extra fund-raising activity will make a critical contribution. The organization will be attempting to raise funds above its ordinary annual operating levels and will need to find ways to stimulate the membership's attention and excitement and to raise the extra money needed to fulfill its pledge commitment.

Membership Development Strategies

A membership association must give first priority to its own member recruitment and renewal programs. Membership development requires a "battle plan" that has mapped out several primary and alternate strategies to be used throughout the year. A second plan projects the activities and programs that will be carried out over a two- or three-year period in order to achieve growth of membership, increased retention rates, and additional revenue production. Such plans must conform to the membership potential and profile of each organization, but Tracy Connors [14] has found that the following guidelines apply uniformly:

1. Figure out how much a member is really worth to you.
2. Set goals.
3. Keep at it.
4. Use a selling theme.
5. Simplify.
6. Sell the benefits.
7. Don't bore people to death.
8. Use a letter with your membership package.
9. Develop a memorable graphic identity.
10. Try new media.
11. Make it easy to join.
12. Don't be afraid to make mistakes.
13. Be keenly opportunistic.
14. Use your members.

Membership Cards and Affinity Cards

Members are usually presented with an annual identification card acknowledging their standing as active members. This card is often a means to access additional benefits—discounts on purchases (tickets, travel plans, and so on) or lowered rates for routine programs and services (special educational and entertainment programs, reciprocal privileges at other membership associations or other nonprofit organizations, and so on). The card usually states an expiration date, a less than subtle reminder of the obligation to pay their membership fee annually in order to continue to receive these privileges. Each of these benefits is especially useful when annual renewal solicitations are made.

Nonprofit organizations have begun to offer their donors and members affinity card privileges. An affinity card is a charge card or credit card that channels a percentage of the charged expenditure (usually, a prearranged figure of 5 to 10 percent (or less) of the gross or the net amount) to the organization as an additional gift. These new dollars are less a gift than a commercial exchange that benefits others more than it benefits the membership association or the nonprofit organization. Affinity cards may also offer a lower interest rate to members, may display the name and logo of the membership association, and may be substituted for the membership card, further enhancing the value of maintaining current membership standing.

Matching Gifts

Several businesses, corporations, partnerships, firms, and professional corporations now provide corporate matching gift programs to their employees, to encourage civic participation and community support. Most will offer a dollar-for-dollar match, up to a maximum amount, to their employees' contributions to selected nonprofit organizations. Some businesses or firms will offer two-for-one matches, again up to a cap amount, to stimulate higher giving levels among their employees. The intent in matching gift programs is to preserve and increase annual giving by employees. Unfortunately, a fairly common practice among employees with access to such programs is to pay half of the required membership dues or gift amount and tap the matching gift program for the other half. The true goal of increasing or doubling the amount given to nonprofit organizations occurs less often. The membership association or nonprofit organization receives the donations and the matching gift, but the income realized falls short of the program's intent and potential.

Business and Corporate Membership Programs

Many membership associations and nonprofit organizations offer business and corporate membership programs—either a category of regular membership prorated for businesses or corporations, or a separate program designed to appeal to business and corporate executives. The membership fee is paid by the corporation, which may justify it as part of its annual corporate gift support. The objectives of the membership association are to gain wide notice within the business community, to attract and retain another source of annual membership dues and gift income, and to recruit the attention and active participation of corporate executives, managers, and employees. When the purposes and goals of the membership association match with one or more of the purposes and goals of a business or corporation, memberships are an attractive decision. They add to corporate visibility in the community and help to demonstrate how business leaders perform valuable levels of community service and contribute support. When the product lines of the business or corporation match with the programs and services of the membership association or its parent nonprofit organization, there is ample opportunity for everyone to benefit. For example, local bookstore own-ers, printers, and publishers may become members of library associa-tions or student bookstore societies in order to further student use of books. In another example, corporate members of an art museum or gallery may be allowed to rent (at discount prices) art works owned by the museum or gallery for display in their offices, a privilege not avail-able to any business or firm that is not a member.

ANNUAL MEMBERSHIP CAMPAIGNS

Considerable effort is required to plan and conduct annual membership campaigns. Membership recruitment and retention are sophisticated enterprises that require experienced and skillful professional managers. When well-defined programs and services are available for the mem-bers, including a full range of benefits and privileges, concentration on these features can be a characteristic of all communications during the annual membership campaign. This campaign is a smaller version of the many other forms of volunteer-led annual giving appeals, including the major capital and endowment campaigns. The same preparations, lead-ership, and expert execution skills are required.

One of the most critical statements in any membership campaign is the "case for support"—a document or paragraph that explains why these members (and their dues) are needed now and what benefits they will provide to others. Most annual giving case statements have had success by addressing new and different projects or priorities that the members have agreed to undertake for that year. The focus on certain projects makes the process of their selection and the annual prepara-tions all the more challenging. A variety of public benefits can be in-cluded in the case statement, but membership associations must attach a hefty roster of member benefits and privileges to these other loftier, and perhaps more distant public benefits. For example, membership gifts that will add books to the special collection section of the local college library can be packaged to allow the members private access to these volumes as a members-only benefit. This same project will be of unique interest to the members of the Friends of the Library Associa-tion and should be effective in encouraging an annual gift that exceeds the normal amount for membership renewal.

Membership campaigns need to be fully planned, and all the details must be carefully scheduled: materials prepared and printed, mailing lists coordinated with mailing packets and their contents, publicity and promotion scheduled for visible support of the drive, personal solicita-tions sequenced into direct mail and telephone follow-up (multimedia) activities, the kick-off and other support activities planned for maximum impact, and much more. Membership campaigns also require enough volunteers to fill the leadership positions and to provide workers for the jobs required. One looming challenge is present in every membership campaign: It has been done before. This is not a new activity, for workers or members, and some amount of creativity and innovation may be required to spark some enthusiasm and excitement. In this area, volunteers can make significant contributions. They know many of the present members' needs and desires; they know friends and neighbors who can be solicited for an annual membership gift. This type of knowledge is a resource that can be tapped during the selection and training of volunteer solicitors, woven into each year's strategy, sprinkled into the several information packages, and added to all the membership materials. Attention to the campaign schedule is essential. Everyone must know what to do and when it needs to be done, and must be trained in how to perform a particular part. A week-by-week countdown suggested by Gaby and Gaby [15] is reproduced in Exhibit 5.9.

Event	Weeks before Opening Day
Preliminary organization meeting	12
[Campaign chairperson] and director secured	10
Campaign office set up	10
[Division chairpersons] secured	8
Meeting of [division chairpersons]	6
Team captains secured	4
Prospect list completed, work cards ready	4
Master lists ready	3
Meeting of captains	3
Membership application cards ready	2
Team workers secured	2
Cards divided or selected	$1^1/_2$
Campaign folder or broadside mailed	$1^1/_2$
Team lists ready	1
Division rallies; cards distributed	$^1/_2$ to 1
Second mailing piece, house bulletin, etc.	$^1/_2$ to 1
Opening meeting of the campaign	

Exhibit 5.9   Planning Schedule for Annual Membership Campaign [15]

Volunteer Preparations

When all the preparations are completed, the campaign has to be begun and carried out according to the plan. Here is where leadership and experience come to the fore. Volunteers have to be prepared for their assignments. Training sessions need to be an enjoyable experience so that they will be well attended. The information about this year's campaign objectives, strategy, and available materials (and how to use them) must be transferred effectively so that each volunteer will be successful in solicitation visits with new or continuing members. Once the campaign is begun, the volunteers will need some encouragement to complete their tasks. Those in leadership positions (board members, committee chairs, management and professional staff) must help by making their gifts first and by motivating the members to complete their assignments. As is true in all other forms of fund-raising, the best method for membership solicitation is a face-to-face presentation. A telephone discussion is second best, and sending requests through the mail brings up the rear. Gaby and Gaby [16] have compiled general guidelines for training sessions for volunteer solicitors (see Exhibit 5.10).

Report meetings are scheduled to allow time for any needed remedial action that will bring in the results by the deadline. Members who have completed or exceeded their assignments should be recognized and rewarded at each meeting. Membership drives have start and end dates; the concentrated action causes everyone to give the assignment some priority. Besides, no one likes to fail when the results are so visible. Progress toward the multiple goals—volunteer solicitations completed, number of memberships achieved, and dollars raised—is tallied, displayed, and reported to all members involved in the campaign. The final date on the schedule is the end date of the drive, the deadline for everyone to have completed his or her assignments. This event, usually designated as a victory celebration, is a stimulus for everyone to complete the work in time to be counted in the final campaign results. (Full details on volunteer campaign management are provided in Chapter Eight.)

Follow-up activities, after the membership campaign deadline, include the routine duties of collections, thank-you letters with new membership cards enclosed, and recognition activities for the leaders and workers who participated in the drive. It is valuable to perform a campaign critique. The best method is to survey all the volunteers for their comments on the campaign plan, materials used, effectiveness of the case statement, and any other topic of their choice. Final tallies are made of all results, and preparations begin for compiling the new membership directory. In some organizations, the campaign critique takes the form of a brief questionnaire mailed to members. Gaby and Gaby [17] recommend

1. Always call beforehand to set up an appointment. This is simple courtesy, since your dropping in unannounced could easily inconvenience your host. He might very well be busy.

2. Tell him exactly why you want to see him while you're on the phone. Downplaying the object of your visit undercuts its importance and therefore the importance of your organization. But don't try to close the deal on the phone.

3. When you see your prospect, thank him for allowing you some of his time before you do anything else.

4. Be sincerely enthusiastic about all the benefits your organization offers him. But don't promise him things it can't deliver. That kind of oversell is one of the prime causes of nonrenewals. You want a member who will *stay* a member.

5. Don't go too fast. Give each point time to sink in.

6. Don't make the mistake of doing all the talking. People who've made up their minds not to buy something generally say nothing. Elicit questions and responses.

7. Try to find the real reasons behind his sales resistance (dues too high? the press of other business too great?) and refer to specific features in your organization to show they don't apply. Counter every objection with a corresponding benefit.

8. Thank him for his time again when you leave. Leave printed matter behind.

9. Always follow up with a call. He may be conferring with associates about joining, and hearing from the salesman again in a week or so can be the final clincher.

Exhibit 5.10 Guidelines for Training Volunteers to Be Solicitors [16]. Reprinted with permission.

forming a few focus groups among volunteers (new and old members) to ask the following questions:

1. Did you enjoy participating in this campaign?

2. What phases of the campaign did you particularly like?

3. What phases would you criticize?

4. Do you have any suggestions to improve the conduct of future campaigns?

5. Any suggestions about the programs at report meetings?

6. Any suggestions about workers' materials, awards, and so on?

7. What do you consider to be the chief benefits accruing to the association from the campaign?

8. Do you think the campaign had any harmful results?
9. Would you be willing to work in one next year?

Mail and Telephone Campaigns

Why is the volunteer-led, volunteer-staffed annual membership campaign recommended above all other methods? Because it has the highest rate of success, for number of members and dollars, in both new-member acquisition and member retention. If volunteers cannot be recruited from among the membership to perform these tasks, the membership organization may be in distress. The fall-back position is to rely on the mail or to use a combination of letters and telephone calls. The results will drop off, and costs to support these efforts will increase, which will reduce net revenues to the membership association and nonprofit organization. The whole purpose of membership associations, which is to encourage and facilitate individuals as active members in their own association, is soon lost. (Details about how to organize and mount direct mail campaigns were presented in Chapters Two through Four.)

Before giving up on members or on personal solicitation, a distressed organization might try taking some creative risks. Fund-raising is a relationship business; to get people's attention these days, some inventiveness is needed. How important to the association and the nonprofit organization are the members? When the efforts to acquire new members were adequately high, is it possible that too little attention was given to fulfilling member services? The first year is especially critical. "Once people renew after the first year we keep them around for a long time," says Mike Mueller, who manages renewals for the 370,000-member United States Golf Association. "Retaining members year after year can also be a tricky affair, often requiring a subtle balance of persuasion, persistence, and humor" [18]. Here is an especially effective example from another membership association [19]:

> The Los Angeles County Museum of Art seems to have captured that balance. Membership Director Melody Kanschat recalls that in the past, the museum sent out four direct-mail notices to its 80,000-plus members. But in the last year or so, Kanschat began sending out six notices—some with a rather distinct spin.
>
> One of the early notices arrived in the form of an invoice rather than the old personal plea to renew. While some members were no doubt stunned to find a "bill" inside a museum envelope, many responded affirmatively. Kanschat says the strategy pushed renewal rates up "a couple of points." Another early notice arrived in an envelope featuring a picture of the Madonna staring at a lighted candle. The copy read, "We're still waiting to hear from you."

Those who did not respond received more gentle nudges. The fourth notice offered three months' free membership for renewing within 15 days of
receiving the letter. It also featured a photo of an armless sculpture on the
envelope, below a headline stating, "We'd give anything to get you back."
The fifth notice included an old art catalogue the museum had in stock and
wanted to discard anyway. The sixth and last notice went back to a personal
appeal from the museum director. In all, the strategy worked, Kanschat
says, and last year the museum won awards from the American Association
of Museums and the Direct Marketing Association for its efforts.

"It's extremely critical to retain members," Kanschat explains. "The best
customer is the one you already have."

OPERATING COSTS FOR MEMBERSHIP PROGRAMS

To review quickly, the chief advantage of a membership association is its
ability to define solid reasons for people to join and to remain active supporters of a nonprofit organization. The "linkage" and "connection" are
visible through delivery of member services packaged as benefits and
privileges; they are the "glue" that holds members close year after year.
Members' annual gifts provide crucial dollars for annual operations. Every nonprofit organization needs them. The advantage of a membership
association is that members bring their time, energy, and talents, in addition to their dollars. Without all of these, the association could not long
survive.

There is a full range of operating costs for membership associations.
Delivery on member services requires professional and support staff
who receive salaries; paid vacations; health, dental, and life insurance
support; pension funding; and other basic employment benefits. The
cost of office operations will usually match or slightly exceed salaries
and benefits. The biggest budget items are (1) the heavy printing and
promotion costs for membership acquisition and renewal and (2) member services. When all operating expenses are known, they must be
measured against anticipated membership gift income. If these costs
are charted on a graph, there is a point at which the revenues and expenses lines meet. Above this point, excess revenue is generated; below
it, losses occur, just as in any other business. It is essential to know
where these two lines meet and whether there will be enough income
to exceed the break-even amount. As an example, if membership dues
in a 3,000-member association are $100 per year and the operations and
member services cost around $50 per member, the "profit" point on the
chart is at 1,500 members. The "material value" of the member services
delivered causes many membership associations to experience great
difficulty in their annual financial operations. A bit of help can come

from calculating the members' tax deduction for their annual gift. (The Internal Revenue Service (IRS) is credited with this solution.) "A museum, for example, has determined that the first $50 of a member's dues must be considered as quid pro quo—for the services a member is provided—and that only what he pays above that amount can be considered a contribution" [20]. If the annual membership gift is $100 and half that sum is allowed as a deduction from personal income tax, then all operating costs need to be contained at $50 per member as a matter of operating policy. If membership gift levels are below $100, the association has three options to resolve the situation: (1) raise gift levels, (2) cut member services, or (3) do both of the above. No more agonizing issue will be faced by any membership association than choosing from among these three options.

The course to pursue is the one that will overcome membership instability. It takes a considerable effort each year to maintain a 3,000-member association. If only a 5 percent annual attrition rate occurs, 150 members will be lost each year. To replace them may require recruitment of an average of two to three candidates for every new member signed. Identifying 300 to 450 new member candidates and successfully signing 150 of them is an aggressive recruiting program that will be difficult to achieve year after year. A comparison of the attrition and recruitment rates will help demonstrate this challenge:

Present Size of Membership	Attrition Rate (Percent)	Candidates Required
1,000	@ 5% = 50	100 to 150
	@ 10% = 100	200 to 300
2,000	@ 5% = 100	200 to 300
	@ 10% = 200	400 to 600
3,000	@ 5% = 150	300 to 450
	@ 10% = 300	600 to 900

Renewal at a 90 to 95 percent performance level is exceptionally high. The rate for most membership associations is between 80 to 85 percent, which means a large number of new members will have to be found *each year*. Maximizing membership retention should be the first priority, and, because current members are a control group of modest size, continued membership services with all benefits and privileges must be stressed. These same services, benefits, and privileges must be cost-effective and must meet the 50 percent IRS tax deduction test as well. The mission of the membership association is to fulfill its charitable purposes; at a 50 percent cost of operations, an equal 50 percent goes to programs and services of public benefit. All these calculations are necessary in order to know how many total members (and at what membership levels) are required for the association to achieve a break-even or better financial return on both its 50 percent for operations and 50 percent for charity. If any new projects or new expenses are suggested, each must be matched with an equal source of new revenue that will contribute to improving the 50 percent break-even minimum.

The lessons from such basic mathematics are clear and illustrate why membership associations are always in search of alternate revenue sources (affinity cards, travel tours, T-shirts, coffee cups, insurance plans, and so on) along with constantly aggressive membership acquisition and retention activities. Their alternative is to consider raising the annual dues, possibly disguised as new (higher) membership levels with added benefits and privileges, which incur increased costs for member services. However, any raise in membership dues is always unpopular, no matter how valid and urgent the reasons. This plan also will result in a bit of attrition and will slow new membership recruitment. The best rule is: Examine all reasonable alternate revenue sources and restrain the value of member services "given away" each year.

One novel answer to the operating budgets problem is joint ventures or purchasing alliances. Allied membership organizations can join together to pool several areas of annual operating expense and achieve higher efficiencies at lower unit costs. Just such a program, the Metropolitan Cultural Alliance, was begun in Massachusetts in 1969 by a half-dozen cultural organizations. Standard services included the following: "Management training workshops and seminars, a monthly newsletter, a library, group purchasing, employment listings, and health insurance plans" [21]. Additional benefits can be developed where the members share common operating needs. The arts and theater members, for example, joined together in a central telephone answering service for ticket sales, negotiated with local hotels to get group rates for traveling artists, and contracted for joint use of advertising, graphics, publicity, and printing firms.

The Future for Membership Programs

Every nonprofit organization must commit time and money to building and maintaining a constituency of new and old friends and supporters. Even a cursory review of our fast-paced society reveals that competition for people's time and money will only increase, suggesting that the membership attachment will grow in importance. Budget pressures will tempt reductions in acquisition, donor communications, and retention activities in favor of "easy money" and "quick cash without effort" proposals, which are likely to be poor decisions in the end. What are the trends? Richard Trenbeth [22] forecasts the following as a baker's dozen of changes:

1. Older people are an expanding market
2. More research is being done
3. Travel benefits will boom in popularity
4. Upscale memberships will increase
5. Direct marketing will grow in importance
6. Computerization will leap ahead
7. More catalogs and merchandise will be offered
8. More insurance and investment opportunities
9. More newsletters and technical publications
10. Social events for members will increase
11. Adult education will grow as a benefit
12. People want recognition
13. Accountability will be stressed.

Each membership association must identify the changes that are most significant to its membership program plans for the future and act on them.

Let us return now to the CCUA Clean Up Cleveland Chapter and see how the new membership association, The Circle of Champions, is doing.

Focus: CCUA Clean Up Cleveland Chapter

The Circle of Champions program was able to recruit additional members at the $100 gift level. The initial test mailings produced 118 members out of 1,504 respondents (8 percent). However, the first renewal request sent to these donors this past spring succeeded in retaining only 78 of these active members (66 percent), a cause for some concern. In addition, the spring mailing to 1,504 current donors from last fall resulted in only 6 new members of The Circle of Champions at the $100 level (less than 1 percent). The full spring "roll out" campaign was more successful: another 76 new members were added to the Circle out of 3,653 donors, but this level of response (2 percent) also was a bit disappointing. Total membership stands at 160 as planning for the second fall campaign begins.

In her analysis of all these results, Karen Anderson, Director of Development for the CCUA Clean Up Cleveland Chapter, has several concerns. Why was the charter membership response to the first test mailing so high (78 out of 1,504 donors, or 8 percent)? Why did 40 of these new members decline to renew their membership in the spring? There should have been more new members at $100 from the 200,000 residents solicited in the spring. In consultation with other fund development professionals around town, Anderson has learned that some of the answers to her concerns might lie in the fact that the initial 118 members had made their first gift during the July test mailing, which was sent to a highly selective prospect list. Their gift decision was that year's tax deduction; the fall resolicitation appeal came in the same tax year. Perhaps other donors who made their first gifts last fall realized that they had given six months earlier; they may have believed their annual membership renewal gift was not due again until the fall, and bypassed the spring appeal. Anderson concludes that the coming fall solicitations should help to resolve these concerns.

Anderson prepares a gift report of total mail results (Exhibit 5.11). A solid response has been achieved from the community at this early point. A total of 3,653 new donors was acquired in the spring "roll out" mailing, a sure sign that residents have become more aware of the Clean Up Cleveland campaign. Anderson believes that these 3,653 donors will benefit from a progress report from Harvey Clout (Exhibit 5.12), which will be mailed to all donors in late August. She also believes she must intensify the charter membership in The Circle of Champions for each group in the fall mailing cycle. She decides *against* adding any new resident mailing lists for the coming fall program. The current lists appear to have a lot of potential left in them, and some savings can be realized by reusing them. She has already received approval to renew the offer of complimentary tickets to a second Cleveland Orchestra concert and Cleveland Play House show to be held

Letter	Program	Number Mailed	Replies Number	Replies Percent	Gift Income
Acquisition Phase					
A & B	Test Mailing (July)	30,000	348	1.16%	$ 8,527
B	Full Test List Mailing	80,575	1,156	1.43	35,758
B	Spring "Roll-Out"	200,000	1,831	0.91	56,936
C	Spring Follow-Up	194,467	1,822	0.94	59,975
	Subtotal	505,042	5,157	1.02%	$161,196
Donor Renewal Phase					
D	First Renewal Request	1,504	914	66.77%	31,064
	Total	506,546	6,071	1.20%	$192,260

Exhibit 5.11 Gift Report on Total Mailing Program Results

The Campaign to Clean Up America
Clean Up Cleveland Chapter

Summer 199X

Dear Compatriot in the "Clean Up Cleveland" campaign:

Our first year of operations is completed and I want to report to you on all the progress we have been able to make, thanks to you.

First, we have written to over 500,000 Cleveland-area residents to invite them to join in the "Clean Up Cleveland" campaign. A total of 5,157 agreed to our request and sent in a contribution. Total dollars raised to date come to $161,196. Thank you!

Second, our 1,504 earliest donors who gave last summer already were asked to renew their support for a second year. To date, 914 have done so, a marvelous 67% performance. Adding their gifts to our total, we have raised $192,260. When you receive your request to renew your gift later this fall, please continue to support our efforts if at all possible.

Third, we have just introduced The Circle of Champions membership association. This new program encourages gifts at $100 or more to help us to finance the energy conversion plant as soon as possible. The first donors who join will be known as "charter members." We will be offering charter memberships this fall; you should think about becoming one of the first members of The Circle of Champions (see the information card attached to this letter for full details).

Fourth, we have been making progress on site selection for the energy conversion plant. Four sites have been identified and are under review. Quite a few federal and state agencies have to be involved in these proceedings, as are a number of citizens' groups including several environmental and conservancy groups. We are proceeding on schedule and hope to be able to announce the final site early next year.

Fifth and last, we are seeing more of our "Clean Up Cleveland" bumper stickers around town every day. Add yours to your car or truck to help spread the word. If you need additional bumper stickers, just call our offices at (216) CLEAN UP and we will send you as many as you like.

Have a great summer and thanks again for your support of our campaign. We are making a difference; our streets are looking much cleaner already.

Sincerely,

I. Harvey Clout
Chair of the Board
Cleveland Cast Iron Works

Encl.

Exhibit 5.12 Progress Report Letter to Current Donors

next summer. This offer was well received during the summer; quite a few donors called afterward to ask whether the offer would be repeated.

Anderson's fall mailing program will include three areas of concentration:

1. Continue the charter membership offer in a two-part acquisition mailing (Letter E, Exhibit 5.13), to resolicit the 200,000 residents in the seven select communities of Cleveland who have not yet responded;

2. Stress the charter membership offer in a two-part renewal mailing to all 5,157 current donors (Letter F, Exhibit 5.14), using first-class, computer-generated personally addressed letters and envelopes;

3. Send personal letters to the 160 currently active members of The Circle of Champions, asking them to renew their membership. Follow up telephone calls from members of the board of directors will encourage their renewal and invite them to upgrade their annual gift, if possible. A sample telephone script is available for board member calls, if needed (Exhibit 5.15).

The Campaign to Clean Up America
Clean Up Cleveland Chapter

Fall, 199X

Dear Concerned Resident,

You will recall our letters last spring. We sent you a bumper sticker and invited you to join in our "Clean Up Cleveland" campaign. Over 3,600 residents replied with a gift to our cause.

We also invited every resident to join in our effort to clean the trash off our city streets. We will use 75 percent of your gift to help build a new energy conversion plant to burn our trash and convert it into electricity for our use. We estimate this new plant can lower our electric bills by *$12 a month* and *$124 a year.*

The other 25 percent of your gift goes to support our public education campaign to ask everyone to stop being a "trasher," and to pick up after themselves. I've noticed a lot of improvement already; our streets are less cluttered; even the areas around our homes and offices are cleaned up. Thank you for helping our cause.

Our campaign is continuing to gain public support. We now offer a charter membership in our new membership association, The Circle of Champions. Every donor of $100 or more will also receive two free tickets to the Cleveland Orchestra and a show at the Cleveland Play House.

Join us today. Put our bumper sticker on your car and help spread the word to "Clean Up Cleveland." Together, we can do it!

Sincerely yours,

I. Harvey Clout
Chair of the Board
Cleveland Cast Iron Works

Encl.

Exhibit 5.13   Letter E: Second Charter Membership Offer

The Campaign to Clean Up America
Clean Up Cleveland Chapter

Fall, 199X

Mr. and Mrs. (personal letter; donor name and address printed here)

Dear (donor name):

I want to thank you again for your contribution this past year. Your support has been part of our success. Let's keep up the good work!

Our campaign has begun with a strong reply from our friends and neighbors. Over 6,000 residents are participating in our campaign with their contributions and with their own clean-up activities.

Total funds raised to date are $192,260. The first 75 percent of this money (that's $144,195) has been set aside in our account at National City Bank for construction of the energy conversion plant. Our contribution target is $1,250,000 and we are 12 percent on our way toward our goal.

I hope you will continue your support with a second gift at this time. Please consider a gift of $25 or more if you can; the sooner we reach our goal, the sooner the plant will be constructed and can begin to burn our trash to give us more electricity at lower rates.

Let me also alert you that charter memberships are still available in our Circle of Champions membership association. Gifts of $100 or more are requested. Full details are provided on the enclosed card.

We are off to a great start, thanks to you. Together, we can finish this campaign and clean up our streets at the same time. It's a worthwhile effort.

Please call our offices at (216) CLEAN UP if we can provide you with additional details on our clean-up campaign and about membership in The Circle of Champions.

Thank you again for your past support. I hope you will continue to be one of the pioneer contributors to this communitywide effort.

Sincerely yours,

I. Harvey Clout
Chair of the Board
Cleveland Iron Works

Exhibit 5.14   Letter F: Offer of Charter Membership in Circle of Champions to Prior Direct Mail Donors

Good evening;

This is [state your name], a member of the board of directors of the Clean Up Cleveland campaign.

I'm calling to follow up on the letter you received from us last week. You may have noticed that we have raised over $192,000 toward the energy conversion plant, which is 12 percent of our goal. That's a pretty fair start, but we have some work left to do, don't we?

Let me ask if you have any questions about our campaign. Can I answer your questions? [pause]

You were one of our earliest donors and I wanted to call and thank you for your support. We truly appreciate your help on this project. Also, you are a charter member of our Circle of Champions membership association.

By chance, were you able to join us for the Cleveland Orchestra concert at Blossom last summer? How about the show at the Cleveland Play House? I certainly enjoyed both evenings. I am pleased to tell you we will be repeating both programs next summer.

The purpose of my call this evening is to invite you to continue your support of our campaign to clean up our city streets. Can we count on you to renew your membership in The Circle of Champions? [pause]

(If Yes, ask) Will it be possible for you to increase your gift at this time? The annual dues remain $100.

(If Yes, ask)How much do you think you can give? [pause for reply] That's terrific!

We will send you a confirmation of your renewal pledge tomorrow. It was nice to talk with you. Thank you again for continuing your support of our clean-up campaign. Good evening.

Exhibit 5.15   Telephone Script, Circle of Champions Renewal Follow-Up

CHAPTER SIX

Groups, Guilds, and Support Organizations

There are a multitude of affiliation models for donors and volunteers in addition to membership associations. The purpose of each is to help the parent nonprofit organization and its annual giving programs, using different methods and techniques designed to provide for higher levels of annual gift support, higher levels of personal involvement, or both. The overall plan for an annual giving program, as outlined in this book, begins with identifying and acquiring first-time donors in order to expand and enhance their relationship with a nonprofit organization through volunteerism and gift renewal year after year. Creativity, persistence, and reward are required when asking volunteers and donors to continue to give their time and personal resources again and again. One of the best such methods is through a membership affiliation, as described in Chapter Five. Other methods are offered through groups, guilds, and support organizations, the next plateau in annual giving.

Groups, guilds, and support organizations offer opportunities to become personally involved in the daily life of a nonprofit organization. Each individual should be invited and encouraged to expand the relationship in any of several directions that will help the organization to succeed in meeting its mission. An active relationship may feature one or more of the following characteristics:

1. Concentrates on friend-raising along with fund-raising;
2. Personalizes the relationship;
3. Invites and encourages active participation;
4. Invites and encourages additional gifts during each year;
5. Offers a variety of voluntary assignments and active roles;

6. Defines leadership positions and develops leadership candidates;
7. Communicates progress in meeting priority projects of need;
8. Trains volunteers to solicit others and to conduct support activities;
9. Identifies candidates for major and planned gift opportunities;
10. Provides for special recognition to encourage continued support.

This expansion of interest, involvement, and participation is made possible through a variety of forms, vehicles, or models. These models are distinguishable from membership and membership associations by their concentration on higher levels of annual gift support, their emphasis on personal involvement through voluntary service, their semiautonomous nature and self-management style, and their extra recognition opportunities. The operating style of these models is to be active (not passive) groups, and to take, as their own enterprise, responsibility for the welfare and success of the group, guild, or support organization. They can and do provide advice and counsel from time to time, but their primary energies are directed toward managing activities that promote and enhance their own image and that of their parent nonprofit organization. In their official names, these formal and informal voluntary organizations use a variety of words and terms, most of which appear to have similar meanings (see Exhibit 6.1). Their overlap can be confusing to someone attempting to understand the purposes of these entities and how they are distinguishable from one another. The words available for their names are close to synonymous, but the name chosen is important as an indicator of the degree of separateness from the sponsoring nonprofit organization. Each group, guild, or support organization is distinguished by the degree of its dependence on the parent or sponsoring nonprofit organization for routine operating support.

Regardless of their names or their degree of independence, most of these entities will share one or more of the following objectives:

1. They have a single purpose or mission;
2. They ask for a commitment of time, money, or both;
3. They offer enhanced benefits and privileges;
4. They offer contacts and networking opportunities with select audiences;
5. They feature recognition and reward;
6. They operate in a semi-independent style;

7. They are more volunteer-led than staff-directed;

8. Their image enhances that of their parent or sponsor;

This chapter describes how these objectives are pursued in four distinct but typical entities: (1) the auxiliary, (2) the guild, (3) donor clubs, and (4) support group organizations. A variety of features may be incorporated into each entity's routine operating programs, as indicated

Alliance	Any union or connection of interests.
Association	A society of members united by mutual interests or for a common purpose.
Auxiliary	A group that is subordinate to another organization, helping or aiding, and giving support.
Circle	A group of persons or friends who have a common tie.
Club	1. A select group of persons who are in the habit of meeting for the promotion of some common objective such as athletics, literature, science, politics.
	2. A group of persons who participate in a plan wherein they agree to make regular payments or purchases in order to secure some benefits.
Coalition	A voluntary union of individual persons, parties, or states for a common objective or cause.
Company	A number of individuals assembled or associated together; a number of persons united or incorporated for joint action.
Fraternity	A group of people gathered for a common purpose.
Group	A number of persons, as in a community, who are united by common ties or interests; a number of persons or things ranged or considered together because they are perceived as being related in a scientific, natural, or other way.
League	A combination of parties for promotion of their mutual interests and goals; the covenant or compact by which these parties are joined.
Organization	A body of persons united in working toward some end or purpose.
Society	A group of persons united for the promotion of a common aim, typically literary, scientific, political, religious, benevolent, or convivial.

Exhibit 6.1   Common Names for Supportive Organizations

Active Programs	Auxiliary	Guild	Donor Club	Supportive Group
1. May operate with separate tax-exempt status	X	X		X
2. May maintain separate financial records	X	X		X
3. Requires staff and operating support from parent	X		X	X
4. Accepts annual fund-raising goals from parent	X	X		X
5. Is focused on friend-raising	X	X		X
6. Is focused on fund-raising		X	X	X
7. Is focused on recognition and reward	X		X	
8. Is focused on benefits and privileges			X	X
9. Is focused on volunteerism and service	X	X		X
10. Requires annual membership dues or gift	X	X	X	X
11. Requires active participation	X	X		X
12. Prefers self-management style	X	X		X
13. Elects its own board and officers	X	X		X
14. Appoints its own committee chairs and members	X	X		X
15. Trains its volunteers in their assigned duties	X	X		X
16. Trains volunteers in personal solicitation		X		X
17. Conducts performance evaluation of volunteers	X	X		X
18. Keeps track of hours of service	X			
19. Conducts annual membership recruitment and renewal drive	X			X
20. Maintains active leadership development program	X	X		X
21. Conducts its own fund-raising benefit events	X	X		X

Exhibit 6.2 Common Program Features for Supportive Organizations

Active Programs	Auxiliary	Guild	Donor Club	Supportive Group
22. Publishes its own newsletter and membership directory	X	X		X
23. Conducts its own annual meeting	X	X		X
24. Conducts member activities to enhance participation and renewal	X	X		X
25. Performs legislative advocacy and lobbying support	X	X		X
26. Performs community education programs		X		X
27. Performs community service activities	X	X		X
28. Participates in parent's marketing and promotion activities		X		X
29. Promotes direct involvement with parent's delivery of programs and services	X			
30. Permits fund-raising events in its name by others		X		X

Exhibit 6.2   *(Continued)*

in Exhibit 6.2. The adoption of one or more of these features will depend largely on local preferences for operating style, the priority of needs and wishes of the parent nonprofit organization, and the personalities of the charter members.

THE AUXILIARY

An auxiliary is a volunteer-led association of members whose principal activities assist the parent nonprofit organization in the delivery of its programs and services to the public. In its management style, this model features a board of directors and as many operating committees as there are programs and services within the parent where volunteer workers can be used. The primary purpose is to recruit, train, and develop men and women who will take it as their personal obligation and responsibility to assist with the actual delivery of programs and services to the public. Their acceptance of this level of responsibility is the essential feature that distinguishes them from members of other groups because it requires a commitment to be present at assigned times to perform their service, whether day or night, weekend or holiday. This personal style of direct service to others is the key attraction to the volunteer, the chief motive for active participation. The result is a higher level of personal "high touch" than staff can offer, which adds to the competence and quality of the service provided. For example, hospital auxiliary members can be found in nearly every area of hospital service where their primary attention can be directed toward support of hospitalized patients and their families. Hospitals could never afford to hire enough employees to perform these same assignments, much less be able to motivate them to be as caring and friendly. In another example, auxiliary members in a rehabilitation center will "work directly with patients through physical therapy, occupational therapy, or therapeutic recreation. These activities include assisting with patient exercise and wheelchair skills classes, adapting patient clothing by sewing adaptations for easy dressing, and accompanying patients on recreational outings and in leisure time activities" [1]. These extra services are possible only if the hospital is able to organize the auxiliary model of voluntary participation and offer it to local residents as an opportunity to help. Improved and enhanced support services that assist patients and their families to regain self-confidence and to maximize their remaining skills despite health-imposed limitations are the very visible result.

The essential feature of an auxiliary is its ability to provide a variety of volunteer assignments that offer a large amount of personal satisfaction in return for a few hours of service each week. People helping people is the attraction and the chief reward. An auxiliary may also be able to offer a variety of subgroups, each with their own leadership and committee system, that can appeal to a wide array of volunteers' interest areas. Using a hospital as an example again, its auxiliary may offer one group of committees linked to a specific area of healthcare service. A favorite is the modern childbirth center with its labor-delivery-recovery (LDR) rooms and accompanying neonatal intensive care and well-baby units. Who can resist the opportunity to help a new baby feel loved? Another group of auxiliary volunteers may be interested in supporting the special needs of preschool-age and adolescent patients and their families. Whatever the area of service, a sensitive volunteer with "extra" time to spend with each patient is enormously welcome and valuable. Other auxiliary volunteers may prefer to work in the coffee shop or gift shop, take the book-and-game cart around, staff the information or customer service desk, perform escort and transport services, or donate their clerical skills in administrative office support. Many volunteers contribute professional skills that the nonprofit organization would otherwise have to pay employees or consultants to perform. Other volunteer-led areas of activity may include planning and conducting the auxiliary's membership recruitment program, giving orientation and training to new volunteers, conducting tours of the facility, participating in the speakers bureau, or assisting with the newsletter's design, writing, and preparation for mailing. Some members, after appropriate active service and experience, aspire to committee leadership and membership on the board of directors. To satisfy their needs, volunteers should be placed in assignments that are well-matched to their interests and competency. Just about every area of hospital activity offers opportunities for trained volunteers to lend a helping hand for a few hours each week, which may explain both the popularity of hospital auxiliary work and its remarkable success. When hundreds of volunteers are involved, the effect on the quality and quantity of care provided is enormous.

Training

Auxiliary members find it attractive to be able to work within a nonprofit organization. Most come with preferences of where they want to spend their time. When multiple areas within an institution need support, auxiliary leadership and institution staff must prepare and offer a well-defined orientation program that will encourage members to consider several worthy areas where their time will be equally valuable and rewarding. Not everyone can play with the new babies! Comprehensive training programs are needed for all areas of service. Included in the curriculum will be details about the operating rules and procedures, the policies and guidelines of the nonprofit organization, and the protocols of the assigned work area. Each auxiliary volunteer must understand and observe these parameters. Treating volunteers the same as employees has great merit in building their loyalty for faithful service, reinforcing their commitment to their assigned tasks, and enhancing the personal satisfaction they receive in return. The employees in nonprofit organizations may need to be reminded that volunteers are *not* employees, that personal circumstances may limit their available time, and that they will not always be there when expected. Well-defined orientation sessions and professionally conducted training programs will go far in ensuring the nonprofit organization that its auxiliary volunteers are a reliable and satisfactory work force.

Dues and Other Revenue

Annual dues for auxiliary membership and payment of a uniform fee may be required, but these amounts are usually modest ($10 to $25 per year). A life membership plan may be offered as a one-time gift option at

$100 to $150. Fund-raising is not an auxiliary's chief purpose. All funds raised from dues, fees, and other sources should be delivered directly to the parent nonprofit organization. If the auxiliary is a separately incorporated tax-exempt entity, its income in excess of expenses, reported in its annual financial statements, is transferred to the parent organization. A variety of fund-raising activities may be organized to provide additional revenue, but raising money is usually a secondary goal. The volunteers' preference for "hands-on" participation in direct service comes first. When a fund-raising program is defined, it is often accompanied by a formal process that allows the auxiliary board to select a project for sponsorship after evaluating several current priorities of need identified by the nonprofit organization. This procedure enables the volunteer members to decide where the money they raise will be used. Their decisions are commonly directed toward areas where the public receives programs and services, because auxiliary members often work in these areas and are knowledgeable about the value of services provided there. The role of professional and support staff (when required) is largely administrative: facilitating the scheduling of volunteer assignments, conducting or supervising orientation and training programs, keeping the records of each member's hours of service, assisting in management and clerical tasks, and engaging in "other duties as assigned." Service is recorded faithfully in half-hour increments, for proper recognition of accompanying honors; volunteers' time is valuable, no matter where they give their service. A failure to recognize, honor, and reward volunteers for the services they provide is a huge mistake. Volunteers may decide to give their time and energy to another organization that will be more appreciative of their many contributions.

THE GUILD

The chief difference between an auxiliary and a guild may be that guild volunteers often do not work inside the organization. They prefer to support the organization through activities conducted outside, away from its direct programs and service facilities. A guild and an auxiliary are alike in asking volunteers for their time and service, but the guild will direct this energy toward preparation and management of social activities, educational programs, or public service. A guild may define specific tasks for its volunteers and focus their activities in support of one or two major areas of activity rather than try to cover the breadth of services an auxiliary is committed to fulfill. Volunteer satisfaction is derived from the faithful completion of a mission or an assigned task each year and from the amount of visible recognition received. For example, a theater or orchestra guild may set annual goals that include each member's promotion and sale of a certain number of season passes or series tickets. Members may also take responsibility for an assignment in one or more fund-raising activities, such as a benefit event that has a goal of $50,000 or $100,000 in net proceeds. The guild may define all of its annual goals and decide how these net proceeds will be used—for general operating purposes, for a specific area of theater or orchestra activity that the guild "adopts," or for seeding and growing a permanent endowment fund to ensure that activity's future financial security.

A guild membership recruitment and renewal program may include an annual gift of perhaps $25 to $100. Emphasis may be placed on each member's buying at least one ticket to the guild's benefit event, accepting one active volunteer assignment in one of the guild's programs or committees, and attending one or more of the professional programs offered by the parent nonprofit organization. New members may be required to visit and tour the facilities of the sponsor within a year of joining. All members are invited to an annual meeting (which often features a speaker from the nonprofit organization) at which officers and directors are elected and recognition awards for volunteerism and service are conferred. A guild may circulate a membership directory, prepare newsletters, and offer other amenities. The members will work hard to obtain media coverage for their events and activities, their financial success, and the specific programs and services their funds support. They may not require any administrative or staff support from the parent nonprofit organization, preferring to manage their own affairs.

Guilds can be organized in a variety of ways, using either a social or a business format. They may develop subgroups or chapters composed of select professionals (doctors, lawyers, accountants, and so on) or of people who are living in a specific area of town or in a geographic area that is separate from the sponsor's principal location. The overall mission is to develop a reliable group of men or women (sometimes both) who share a willingness to commit their time to the sponsor's cause, who value the friendship and company of the other guild members, and who will act together to complete the mission and goals assigned. Guild members often select their leaders and board of directors from among their more active members (and those who aspire to leadership). The board will elect the guild's officers, appoint all committee chairpersons and members, set annual goals, and oversee routine operations, including financial affairs during each year. Rotation of the members to serve in board and committee positions is expected and often aspired to. Support provided by the parent nonprofit organization may be on an "as-requested" basis and can take the form of management, clerical assistance, or direct financial support. Often, such support is minimal because guilds may prefer (and take pride in) being independent and self-sufficient. They may choose to maintain their own membership lists, perform their own volunteer recruitment and renewal efforts, and provide all their own communications—a newsletter, contact letters, and the invitations and reservations required for attendees at the annual meeting and at benefit events. The guild will provide its roster of volunteers and members to the parent nonprofit organization so that every guild member will receive all the regular communications sent to other volunteers and donors. Funds raised through membership fees, activities, and benefit events should be delivered directly to the parent nonprofit organization unless the guild is a separately incorporated tax-exempt entity.

DONOR CLUBS: THE BENEFITS OF ORGANIZING DONORS

Faithful donors appreciate recognition and respect for their generosity; they place a value on the courteous and consistent treatment their gifts have earned for them. They are not offended when offered opportunities for increased personal activity or association with their chosen nonprofit organization. Many organizations group their faithful donors together in order to manage the relationship optimally. A society of donors or a donor club enhances the association, confers a special identity on each qualified donor, and provides donors with the added opportunity of associating with others whose levels of commitment and generosity match their own. It is a courtesy and a privilege to be invited to join such a distinguished and select group.

> The first purpose of donor clubs and associations is to convey gratitude for higher contribution levels; they must then perpetuate a privileged association with the organization in order to encourage faithful participation each year. Donor clubs represent one of the best means to demonstrate an institution's commitment to expressing honest gratitude. Offering a list of benefits and privileges to donors whose annual gifts begin at $1,000 gains their appreciation, helps to retain their interest, and cultivates the potential for other gift opportunities in the future. [2]

Donor clubs (often called gift clubs) possess several unique features that can be offered to their participants and to the nonprofit organization they support. For annual donors, the chief attribute is increased benefits and privileges based on a higher level of giving or on the cumulative total of all gifts received in one year (see Exhibit 6.3). Thomas Broce calls donor clubs "the fastest way to increase the annual gifts total and is also the best method of raising donors' giving levels. Each year the gift evaluation should automatically encourage each donor to

Gift Amount*	Club Name	Benefits and Privileges
$ 100	Circle of Champions	Quarterly newsletter Annual report Invitations to benefit events
500	Ambassadors	All of the above *plus:* Name listed in annual report donor roster
1,000	Friends	All of the above *plus:* Name added to main Donor Wall VIP identification card with 10 percent discount in gift shop Invitation to annual meeting
2,500	Sponsors	All of the above *plus:* Name added to Sponsors plaque at main entrance Invitation to annual recognition luncheon Subscription to *President's Letter*
5,000	Patrons and Life Members	All of the above *plus* Name added to Life Member plaque at main entrance Two tickets to annual black-tie ball Personal gift

*Multiple gifts within the same year will be counted together in order to qualify the donor at the highest level of donor privileges achieved through cumulative giving. The donor will be honored throughout the following year at this cumulative total.

Exhibit 6.3 Donor Club Annual Giving Benefits and Privileges

move up to the next category. No one has ever been offended by being asked for too much (though by the same token few donors have suggested that the solicitor didn't ask for enough!)" [3]. A donor club encourages present annual donors to give at higher levels and offers them recognition and rewards in the form of extra benefits and higher visibility. Those who respond by giving at these higher levels may qualify for extra recognition and reward from the parent nonprofit organization. Donor clubs also can request higher levels of active personal involvement and voluntary participation to retain full standing. Most are designed to reinvest the recognition and reward given to donors based on the amounts they give each year. Whenever possible, nonprofit organizations should tie the uses made of these gifts to the highest-priority needs, especially when the gifts support a program or service that is highly visible to others outside the organization. This added element of urgent need helps to preserve the relationship, especially when the success of the programs and services funded is attributed to the principal donors. Donor recognition honors the contributor and, in so doing, lets others witness how faithful and generous donors are treated. The maxim "It pays to advertise" can be put to good use in recognition programs used for donor clubs.

Many donors will welcome the association and status connoted in belonging to a donor club. Formalization of their association with donor gift levels (and their related privileges) adds the appearance of a membership relationship. Membership status can be defined to include the usual array of member services and benefits, all designed to hold the attention of the donor and to secure continuous commitment of faithful annual support. However, a donor club can be more aggressive about the level of gift support required and the direct relationship of gift size to membership status. A clear focus on higher gift levels will help to preserve the special attention given to those who participate at these prescribed rates.

A lesser known fact about donor clubs is their exceptional record of cost-effectiveness and high profitability. Broce [4] comments:

> One of the most successful means of soliciting significant annual gifts is through donor clubs. First let me say that in today's economy few organizations can afford to make solicitations for gifts of less than $100. All gifts below that amount should be solicited by mail. Even telephone solicitations should be for $100 and above. We should not waste valuable manpower on small gifts; moreover, most organizations should set their minimum gift level at $100 (though many prospects may respond with less than $100). This is difficult for many people to accept, but it makes good business sense.

Donor clubs are profitable to operate because they require only limited amounts of direct budget support for annual solicitation and maintenance. The costs of recognition elements are typical budget items: sending members copies of newsletters, annual reports, invitations to annual meetings, and the like; purchasing paperweights, certificates, plaques, and other mementos of appreciation. With advance planning and wholesale buying, these articles can be acquired at reasonable expense. The Internal Revenue Service (IRS) rule on "give backs" (recognition to donors) limits them to 2 percent of the original gift value and is a helpful guide for how much to spend on recognition gifts.

Nonprofit organizations can and should maintain one or more areas within their facilities for donor recognition displays. Annual maintenance costs of such areas, once established and furnished, are reasonable. Designated donor recognition areas also serve as active advertising space for the importance attributed to larger gifts from donors and for the cumulative giving history of faithful contributors. Inquiries about the amount required to add a name to a donor recognition display are usually followed by new gifts of just these amounts, and a steady stream of new gifts more than offsets the costs of maintaining the display programs. Other recognition elements, such as citations and plaques, also are important to donors and to the organization. In offices and homes, they are often displayed with pride. The wider public sees these symbols of giving as a statement on how each nonprofit organization treats its more important donors.

> Tell your members that you love them. Tell them as often as possible and in as many ways as possible. Let them know your plans and ideas. Involve them in these activities. Use them on your committees and programs. Herald their accomplishments in your publications. Remember their birthdays and anniversaries. Send them invitations to special programs and events. Show how easily, and at what little cost, the needs to feel important, appreciated, and loved can be satisfied through membership in your institution's gift club, and your contributors should become your best friends. [5]

An association of donors or the members of a donor club may well become the most committed friends a nonprofit organization can hope to have. Their faithful generosity will attempt to attain levels of giving that are well above the average gift size required in every other annual giving program and activity. Their faithful support represents the source for the largest percentage of annual gift income received each year. These VIP donors are important financial security for any parent nonprofit organization. They should be given extra good care at all times.

Donor Records

Keeping records of donors' prior gifts is important for many reasons; primarily, their annual and historic (lifetime) giving is linked to a formal donor recognition program. Each gift made—no matter when, for what purpose, or in what form—should be added to the donor's permanent gift history. Over time, each donor's cumulative total can build to an amount that qualifies him or her for the extra benefits and special privileges defined in the donor honors and recognition policy (see Exhibit 6.4). Cumulative tallies are not at all difficult to maintain

Qualifications: All donors whose cumulative contributions add to $1,000 or more will be recognized on the main Donor Wall as follows:

Category	Amounts			
Friends	$	1,000	to	$ 2,499
Sponsors		2,500	to	4,999
Patrons/Life Members		5,000	to	9,999
Benefactors		10,000	to	24,999
Meritorious Benefactors		25,000	to	49,999
Honored Benefactors		50,000	to	99,999
Distinguished Benefactors		100,000	to	999,000
Preeminent Benefactors		1,000,000	or	more

Types of Gifts:

1. Donations of cash, bonds, securities, and real estate will be included. The value of each gift to be recognized will be based on the charitable contribution deduction amount.

2. For planned gifts and estate planning arrangements, donors whose gifts are in the forms of pooled income funds and future interest gifts (irrevocable gifts in trust, life estates, and gift annuities) will be included. The value of each gift to be recognized will be based on the charitable contribution deduction amount. Individuals who present documentary evidence of a future gift will be listed on the Endowment Society section of the main Donor Wall.

3. Gifts of life insurance will be recognized at cash value until maturity of the policy. Individuals who provide a copy of a policy with a minimum value of $10,000 directed to this nonprofit organization will be listed on the Endowment Society section of the main Donor Wall.

Commemorative Gifts: The names of those individuals in whose memory or honor a gift of $1,000 or more has been received will be listed on the Commemorative Gifts section of the main Donor Wall.

Recognition: Other forms of appropriate recognition will be given to qualified donors by action of the Board of Directors in accordance with the Donor Honors and Recognition Policy.

Exhibit 6.4 Sample Donor Honors and Recognition Policy

today, thanks to reasonably priced office computers and software. The data stored may indicate the areas of special interest favored by each donor; the preferred solicitation methods (where, when, and to what type of appeal this person responds best); other invitations extended and the responses received each time; giving levels and interests preferred, as indicated by annual support; participation at benefits and public events; special project and major campaign gifts; pledge history and record of payments (including assets used); and estate planning interests and activity. This type of profile of each donor is a valuable guide to staff and volunteers when they must assess likely candidates for ability to manage areas of need and new and changing priorities; for volunteer assignments; for positions that require a record of training and proven experience; or for leadership. All these data help the organization and its volunteer fund-raising leaders to determine the interests and aspirations of their best donors. Each such donor deserves an annual evaluation of how well his or her interests are being served, and should be considered for any opportunities that may offer expanded ways to fulfill his or her preferences. Additional enhancements through the benefits and privileges in a donor club should be part of these analyses. One donor may be prepared to consider a major gift opportunity; another, who is approaching retirement, may be interested in an estate planning interview. Donor records and gift histories reveal all the information necessary to help guide the nonprofit organization in selecting options to offer its major donors. What will assist them in fulfilling their long-term preferences, even their lifetime aspirations, and yield a maximum level of financial support to their favorite nonprofit organization?

The most practical use of a donor club is in helping to retain as many prior donors as possible each year. Current donors should be encouraged to increase (upgrade) their annual gift whenever possible. Donor clubs provide substantial advantages to all who can give or who choose to give at higher levels. Every current participant should be rewarded equally. A recognition plan that is tied to uninterrupted annual giving should recognize those who have been faithful over many years. Other advantages from a well-defined donor club program are:

1. Increased potential for continued (secure) gift income;
2. Identified and qualified prospects for major gift support when a special-project or capital campaign gift is needed;
3. Likely candidates for volunteer and leadership duties;
4. Active community advocates and ambassadors for the organization;
5. Likely candidates for estate and planned giving opportunities.

Donor club members may have a variety of reasons for choosing to continue their current level of support. Feeling good about being treated well, being part of a valued group, and enjoying special benefits and privileges are important incentives, but these may not be their motives for giving. One way to understand motives is to picture a $1,000 donor standing outside the front door, waving his arms, and yelling, "I like you a lot! Pay attention to me!" These should be the steps taken in response:

Get to know this person and others like him;

Meet with them and listen to their thoughts about why they give so much to the organization and what they would like to receive in return;

Find out what else they might be willing to do;

Introduce them to volunteers, management and professional staff, and board members;

Continue to offer them privileges, such as access to the organization and benefits they can use in exchange for their generous level of support;

Invite them and their spouses, plus any special friends they might choose, to be guests at the next major benefit event or public meeting;

Show them appreciation in a personal way at least once a year: call on them or give them a telephone call, or send them a birthday or anniversary card.

William Grasty and Kenneth Sheinkopf [6] gave this summary:

The basic purposes of gift clubs are to:

- Involve a very special group of institutional friends who will give mainly unrestricted funds, which are the most difficult to get, and the most useful to have;
- Encourage an increased level of giving by current donors;
- Attract a high level of annual support;
- Upgrade donor gifts;
- Recognize and honor the individuals who have supported the institution financially;
- Attract new contributors who are influenced by the individual recognition given the more generous donor;
- Inform and involve the membership in the purposes and plans of the institution;
- Develop volunteers for their effective use as ambassadors, advisors, and fundraising leaders in support of many important projects . . . .

SUPPORT GROUP ORGANIZATIONS

What exactly is a support group organization? It combines many of the features of a membership association, an auxiliary, a guild, and a donor club, all put together in a single entity. It is a highly structured program designed to facilitate constituency building, to conduct friend-raising, to offer a membership affiliation, to enhance and invigorate volunteerism, to develop leadership candidates, to market and promote a cause, to facilitate community relations, to prepare and produce fund-raising activities and benefit events, to undertake major fund-raising objectives, and to identify, recruit, and develop major gift candidates. A support group organization will include all of these features in a volunteer-led, self-management style that provides multiple opportunities for and direct benefits to the nonprofit organization that is its sponsor. Harold Seymour [7] cited a famous college alumni association as an example of a successful support group organization:

> Our oldest alumni fund is at Yale, where in 1890 they agreed on these principles: that the funds should be unrestricted; that the appeal should be universal; that emphasis on numbers would actually encourage larger gifts; and that the primary objective should be to persuade the alumni to give annually, with such a steady flow of contributions that the alumni themselves might properly be regarded as an endowment, with the fund's yearly receipts as the income.

One hundred years later, not much has changed from this original prescription for success. Funds raised are for annual operating purposes and for promoting growth in the number of donor participants; these remain the priority objectives. The funds raised *each year* are equal to the investment earnings achieved by an operating endowment worth more than ten times the annual gift total.

Support groups are usually formed under the tax-exempt umbrella of privileges granted to their parent nonprofit organization. Separate tax-exempt status is not required or recommended. As an semi-independent organization, each support group will need to operate within written guidelines (called "Operating Rules and Procedures" instead of "Bylaws") that are approved by the parent, to whom they owe their allegiance. Funds are raised in the name of the parent and should be delivered directly to it. (The procedure is the same for an auxiliary, guild, or donor club.) The uses made of these funds can be determined jointly with the parent, according to its current roster of priority needs. The project or program selected becomes that year's or that period's official objective for the support group. All its activities are dedicated to the successful completion of the assignment; all funds received (membership fees, benefit event net proceeds, "something extra" annual gifts from members, and so on) are counted toward the support group's annual gift. Acceptance of these responsibilities each year is one of the distinguishing features of support groups, chiefly because of their self-management style and their ability to undertake important tasks on behalf of the parent nonprofit organization. Such independence fosters, among the members, greater pride in their past accomplishments as a group working together and in their continuing commitment.

The key feature for successful operation of a support group organization may lie in a combination of self-management and volunteer-led participation. Support groups offer varied opportunities for public service, from board membership to a great variety of active committees (see Exhibit 6.5). Every function and every activity can be facilitated through one or more of the group's active committees. Most committees also offer a variety of subcommittees to support their overall assignment. A benefit event committee can maximize its potential to raise funds by delegating several assignments to subcommittees on sponsor and underwriter gifts, on ticket sales, on in-kind contributions (food, beverages, decorations, flowers, printing, entertainment, linens), and on recruiting auction and raffle prizes.

The balance of committee members can be organized to help with the design, printing, and addressing of invitations, with creating and tasting the menu, with planning the program and entertainment, and with putting up the decorations. The list of assignments is purposely made long so that as many people as possible will have a responsible task to perform. A committee work plan requires a host of volunteers, with several volunteers in leadership positions. Several months will be required to organize and produce this event, but the work is spread around so that no one person has too heavy a burden. If any volunteer senses that he or she has too much to do, help should be requested from other volunteers. Among the results of this operating style are: high attendance at the function (all volunteers will, of course, be expected to attend), and the enormous value each support group organization can offer to its parent nonprofit organizations. Large nonprofit organizations may sponsor more than one support group, with each support group designed to match the needs of several standing programs or service areas within the institution. Because of their visibility in staging public activities considered beneficial to others in the community, support groups provide substantial marketing, promotion, and communications enhancements to the programs and services they sponsor.

Operating styles may vary, but most support groups prefer to have a major voice in managing their own affairs. They conduct all their activities within a prescribed set of "Operating Rules and Procedures" (see

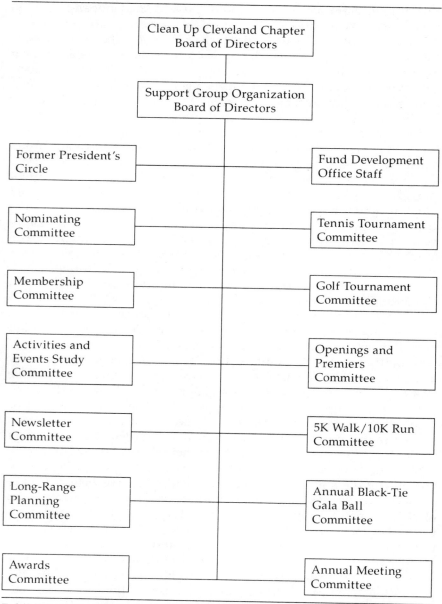

Exhibit 6.5   Sample Support Group Organization Chart

Appendix A for complete sample text), recruit new members and renew prior members, plan their many activities and events, critique their performance, publish their newsletters and annual membership directory, study and make comprehensive plans for their own future, recruit and train new volunteers to their methods and style of operation, identify and prepare future leaders for larger assignments, handle cash and other forms of contributions, and conduct annual business meetings for the orderly transfer of leadership to their successors. They utilize many if not all of the features previously described in this book for (1) how to identify and recruit new friends by mail, (2) how to recruit and renew annual donors, (3) how to prepare and conduct successful membership activities, and (4) how to operate in a semi-independent style endorsed by the sponsoring nonprofit organization. Support groups may augment some or all of these features in their own operation, and may explore and adopt others completely new to the parent nonprofit organization. Support group organizations may be asked to take an active role in community service, similar to that of a civic or fraternal association, depending on local conditions and circumstances. In times of community need, the organizational skills plus the strength and caliber of support group members may be needed for broader purposes, such as collaborative activities with other nonprofit organizations and civic associations. Where such additional efforts also serve to advance the mission and purpose of the parent nonprofit organization, they are undertaken willingly. Support groups remain alert to community relations opportunities that will promote their own activities and those of the parent nonprofit organization. They may engage in legislative action and lobbying from time to time, especially when there is a need to address issues, laws, and regulations that affect their ability or their sponsor's ability to fulfill their mission. They also remain conscientious about being visible in the community through media coverage of their activities and events. Their members are a constant example to others of the spirit of volunteerism, leadership, personal commitment, and gift support of the mission, purposes, goals, and objectives of their own organization and of their parent nonprofit organization.

Activities Other Than Fund-Raising

Support groups need to offer their members several opportunities for personal participation in addition to voluntary service and personal gift support. These might include activities sponsored by the parent nonprofit organization, such as public tours of facilities, lectures on topics of public interest by professional staff, and invitations to public events (an annual picnic, ground-breaking ceremonies, new-building dedications, and so on). Any routine activity open to the general public should be offered to support group members in a personal, VIP manner. The purpose of these invitations is to permit those members who prefer a less active role than voluntary service to participate at a level where they are most comfortable. Other forms of activity may be included as routine membership benefits. These types of offerings—affinity credit cards, supplemental insurance plans, group travel tours, and estate planning seminars—are designed to encourage members to remain active participants in the support group each year, no matter what their level of personal participation or giving may be.

Throughout each year, a volume of information is sent to all members—their own and the institution's newsletters and annual reports, plus other materials selected for all other donors and active volunteers. The purposes are: to offer direct education in areas where the sponsor has expertise, to increase the members' information about the charitable good works their gift dollars help to provide, and to report on all the activities and events the support group has completed and is planning for the future. Special activity reports, newsletters, membership directories, and annual reports are forwarded on a steady schedule to maintain member awareness of all these activities, to continue to invite their active participation, and to honor and reward those who choose to participate.

Independence

The basic mission of a support group organization is to enhance the image and reputation of its parent and to raise friends and funds that will assist in the fulfillment of its sponsor's mission. Good communication, coordination, and cooperation are necessary to both entities, but a support group may be more capable of undertaking broader areas of responsibility than an auxiliary, guild, or donor club could perform. Support groups are designed to develop and retain their own membership, manage their own activities (including financial transactions), reward those whose voluntary service has been distinguished, undertake new as well as routine programs and services, and recruit and train volunteers who will move on to other roles on behalf of the sponsor. Their flexibility is one of their greatest assets, alongside the talent and commitment of their members. They are given fairly extensive amounts of responsibility for their own conduct; for the choice of their officers, board members, and committee chairpersons; for the quality and success of their activities, events, and publications; for their relations with the media; and for charting their own destiny and future plans in concert with their sponsor. To fulfill these responsibilities, they require defined amounts of independence. Autonomy is a double-edged proposition; it includes tests of accountability and performance evaluation while it shares the image and reputation of its sponsor. Independence requires an ability to make tough decisions when necessary, and a flexibility that can respond to changing economic conditions while still fulfilling the purpose of helping its sponsor to meet changing priorities. Changes to the group's well-made plans may be required when the priorities of the parent organization conflict with those of the group. Support groups must (1) be exacting in their management of all funds entrusted to them in the name of their sponsor; (2) ensure that no member uses an appointment or position for self-promotion or derives personal financial gain from the funds received for charitable purposes; (3) ensure their own continuity through continuous dedication to enhancing friendships and gift support that will benefit the parent nonprofit organization.

Important legal and accounting requirements need to be honored voluntarily by each support group organization.

> [E]very person and every entity involved, no matter what its relationship or its distance from the parent corporation, must operate within the purview of the board of directors, chief executive officer, and fund development office of the parent corporation. The controlling factor is the use of the official name of the parent, which holds the original charter and without which all the others would have no reason to exist. [8]

Two of the more important reasons to faithfully observe such a close relationship on behalf of all donors are:

1. A donor who makes a contribution to a support group organization assumes that the funds will be delivered to the parent nonprofit organization and will be used for charitable purposes. An official acknowledgment of each gift from the parent is essential to preserve this bond of trust.

2. Each donor may be entitled to a tax deduction for his or her contribution. Tax advantages are an important motive for continued giving; they reinforce the need for proper acknowledgment and record-keeping of all gifts received by the support group organization.

(For additional details on the cooperation and coordination necessary to manage ownership and authority, setting goals and objectives, financial accounting and reporting, and donor relations in related organizations, see my earlier text [9].)

Recognition

Support group organizations offer a variety of extra opportunities to honor, recognize, and reward volunteers and donors for their work and for their gifts. It is important to acknowledge as many of these valued participants as can be qualified for rewards. Considerable pride builds up within support group organizations, and they should be showcased by the parent nonprofit organization. Just as the loyalty that donors develop for the parent and its cause can be strong and enduring, volunteering and contributing through a support group can inspire similar "warm feelings" toward the group itself, toward its mission, which all who join can share, and toward the charitable purposes that their efforts help to fulfill. The benefits that gifts achieve each year need to be published. Gift levels and historic giving also should be recognized by the parent organization in accordance with its official policy and procedure (see Exhibits 6.3 and 6.4). These same benefits and privileges can be extended to qualified support group members and to participants in the activities and events. A range of membership levels and gift sizes can be keyed to correspond to the donor club gift levels. Consistency in the benefits and privileges provided to all donors by the parent nonprofit organization is paramount. Support group members should be accorded the same benefits and privileges that donor club members receive. These benefits can be marketed as "double the value" opportunities—additional features that will encourage the members to continue their active levels of participation. Benefits offered to donors for their gift of $100 should be equivalent to the benefits of annual membership in the support group organization (see Exhibit 6.3). With proper coordination, the parent nonprofit organization can arrange to have its honors and recognition policy administered to all its donors on a fair and equitable basis. Support group members will receive all of these privileges in addition to the special benefits arranged for support group participants only.

In some circumstances, special treatment of gifts made through support groups is appropriate in addition to recognition opportunities for volunteerism and leadership service. For example, special handling is required in the area of contribution value and donor "credit" for the specific tax deduction amount allowed for event tickets. The amount of contributions "credit" (the same as charitable contribution deduction value) must be clearly defined and explained in all of the event literature because the contributions credit and gift deduction value of tickets purchased for benefit events are not the price paid for the ticket. The Internal Revenue Service (IRS) has published a guide instructing nonprofit organizations to advise each purchaser of special-event tickets that the price paid for the ticket is not the amount that can be claimed as a charitable contribution. The donor must deduct the "material value" of the cost of goods and services (food and drink) consumed at the event [10] to arrive at the gift deduction value the donor may claim at income tax time. This same value is the correct amount that can be credited to the donor's gift records. The net proceeds from the event, or the "profit" delivered to the parent nonprofit organization, is credited as a separate gift from the support group organization, and the amount is added into its tally of total contributions provided each year.

Recognition for Volunteerism

Honors and recognition for voluntary and leadership service are additional features that can be offered to members, volunteers, and leaders of support group organizations. The chairperson of each event committee should be recognized following the successful completion of the event. This ceremony can be scheduled for the time and place where the net proceeds check is presented or for the annual meeting. The form of this recognition may be a personal gift, such as a clock, glass figurine or memento, or similar gift or favor. Board members are usually honored at the conclusion of their term, and special awards are reserved for the elected officers. Another awards program may be held by the parent nonprofit organization. For example, each auxiliary, guild, donor club, and support group organization can be invited to nominate a candidate from among its distinguished members for a volunteer service award to be presented by the parent. The occasion may be the nonprofit organization's annual meeting, at which distinguished donors are also recognized for their accomplishments. A combined event for these awards for volunteerism and generosity sends a message that the parent institution values its volunteers and its donors with equal merit and distinction.

MANAGEMENT OF GROUPS, GUILDS, AND SUPPORT ORGANIZATIONS

This chapter began with a suggestion that auxiliaries, guilds, donor clubs, and support group organizations are valuable because they can concentrate on the promotion of individual donors into more active levels of both personal involvement and gift support. Each of these entities has its own separate style and structure, as it should. Yet each must be sufficiently modified in style and structure to "fit" within the overall program of annual fund-raising of the parent nonprofit organization and within the voluntary and giving styles of the local community. Professional management of these programs is required and should be provided by the parent nonprofit organization; they will not be able to achieve their maximum levels of productivity and efficiency if they are operating alone and outside the institution. They are part of an overall program designed to develop reliable annual contribution support for the parent nonprofit organization. Their activities must be coordinated with those of all of the organization's other annual giving programs. Participants will benefit from communications from the parent that keep them well-informed of its progress, its concerns, and its future plans. Their professional direction, which must take into account the somewhat separate nature of each entity, will require routine support features that should be provided by the Fund Development Office, as follows:

1. A professional staff member assigned responsibility to supervise their daily operations, to provide professional guidance and direction, and to provide whatever clerical support is required;
2. Maintenance of up-to-date and complete mailing lists of current and past participants;
3. Gift acknowledgment and appropriate posting to each donor record;
4. Preparation of gift reports and analysis of results, by event, activity, and group;
5. Advice and counsel to all volunteers in leadership positions, to assist in their success;
6. Inclusion on invitation lists for institutional public activities and events;
7. Inclusion on mailing lists for institutional newsletters, marketing pieces, and annual reports;
8. Inclusion in the institution's honors and recognition program for all who qualify as distinguished volunteers or as generous donors.

These routine functions can be centralized in the Fund Development Office, but it is important for each auxiliary, guild, donor club, or group to maintain a strong sense of its separate and independent nature. Individual activities and programs should retain their separate identity, represented in the use of unique logos, graphics designs, stationery, invitations, newsletters, and so on. For many auxiliaries, guilds, donor clubs, and support group organizations, their separate image and reputation are among their main assets in the community. To many of their leaders, volunteers, and members, this identity *is* their cause, their association. All that the parent nonprofit organization need insist on is that the affiliation with their sponsor be visible at all times. A unique partnership is at work here; both sides benefit from public awareness of the relationship. The parent nonprofit organization should always give proper credit to each of its supportive organizations for all that they do, including the public-recognition opportunities that they make possible. Neither the public nor the individuals affiliated with any of these groups benefit from being confused about how the nonprofit organization is related to or benefits from these separate entities.

Competition among groups must remain friendly and positive. Generally speaking, each group has its own record of prior performance to measure itself against. It is normal for this year's board and committee chairs to want to do a better job than their predecessors. This point of view is not a negative report card on prior years' performance; wanting to do as well or better is a valid objective. However, it is important to guide these comparisons into areas where performance is measured positively and no individual member is embarrassed. A positive approach would be to count the increases in:

1. Number of new members recruited;
2. Number of prior members retained;
3. Public attendance at activities and events;
4. Number of volunteers who participate on committees;
5. Number of members who attend activities and events;
6. Training and experience for future leadership candidates;
7. Attention to budgets, to achieve greater efficiency and productivity;
8. Total in net revenue delivered to the parent nonprofit organization.

When more than one auxiliary, guild, donor club, or support group organization is active in support of the same nonprofit organization, there can be circumstances that cause friction, but there are more opportunities for the groups to work together, in a spirit of coordination, cooperation, and communication. For example, all the entities could adopt the same fund-raising goal or program area as their objective for the next year. From the organization's point of view, this concentration may greatly increase public awareness of the designated program area and may attract new clients. However, one group could feel unsuccessful if its results are not equal to or greater than those of the other groups. Competition can be healthy if the teams are fairly equal, but the last thing a parent nonprofit organization wants to encourage is an unfair or unequal situation where one or more of its auxiliaries, guilds, clubs, or support organizations become discouraged because they were unsuccessful or inadequate to the challenge. Most nonprofit organizations have a long list of program and service areas that need attention and support from these entities; they also have a variety of fiscal needs that can be defined as annual goals and objectives. Each of these program areas and service needs should be reviewed for its added value as a marketing opportunity and evaluated for one or more recognition opportunities to be used when the project is fully funded by the entity. Most of the time, each entity has a preferred area that it chooses to sponsor. Once these choices are established, other groups will need to respect the stated wishes and commit their support to other parts of the nonprofit organization.

Management skill is required to engage volunteer groups in accepting guided self-direction. Their founding purposes and their operating rules and procedures will spell out their basic mission, which is to provide support to the parent nonprofit organization. Armed with that statement alone, volunteers in leadership positions have the duty and the responsibility to preserve and enhance the relationship, not redirect it away from this mission. New and revised mission statements can and should be prepared so that supporting organizations are always in step with changes in direction made by their parent nonprofit organization. Group management is possible only through the active cooperation of the volunteers who are in leadership positions. At times, individuals may come forward and seek these positions in order to achieve a personal goal or to espouse a new or different point of view. Controversy seldom makes friends, and although democratic procedures are valid to address questions of change or redefinition of mission, the overriding objective should not waver from faithful support to the parent nonprofit organization.

Because auxiliaries, guilds, donor clubs, and support groups bring a wealth of talented people into active roles within the family and life of nonprofit organizations, they are of enormous value. Several additional objectives can be achieved through this joint relationship:

1. Improved communications, image enhancement, and understanding, within the community of the parent nonprofit organization and its mission;
2. Increased marketing opportunities and market penetration;
3. Improved community relations and public participation in the life of the nonprofit organization;
4. Increased media awareness and responsiveness;
5. Improved volunteer participation and training;
6. Increased avenues for leadership development to meet future institutional or agency needs;

7. Improved public relations with corporations, business executives, community residents, and government officials at all levels;

8. Increased contributions revenue.

Another important area where support entities contribute positively to the parent nonprofit organization is in reduced cost of operations. Volunteers who bring time and talent to work areas may substitute for paid employees, and they may be equally efficient and effective in carrying out the work assignments. Volunteer support to nonprofit organizations may allow salaried staff to spend more time in directing programs and providing services. Volunteers can improve the overall quality of programs and services rendered. They can also add contributions revenue not otherwise available, especially when they become involved in soliciting their friends, neighbors, business colleagues, and fellow club members. As a result, the costs to provide programs and services and to raise funds are lowered. Improved cost–benefit ratios may occur in every program in which volunteers are actively involved, which means more gift dollars are available for programs and services.

Auxiliaries, guilds, donor clubs, and support group organizations, when teamed with a mature annual giving program, can be a much broader area of public influence than most people appreciate. Volunteer solicitors can approach many more people than fund development staff can hope to see, and they often are more successful in their solicitations. In addition, volunteers can identify new candidates for other annual giving activities and can achieve corporate and foundation solicitations, special project efforts, major gift campaigns, and estate and planned giving programs. Further, and perhaps most important, volunteers can motivate others to join them in active support of the parent nonprofit organization. They can conduct orientation and training programs for newcomers and communicate their enthusiasm. They can help newcomers to integrate their time, talent, and energy into the activities of the organization. Leadership development is one of the more important areas of volunteer support to nonprofit organizations. The experience that volunteers gain through a variety of roles within auxiliaries, guilds, donor clubs, and support group organizations greatly enhances their visibility to others. These activities serve to demonstrate their ability and skill to work within organizations and to lead others. Such volunteers are being prepared to become the future leaders of nonprofit organizations. Their knowledge of annual giving and fund development programs, activities, principles, and practices will aid them if they rise to a senior management level. Their background and training will greatly enhance their ability to be influential and effective when major fund-raising objectives need to be planned and carried out successfully.

Focus: CCUA Clean Up Cleveland Chapter

It is now mid-January and the fall annual giving activities have been completed. Karen Anderson is tallying final year-end giving results for a report to the board later in the month. Three main programs were held this past fall:

Program A. The original roll-out list of 200,000 prospects solicited for the first time last spring was contacted twice more (minus those who had made a gift), to ask for a first gift. Anderson used Letter E (Exhibit 5.13, page 181) and included a second invitation to charter membership in The Circle of Champions donor club.

Program B. All 6,071 prior donors to the program who had given under $100 (she excluded only the 160 who had given over $100 and were already members of The Circle of Champions) received Letter F (Exhibit 5.14, page 182), encouraging them to upgrade their gifts to $100 and to join The Circle of Champions.

Program C. The board conducted a personal letter-and-telephone follow-up campaign to ask each of the 160 first-time members of The Circle of Champions to renew their important annual gifts at $100 or more; this appeal was their first renewal opportunity.

The results of all these activities were as follows:

Program A. Letter E to 200,000 community residents. (See Exhibit 6.6 for complete details of all these results.)

1. A total of 4,192 new donors was acquired!
2. A total of $106,396 was received!
3. An average gift of $25.38 was achieved!
4. A total of 226 persons joined The Circle of Champions; they gave a total of $28,250, for an average gift of $125.
5. Mailing costs for Letter E were $94,824 ($0.2475 × 383,128).
6. Net acquisition mailing proceeds were $12,574 ($106,396 − $94,824).
7. Cost-per-dollar-raised ratio was 0.89 percent.

Program B. Annual donor renewal and Circle of Champions first renewal request.

1. The number who renewed was 4,383 (66 percent)!
2. A total of $126,536 was raised!
3. The average gift was $28.87!
4. The cost of these renewal mailings was $12,707 ($1.215 × 10,458).
5. Net proceeds were $113,829 ($126,536 − $12,707).

6. Cost-per-dollar-raised ratio was 0.10 percent.

7. A total of 78 persons agreed to join The Circle of Champions; they gave a total of $8,979, for an average gift of $115.

8. The first Circle of Champions renewal mailing and telephone follow-up resulted in 138 out of 160 renewal gifts (86 percent), for a total of $16,836 and an average gift of $122.

Program C. Combined and Total Gift Report. Combining all the fall mailing results, both acquisition and renewal, as of year-end, Anderson will report that a grand total of 14,784 community residents are now active participants in the Clean Up Cleveland campaign. Also, a total of $249,768 was received this fall; added to all other prior gifts received, the grand total is $442,028 (see Exhibit 6.6).

As part of Anderson's summary report, she plans to recommend that the board of directors consider two new activities to be held in the first half of the new calendar year. These could be separate activities or combined into

Letter	Program	Number Mailed	Replies Number	Replies Percent	Gift Income	Average Gift
E	Fall second mail acquisition	192,116	2,216	1.15%	$ 54,276	$ 24.49
E	Fall follow-up mail acquisition	191,012	1,976	1.03	52,120	26.38
Subtotal/Average		383,128	4,192	1.09	106,396	25.38
F	Second renewal request	6,661	1,864	27.98	81,872	28.58
F	Second renewal follow-up	3,797	1,519	40	44,664	29.40
Subtotal/Average		10,458	4,383	66	126,536	28.87
Circle of Champions renewal (letter: + phone)		160	138	86	16,836	122.00
Fall Mail Total/Average		393,746	8,713	2.21%	$249,768	$ 28.66
*Cumulative Total/ Average		900,292	14,784	1.64%	$442,028	$ 29.90

*Includes figures brought forward from all prior mailings, described in Chapters Two through Five.

Exhibit 6.6   Gift Report 2, Cumulative Program Results

one major event. The first suggestion is to stage a major benefit designed to achieve wide media attention and public awareness of the chapter and the campaign. The second suggestion is to conduct the first annual meeting of the chapter, as a vehicle for a progress report to the community. Each will be organized to pay for itself through sponsorship and underwriting, gifts-in-kind, and ticket sales, and should yield a modest profit. A large portion of Anderson's time will be required to support preparation of both events.

Anderson arranges a meeting with Harvey Clout and Harold Connected, to review her gift reports and to present her recommendations for the two new events. They like the results and, after discussion, agree to ask the board for approval of a combined major event. They will also ask the board for help to identify a prominent community member who can be recruited to serve as chairperson for a combined annual meeting and benefit. They know this major affair will require someone with proven leadership experience who will recruit a solid working committee of volunteers to do most of the work. Connected also suggests including a number of local sports celebrities from the Cleveland Browns, Cavaliers, and Indians, for a "Dinner with Cleveland's Circle of Champions." Clout also likes Anderson's idea of using this first annual meeting as an opportunity to recognize all the charter members in The Circle of Champions, and to present them with membership certificates. Clout tells Anderson and Connected that he is making fairly good progress with all the agencies involved in approving the selection of a site for a new power plant; they might even have a decision by April 15. Connected suggests that the event be scheduled between April 30 and May 30, if possible. With luck, all these ideas might come together at the same time to make for a grand first annual meeting of the chapter. All agreed that the combined event will serve as a major opportunity for the chapter to achieve a number of its own objectives plus maximum media coverage for its efforts to clean up the city streets.

At the board meeting, following the gift report and annual meeting presentations, everyone is surprised when Mary Moneybanks immediately speaks up in support of the combined annual meeting and benefit proposal. They are then delighted when she volunteers to chair the committee and to take responsibility to produce this "gala benefit event," as she has already begun to call it. She asks Trafalgar ("Telly") Temple to join her as co-chair of the Benefit Committee and suggests that Temple set up a meeting with Iris B. Radiant, a prominent businesswoman who owns a chain of Ohio department stores, to ask her to join them as the third co-chair of the committee. With Moneybanks' experience, her two co-chairs, and their combined business and social contacts in the community, everyone feels the success of this premier annual meeting is virtually assured.

CHAPTER SEVEN

Activities, Benefits, and Special Events

Activities, benefits, and special events are what many people think fund-raising is all about. After direct mail, these functions and occasions are the most pervasive forms of public solicitation in current practice. Visibility appears to be their primary objective; raising money for charity is the excuse to have a party. They are popular with the many volunteers who plan them and with the people who attend. We read about them in the papers and see photographs of the dedicated people who planned them and the celebrities and distinguished guests who attended. We read and see less about why they were held or what the funds raised will do.

Why are activities, benefits, and special events held? Nonprofit organizations seem to favor them a great deal; they conduct many of them during each year. What are their advantages, their values? Do they actually raise any money? Are they worth all that effort? There are several good answers that validate keeping these activities and occasions on the annual calendar of events; there are also several good reasons why nonprofit organizations should cross some of them off. This chapter will discuss activities, benefits, and special events, defining their many purposes and describing their many forms. They are a rich and valuable addition to a comprehensive annual giving program. They are an asset because of their ability to enhance and reinforce direct mail and membership acquisition and renewal objectives and to further the goals of auxiliaries, guilds, donor clubs, and support groups. Each of these annual giving methods is repeated again and again, year after year. Activities, benefits, and special events can add spice, vigor, and zip to these repetitious programs while they serve many other valid purposes on their own.

A complete list of all the types of activities, benefits, and special events that can be held would be long and not especially enlightening,

215

except as proof of the human creativity and experimentation invested in gathering people together. Examples range from camel races to rat races, from auctions to raffles, from Las Vegas nights to Monte Carlo nights, from chili cook-offs to cotillions, from 10K runs and 5K walks to golf and tennis tournaments, and (saving the best for last) from pancake breakfasts to fashion show luncheons to black-tie, gala dinner dances. This brief list is ample evidence of how men and women can invent activities, benefits, and special events and offer them to other people as exciting "fun things" to do, especially if they are held for "a worthy cause." Exhibit 7.1 illustrates some of the primary purposes for nonprofit organizations' use of these functions.

I have chosen to segregate activities, benefits, and special events as three distinct entities for presentation in this chapter. The terms are similar, and some people use them interchangeably. By distinguishing among the three types, the chapter can cover all of their multiple purposes and their separate utilization in a comprehensive annual giving program.

Activities, benefits, and special events can be staged by nearly every form of organized human enterprise, whether held for a business, governmental, or philanthropic purpose. They attract attention; they bring

Method	Primary Purposes	Examples
Activities	Communication	Lectures
	Information	Tours
	Support	Memberships
	Advocacy	Lobbying
	Awareness	Community services
Benefits	Friend-raising	Grand openings
	Marketing and promotion	Ground-breaking ceremonies
	Media relations	Sporting events
	Donor relations	Victory parties
	Community relations	Fairs/Open houses
	Volunteer involvement	Social events
	Leadership development	Campaigns
	Fund-raising	Every benefit
	Fun	Every benefit
Special Events	Contacts	Retreats
	Required business	Annual meetings
	Honors and recognition	Dedications
	Public activity	Convocations
	Tradition	Public ceremonies

Exhibit 7.1   Primary Purposes for Activities, Benefits, and Special Events

people together; they convey a message; they promote a purpose or cause; they encourage people to action. Here are some of the purposes that activities, benefits, and special events can accomplish for nonprofit organizations:

1. An increase in visibility and an improved public image;
2. An opportunity for volunteer participation;
3. An increase in community relations;
4. An opportunity for leadership development;
5. An increase in market penetration;
6. An opportunity for testing market response;
7. An increase in cash available for current purposes;
8. An opportunity for honors and recognition;
9. An increase in media coverage;
10. An opportunity to energize donors and volunteers;
11. An increase in corporate contacts and participation;
12. An opportunity to showcase the organization's leadership;
13. An increase in attention to ongoing programs and services;
14. An opportunity to recruit new donors;
15. An increase in multiple annual gifts;
16. An opportunity to cultivate major gifts;
17. An increase in professional staff visibility;
18. An opportunity to promote the mission or cause;
19. An increase in public awareness and general consensus;
20. An opportunity to have fun.

Given all of these potential attributes, is it any wonder that activities, benefits, and special events are held so frequently? No single activity, benefit, or special event could hope to accomplish all of the above purposes, but, like every other endeavor planned by the organization, there should be a list of defined objectives against which an activity, benefit, or special event will be measured. Planning for an activity, benefit, or special event should begin with the selection of several purposes; the greater the number, the greater the value of the activity, benefit, or special event in opening up its nonprofit sponsor to its community of friends, neighbors, clients, and potential clients. Public activities invite people to come inside, to see the facilities, to learn about the programs and services being provided to others in the community, and to consider joining with other volunteers to help the organization accomplish its urgent and necessary goals and objectives. Activities, benefits, and special events serve philanthropy best as means to an end rather than ends in themselves.

VOLUNTEER DEVELOPMENT

Activities, benefits, and special events are exceptional opportunities for volunteerism. To be successful, they need and can use hundreds of hours from hundreds of people working together. They offer opportunities for community liaison, volunteer participation, and leadership identification and development. Converting suspects, prospects, and donors into volunteers is one of the best ways to help an organization to grow and to attract those who will support its needs today and in the future. Active volunteers also become more faithful donors, according to a national survey published by Independent Sector:

> The incidence of volunteering has a direct relationship to the amount of contributions. In 1991, respondents who reported household contributions but did not volunteer (26 percent of all households) reported contributions averaging $477, or 1.4 percent of household income. Respondents who reported household contributions and volunteering (46 percent of all households) reported contributions averaging $1,155, or 2.6 percent of household income. [1]

Involvement increases personal awareness and knowledge of nonprofit organizations, and their many charitable purposes. To volunteer is to begin to learn about an organization's mission and purposes, its need for volunteers, and its methods of fund-raising. Successful nonprofit organizations explain exactly how volunteer services make a difference and how the funds raised by volunteers are used to carry out programs and services that meet public needs. The personal experience of volunteerism should be rewarding, even if it is sometimes hard work begun at the end of a regular workday. It serves a high purpose by helping to make the community, the nation, and the world a better place to live. People want to help; they want their good efforts to make a difference. Satisfaction increases their enthusiasm for volunteerism and sustains their commitment to continued support of a nonprofit organization. When a nonprofit organization asks for volunteers from among the residents of its community, it is serving the public interest and creating a valuable community benefit. Every nonprofit organization needs volunteers to fulfill its mission; it cannot fulfill it alone.

Because volunteers are essential to the success of each activity, benefit, or special event, it is important to review what is involved in finding and training them. Each nonprofit organization must identify and re-cruit volunteers, inform and train them, carefully select their early as-signments, supervise their development, support all of their efforts, evaluate their performance, and honor and recognize them for all they have done. These steps are summarized in Exhibit 7.2. For some volun-teers, their capacity for responsibility will predict their later roles as vol-unteer leaders; they will take a turn at planning and directing nonprofit organizations. Every organization needs volunteers who like to be in-volved with public activities, who can organize and manage a group, whether friends or strangers, and who will support an organization's need to conduct necessary and useful special events.

Identification

Despite its great need for volunteers, a nonprofit organization must be selective about whom it invites to work for it. People who are already active in community work and experienced with activities, benefits, and special events are the best choices. The first criterion to measure is a candidate's ability to join with others and, by working together, to accomplish a common purpose. People with a record of responsibility and performance in support of activities, benefits, and special events at other organizations might be asked to do the same job here. I recom-mend calling other nonprofit organizations where a leadership candi-date has been active, and asking about his or her performance. Was it characterized by cooperation and coordination with the volunteers and professional staff in place, or did the candidate insist on bringing in "my own people" and subordinating those already active on the organi-zation's behalf? Some well-intentioned people have a personal style that drives people away. Will the candidate raise friends and build rela-tionships in the community, and make a successful cadre of volunteers

---

1. Identification
2. Recruitment
3. Orientation and training
4. Assignment
5. Leadership development
6. Staff support
7. Performance evaluation
8. Honors and recognition

Exhibit 7.2 Steps in Volunteer and Leadership Development

into an enthusiastic unit? If not, no matter what the candidate's credentials or past successes, it may be wise to look for someone else. Friend-raising and relationship-building remain the prime directives of the annual giving program.

Do any board members have experience in directing activities, benefits, or special events? If so, they were probably not board members at that time. Board members may not be eager to take on a major project unless they have absolute assurance that the professional and support staff know what they are doing. Given their position as board members, neither they nor the organization can risk any failures. They can, however, be asked to serve as information resources during the planning of an activity, benefit, or special event, and as advisers if problems develop during implementation of the plans. Do they know others who have worked on similar functions? Can they assist in recruiting experienced volunteer leaders, or serve on the committee that will manage the project? How, in their opinion, should the organization proceed with planning each of its activities, benefits, and special events? What functions do they think the public will support? Which ones should be avoided? The experience and intuition of board members who have observed many social activities and benefit events held in the community can be invaluable when choosing the type of function that will be held. Can they nominate or help to recruit people who are experienced and reliable volunteers? The new project will need a few individuals who have succeeded in managing similar functions. Board members will be sensitive to the possibility that the nominees for this function might help to meet other needs of the organization in the future.

The next resource might be current volunteers. Have any of them demonstrated the talents needed for this more demanding assignment? Whose faithful service has gained recognition and earned a new opportunity to serve by leading? Their commitment to a working relationship may warrant turning over to them the staging, producing, and directing of this important new project. Volunteers in current leadership positions are often looking for their next assignment. Who among them has a proven ability to organize and manage both people and the complex components of a financial and social success? These are the organization's own qualified candidates!

Donors might also be tapped. There are always people in the donor files who have not come forward because no one has asked them. Donors with faithful giving histories are telling the organization that they care about it a lot. Consistent performance is the clue here, not how much they have given. Donors come in many sizes and shapes. One donor may have access to others and may be willing to call on them to help the activity, benefit, or special event. Donors who are well-placed in business and commerce and are already active in community and civic projects will have established contacts that can be used in the organization's behalf. Some donors' business or profession may bring them into frequent contact with a suitable audience for the planned function—and may illustrate their leadership ability. Any donor who is in an executive position has the necessary knowledge and experience to accomplish goals by set deadlines. For example, any donor in a sales position is a good candidate to serve on the subcommittee charged with recruiting sponsors and underwriters and soliciting table hosts and individual ticket sales.

Among the new people nominated for service to the organization, are any candidates reported to be well-qualified? These individuals may have already emerged as highly placed volunteers with other nonprofit organizations. Some research will indicate whether these nominees might agree to serve in some voluntary capacity. Motives are still important. Are these people inclined to participate in charitable work only to advance themselves and expand their business and professional contacts? If so, they may have only a minimal interest in the mission and purposes of the nonprofit organization and may abandon a committee or an event if it does not fulfill their personal objectives.

In suspects, or newcomers already identified as probable annual givers, an active interest in the nonprofit organization is already stirring. An invitation to serve in a volunteer role on a committee responsible for a major function will acquaint them with other volunteers and donors and start them at a good pace toward personal involvement with the organization. Their progress can be a gauge of their potential for continued service. Their immediate interest and their willingness to skip the preliminaries and go right into the main event should be appropriately recognized.

The remaining search criteria are tied to the type of activity, benefit, or special event that is being considered. If entertainment is essential, people who are close to the entertainment industry should be contacted. If a social function, the help of men and women who are well-versed in local social customs and possess local social standing should be enlisted. If a sporting event, sports celebrities will give a great lift to the party. When the call goes out for nominees, people will submit names of friends who have connections, of public figures who are "politically correct," and of themselves if the community service will look good on their resumes. Not everyone nominated may know or care about the nonprofit organization or its mission. The perspective, knowledge, and political sense of the board members, the president/CEO, and the volunteer leadership deserve some trust here. Meeting these unique needs is part of their leadership obligation. The organization's name and reputation are inside the package when an activity, benefit, or special event is handed over to a volunteer committee.

Recruitment

After a roster of qualified volunteer candidates has been assembled, the volunteers nominated should be evaluated against the plan for the activity, benefit, or special event. Do they have the skills that will be needed to manage this project to success? How many of the primary purposes identified in Exhibit 7.1 can be realized with their assistance? Some names may be on the roster only because removing them would send out negative shock waves. Politically correct favorites will also need to be invited. Some candidates may be more valuable to other annual giving programs and should be set aside for those duties. Others, especially candidates who are not well-known, can be coded for possible selection on a second pass through the list.

The best approach is to identify at least three leadership candidates first: an overall chairperson plus two (or more) nominees for vice chair. The positions of chairperson and vice chair are crucial, and board members and other key volunteers close to the organization can be enormously helpful in resolving this choice. They should be asked to review the leadership candidates identified for each project and to assist in their recruitment. Each of these candidates should be personally interviewed before being asked to serve as chairperson or to take responsibility for a high-level duty on the committee. The candidates' capabilities, interest, and willingness to commit the time required should all be thoughtfully assessed.

> The ideal fund-raising leader is influential in the community, resourceful, creative, and ambitious; has a strong sense of order and is a good administrator; is interested in people and attentive to their ideas; gives others a feeling of involvement; delegates easily and wisely; has a contagious sense of commitment; possesses excellent communication skills; is accessible and discriminating; and is willing to take on a tough challenge for the right cause. [2]

Each candidate should evidence some interest in the organization and prior experience with the type of activity, benefit, or special event being proposed. The names of others who have made a firm commitment to participate and the extent of staff experience and support personnel that will be available should be communicated during the interview.

Careful consideration of vice chair candidates is also required. Where possible, these candidates should be from among the top leadership group of current volunteers and donors, as proved by their commitment and record of service. This position should not be conferred; it should be earned by dedicated work and given as a reward. Each vice chair candidate should understand that selection for this assignment carries the possibility of nomination to chair the activity, benefit, or special event the following year or the year after that. The time spent as vice chair will assist the chairperson in leading the event successfully and will be preparatory for a future term as chair.

Those who nominated the final leadership candidates are usually the most qualified persons to assist in the recruitment process, which can take as long as the candidate search. Securing the nominees' acceptance is crucial; success is riding on their saying Yes. Recruiting leaders and key volunteers is like soliciting important annual gifts. Personal contact will be the most successful method and is highly recommended. Telephone calls may work if a personal meeting is not possible. However, sending a letter to someone qualified for a leadership position is the least persuasive way to gain a commitment of his or her time, energy, and talent.

After the chairperson and one or two vice chairs have been recruited, their work can be launched with a few basic steps:

Bring them together, outline the project fully, and identify all the other areas of responsibility that will need their attention;

Provide this new leadership team with the list of all the other qualified candidates so that they can review them against the suggested tasks that remain;

Supply them with sound background information, and then let them make their own choices for whom they want to recruit and how best to sign up the balance of their committee.

In advance of recruiting volunteers, each role that a volunteer will be asked to fill should be defined, and a brief job description should be written for each assignment area. Summary information should explain the overall purposes of the activity, benefit, or special event and its specific goals—in dollars, attendees, or similar measures of success. After recruitment of volunteers is begun, preparation for responses will involve:

1. A thank-you letter to each person who agrees to serve. This letter will serve as an official appointment, an acknowledgment of the commitment expressed, and a designation of an official assignment on the committee. Those who cannot serve should receive another letter thanking them for considering the request and expressing the hope that they may be able to join in next time. (This exchange is good cultivation; when asked again, they may be more willing to join.) Each of these letters should come from the chairperson of the activity or event, from another volunteer who has

overall responsibility for annual giving, or perhaps from a member of the board of directors.

2. Preparations for the initial meeting of the new committee, which should be scheduled for a day close to the completion of recruiting. Information on the date, time, and place of this first meeting may have been provided at the time of invitation.

Some candidates may ask for a specific assignment or express a clear preference to avoid being asked to work in certain areas. For example, some volunteers love to work on designing the invitations and official program, preparing and tasting the menu and making the wine selections, or choosing the decorations and flowers. These tasks should be diplomatically placed in a perspective that centers on the more significant contribution made by helping to sell tickets, recruiting sponsors and underwriters, searching out donations and auction and raffle prizes, and meeting the essential fund-raising assignments by a set deadline. Volunteers are needed in all of these capacities; the volunteer leaders must be trusted to sort out who will best serve in each area and to help them with completion of their duties as quickly as possible.

Orientation and Training

For all volunteers, including the leadership team, orientation and training are always valuable. The focus should be on the objectives of the activity, benefit, or special event and on the organization and committee structure needed to achieve success. Early projections of the budget, estimates of revenue sources, likely ticket sales volume, expected attendance, calendar openings and dates of competing events, staff capabilities and resources the nonprofit organization will provide, and other details requiring attention should all be ready for presentation at the first meeting. These early details help to identify areas of strength and weakness that need to be resolved, and where, how many, and at what levels of competence volunteers will be needed. Some volunteers may have prior experience that can benefit the planning stage. Others may not have had the opportunity to work with the organization before.

When these preliminaries have been presented, both the leadership and the organization are prepared to invite others to join in this affair. Everyone can help with the basic design of the activity, benefit, or special event and it is always valuable to invite volunteers to help with planning a new activity from the beginning. Everyone's prior experiences will be highly useful as this new activity is designed for success. Experienced volunteers can (1) warn where likely problem areas and mistakes might occur, (2) clarify what pitfalls are to be avoided, and (3) offer realistic advice on operating details. Volunteers will begin to identify the activity as "theirs" and to take ownership of it.

Committee leaders will want these planning sessions to arrive at an early version of a fundamental action plan directed toward meeting the desired objectives. This preliminary plan will be shared with the non-profit organization for review and approval. The orientation of volunteer committee members should begin with a general overview of the non-profit organization and its mission and purpose. It should clarify the specific primary purposes or aims, the goals (in dollars or numbers), and the objectives (the features that can be achieved) that this activity, benefit, or special event seeks to accomplish, the plan of action and master schedule ("time line") to be followed, and the planned use of any funds that will be raised. Typically, once these preliminary details are introduced, everyone is invited to add thoughts and suggestions. The activity, benefit, or special event is then ready to be turned over to the volunteer committee, which will proceed according to an agreed-on schedule.

Assignments

All the possible areas of support need to be identified early. Some tasks stand alone but most are interrelated. Some completed assignments (for example, the design of a printed program) may remain in limbo for weeks because other work (the written content of the program) has not been done. A master schedule or time line is essential for each activity, benefit, or special event. Deadlines are a firm reality (see Exhibit 7.3), and certain tasks must be completed on time if others are to meet their deadlines. Support tasks are usually assigned to subcommittees, each of which has its own appointed chairperson, a vice chair or two, and a team of worker-assistants. Given the numerous details associated with an enterprise of this sort and the possibility that the chair or vice chair may not be present during hours when volunteers are working and have questions, a brief written description of each assignment is recommended. A simple paragraph can specify exactly what will be required, when the work must be done, and where the assignment fits into the time line.

Before volunteers accept assignments, they will want to know what they are being asked to do, who else is available to help them (or if they can recruit their own team), when their task must be completed, and what support they can count on from the committee, its leadership, and the staff at the nonprofit organization.

Subcommittee chairs and vice chairs should be members of the organizing committee or the executive committee. Subcommittee members need not attend these larger sessions, but the chairperson, a vice chair, or another representative should be present at each meeting to make a

Assignment/Task	Deadline	Date Completed
1. Goals and objectives (set by board)	9 months prior	
2. Leadership selection	9 months prior	
3. Vice chair selection	8 months prior	
4. Subcommittee chairs	8 months prior	
5. First organizing meeting	7 months prior	
6. Training and orientation	7 months prior	
7. Budget completed/approved	7 months prior	
8. Sponsor/Underwriter lists	7 months prior	
9. Resolution of critical details	6 months prior	
a. Date/Time	6 months prior	
b. Place/Space	6 months prior	
c. Theme	6 months prior	
d. Program plan	6 months prior	
e. Entertainment	6 months prior	
10 Begin monthly committee meetings	6 months prior	
11. Sponsors/Underwriters letters	6 months prior	
12. Site inspection conducted	6 months prior	
13. Notice to area master calendar	6 months prior	
14. Invitation list	5 months prior	
15. "Save the Date" notice mailed	5 months prior	
16. Invitation design	5 months prior	
17. Sponsor/Underwriter gifts/pledges	4–5 months prior	
18. Invitations delivered	4 months prior	
19. Invitations addressed	3 months prior	
20. Decoration/Flower plans resolved	3 months prior	
21. First invitations mailed	2 months prior	
22. Media/Press invitations sent	2 months prior	
23. Menu/Wine tasting and resolution	2 months prior	
24. Second invitations mailed	5 weeks prior	
25. Program text/design finalized	5 weeks prior	
26. First draft agenda plan/script	4 weeks prior	
27. Phone-bank invitation follow-up	3 weeks prior	
28. Site plan walk-through	3 weeks prior	
29. Second draft agenda plan/script	2 weeks prior	
30. Media/Press kit plan resolved	2 weeks prior	
31. Volunteer "on site" duties confirmed	2 weeks prior	
32. Final program text completed	1 week prior	
33. Critique meeting held	1 month after	
34. Critique report sent to board	1 month after	

Exhibit 7.3 Model List of Deadlines for Master Schedule ("Time Line")

report on ongoing activities and the progress of the overall activity or event. Coordination of all the necessary details is an essential function of the project's leadership; monitoring progress, an assignment that usually belongs to professional and support staff, also requires attention. The risk in failing to maintain good communications with everyone is that duplicate efforts, mistakes, failures, and other errors will surface after it is too late to head off their harmful effects.

Regular meetings of the organizing committee should begin six to nine months in advance of the date of each activity, benefit, or special event. The committee's purposes are to organize leaders and teams to handle all of the assignments (see Exhibit 7.4) and to be able to monitor everyone's progress according to the master schedule. One meeting of the full committee each month is usually adequate; subcommittees will establish their own work schedule, as necessary. Teamwork is the preferred method to manage a large group of tasks assigned to various volunteers. Committees, holding regular meetings, are necessary to keep everyone informed and motivated, to spread the work among many volunteers, and to keep everything and everyone moving forward on schedule. It is much harder to manage an event if there are no regular opportunities to bring everyone together to review progress and make decisions on the issues that require resolution. Within the group, consensus on major decisions is important, as is agreement on style, price, location, time of day, time of year, and a host of other important details regarding the activity, benefit, or special event. Once these details are resolved, the work will go forward more easily.

Leadership Development

Managing an enterprise that is comprised of several volunteers, each with a different assignment, demands that someone must be in charge. Leadership of a committee of volunteers is a unique skill. The all-important duty of the chairperson is to be able to orchestrate different individuals toward a common objective, giving everyone room to play a part, managing to get everyone to complete an assignment on schedule, and directing everyone's enthusiasm and motivation toward achieving a success. Leading and managing a committee that is responsible for putting on a public activity, benefit, or special event might be compared to being a conductor of a symphony orchestra. Between 40 and 80 musicians will be recruited to play, but each plays a separate instrument and has a different level of experience and knowledge about the music. Each player wants an opportunity to play a solo part that will feature his or her talent. Rehearsals are required to bring the group together, to practice the music, and to learn to play with perfect synchronization so

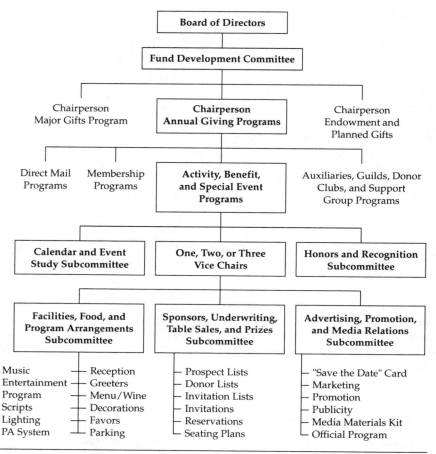

Exhibit 7.4   Sample Organization Chart for Volunteer-Led Committee to Prepare an Activity, Benefit, or Special Event

that they can achieve the best quality of concert possible. Everyone must follow the conductor's direction and play the parts as written in the musical score. Making great music together is a far greater challenge than playing a solo to perfection. The group preparation takes practice, patience, and hard work. The live performance gives immediate results. The public will express appreciation of all the hard work by buying tickets to fill the house and with their applause after each piece on the concert program and when the performance is concluded.

Each volunteer who accepts a committee assignment has an opportunity to learn how to be an integral part of a voluntary work project, how to perform new tasks, and how to work with others. Volunteers do not come to an organization pretrained in exactly the fashion each organization needs or with mastery of the skills with which assignments must be performed. Many people willing to give their time will be satisfied being working members of the team, doing their assigned part, and sharing in the results. They enjoy the project and the company of the other volunteers, and they believe in the cause they are serving. A few others are willing to provide leadership and direction to their assigned area, to delegate the work to others who wish to learn, and to supervise these assignments. Experience is a great teacher; leadership skills can be learned. Those who enjoy the work they are asked to perform and are willing to take some responsibility for its completion should be invited to serve again. Those who work well with others and demonstrate that they can encourage others to perform their tasks as required are leadership candidates. They should be asked again and perhaps given more responsibility. Committee work is one of the best ways to identify and train future leaders of volunteers. A leadership development program, with a variety of job assignments for those who are qualified and eligible, should be formulated and offered to selected people. Without a follow-up assignment, the most competent and experienced volunteers are likely to leave the organization and seek one that has a greater need for their talents and willingness to work.

Staff Support

Volunteers will require some level of staff support. The exact amount and extent depend on their prior experience with the organization, their knowledge of its culture, style, and history, their training and orientation to their specific assignment, and their understanding of the purpose and objectives of the activity, benefit, or special event. Prior experiences in these assignments have taught volunteers where they need assistance and what kind of help they will require to succeed with their tasks. Staff must remain flexible in their response to the variety of support volunteers may require. They must be experienced and knowledgeable enough to be able to assist volunteers with the specific area assigned, without performing the duties for them. In a successful committee of team players, the support staff are identified as advisers to the project. Volunteers can expect to receive the staff support they require, and the staff can expect volunteers to conduct their assignments with energy and independent effort. For a volunteer to accept an assignment and then expect the staff to do the work is not acceptable. The staff may have little choice but to fill the work gap because the task has to be met. Committee leaders should be made aware of this kind of nonperformance; they should not be led to believe that the volunteer is fulfilling all the assignments independent of staff help.

Performance Evaluation

Everyone performs better when someone else will be measuring the results. Volunteers to nonprofit organizations do not expect any degree of personal performance evaluation, which is correct. Their task will be evaluated by their peers, who will also review the overall success of the activity, benefit, or special event. Judgment of one's peers is an adequate motive that can be pointed out to volunteers when they accept their assignments. Other forms of analysis also can assist everyone involved. The objectives are to be fair, to not embarrass anyone personally, and to identify areas where the task or project can be improved. All members of the committee should be asked to participate in a critique meeting following the project's completion (Exhibit 7.3). This final meeting is an excellent time to express praise for individual and collective accomplishments. Volunteers who judge their own results are usually honest and fair in suggesting areas for improvement, especially when the suggestions come from the volunteer in charge of a function. Each assignment area should be reviewed in turn, and suggestions about future roles and the desired performance should be welcomed. This review should also be forthright in assessing all the purposes and attributes for the activity, benefit, or special event, including whether the function should be continued and, if so, what recommendations are valid for its goals next time and for its volunteer leadership candidates. Agreed-on recommendations should be recorded for use by the next committee (and shared with the next group of volunteers assigned to these tasks), and the critique report should be forwarded to the board of directors.

Honors and Recognition

It is essential to provide proper recognition and reward for volunteers who support activities, benefits, or special events. This duty is so important that an honors committee should be created for every project. The multiple purposes and attributes that can be accomplished through activities, benefits, and special events are of enormous value to a nonprofit organization, which can never produce or achieve these results on its own. The board of directors should establish suitable guidelines for honors and recognition for each project in which volunteers are invited to participate. As has been mentioned earlier in this book, the certificate, plaque, or personal gift that is presented to a volunteer is not what counts the most, although these gifts are appreciated. Of true value to volunteers are: the proper occasion at which they are recognized for what they have done, the people (especially the organization's leadership) who are present and express thanks, and the honest feelings of appreciation and gratitude that are conveyed. For example, if each volunteer received a letter of appointment to an assignment from a board member when the project began, that board member should now participate in their honors and recognition ceremony. The board should also send a special thank-you letter to each volunteer who served in a leadership position. Everyone likes to be thanked for work done, especially when it has been done for others and done voluntarily. Volunteers will not return if they believe their efforts have not been appreciated. The challenge to nonprofit organizations is to thank their volunteers properly and thoroughly. When honors and recognition are established as a visible part of each activity, benefit, and special event, volunteers know that their efforts were seen and were honestly appreciated, and they will be more than willing to serve again and again.

DEFINITIONS AND DIFFERENCES

Before beginning the separate examination of activities, benefits, and special events, I offer here the two approaches that I have chosen to distinguish these types of functions from one another. The first approach is to separate them based on their definitions and purposes. What are activities, benefits, and special events and why are they held?

	Definition	Purpose
Activities	Occasions whose chief goals are to communicate person-to-person, to convey a message, or to demonstrate a worthwhile charity. These goals are carried out in lectures, meetings, rallies, tours, and other forms of public gatherings. There is no charge or fee to participants who attend and receive the information or service provided.	To gather people together to inform them or provide them with a service.

	Definition	Purpose
Benefits	Occasions that request attendance, for a fee or ticket charge, but offer in exchange some form of entertainment.	To stage a function for public enjoyment and to provide financial support to the organization's cause.
Special events	Occasions for which no admission fee is charged because the official business to be conducted needs a crowd.	To convene people for business or official endeavors.

Nonprofit organizations often stage several versions of all of these functions during each year. Guests who attend, and others who receive invitations, are likely to interchange the terms activity, benefit, and special event. All three types of function share similar goals—to communicate, to entertain, and to conduct some business (which may include fund-raising). I distinguish them from one another according to their primary purpose, which is a decision made by their sponsors. Most of their other features are added to help attract a crowd.

The second approach I use to distinguish activities, benefits, and special events from one another is to pose four questions of each:

1. What details are required for success?
2. How can each aid annual giving?
3. How and where can volunteers help?
4. How can success be measured?

The replies will address how each function contributes to the annual giving program. Whatever they may be called and however these similar functions may be put to use, activities, benefits, and special events possess different features and attributes that make them useful to an annual giving program's continuous success.

ACTIVITIES

The primary purpose of an activity is to achieve public participation. Attendance at an activity is encouraged through invitations, advertisements, promotions, and the like. Potential guests may learn about an activity from their family, friends, business associates, and social contacts. Activities should be scheduled at times when those invited are likely to be able to attend. The sponsor has a message to share or something to offer every person who attends; the activity should get right to the point as soon as it begins. Those who respond make a decision to attend so that they can hear the message, an important fact to consider when attempting to understand and to forecast public response. Why will people attend? To hear the message, to be seen, to learn something, or to receive something (a public service) that is promised?

An an illustration of how a variety of activities can be used, hospitals' message of AIDS prevention can be communicated through multiple channels. Information about AIDS prevention must be transmitted repeatedly, in various forms, in an effort to reach all of the hospital's targeted audience. This objective is too massive for one activity or message medium; multiple means of transmission are needed, to handle constant repetitions of the same message. The next objective, influencing human behavior, is even more difficult. Mass communication techniques, even in this age of instant news traveling on "information highways," are dedicated to trying to motivate people and stimulate them to action. Influencing human behavior is much like a crusade. To be effective, hospitals must first prepare a variety of activities that will help to communicate their messages about AIDS prevention—lectures, meetings, videos, speakers bureaus, rallies, perhaps even tours of hospital areas where AIDS treatment is provided.

Delivering healthcare to any community involves more than taking care of those who get sick. To be maximally effective, hospitals must become proactive, taking on ancillary activities and expanding the available channels and modes of communication. Parents-to-be, preparing for their new arrival, might be offered classes on how to care for their newborn after they take it home. The hospital might set up mobile clinics in shopping centers to administer flu shots, screen for glaucoma, or hand out skin cancer protection advice and free sunscreen lotion. Hospital staff might visit offices, plants, and schools to lecture about the risk factors in heart disease (to pick only one topic). They might conduct tests for high blood pressure, excess weight, cholesterol levels, and stress, and provide instruction and information materials on early warning signs of heart disease. Exercise, smoking cessation, healthy eating habits, and proper rest can be promoted in continuous running videos and in posters and handouts. All of these activities, repeated over months and years, are necessary to get the attention of the public. One such campaign is having success: the incidence of heart disease in America has decreased within the past 20 years. The consistent message, warning of the risk factors in heart disease, has been heard. Such an enormous overall effort is expensive, but making people healthier is worth the cost. One might wonder why it is so difficult to get people to pay attention to their own life-style and to protect their own health. Preventing disease contributes to increased productivity, a longer and happier life, and less need for healthcare intervention (hospitalization) later on. Message-delivering activities are now second-nature to hospitals and other healthcare institutions across the nation, because they do raise people's awareness. But hospitals had to learn how to use these activities for best effect.

When a nonprofit organization must reach selected audiences, it has to rely on the same communication channels it uses for all of its other messages. An invitation is reliable for getting people's attention and stimulating the desired response because an invitation is a personal message. Nonprofit organizations offer community benefits to the public, but lack the financial resources to get all their messages to everyone intended to receive them. Some well-known activities will attract a high response without much extra work. Examples are the rich variety of classes, lectures, exhibits, and cultural and athletic events that are held by colleges and universities, galleries, libraries, museums, performing arts centers, theaters, and similar organizations. These activities are known to be open to the public and they have value for those who attend. Except when an admission fee may be required, there are no restrictions or special qualifications to attend. A person has only to decide to go and arrive in time to participate. For galleries, libraries, and museums, attendance fulfills their very purpose. All who choose to attend these activities receive the information prepared for everyone. Those who do not attend are aware that the activity remains open to them at another time; they have only to decide when they wish to attend.

Activities with larger attendance can become more complicated to plan and execute than others. Reservation forms may be needed when a location's capacity limits how many people can attend at any one time. Popular activities may require extra planning for parking, crowd control, refreshments, and other details. Expenses will be incurred, and some prior experience with these detailed arrangements may be needed to achieve the desired objectives for the activity.

Activities are opportunities to improve a nonprofit organization's public image and to enhance public understanding of its mission to fulfill charitable purposes. Activities showcase the programs and services offered for public benefit and help to improve an organization's reputation among the people invited to attend. These same people may eventually choose to support the organization in other ways beyond attendance. Media attention is an important priority because extended communications offer the bonus of spreading the message to those who were unable to attend the activity.

When so many positive attributes will result, early planning must not neglect the time and attention needed to develop a well-planned, well-coordinated publicity campaign to support each activity. The objective is twofold: (1) to advertise the activity in order to deliver the primary message about the need, cause, or charitable purpose the non-profit organization espouses, and (2) to spread the word widely about the activity itself, promoting interest and attendance while letting the public know the organization is alive and kicking and is working on their behalf.

> Press, radio, and TV coverage will give you credibility and legitimacy. Most radio stations and many TV stations are willing to broadcast public service announcements of community events. Ordinarily, these announcements are 15-, 30-, or 60-second spots resembling commercials; therefore, the announcement must be brief. When writing the announcement for the station, include only the who, what, why, where, and when. . . . In addition to media coverage, other ways to publicize an event include posters, flyers, handbills, buttons, balloons, marquee messages, and store counter displays in banks, cafes, and other viable outlets. Excellent publicity can also be obtained by getting banks, utility companies, and department stores to let you include a "statement stuffer" in their monthly statements. [3]

Activities can expand rather easily. A once-a-month lecture series that features interesting speakers can grow overnight into a major activity if the speaker, who may have been selected months earlier, suddenly becomes famous. An auditorium with multiple audiovisual aids may be needed, and the speaker may be asking for a generous honorarium plus travel and living expenses. Such good fortune is a nice advantage; a routine activity has the potential to achieve several extra attributes as bonus values—wider media coverage, a larger audience, evidence of the urgent need for volunteer help, major image enhancement, donor cultivation potential (especially if selected donors are invited to a private pre- or postlecture reception with the speaker), improved market position, new member recruiting, and much more.

What Details Are Required for Success?

For starters, common courtesy. The people invited should be treated as guests in the organization's "home." Advance arrangements for their participation must include adequate parking, door attendants, comfortable seating, refreshments, a program with an agenda, and information about the organization. Every activity requires planning, preparation, personalization, and attention to a myriad of details; makes good use of volunteers; and needs a bit of luck to be carried off without a hitch (see Appendix B for a master checklist). Attention to these details will make guests feel welcome and allow them to fully appreciate the activity. Invitation lists, an important detail, must be guided by the selection criteria. Anyone who is interested may be welcome at a public activity, but a number of others deserve to be invited as special guests, whether or not they can be present. Friend-raising begins with personal invitations that are designed to lead to involvement; involvement results in participation and can yield gift support.

How Can Activities Aid Annual Giving?

Donors are more inclined to make annual gifts to organizations they know something about. After an organization has invited people to be guests at several of its activities, it will know how they replied to each invitation and whether they attended. If they did attend and found the activity worthwhile, their willingness to consider financial support has multiplied. Activities communicate effectively to all those who participate. Because the guests are often people who live nearby, they can return again and again. To convert interested people into donors may require only asking them for a gift. All the annual giving methods presented in Chapters 2 through 6 can then be put to use. The request can be tied to the activities they have attended or have been invited to attend, with a few simple messages:

Tell them how these programs are linked to the mission of the organization;

Explain the programs and services in terms of what the organization has accomplished for others and its commitment to continue to do so;

Tell them how gift money is a way to achieve improvements in the volume and quality of programs and services delivered to the community;

Using as an example the type of activity they just attended, show how funds received can be used to repeat the activity, to improve on the quality of speakers, and to maintain the facilities used.

When personal invitations are involved, the mailing list becomes a reasonable prospect list for annual gift solicitation, *after* the activity. A bit of homework will reveal something about who is on the invitation list, and an appeal message matched to their interests can be prepared. It helps to remove from solicitation lists the names of those who are already donors—and the names of anyone who has asked *not* to be solicited. One to two weeks should pass between the activity and the gift appeal. Solicitation timing is always a delicate judgment call. The memory of the activity must still be fresh, but the activity should not appear to have been staged just to "set up" guests for a money touch! If the activity is successful in building a faithful following, the invitation list can become the heart of a new membership association. Common courtesy is the best guide; people who are treated well will respond with friendship and support for years to come.

How and Where Can Volunteers Help?

A variety of tasks and a multitude of details are involved in arranging and carrying out activities for the public. Most nonprofit organizations cannot afford to hire professional and support staff just to manage activities; employee positions are fully committed to providing programs and services. Employees who have their paid responsibilities, however, can be asked occasionally to volunteer some of their personal time to help their employer. Requests to employees to volunteer their time must be carefully limited, or the employees will feel they are being put upon. If they believe these tasks are within their job descriptions, they may correctly ask to be paid for these extra hours at an overtime rate; volunteerism should not be, legitimately, "extra work" for them. Volunteers who believe that their time, energy, talents, and contacts are of value must be entrusted with duties and responsibilities that require a high level of performance—actual leadership and direction of an activity, selection of other volunteers who will help, and delegation of specific duties to perform. Other volunteer tasks may be less demanding or may appear to be minor work projects; all must be identified as necessary for the event to be successful.

A committee system is recommended to provide some order and structure to any activity (Exhibit 7.4). A committee is a democratic system for planning, preparing, and conducting activities. People are quite comfortable with committee work; it is a normal experience. They also understand that working together as a team is how a committee functions best; committee members join together and share a sense of true responsibility for their overall performance. A committee system also helps a nonprofit organization to use its volunteers well. Activities allow volunteers to manage themselves toward accomplishing a valued assignment in support of "their" organization. The tasks volunteers may identify for themselves include all of the following:

1. Assist in planning the activity;
2. Assist in making all the arrangements;
3. Provide names for the invitation list;
4. Prepare and address the invitations;
5. Promote attendance in the community;
6. Contact the media and enlist their coverage;

7. Bring friends and colleagues to the activity;
8. Greet all guests on arrival;
9. Evaluate the results;
10. Assist in planning the next activity.

To succeed with volunteers in any assignment, a nonprofit organization has to be willing to entrust to them the work it asks them to perform. The organization is also entrusting them with its good name and reputation, which volunteers respect and will honor. Some volunteers come with a lot of experience in performing these assignments; these are primarily the people an organization seeks. Volunteers who are trained, motivated, and well-led will perform well. A nonprofit organization's professional staff provides guidance in identifying, recruiting, training, and managing volunteers who can lead and direct others. Working through a committee system, volunteers can plan and carry out a variety of activities with high success each year. The organization must identify the goals and objectives for each of the activities it will ask volunteers to conduct, and provide clearly stated policies and guidelines to be followed by everyone involved (see Exhibit 7.5). The board of directors, professional and administrative staff, and employees should appoint volunteers to their assignments, identify and often select those who will be chairpersons, ask for progress reports during the preparation stages, and require a critique report after the activity is concluded. Volunteers must understand that clear accountability is their obligation to the organization. In their working partnership, both parties must appreciate that close coordination, cooperation, and communication are required for success in working together.

How to Measure Success

Nonprofit organizations should set the standards of performance for all their activities. The board of directors should establish and clarify expectations for each activity to be carried out in the name of the organization. The criteria to be used for performance evaluation should be prepared and approved by the board, identified and expressed as specific goals to be achieved, and made known to those who will be evaluated. Unrealistic expectations neither encourage nor inspire volunteers. A balance must be struck and a consensus achieved in order for appropriate measurement criteria to be accepted.

Because activities are directed at people and intended to elicit their response in some way, measurement should focus on how the process performed as well as on the numerical results. Evaluations should never

---

New Activity, Benefit, or Special Event

---

1. Primary purpose(s), goals, and objectives
2. Availability of volunteers; number required
3. Identified volunteer leadership
4. Marketing and communications attributes
5. Community relations and community benefits attributes
6. Conflicts with known calendar of local functions
7. List of sponsor and underwriter prospects
8. Estimate of attendance and ticket sales revenue
9. Preliminary budget (revenue and direct costs)
10. Staff support required; prior staff experience
11. Potential for conflict with ongoing annual giving programs
12. Review and approval by board of directors

Approved and Existing Activity, Benefit, or Special Event

---

1. All of the above criteria *plus*
2. Critique report from previous function(s)
3. Final report on prior budget, net proceeds, and name of project funded with proceeds
4. Marketing and communications assessment
5. Community relations and community benefits assessment
6. Preliminary operating budget with estimate of net proceeds
7. Priority project for use of net proceeds identified
8. Potential for new leadership and volunteer development
9. Potential advantages to ongoing annual giving programs
10. Potential for volunteer and donor honors and recognition

Exhibit 7.5 Policies and Guidelines for Activities, Benefits, and Special Events

be punitive exercises. They are held after the fact; they are most valuable for future planning purposes and as learning experiences. Here are a few measures that can be used in performance analysis of an activity:

1. Were the goals and objectives clearly stated?
2. Were leadership candidates recruited early enough?
3. Were committee members trained to their tasks?
4. Was adequate staff and budget support provided to the committee?

5. Was there a communications channel between volunteers and the organization's leadership?
6. Was the date selected in conflict with other, similar activities in the community?
7. Were advertising and promotion communications adequate in relation to public response and attendance?
8. Were the names and addresses on the invitation list accurate?
9. Were the invitations mailed on schedule?
10. What percentage of invited guests attended?
11. Was a record made of attendance by the special guests who were invited?
12. Were the facilities adequate to support the speaker, the program, and the audience?
13. If media coverage was important, what results were achieved?
14. Were postactivity assignments completed as planned?
15. Did the committee hold a critique session after the activity?
16. Was the committee's critique report delivered to the board of directors?

Success can be measured in many ways. A complete list of appropriate evaluation criteria should be prepared in advance for every activity, to clarify for everyone involved the areas that have been identified as important goals.

BENEFITS

Benefits are best known for their popularity with volunteers, their high visibility, and the money they raise for charity—usually in that order. They share some of the primary objectives of activities: they communicate widely and they motivate people to respond with attendance. Benefits add monetary goals for worthy purposes. A money goal requires (1) considerably more attention to fund-raising techniques and (2) exact financial management of all expenses so that net proceeds can be delivered to the nonprofit organization. Marilyn Breutlinger and Judith Weiss [4] expressed their opinion of benefits this way:

> [T]he only way to determine the degree of success a benefit attains is to establish clearly defined financial and promotional goals in advance. If we have one message to convey, it's that benefits are indeed a business. Unless you approach them in a businesslike manner, your charitable intentions may go out

the window. Therefore, to further refine the definition of a benefit, our "special occasions" must also meet the following requirements:

1. *They make significant amounts of money.* Net profits (from ticket sales, contributions and other income, minus expenses) should be no less than $50,000 or 10 percent of the organization's annual fund-raising budget. An event that earns less than this is not worth the time, effort and expense of putting it on.

2. *They have a high ticket-price structure,* relative to the actual cost of food, entertainment and incidentals. These costs should be reduced by underwriting and by the donation of professional managerial and clerical services by volunteers.

3. *Tickets are presold*, through personal solicitation by committee members. Walk-ins or box-office sales are not anticipated, except for those benefits that offer a large number of "performance only" tickets at considerably lower price than the complete package.

4. *They are deliberately targeted to a well-defined market segment* that includes those individuals who can afford and are willing to pay a premium for an evening out in order to demonstrate a high level of support for a worthy cause.

5. *They promote community involvement and continuing support for the sponsoring organization,* not only through publicity surrounding the event, but through a planned campaign that includes follow-up contact with individuals introduced to the organization through the benefit.

6. *They are carefully planned and executed, right down to the last detail,* so that the event itself goes smoothly and nothing is left to chance. Those who attend have a satisfying experience, those who hear about it afterwards wish they had been there, and all concerned go away with a favorable impression of the sponsoring organization.

Careful planning is essential to selecting the kind of benefit that has just the right style to inspire contributions and attendance from the people who can afford to participate. Benefits have an inherent potential to expand as preparations progress, chiefly because of the energy and enthusiasm of the volunteers who become truly involved. Committee leaders must be alert to the effect new ideas can have on the overall plan, especially on the budget. Clear guidelines will help to keep everyone focused on the plan (see Exhibit 7.6). To be successful, benefits must appeal to some of the people all of the time. Benefits can be planned, prepared, conducted, and evaluated in weeks, months, or years, depending on their history, tradition, magnitude, and complexity, and on the availability of adequate numbers of trained and dedicated volunteers. Once a benefit is held, most organizations begin preparations for the next one, which is why benefits fit well in the overall program for annual giving.

No event should be undertaken without careful thought. Every angle should be considered. This is best done by a planning committee composed of dedicated individuals who understand the organization's needs and objectives.

1. Do no benefit that will net less than 50 percent of gross income.
2. Eighty percent of the tickets should be sold before the invitation goes out.
3. Do not expect the invitation to sell the benefit. Mailing to a list of people who know and like the organization will produce a response of about 2 percent. A mailing to people unfamiliar with the organization (a purchased list) probably will not produce enough income to pay for the mailing.
4. Plan to sell about five tickets for every volunteer who is actively selling tickets through personal solicitation.
5. The vast majority of people who will attend the benefit will come from the organization's family, so:
   a) Make sure the benefit is within the means of the majority of them.
   b) Make sure it will be of interest to most of them.
   c) Make sure it will take place at a location and a time that are convenient for them.
6. Do not mimic another organization's traditional benefit. A traditional benefit sells itself; the new benefit will not, and a comparison will make the new benefit appear to be a failure.
7. Never hire a promoter who charges a percentage of gross receipts as a fee to conduct a benefit.
8. Never ask a sponsor or underwriter to subsidize attendance (i.e., reduce the price of the benefit tickets because some expenses are being underwritten).
9. Never say something is tax-deductible if it is not. Seek the advice of a tax accountant or tax attorney on how to explain to purchasers of benefit tickets the IRS regulations that limit the charitable deduction amount to only a portion of the price of the benefit tickets.
10. Always prepare a detailed budget in advance, and stick to it. Do not guess what the expenses will be; ask for quotations on prices and hold vendors to them.
11. Make the benefit fun so that people will want to attend next year. To do so:
    a) Do not try to force people to spend more money than they expected.
    b) Do not belabor them with speeches about how great the organization is.
    c) Do tell them how great they are for participating actively.
    d) Do tell them how the proceeds will be used and what good works are expected.
12. Design the benefit to make friends first, then raise funds.
13. Do not decide unilaterally what the organization needs money for. Ask the organization about currently urgent needs, then raise funds for that priority.

Source: Adapted from "Guidelines for a New Special Event," by Frank R. Hall, St. Jude Medical Center, Fullerton, CA, with permission.

Exhibit 7.6 Thirteen Rules to Guarantee Success with Benefits

They should know that almost every fundraising event takes a lot of work, many transactions, and a lot of volunteer help. Since volunteers have a limited amount of time to spend on any organization, the goal is to maximize the dollar return per every volunteer hour expended. For example, if the need is for $10,000, it may be a better investment of time to ask ten prospects for $1,000 each than try to sell 400 dinner tickets at $25 each. [5]

Benefits are much more challenging to conduct than activities because of the financial obligation to produce a profit. More time and attention must be paid to the invitation and the invitation list, to the choice of facilities and their decoration, to having a program that entertains enjoyably, to the menu and beverages, and so on. (See Appendix B for a master checklist.) Activities are a function to be carried out; benefits are a performance to be staged. Employees may be asked to plan and stage a benefit alone, but complete success can be achieved only through volunteer leadership and participation. Benefits, more than either activities or special events, are public enterprises and attractions because their primary goal of raising money demands that they fulfill high public expectations.

Financial goals aid the participants in defining success, and in achieving a sense of reward and accomplishment at the termination of the event. Specific goals stimulate and challenge participants to stretch imagination and efforts beyond their intended limits. If the committee has invested themselves in the benefit effort,they will desire the esteem associated with a job well done, and will "get" or "give" the resources required to meet that goal. [6]

Benefits are also more of a business venture and require commercial decisions not usually needed for activities or special events. Benefits require negotiating for prices and contracts, recruiting in-kind gifts and donated services, seeking contributions of products to be used as prizes and auction items, sales effort to secure sponsorships, underwriting, and table sales, and astute expense management.

Certain costs are highly specialized. For example, you may want to take out liability insurance on an event to protect your organization from unavoidable accidents. Other costs often are not normally considered, but should be. For example, rarely will an organization identify costs of a regular employee's time. If a salaried staff person devotes half time for a 3-month period in planning an event, it is the unusual organization that earmarks this portion of the staff person's salary as an expense of the event. If this were done more frequently to reflect actual costs, many organizations probably would not undertake fund-raising events, because costs would appear to be excessive. [7]

Benefits are intense fiscal projects from start to finish. There is no room here for inappropriate fiscal management, inattentive accounting, or private inurement practices; to permit any of these is to encourage failure.

Benefits offer additional opportunities that can be shared with local area businesspeople, companies, partnerships, and firms. These expanded contacts, which build relationships that can aid other annual giving and major-gift fund-raising goals, are a result of the commercial nature of benefits. Company executives can be asked to serve as volunteer leaders on the benefit planning committee. The businesses, corporations, and firms receive *quid pro quo* exchanges from advertising, marketing, public relations, promotions, plus the civic and community-relations visibility that corporate sponsorship and underwriting gifts can deliver in exchange. When business and corporate leaders are involved, expectations for professional management of benefits are higher because company names and the names of their executives are going to be widely broadcast. These features are all on the plus side. To examine the potential negatives, only a look at the law is required.

Laws, Regulations, Licenses, and Permits

Because soliciting money from the public is a part of every benefit, every such function must observe local ordinances. Legal requirements vary among the several states, counties, and cities, and time and patience are needed to search them out. Most authorities require the sponsoring organization to file an application in advance of conducting the benefit. A permit is issued after providing certain details about the planned benefit and paying a filing fee ($25 to $50 for each benefit). Some jurisdictions may add specific requirements for traffic control and police security, site inspection and approval by the fire marshal, and on-site paramedics. If alcohol is to be served or sold, a one-day liquor license may be required from the local Alcohol and Beverage Control authority. If the benefit will involve any form of sweepstakes, lottery, or other game of chance, or will be a Las Vegas or Monte Carlo night, several authorities may specify operating procedures. They will have a keen interest in fiscal control procedures in particular. A complete financial statement showing all income and expenses will need to be filed following the benefit. A tax may be assessed on a percentage of the net proceeds.

The federal government becomes an invited guest at every benefit because a charitable contribution deduction may be allowed for a portion of the price of the ticket. The nonprofit organization is responsible to inform donors *on the invitation* what amount of the ticket price is deductible (the rest cannot be claimed as a tax deduction) [8]. This deduction figure is the difference between the amount of "material value" received by the donor who attends the event (cost of food, beverages, and favors such as taking home the floral centerpiece) and the price of the ticket. Federal tax rules on deductions for auctions are clear: No deduction is allowed except where the value of the auction item is exceeded by the bid price. No tax deduction is allowed for raffle tickets and door prizes.

Another area of increased legal sensitivity is the use of professional (also called paid or commercial) solicitors who can be hired to conduct fund-raising benefits. Several court cases have resulted when state authorities pursued fraudulent and deceitful solicitors whose operating method was to conduct benefits in the name of a nonprofit organization. These solicitors often propose to make all of the arrangements for a benefit—sell the tickets, book the talent, sell the advertisements, print the program book, handle all the money, pay all the bills (including their fee for marketing, promotional, and professional services)— and deliver a check for the net proceeds to the organization. There are several problems with such a proposal; chief among them is the amount of the net proceeds, which is usually less than 20 percent of gross revenue [9]. More than a few nonprofit organizations have experienced benefits conducted as illegal enterprises or scams. The public is increasingly suspicious of high-pressure sales techniques (telephone "boiler rooms" for ticket sales with "runners" to collect the money). This kind of benefit activity hinders all the efforts of sponsors of legitimate benefits. Their volunteers may use the phone to encourage public participation, only to be met by suspicion. Several states and local jurisdictions have well-defined regulations just for this narrow area of fund-raising practice: They require annual registration of any organization, business, firm, or private contractor who engages in professional, "paid," or commercial solicitation of the public. A registration fee, posting of a bond, and a copy of each contract for service to a nonprofit organization will be required before a "paid" solicitor may begin to practice. The contract, signed by an officer of the nonprofit organization, must disclose details about the benefit, such as how the solicitor will be paid (straight fee, a commission for each sale, or a percentage of net proceeds). The contract must also specify where the money will be received and deposited, who has approval authority for expenses, and who can sign checks. A complete financial statement must be filed within 30 days after the benefit, and all these details must be made public upon request. Behind such extensive regulations are abusive practices by entrepreneurs who trade on the public's confidence and trust in charitable giving. To be fair, a number of legal and legitimate professional fund-raising firms and solicitors provide complete services to stage a benefit. However, suspicions about their trustworthiness persist because of others' illicit practices.

The board of directors has the responsibility to be certain that every legal and regulatory requirement associated with benefit fund-raising is fully and completely observed. Much is at risk, beginning with public confidence and trust in the name of the organization. No board member, volunteer, donor, or staff member wants to read in the morning paper or see on television that a lawsuit has been filed against the nonprofit organization or against the firm hired to conduct a fund-raising benefit. The media appear to have a high interest in reporting scandal and abuse, and will put special focus on the fees paid to solicitors whose purposes appear to be more directed at attempting to defraud the public of its money than at raising money for charitable purposes. If illegal acts are proven in a court case, the subsequent legal action could result in the loss of the nonprofit organization's tax-exempt status. The public loses, the charity loses, and a valid fund-raising method loses; only the paid solicitor wins. As a general rule, when looking this gift horse in the mouth, one should examine every tooth!

What Details Are Required for Success?

Strict financial management that will produce the highest net proceeds possible for charity is essential. If a benefit does not possess the ability to yield *at least* 50 percent of its gross revenue after direct costs to the nonprofit organization, it should be challenged to prove it can do so or be discarded. Each new benefit should not be held immediately accountable to this level of success; a minimum of three years should be adequate to achieve this goal. The 50 percent standard requires that budget be prepared, approved, and used to manage the benefit (see Exhibit 7.7). The budget will help keep everyone's attention on the primary objective. This fiscal requirement also helps to achieve a clear understanding that each benefit should be able to document its potential to achieve the 50 percent level of performance after three years. If it cannot, it should be set aside for another benefit that can deliver at that level.

An organization's officers should pay close attention to benefits sponsored by other organizations in the community and to those sponsored by outsiders to benefit other organizations. Many civic, community, and service organizations that conduct benefits for charitable purposes are committed to civic improvements that will help to meet community needs and are led by responsible community residents, but there are others that are in business for themselves. (See Exhibit 7.8 for professional guidance [10] on how to work with outside organizations in sponsorship

	Approved Budget	Actual Costs
A. Projected Cash Receipts (Revenue)		
Ticket sales	$	$
Sponsor gifts		
Underwriter gifts		
Auction receipts		
Raffle receipts		
Other revenue		
Contributors		
Donated materials (gifts-in-kind)	<____>	<____>
Subtotal	$	$
B. Projected Cash Expenses (Costs)		
Cash expenditures (itemized list):		
Printing	$	$
Postage		
Facility fees		
Food and beverages		
Decorations		
Flowers		
Favors		
Entertainment		
Miscellaneous		
Auction/Raffle prizes purchased		
Temporary staff hired		
Consultant fees		
Subtotal	$	$
C. Projected Net Proceeds (A minus B)	$	$
D. Percent Proceeds	____%	____%

Guidelines and Instructions

The Budget Worksheet is designed to assist benefit committees in achieving *successful fiscal management*, which is defined as achieving net income for a benefit equal to at least 50 percent of the gross proceeds for the benefit, after excluding contributions and donated materials, in-kind gifts, and so on, from gross income.

Definition of Terms

Benefit budget   An estimate of all planned income and expense categories, prepared and submitted for approval by the board of directors, to represent projected income and expenses required for the benefit to function successfully.

Exhibit 7.7   Benefit Event Budget Worksheet

Definition of Terms

Cash receipts	Direct income from ticket sales plus donations from those unable to attend.
Sponsors and underwriters	Donors who make a special-level gift and qualify for visibility in the official program, on the invitations, at the benefit site, and so on. The benefit committee sets the levels (there can be several), and this revenue counts in the 50 percent test.
Auction receipts	Auction revenues shall be reported in the amount of actual receipts at the auction. The purchase of auction prizes is not recommended.
Raffle receipts	Tickets purchased for raffle sales shall be reported as raffle revenue. If raffle prizes were purchased (which is not recommended), these costs shall be treated as expenses. Donated prizes shall be treated as donated (gifts-in-kind) materials.
Contributors	Donors who "purchase" an item on the expense budget as their special contribution, either with cash or an in-kind gift. The value does *not* count as gross revenue.
Cash expenses	Items bought or directly paid for out of the benefit expense budget, in direct support of the benefit.
Temporary staff	Benefit chairpersons and committees may require direct staff support that exceeds the time available from employees to support the benefit. The decision to hire temporary staff will be considered by the board and development officer. If approved, staff will be hired by the development officer and all expenses for their employment will be added to the benefit budget as an expense.
Consultants	If professional experts should be required to supplement volunteer and staff talents in order to succeed with a benefit, the hiring of any consultant shall be with prior approval of the board and the development officer, and shall be engaged in a written agreement (fee payment basis only), with all costs added to the benefit budget as an expense.
Miscellaneous costs	Staff time (salary, benefits, and so on) and other expenses incurred by the organization in support of benefits are considered "indirect costs" and are not billed against benefit budgets. These hours and costs will be applied to the annual productivity analysis of all activities, benefits, and special events.

Exhibit 7.7   *(Continued)*

Participants in joint-venture marketing should include the following elements in their campaigns if they wish to ensure the charitable organization's compliance with the voluntary CBBB Standards calling for charities (1) to establish and exercise controls over fund-raising activities conducted for their benefit and (2) to include certain information in solicitations made in conjunction with the sale of goods or services:

1. A written agreement that gives (a) the corporation formal permission to use the charity's name and logo and (b) the charity prior review and approval of all joint-venture solicitations that use the charity's name, and

2. Joint-venture advertisements that specify (a) the portion of the product or service price or the fixed amount per sale/transaction to benefit the charity and, if applicable, the maximum amount the charity will receive, and (b) the full name of the charity, (c) an address or phone number to contact for additional information about the charity or the campaign, and (d) the term of the campaign.

The additional suggestions listed below are not required to meet the CBBB Standards. However, in the interest of full disclosure and public accountability, PAS [Philanthropic Advisory Service] recommends that corporations consider the following questions:

- Some states now have specific guidelines for sales made in conjunction with charities. Does the promotion follow these suggestions?
- Does the written agreement: (a) indicate how long the campaign will last, (b) specify how and when charitable funds will be distributed, and (c) explain any steps that will be taken in case of a disagreement or unforeseen result with the promotion?
- Does the corporation have financial controls in place to process and record the monies received to benefit the charity?
- Will the corporation issue a financial report at the end of the campaign (or annually, if the campaign lasts more than a year), which identifies: (a) the total amount collected for the charity, (b) any campaign expenses, and (c) how much the charity received?

Exhibit 7.8   Council of Better Business Bureaus (CBBB) Guidelines for Sponsorship Involving Charities and Companies [10]. Reprinted with permission.

arrangements.) Some of these service organizations plan only to stage promotions at their place of business and to attract a crowd who will buy their products. A percentage of sales is advertised to be assigned to the nonprofit organization, which has agreed to use of its name in the promotion. These "cause related marketing" efforts have raised money for a few nonprofit organizations, but their purposes are neither charity nor relationship-building. They yield only increased sales for the business.

Commercially sponsored benefits depend on the public's confidence and trust that some of the money will go to charity; a typical promotion offers 5 to 10 percent of all sales. Because these benefits are conducted outside the management control of the nonprofit organization, accounting for all the money exchanged is difficult. The preferred method for managing a benefit is to organize it in-house and invite volunteers to help with achieving a 50 percent profit margin [11].

With agreement and acceptance of the financial objectives, the details required for success are now quite clearly stated. The names of suspects and prospects for sponsorship and underwriting gifts are the first priority, as are candidates for in-kind gifts and donated services. The invitation list must include current and past donors and candidates for contributions, especially those who seem capable of strong support of the nonprofit organization. Attention to detailed planning and management of the benefit will achieve a balance between appealing to those invited at a reasonable expense and being sure that everyone has a good time at the party.

How Can Benefits Aid Annual Giving?

Successful benefits add revenue to meet annual operating needs. They also draw attention to nonprofit organizations because of their high visibility. Benefits can help to promote the same priority of needs for which other annual giving appeals are soliciting public support. No single solicitation program is likely to produce all the funds needed each year. Prospects for other annual giving programs, if they live nearby, can be invited to attend benefits; a portion of their ticket price becomes an annual gift to the organization, and this amount may be a larger gift than the organization would have received in response to a direct mail letter or a membership invitation. Corporations that are frequent prospects for other areas of annual giving will be prime candidates for sponsorship, underwriting, table sales, and "in-kind" gifts to benefits. Current and prior-year annual donors should also be invited to benefits. Many donors are likely to attend because they are already aware of the organization and have begun to invest their money in its current needs and future plans. A few may object to another solicitation, but when everyone is being invited to the party, they cannot be left off the invitation list. This "extra" solicitation only asks them to attend a social or sporting occasion that they might enjoy and that helps to support the organization; they do not have to attend. Current and past major-gift donors should be invited and treated as special guests; a portion of the program might be set aside to honor and recognize their exceptional support. This highlight will send an important message to everyone present: "To those who are able to do more for us, we are pleased to give recognition and reward before their friends, neighbors, colleagues, and peers." The *brief* official program should not be expanded with a detailed "message" of why the benefit was held and the good uses intended for the money raised. This message should be transmitted in press releases and media coverage. The media should be encouraged to report on (and photograph) the party, the names of those who attended, what they were wearing, and the cause they were supporting.

How and Where Can Volunteers Help?

A benefit is one of the most popular forms of volunteerism available to nonprofit organizations. A benefit realizes the most intensive and extensive use of volunteers among all the annual giving fund-raising methods available today. Volunteers can do it all for a benefit, start to finish (see Exhibit 7.9). To the extent that they can and do plan and

---

Anniversary of founding
Art show/Exhibition
Auction (live and silent)
Bake sale
Ball/Banquet/Cotillion/Dinner dance/Gala
Bingo
Breakfast/Luncheon/Dinner
Car-wash
Concert
Contest
Fashion show
House party
"Kick-off"
Las Vegas/Monte Carlo night
Opening night/Premier
Picnic
Race/Run/Walk
Raffle
Rally
Roast
Sporting event
Testimonial
Tournament
Travel tour
"Victory celebration"

Exhibit 7.9   Selected Fund-Raising Benefits That Need Volunteers

execute successful (profitable) benefits year after year, volunteers' willingness is of enormous value. Nonprofit organizations are not expert in staging social or sporting functions; in contrast, most volunteers began and have developed their community service career through benefits. They bring strong views based on their experience working with other organizations. They choose to support organizations that have the capability to assist them in these duties; no one wants to run the risk of being associated with a failed benefit.

A committee of volunteers supported by professional staff is the recommended method for managing and conducting benefits. All of the details required can be organized around subcommittees, and the work can be delegated for performance according to a master schedule (see Exhibit 7.3). To succeed with benefits year after year, the nonprofit organization must provide volunteers with adequately trained and experienced professional and support staff and a reasonable budget. It should also provide policy guidance and direction on the functions preferred and the results desired. A benefit committee is a marvelous vehicle for the identification, recruitment, and training of volunteers for all the duties and assignments that make a benefit successful—organization and planning, teamwork, attention to detail, list building and friend-raising, corporate and major-gift solicitation, fiscal responsibility, marketing and promotion, honors and recognition, and attention to other details. Benefit committees are also exemplary training grounds for leadership at all levels. Hard-working volunteers one year should be asked to take charge of another area the next year. Volunteers need to know they can work their way up to the chairperson role. Some may prefer just to be involved and to help make the benefit a success; others will want to take on more responsibility. Both groups of volunteers are essential, and both need to be recognized and rewarded.

There may be circumstances where access to volunteers, especially those with prior experience and training, is limited. New nonprofit organizations require a year or two of operation to build a reputation for validity and successful management that will attract friends and donors. Some history is also required before the new organization can expect to marshal enough volunteers to support activities, benefits, and special events. The organization's current and future management plans must be defined well enough to be able to hire professional fund-raising staff (either as consultants or as employees) during these early years. No matter how honest their assessment, the leaders of every nonprofit organization should be aware that a conclusion that "We can do it alone" can be a trap leading to poor decisions. Fund-raising is not only an expertise in holding benefits that produce money. Each of the other methods and techniques of annual giving described in Chapters Two through Six possesses greater efficiency and effectiveness at raising money than do benefits. Benefits *add to* the annual giving program; they are not a substitute for mailings, memberships, and volunteer-led groups that contribute to the primary objectives of friend-raising and relationship-building for a new organization.

> Small, new organizations may complain that they cannot raise money without hiring outside help in the form of a professional solicitor who is not a fund-raising executive or a professional consultant. One of the primary responsibilities of every board member in any nonprofit organization is to initiate professional fiscal methods and controls. Hiring out this responsibility is a mistake and a lapse in stewardship.
>
> Special and benefit events, like every other method of fund-raising, take time and expertise. There are no easy dollars or quick fixes. Poorly run events will not build a quality reputation for an organization nor will they motivate a cadre of committed volunteers and donors to return for another event next year. [12]

The ability of the community to support annual giving programs by nonprofit organizations in the future may well depend on the cooperation between community residents who are willing to volunteer their time and talent and nonprofit organizations that can provide the means to utilize the volunteers' commitment well. Benefits and committee work offer multiple ways to accomplish all these objectives, especially if the organization remembers to recognize and reward those who freely give so much of their time to serve.

How Is Success Measured?

Because one of the primary areas of emphasis for benefits is their financial success, several measurements can be made of their monetary performance. The board of directors should set up fiscal signposts, such as the need to achieve 50 percent net proceeds within three years of operation. The board also needs to define a firm policy on the use of the official name of the organization for any benefit purpose, internal or external. Performance measurement is not intended for punitive reasons; it distinguishes the factors that led to success from those that did not. Measures that can be applied to benefits include the following, all of which can be compared with prior year(s) performance:

1. Was the budget prepared in advance and approved?
2. Was recruitment of sponsors and underwriter gifts successful?
3. What percentage of total revenue did sponsors and underwriters represent?

4. Were the materials used in sponsor and underwriting sales valuable to volunteers making these solicitations?

5. Were the sponsors and underwriters satisfied with the visibility their higher gifts promised?

6. What was the number and estimated value of in-kind donations and auction or raffle prizes received?

7. What was the amount of auction (live and silent) and raffle income?

8. Were the invitations mailed on schedule?

9. What percentage of those invited purchased tickets and attended?

10. What percentage of those invited did not attend but made a gift to the organization anyway?

11. What was their average gift size?

12. Were acknowledgment letters sent to all who purchased tickets and did they specify the income tax contribution deduction value?

13. How many guests did those invited bring with them?

14. How many tables were sold?

15. Who were the people who sat at the sold tables? Were the names of all these guests recorded?

16. Were all bills for services paid quickly? Were expense levels according to budget?

17. What were the unexpected costs?

18. What were total net proceeds and their percentage of gross revenue?

19. Was the net proceeds check delivered to the nonprofit organization?

20. Was the critique report delivered to the nonprofit organization?

Many other areas of performance measurement should be studied to understand the success of each benefit. Those listed above focus on items related to fiscal performance. Every detail of the benefit should be reviewed to learn from the experience and to recommend improvements for the future. Benefit evaluations should also try to learn how the guests enjoyed the affair. Benefits are a form of market research to survey fundraising attitudes in the community. If sponsorship, underwriting, in-kind gifts, donated services, table gifts, or individual ticket sales declined from prior years, the cause of such losses must be learned. The committee and staff should analyze every factor in an attempt to understand this change in response. The economy may be in recession, but this excuse is too easy. More serious issues may be a lack of proper training for solicitors, late delivery of invitations, no telephone follow-up to personally encourage those who attended in prior years, no media coverage, rising prices, poor financial controls, or inadequate staff and budget support from the nonprofit organization. All of these will affect overall performance and should be understood. Other less quantitative areas to measure for success include the extent to which invitations, media coverage, and the messages about the nonprofit organization and its needs were communicated through this benefit. Each invitation to an activity, benefit, or special event is another means of communication to the community and should add to the fund-raising ability of other requests for gifts during the year. Was there good coordination with the other annual giving programs regarding the invitation and sponsor lists? Was there any follow-up to the benefit by another annual giving area; for example, were membership applications mailed to nonmembers who were attending? Is there any evidence that the benefit siphoned off important gifts from other annual giving programs? How well did the advertising, promotion, and media relations plan work to communicate the priority needs these funds will support? What effect will these efforts have on the next request to the media for their attention and coverage? These questions about the value of benefits are worth exploring in depth. A great effort was required to produce the benefit, and it is important to measure as many of its attributes as possible. Only with a full understanding of the potential of benefits to communicate needs and establish warm feelings can they achieve their full potential to assist the other annual giving programs.

SPECIAL EVENTS

Most special events are conducted for an official business or ceremonial purpose. This purpose may be their primary objective, but the special events can be quite flexible in their design and useful to the overall annual giving program. The most common example of a special event is the annual meeting. Nonprofit organizations are required in their bylaws to conduct, each year, a meeting at which they elect the board of directors, amend the bylaws (if needed), and conduct such other business as may come before the organization. This agenda of necessary business usually does not require much time, but the program is deadly dull for the public. The remedy is usually a dual-purpose program plan. The annual business meeting is held first and, after adjournment, the board of directors invites the public to join in an expanded annual event. This affair often emerges as a social occasion (luncheon or dinner) to which spouses and several groups of guests are invited. In a brief program planned for this segment, the board of directors, chief executive officer, and others may present their annual reports. The accomplishments reported should inspire confidence and instill enthusiasm for continuing these good works. The program part of the annual meeting is also the perfect occasion to honor retiring board members and introduce newly elected ones, and to recognize donors and volunteers. Annual meetings are anniversary celebrations, and extra features can be added at five- and ten-year milestones of the organization's history.

Convocations, dedications, ground-breaking ceremonies, employee picnics, planning retreats, and certain public presentations are other examples of special events. These special occasions in the life of an organization offer the opportunity to celebrate accomplishments; to thank volunteers, donors, and employees for their services; and to announce the beginning of major new initiatives. Invitations to attend these events are often extended, even though they are convened so that the public may join in the festivities. Dedications and ground-breaking ceremonies are public events because they represent major accomplishments in the life of an organization that were made possible with public support. Convocations and retreats have an additional purpose: to bring decision makers and members together to achieve consensus on major issues and future plans. Special events may also be used to inaugurate a new board chairman or chief executive officer; military organizations conduct change-of-command ceremonies to formalize such transitions. Religious organizations, colleges, and universities possess long traditions of special events celebrated through public ceremonies, such as religious holidays, charter days, and graduation exercises. Most of these ceremonies reflect decades-old, or even centuries-old traditions of pomp and circumstance that are reenacted and observed. Whatever their primary purposes, special events are superior opportunities to invite wide public participation that will further the objectives of annual giving programs.

What Details Are Required for Success?

The first decision is whether a special event is required or optional. If required, what demands must it accomplish? If optional, what purposes and extra attributes does the organization wish to accomplish? In either case, the special event becomes an opportunity. With the primary purpose clarified, the next group of decisions relates to date, time, place, featured speakers, size of the invitation list, other agenda items that can be accomplished, and estimated cost. These details and the process to accomplish them are the same as for activities and benefits, and will not be

repeated here. (See Appendix B for a master checklist.) Often, a committee of employees is formed and charged with planning all of the event's
details. However, when a volunteer advisory committee is appointed instead, the nonprofit organization can profit from the volunteers' experience in staging successful public affairs. Most special events are not
designed to serve as fund-raising benefits, although close attention to
budget planning and financial controls is certainly appropriate. Some
special events may lend themselves to sponsorship and underwriting as
well as in-kind gifts and donated services, but they may then compete
with other appeals to the same donors for funds needed to support
scheduled benefits.

One area of detail that always deserves special attention is the invitation list. Friend-raising and relationship-building continue to be the
list's prime directives. Because special events are more open to public
participation (especially where no admission fees are required), the
regular invitation list may need to be expanded. Many segments of the
community, including employees, are not regularly invited to many of
the activities and benefits that an organization may sponsor for a fee
during the year. A special event is an opportunity to balance their access to the nonprofit organization's official functions. Invitation lists
for special events must be attuned to political issues and to a wide selection of elected officials, many of whom are accommodated at other
public activities and benefits as well. Compiling invitation lists and
maintaining them accurately to support all of the organization's activities, benefits, and special events is a major responsibility. This duty can
be assigned to the fund development office because of its ongoing attention to the maintenance of other lists of volunteers, donors, and
prospects. When this department keeps the master mailing list, all of
these resources for friend-raising and relationship-building purposes
can be used throughout the year.

Despite all the careful planning and preparation, something can be
expected to go wrong. The wine may have been ordered weeks before
but, just days before the event, the vendor calls to say that the supplier
has delivered a different wine. The invitations are delivered late, which
leads to late mailing and reduced attendance. These mistakes are comparatively easy to live with; few people will even know they were made.
Other things that can go wrong are true disasters. The speaker fails to
arrive, the electricity (lights, air conditioning, and PA system) goes off,
and (worst of all for outdoor events), it rains all day! In the events business, being prepared will avoid preventable errors and mistakes, but
natural disasters and "acts of God" require back-up plans. Grasty and
Sheinkopf [13] compiled this list of ruin-preventing suggestions for
special events:

- Proper insurance
- Receipts
- Cash boxes with cash in proper denominations for each box
- Emergency numbers for police and fire
- First-aid kit
- Pens, tape, poster board, and markers
- All phone numbers for key participants, including band, speakers, master of ceremonies
- Fire extinguisher
- Enough bags, if you are selling something
- Sound system that works
- Runners for emergencies and all things forgotten.

How Can Special Events Aid Annual Giving?

Any occasion in which suspects, prospects, donors, and volunteers can be involved as active participants is a positive opportunity for one or more of the traditional annual giving programs. It is essential to be able to invite people to respond to an organization in other ways besides donations—perhaps to answer a call for advocacy, attendance, giving, or volunteerism. Special events are valuable in much the same way as activities: they communicate information and raise awareness of the mission and purposes of the organization; they offer a balance for the fund-raising invitations extended to the public. The more opportunities offered to the public to be active participants, the better. Activity leads to information, which leads to education, which leads to commitment. The annual giving continuum moves on.

How and Where Can Volunteers Help?

The use of volunteers in support of special events may be limited where these functions are organized and carried out by the nonprofit organization itself. Several special events (convocations, dedications, and ground-breaking ceremonies) are highly appropriate for joint committees with volunteers, particularly where volunteers have been involved in the project that is being celebrated. Ground-breaking and dedication ceremonies tied to fund-raising campaigns are special events for which both donors and volunteers should be asked to assist in the planning and preparation. Voluntary advisory committees are valuable to other types of special events as well. A good rule of thumb is: Whenever the public will be invited to participate in a function, it is wise to call on the organization's friends in the community to assist in planning for the public's active participation.

How to Measure Success

Because most special events do not have any direct financial objectives, performance evaluation should be focused on the areas where qualitative analysis will be useful. How did the mailing list, invitations, and reservation system work? What improvements can be suggested? Annual business meetings usually need remedies for their length, a lack of sparkle or humor, and failure to inspire people with their message. Retreats and convocations should be measured on their ability to conclude with a plan of action that is an agreed-on vision, for both the coming operating year and the next three to five years. Dedications and ground-breaking events should be measured on how well they serve to honor and thank all those volunteers, donors, and staff who contributed to their accomplishment. Public ceremonies also should be measured on how they acknowledge the accomplishments of others and how well they confer rites of passage on those around whom the event was centered. Other approaches to qualitative evaluation might include:

1. Were the support arrangements well prepared and conducted on time?
2. Were accommodations for guests (parking, access, greetings, seating, public address system, refreshments, bathrooms, exiting, and so on) suitable and did they perform satisfactorily?
3. Were accommodations for speakers suitable? Was each speaker adequately prepared regarding his or her role in the special event?
4. Did the planning committee include enough people for all the detailed tasks required?
5. Did other employees cooperate with the extra demands the special event placed on them?
6. Were media objectives attained and was the coverage evaluated?
7. Were the ceremonies filmed and were the comments of featured participants recorded for use in the future?
8. Did the committee complete its tasks within budget?
9. Did the committee conduct its critique and evaluation?
10. Was the critique report submitted to the board of directors?

One important area that is difficult to measure is the level of interest (or tolerance) of the public for all of the activities, benefits, and special events offered each year. Attendance and participation are valid measurement criteria of response, but more information may be needed for assessment in the future. Everyone invited is not expected to attend everything, but when these functions are prepared in the belief that they offer value to those who participate, it is important to learn the public's opinion on the outcome. During times of economic stress, the price to attend any activity may need to be lowered, so that as many people as possible may still attend. At times, board members and staff grow weary of the burden of being required to participate in everything. They may raise critical questions about the need for special events, especially those that are not well-managed and well-executed. The board is correct to question the value and worth of every activity, benefit, and special event held, and should be reading the critique reports submitted after each affair. Performance measurement is designed to document the number of attributes attained as well as the problems encountered. If special events are not contributing to the mission of the organization and cannot be kept fresh and exciting to the public, they may be discontinued.

MANAGEMENT AND PERFORMANCE MEASUREMENT

Knowledge, experience, and skill are required to manage activities, benefits, and special events. Professional and support staff in marketing, public relations, fund development, and other offices cannot achieve maximum results working alone; there is a need for volunteers to assist in preparing public functions. Performance measurement is a valid method of evaluating each activity, benefit, and special event; each should be able to demonstrate its effectiveness and efficiency in achieving its own goals and objectives and in contributing several attributes of benefit to its nonprofit organization. Functions that involve fund-raising should be able to demonstrate their cost-effectiveness in their delivery of profits as net proceeds for charitable purposes. Final judgment turns on this question: Does everyone want to do it again? Several areas of management and performance measurement have been examined in this chapter. This final section assesses the factors that contribute to the success of activities, benefits, and special events.

Nonprofit organizations should set goals for their use of activities, benefits, and special events. They should also support adequately any occasions that will serve their purposes. Budget and staff resources are required if activities, benefits, and special events are to be successful, but these resources will be limited. Because restraint is necessary, decisions on which functions to approve, and at what financial levels, must be based on how they demonstrate their potential to assist the organization in achieving its mission, purposes, goals, and objectives. To do so, they must be able to meet performance standards set by the board of directors. The board, the source of the organization's goals and objectives, should define goals and objectives for each activity, benefit, or special event it approves. The board should also establish the standards of performance against which each function will be measured. The plans proposed for each activity, benefit, or special event, repeated or new, must begin with a statement of goals and objectives (see Exhibit 7.10) and be accompanied by a preliminary budget (see Exhibit 7.7). To evaluate actual performance, the board must receive and read a post-function critique report that includes recommendations from those closest to the function—its volunteers and participants. Among the areas of emphasis for evaluation are:

1. Progress in volunteer recruitment and training;
2. Progress in leadership development;
3. Success in prospect and donor identification;
4. Financial performance against the approved budget;
5. Benefit net proceeds of at least 50 percent of gross revenue.

Planners of activities, benefits, and special events should analyze in their postmortem the potential for burn-out among volunteers and staff if aging activities, benefits, and special events are repeated too often. It is not easy to remove a function and it certainly should not be done without adequate documentation. Each public affair will have its proponents and faithful followers whose goals and analysis of their achievement may differ from the more objective view of the board of directors. Performance evaluations and critique reports document how and why each function is successful and reveal where others need to be fixed. Steps to revise or freshen those that can become more successful should be given active consideration and, if viable, be allowed to be implemented once more and given the support needed to achieve the newly projected potential for success. If performance does not improve sufficiently, there is documented reason to retire the event. Keeping a public event on the calendar for sentimental reasons may be its worst sentence. If it must be retired, it is best to let it go. Another function should not be allowed to take its place on the calendar *unless* it can demonstrate the potential to attract a wider public audience, achieve more attributes that benefit the organization, *and* deliver increased financial support to meet priority needs. If any function cannot achieve

Name of Activity/Benefit/Special Event: _____

_____

Current Chairperson/Vice Chairs: _____

_____

Proposed Next Chairperson/Vice Chairs: _____

_____

A. Description of Activity/Benefit/Special Event:

B. Primary Purposes/Goals/Objectives of the Function:

C. Proposed Date and Schedule for Planning, Preparation, and
Implementation:

D. Estimate of Volunteers and Staff Required:

E. Estimated Budget Worksheet (Attached):

Exhibit 7.10   Sample Proposal Form for Goals and Objectives for Volunteer-Led Activity, Benefit, or Special Event Committee

all three of these critical criteria, there is no good reason to offer it to the public in the name of the organization.

Conducting performance measurement can be as easy as counting the number of people attending. Evaluating how many (and who) were there is evidence of the public's confidence that the organization will conduct satisfactory functions. Raising friends and building relationships can be traced through public participation in every annual giving program offered. Gathering the direct opinions of this same public is essential and easy: people just need to be asked what they think. Gathering opinions from guests, which is well worth the nominal time and expense involved, can begin with placing addressed postage-paid evaluation post cards in their seats or distributing them randomly in the crowd. The assessment of the public's reaction needs to separate their enjoyment of the affair from the committee's ability to manage the benefit so that it passes the 50 percent test. If a benefit does not have strong public support (comparing prior-year attendance figures will yield the answer), it is consuming precious resources that other annual giving programs can use to increase their profitability and their achievement of other measurable attributes. Volunteers' opinions are valuable, but their enthusiasm has been known to cloud their judgment. If they are tired, lack enthusiasm for a function, and do not come back to help next year, there must be a method to hear that message. It is just as important to achieve volunteer satisfaction as it is to realize a successful event. No activity, benefit, or special event is worth keeping at the risk of losing the enthusiastic commitment of volunteers.

Activities, benefits, and special events can prove their value in many quantitative and qualitative performance areas. More than 65 specific criteria have been listed in this chapter. These public functions have the ability to cement positive relationships with people (volunteers and donors) and to stimulate those who support the organization to do so again and again. That's why nonprofit organizations hold public-participation functions! Tracking the performance of each annual giving method over many years will chart its progress in providing the additional attributes the organization needs, beyond friend-raising, relationship building, and financial support. A combination of well-defined plans, carefully defined attributes, and realistic goals and objectives can supply quite satisfactory tools for monitoring progress and demonstrating effectiveness, efficiency, and profitability.

As first outlined in Chapter One, the prime directive for the entire annual giving program is raising friends and building relationships and then raising money for annual operating needs. Activities, benefits, and special events have the potential to contribute to this directive. Direct mail was advocated in the acquisition and renewal of new, first-time donors in Chapters Two through Four. Invitations to activities, benefits, and special events can enhance the responsiveness of these new friends and donors. The membership associations discussed in Chapter Five used activities, benefits, and special events to maintain members' interest and enthusiasm, which aided membership renewal gifts. The auxiliaries, guilds, donor clubs, and support groups described in Chapter Six could serve as active sponsors and provide the volunteers needed to conduct activities, benefits, and special events. Opportunities for personal participation add to these volunteers' self-worth and enthusiasm and encourage their active support. Every annual giving program can be made more successful through a wise and balanced use of activities, benefits, and special events. The conclusion is overwhelming: Activities, benefits, and special events are among the most effective means for nonprofit organizations to make friends, build relationships, invite participation, deliver information, achieve involvement, and realize commitment and loyalty from the public. With meticulous management, they can make money too.

FOCUS: CCUA Clean Up Cleveland Chapter

Following the board's approval in late January of a plan to combine the first annual meeting and the first benefit event into a "Gala Benefit Evening," Karen Anderson began planning the balance of the chapter's spring fundraising activities. The resident mailing list for Cleveland and six of its suburbs has continued to respond well and will be used again for a two-part letter that includes a final offer for charter membership in The Circle of Champions. Anderson has also made a list of previous donors who did not renew their prior gift before December 31. She knows that she has to make an extra effort to encourage these important donors to renew their first gifts to the Clean Up Cleveland Chapter; their next gift decision will be critical to their willingness to continue their support for several years afterward. She makes plans to invite some active donors to become volunteer solicitors who will make telephone calls to as many of these nonrenewed donors as possible; personal contact is most important at this point.

Solicitation messages this spring will highlight the combined first annual meeting/gala benefit evening, to help spur results and ticket sales. Anderson plans to close out the charter membership feature after these spring appeals; this introductory offer has been in place for a full year. She also adds a proposal for a "discount plan"—a "special sale" offer of two complimentary tickets to the gala for any charter membership gift of $100 or more received *prior to* the date of the benefit. This discount offer will be announced in all of the promotional activities and publicity releases for the gala.

With her spring solicitation plans in place, Anderson begins work on the combination annual meeting and gala benefit evening to be held sometime between April 30 and May 30. After calling to check available dates against the Women's City Club community calendar and the Greater Cleveland Convention and Visitors Bureau, Anderson discovers that every major hotel and auditorium, including the Cleveland Convention Center, is already heavily booked for every weekend; a weekday evening will have to be considered. Anderson believes that if the program begins at 6:00 P.M. and is over by 9:30 P.M., the choice of a weekday will work out. She calls Harvey Clout and Harold Connected about their availability to attend the gala on weekday dates between April 30 and May 30; several dates are good for both of them. They both ask her to call Mary Moneybanks right away; it seems that Moneybanks and Trafalgar ("Telly") Temple have talked with the owners of Cleveland's three professional sports teams and have come up with a "fabulous idea" for the gala's entertainment program. Neither Clout nor Connected will say anything more about this idea and, with more than a little fear in her heart, Anderson calls Moneybanks but is forced to leave her name and number on Moneybanks's message machine. Anderson resumes studying the benefit master checklist in the manual from The Campaign to Clean Up America. [See Appendix B.]

Moneybanks calls back within the hour and is quite excited. "All three teams have agreed to join our gala and we have the greatest idea for the entertainment—a variety show." Moneybanks tells Anderson about a breakfast meeting she and Temple has two days ago, adds that she has called the executive director of the Play House Square Foundation, and reports that she has a tentative "hold" on the State Theater for Thursday evening, May 15. Moneybanks then returns to telling Anderson about the variety show idea. Moneybanks believes the combined annual meeting and benefit is the perfect opportunity to ask Cleveland's professional athletes to get involved in the Clean Up Cleveland campaign. "Let's have a variety show!" Moneybanks told Temple. "Let's ask each of our three Cleveland professional teams to prepare at least one act apiece, and to compete against one another for the best performance, like the old-time vaudeville acts but in a live contest with the audience serving as judges. With so much television today, we never get to see live acts any more." The deal was struck. Anderson's summary to herself, later that evening, was that the future of the first annual meeting and first benefit event for the Clean Up Cleveland Chapter now rested on the thespian talents of professional ball players.

By 10:00 A.M. the next morning, Anderson had heard from Clout, Connected, Temple, and Moneybanks again; each asked her what she thought of the variety show suggestion. Anderson had to admit that her leaders were certainly excited about the idea. Moneybanks told Anderson that she and Temple were having lunch at the Union Club on Thursday, and asked Anderson to join them. Moneybanks added: "I forgot to tell you earlier that Telly and I saw Iris Radiant at the orchestra concert two nights ago and asked her to join us to co-chair the gala. You know Iris; first it's 'No, I don't have the time.' Then it's 'Maybe, because I owe you both for all you've done for my charities.' Well, we waited to hear her out, then dropped the idea of the variety show on her, and she went for it like a trout! I'm so glad she liked our idea; she can get a lot of sponsors and underwriters as well as corporate executives to buy tables and to fill them too! Oh yes, Iris will be joining us for lunch on Thursday too. Do you think we could see a preliminary budget and program agenda? Can you piece together a few details for the luncheon? Thanks so much, Karen. See you Thursday. Bye." Anderson thought to herself, this train is out of the station already!

The Thursday luncheon was one of those rare moments, Anderson realized afterward, when the right people were matched perfectly with the right idea at the right time. Moneybanks began, as soon as everyone had arrived, with all the reasons she knew why the variety show would be a big hit. She had talked with the majority owners of each of the three teams; all were enthusiastic about the idea but raised questions about the date. "The Cavs could be in the NBA playoffs with Chicago, the Indians will be in Spring training in Florida, and the Browns are on vacation," Temple added, "but I assured them it would work out fine. The NBA division championships should be decided by the first week in May, and flying a few baseball players home from Florida for a day is easy enough." Moneybanks added that she had the Play House Square theater "on hold" for May 15, a Thursday evening, from 6:00 P.M. until 10:30 P.M. Moneybanks asked Anderson to show everyone her draft budget and program plan (Exhibits 7.11 and 7.12). Anderson reported that she had faxed copies that morning to both Clout and Connected, but had not heard from them before the luncheon. The budget plan showed a potential gross revenue of $104,500, expenses of roughly $45,000, and an estimated net profit of $59,500 (57 percent). Radiant commented on how ambitious these figures were for a new event, especially with the gold and silver medalist levels set at $2,500 and $1,000 respectively. After discussion, the group agreed that sponsorships and underwriting were essential to a financial success. They also agreed they had a good case for keeping general admission at $25 per person. Everyone next offered suggestions about where to get many of the expense items at good prices and named some candidates for in-kind donations. They next reviewed Anderson's draft agenda plan. They were concerned about the length of the program, but agreed each of the agenda items was necessary. They also agreed with Anderson's list of five goals and objectives for this first public function of the chapter:

1. Attract a minimum of 700 people as paid attendance;
2. Achieve a better than 50 percent net profit;

3. Achieve newspaper, radio, and local television coverage;

4. Announce the early fund-raising success;

5. Significantly heighten public awareness of the mission and purposes of the Clean Up Cleveland Campaign.

Anderson articulated her conviction that the success of this first public event would depend on the people present at this luncheon, and on the number of their friends they could recruit to assist as volunteers. Everyone agreed this was a personal obligation. "That's why we're here today," said Radiant. They also agreed the ticket price for general admission must be kept at $25 per person so that nearly everyone could afford to attend. They thanked Anderson for her preparations, and the luncheon adjourned in solid agreement.

Driving back to her office, Karen now understood why Moneybanks, Radiant, and Temple were so successful; they had enthusiasm and clear thinking. She wondered how she and Alice Nice, her assistant, could hope to keep up with these three energetic volunteers. When she returned to her office, she called Titus Brown, president of Clout's public relations firm, to brief him on the entire plan and to ask for his help with the promotion and printing, as the luncheon group had suggested. "Harvey already called me last night," said Brown. "He asked me to assign one of my account executives to this project for the next three months, and charge it to his company. You know Susan White on my staff? Good. I've asked Susan to set up a meeting for the three of us early next week." When Anderson hung up, she had a growing conviction that the combined first annual meeting and first gala benefit evening was going to work out just fine. She turned to her computer and composed the spring appeal letter (Exhibit 7.13) for Clout's signature.

	Estimated Budget	Actual Budget
A. *Projected Cash Receipts (Revenue)*		
Ticket sales (500 @ $25)	$ 12,500	$
Charter member sales (150 @ $100)	15,000	
Gold medalist sponsor gifts (8 @ $2,500)	20,000	
Silver medalist underwriter gifts (15 @ $1,000)	15,000	
Bronze medalist gifts (35 @ $500)	17,500	
Auction receipts	12,000	
Raffle receipts	8,000	
Other revenue	2,000	
Contributors (sent gifts; did not attend)	2,500	
Donated materials (in-kind)	< 1,800 >	< >
Subtotal	$104,500	$
B. *Projected Cash Expenses (Costs)*		
Cash Expenditures List:		
Printing (5,000 invitations/tickets/programs)	$ 12,500	$
Postage		
VIP (@ $0.29 ea)	290	
Donor list (@ $0.08 ea)	320	
Theater fees:		
Sets/backdrop	8,000	
Stage crew	2,500	
Concessions	< 1,800 >	
Clean-up	2,000	
Food and beverages (postreception)	6,000	
Decorations/Signs	2,500	
Certificates (350)		
Printing	2,500	
Calligraphy	1,750	
Frames/boxes	700	
Rental tables/chairs	2,500	
Valet parking (VIP only)	1,000	
Police (2 @ $100)	200	
Committee meetings	250	
Contingency	2,000	
Subtotal	$ 45,010	$
C. *Projected Net Proceeds* (B minus A)	$ 59,490	$
D. *Percent Proceeds*	57%	%

Exhibit 7.11   Budget Worksheet for First Annual Meeting and Gala Benefit Evening

Preliminary Agenda Plan

Welcome and Introductions	Mrs. Mary M. Moneybanks Mistress of Ceremonies
Invocation	Rev. William Smith Pastor, Cleveland Community Church
In Appreciation	Michael M. Activist National Chairman, The Campaign to Clean Up America
Convene Annual Meeting of the Clean Up Cleveland Chapter of The Campaign to Clean Up America	Mr. Harvey Clout Chair of the Board
Treasurer's Report	Mr. Sidney M. Secure, CPA
Election of Directors	Mr. Theodosius Worthy Secretary
Adjourn Annual Meeting	Mr. Harvey Clout
Recognition Program	Mr. Harold Connected Chairman, Fund Development Committee
Charter Members of The Circle of Champions	with Mr. Activist and Mr. Clout
Entertainment Program	Mrs. Mary M. Moneybanks Mrs. Iris B. Radiant
Cleveland Browns Cleveland Cavaliers Cleveland Indians	Mr. Trafalgar Temple
Adjournment to the Reception	Mrs. Mary M. Moneybanks

Exhibit 7.12   Preliminary Program Agenda for First Annual Meeting and Gala Benefit Evening

The Campaign to Clean Up America
Clean Up Cleveland Chapter

April 2, 199X

Dear Concerned Resident:

Thanks to the help of many of our friends and neighbors, our campaign to Clean Up Cleveland is working quite well. There is less trash on our streets than one year ago.

The Campaign to Clean Up America (CCUA) is making progress too. Each one of us wants to be proud of our country, and we want it to be clean.

After just our first year of operations, the CCUA Clean Up Cleveland Chapter has received over 14,500 gifts and $442,000. That's 36 percent of our overall goal of $1,250,000! My personal thanks to each and every one of you, our generous donors.

To celebrate our progress, I am inviting you to our first annual meeting and gala benefit evening to be held on *Thursday* evening, *May 15,* beginning at *6:00 P.M.* in the State Theater in Play House Square. And, do we have a show for you!

Our program will have two parts. First, every charter member of our Circle of Champions donor club will be honored on stage. Second, a variety show will feature entertainment by team members from the Cleveland Browns, Cavaliers, and Indians. You won't want to miss this show or the great dessert-tasting reception that follows the program.

Tickets are only $25 per person. Your income tax deduction is $12.50, exactly what goes toward our project.

Special Discount Offer: Any donor of $100 or more whose gift is received *before May 15* will (a) receive *two* tickets to our gala celebration and (b) be inducted into The Circle of Champions as a charter member. Act now; the State Theater has only 700 seats.

The new energy conversion plant will give each of us more electricity at less cost, just from collecting and burning our own trash. Join us on May 15 to celebrate a cleaner Cleveland; I look forward to seeing you.

Sincerely yours,

I. Harvey Clout
Chair of the Board
Cleveland Cast Iron Works

Exhibit 7.13 Spring Appeal Letter G: Package Plan Offer for First Annual Meeting and Gala Benefit Evening

CHAPTER EIGHT

The Volunteer-Led, Personal Solicitation Annual Giving Campaign

The slogan, "It doesn't get much better than this!" applies fully to the volunteer-led, personal solicitation annual giving campaign. All of annual giving is a yearly campaign, and personal solicitation is the best method to invite volunteers and donors to ask others to *renew* (and possibly *increase*) their annual gifts. Of all the several methods and techniques of fund-raising practice to develop annual gift dollars, the volunteer-led, personal solicitation campaign is "as good as it gets!"

If volunteer-led, personal solicitation is so great, why is it discussed so late in this book? The answer is that it cannot begin until *after* the other forms of annual giving are up and running. For a volunteer-led, personal solicitation campaign to succeed, there first must be:

1. Donors who need to be seen;
2. Trained volunteers who have experience in asking;
3. Leaders who can organize and motivate volunteers;
4. Experienced staff who can guide and direct a campaign;
5. Board commitment, based on conviction that an intense, personal solicitation campaign is necessary.

A volunteer-led, personal solicitation annual giving campaign is the culmination of the overall annual giving program, not its source. Among the advantages and attributes to be realized from the successful introduction of a volunteer-led, personal solicitation annual giving campaign are:

1. It tells current donors that they are appreciated for who they are and valuable for what they have done;
2. It identifies and recruits volunteers who will ask their friends for money;
3. It identifies and recruits leaders who are able to direct others to perform a specific assignment by a deadline;
4. It asks current donors to increase their level of annual support;
5. It invites current donors to become volunteers and actively help the nonprofit organization;
6. It identifies major gift prospects among individuals and organizations;
7. It proves that personal solicitation is 16 times more effective than direct mail, and eight times more effective than use of the telephone;
8. It proves that personal solicitation, at $0.05 to $0.10 to raise a dollar (or less), is the most cost-effective method of annual giving available.

To establish and manage a volunteer-led, personal solicitation campaign every year is not an easy job. Each campaign must follow a strategic plan grounded on well-documented and well-publicized priority needs. The strategic decision to use a campaign model, which is an intense experience for everyone involved, must be fully supported by the board of directors. Board members also must agree to be the first donors to this campaign, with personal gifts that are large enough (as a group) to inspire others to follow their example. Further, one or more board members must serve as volunteer solicitors in the campaign; if the board expects others to work in their behalf, the board must show the way. Several components are required, and all of them are critical to the success of each annual giving campaign:

1. An adequate supply of current donors with a known potential for increased levels of participation and support;
2. An adequate supply of well-trained volunteer solicitors to represent the nonprofit organization while acting as its public solicitors;
3. A few identified leaders who are experienced in organizing and directing volunteers and in motivating them to complete their assigned duties on schedule;
4. A well-prepared campaign plan managed by experienced fundraising professionals in whose advice and counsel leaders and volunteers will have confidence;

5. A tracking and reporting system to evaluate the campaign's performance and to keep everyone informed of progress;

6. A recognition program that will honor donors for their achievements and reward volunteers for their accomplishments.

DEVELOPING QUALIFIED DONORS

Even the smallest of nonprofit organizations, if it has begun its annual giving program by using the mail for acquisition and renewal solicitations as described in Chapters Two through Four, should develop at least 1,000 donors *after* three years. Among these 1,000 donors will be some 10 to 15 percent who have upgraded their original gift amount by the third year. Most of the others (40 to 50 percent) will maintain the same gift level each year. If gifts to donor clubs or membership associations have been requested, some of these donors (10 to 15 percent) will have added another gift or switched from being mail respondents to the donor club or membership program. Another 10 to 15 percent of donors will have brought tickets to one or more benefits within three years. Other donors may have begun to volunteer in some capacity (the final 10 to 15 percent), taking assignments and proving their willingness to help in other ways. Given all these opportunities during the first three years, the majority of donors will have invested between five and ten separate gifts in the organization for a total of $100 to $300 or more. They will have received newsletters and three annual reports and will have a fairly good idea of the progress made and the needs that remain to be addressed. They have proven their loyalty and are prepared to answer the next request.

These donors and volunteers are well-prepared to ask their friends for donations. They have made an extensive personal commitment to the organization. They continue to give because they believe in the mission and purposes of the organization. They remain positive about the value of their investment and have become ambassadors for the cause, perhaps without knowing it. How much more qualified can they be? What can the organization ask them to do next? The answer is: Join the volunteer-led, personal solicitation annual giving campaign and solicit *other donors* (not strangers) for their annual gifts.

If donor development has been well planned, a series of naturally progressing steps brings donors to this decision point. They believed in the organization's services enough to aid it with repeated contributions. They gave their time and talents to help with projects and to serve on committees. They may have been directly involved in a project, taken a leadership role in organizing others, and brought their friends to a benefit event or open house. Their involvement increased without much prodding on the part of the organization, but all according to the development plan. [1]

Despite their qualifications, they may not be willing to ask their friends for money. Some will say they are willing to do *anything* else, even to give five times the amount of time and effort in any other assignment, no matter what it may be. Others will be reticent to solicit anyone, even another prior donor, because they are shy or uncomfortable with the idea. A few may never have "sold" anything before (so they think) and are not sure how to do it. Perhaps they have asked others for gifts before, were turned down, and came away with bad feelings of what they thought was rejection of them. Any volunteer wants to succeed and fears failure most of all, especially in front of friends and for an organization they care about. Each of these attitudes, good or bad, can be addressed during orientation and training, if these donors will first agree to serve.

Assume that at least 250 of the 1,000 donors developed by an organization after three years might be eligible to become volunteer solicitors. What criteria can be used to find 250 prospective volunteers from among 1,000 donors? Eight sure indicators are the following past actions:

1. Gave repeated personal gifts each year;
2. Gave additional gifts, or increased annual gift levels, or joined the donor club, or asked about commemorative gifts;
3. Attended one or more activities, benefits, or special events in each year;
4. Brought friends to activities, benefits, and special events;
5. Requested additional information, whether asking for themselves or "for a friend who wants to know";
6. Volunteered for service to the organization outside the fund development program;
7. Volunteered for service at another organization, possibly in a fund-raising assignment;
8. Was nominated by a board or staff member or by another donor.

"Donors make the best prospects," an old maxim in fund-raising practice, applies as much to volunteers as it does to donors. The next step, *how* to ask them to be solicitors, is all-important; a lot is riding on this request. Summarizing the advice in the first seven chapters of this book: *Do not* write them a letter! What will come back is another check. If they are being asked to perform personal solicitation, the only way to invite them is by *personal solicitation*—by board members, administrators, volunteer leaders, and fund development staff. Without volunteers, there will be no volunteer-led, personal solicitation annual giving campaign.

RECRUITING AND TRAINING VOLUNTEER SOLICITORS

Each volunteer who accepts the invitation to serve as a member of the volunteer-led, personal solicitation annual giving campaign should receive a letter of appointment from a high-ranking officer of the organization (chair of the board, chair of the development committee, president, or CEO). A copy of the letter should be sent to the person who asked the volunteer to serve. The appointment letter should specify the assignment, verify the importance of the work to the organization, identify who is in charge of the project, specify the period of service (the planned length of the annual campaign), and conclude with an offer to be available at any time for assistance. The appointment letter should announce the date(s) and time(s) for the orientation and training sessions and stress that every volunteer should attend (see Exhibit 8.1). It is important to preserve the personal style that is essential to every phase of this project. A confirmation notice with details about the orientation and training session should arrive shortly after the appointment letter and should come from the annual giving campaign chair or vice chair or from a team captain. The volunteer is now enlisted in their effort and will be asked to follow their direction from this point forward.

Each volunteer comes to this assignment with an individual background and varied experience. Not all volunteers will have the same level of knowledge of or comfort with this assignment. Most are likely to have been involved with the organization in some entirely different capacity, especially if recruited from among the roster of donors. A few may have had prior experience in a campaign and may have attended orientation and training sessions. Their new role is being part of a personal solicitation campaign committee. Annual giving campaigns are not military operations, but orientation and training sessions are a command, not an option, for every volunteer, especially in the first years of volunteer participation. Experienced volunteers may be excused from the instruction sessions, but should attend to communicate their enthusiasm and experience to the newcomers. Each volunteer needs to be brought up-to-date on current priorities and to renew his or her enthusiasm for this task.

Orientation and training meetings should be scheduled at a time of day and on a day of the week when most volunteers can attend. People who are unable to attend any session will have to be seen separately by a committee member or staff employee, to be sure they receive the

August XX, 199X

Dear _____;

Thank you for agreeing to join our annual giving campaign committee this year. We are highly dependent on volunteers such as yourself who are willing to meet with our most faithful annual donors to ask them to renew their annual gift.

Please plan to attend one of our volunteer orientation and training meetings next month. These one-hour sessions will provide you with complete information about our campaign plans, the projects needing funds this year, and how to solicit a gift. You will also meet the other members of our committee. The schedule for all sessions, to be held in our conference center at 1234 Main Street, is as follows:

7:30 A.M.	Wednesday	September 22
5:30 P.M.	Thursday	September 23
7:30 A.M.	Friday	September 24

Enclosed is a RSVP card to sign up for one meeting; please reply by September 15. If you cannot attend, we will schedule another time for one of us to meet with you.

Enclosed is a roster of annual donors. Please circle the names of each person you are willing to see about a gift this year. Return the list to us *prior to* September 15. Each volunteer will be assigned *five* donors to see during the campaign period, from October 1 to November 15. You will receive your assignments at the training session.

Please give either of us a call if you have any questions. Thank you again for joining our committee; we look forward to working with you to benefit our community through this, our favorite charitable organization.

Sincerely yours,

Timothy Brown   Rachel Smith
Campaign Chairman   Team Captain
897-6655   545-3211

Encl.

Exhibit 8.1   Letter of Appointment to Volunteer-Led, Personal Solicitation Annual Giving Campaign Committee

instruction they need to fulfill their assignment. Attendance implies acceptance of the accountability to perform as requested. Volunteers will not want to have to explain their lack of performance to others on the committee. It is usually much easier to do the work than to try to explain why it was not done. Completing the assignment is all they are asked to do; the results (each donor's gift decision) are a separate matter and are not always within the volunteers' ability to control. Their job is to meet with each of their assigned donors and to invite his or her continued support.

The orientation and training session is an important part of *every* personal solicitation annual giving campaign. To help stress this point to everyone involved, leaders from the board of directors should attend; some should be included on the agenda (see Exhibit 8.2) as speakers, and others can be introduced and participate in the discussion. Their attendance will count greatly with the volunteers present. Each session should be conducted as a seminar or workshop, using an adult education model. Informality will encourage audience participation. To be effective, each session should be limited to 25 or 30 people; extra meetings can be held if more volunteers are involved. The time span should be one hour, with only 30 to 40 minutes planned for actual presentation. Audiovisual aids

1. Welcome and introductions	Chair, Annual Giving Campaign Committee
2. Importance of annual gift support	Chairman of the Board or President/CEO
3. The project that needs support	President/CEO or senior professional staff member in charge of the project
4. Prospect assignments	Chair, Annual Giving Campaign Committee
5. The campaign plan, timetable, visit reports, gifts reports, staff support available; introduction of team captains	Chair and Vice Chair, Annual Giving Campaign Committee
6. The art of asking for money ("role-playing" exercise)	Chair, Annaul Giving Campaign Committee with successful volunteers from last year's campaign
7. Discussion: Questions/Answers	Chair, Annual Giving Campaign Committee plus all other speakers
8. Adjournment to refreshments	

Exhibit 8.2   Sample Agenda for One-Hour Training and Orientation Session

should be used and refreshments should be provided. The site should be conducive to training purposes and devoid of distractions. Where possible, training should take place at the site of the project or within the nonprofit organization. A successful session will:

Begin as soon after the announced time as possible;

Encourage questions;

Have board members and other representatives from the organization available to answer questions;

Be conducted professionally;

Be thorough in preparing volunteers for all facets of this assignment.

The key reasons why orientation and training sessions are valuable to volunteers can be described by what they accomplish:

1. Provide complete instructions on the project and on how the funds will be used, how those served will be helped, how the cause will be advanced;

2. Explain the benefits to the community that will result from meeting these needs;

3. Explain the recognition program planned for donors at all levels;

4. Explain why volunteers' own personal gift decision must be made *before* they ask someone else for their annual gift, and why they should secure the gifts as soon as possible;

5. Explain how to present the project fairly, without overstatement, and how to ask for a gift without implying any coercion (giving is voluntary);

6. Explain how to invite others to join in support of a project whose value is expressed in terms of helping those in need and fulfilling the mission and purposes of the organization;

7. Explain how the campaign is organized, who are the people in charge, which team captain they will work with, how they are to conduct their assignment, when the campaign begins and ends;

8. Review the contents of the "workers' kit" to show how the information and materials can be used;

9. Explain how the results will be reported, how the overall program will be evaluated, and how their performance will be measured;

10. Provide encouragement, praise them for volunteering to help, and describe how they will be recognized and rewarded for their service.

All that remains is to assign each volunteer the names of the prior donors and prospects he or she is to see and solicit. Assignment is a crucial part of the orientation and training session. Personal solicitation is a delicate and, for many people, a somewhat confrontational experience. Everyone should be asked to take a minimum number of donor candidates (between three and five), and should be provided with basic information on each donor assigned. The information is *confidential* but necessary to the task of asking for the next gift (see Exhibit 8.3). At the orientation, the value of reporting the contents of their discussion with each donor should be stressed; this information is an essential portion of each donor's permanent record. Because annual giving campaigns are scheduled to last only one to two months, it is not unreasonable to ask a volunteer to meet with three to five donors within four to eight weeks. Some volunteers will ask for more than five assignments. Their enthusiasm is commendable, but they should begin with three to five. After these visits have been completed, their results can be studied before they are given additional assignments.

> No formula for determining how many prospects an individual can handle will be applicable to every situation. In an intensive campaign, however, solicitors should seldom be asked to make more than five calls. This is especially true in the campaign that is operating on a genuine deadline (and without a deadline it is not a campaign!). Many well-meaning persons accept too many assignments with the result that, while they may make all the calls, they usually do so perfunctorily and without enthusiasm and determination. Some people can handle only one or two calls well. [2]

After a year or two of experience, those volunteers who can secure more gifts from prior donors can take more than five assignments. Most volunteers prefer to select the names of people they know because they have a higher comfort level when asking their friends or business colleagues for donations. They expect to see these people once or twice in the course of their normal activities during the campaign period. Other volunteers prefer to take the names of people they do not know; they become embarrassed when confronting their friends. Some may take new names for an opposite reason: They want to make new contacts and acquaintances, either for personal or business reasons. Whatever the choice or motive, everyone should accept an assignment of three to five donors to see and to resolicit for their next gift.

The next step is to educate the volunteers about who and what they are representing. One way to get this message across is to weave the information into a monologue that illustrates what the volunteer might say or how the project or cause might be explained to someone the volunteer will call on. A short video in which sight and sound are used together, or

Donor Name:	Mr. and Mrs. Allen B. Constant		
Address:	23456 Chagrin Falls Blvd.		
	Gates Mills, Ohio 44022		
Telephone:	Office: 123-4567	Residence 765-4321	
Giving Summary:	Annual Gifts:	19XX	$100.00
		19XX	150.00
		19XX	150.00
		Total:	$400.00
Suggested Renewal/Upgrading/Gift:			$200.00

Other Gifts:	Date	Amount	Purpose
	3/10/XX	$ 50.00	Memorial gift
	5/12/XX	100.00	2 tickets to BBQ
	9/15/XX	50.00	Memorial gift
	2/21/XX	100.00	Membership
	5/15/XX	200.00	4 tickets to BBQ
	7/27/XX	25.00	Memorial gift

Possible Areas of Priority Interest:

1. Commemorative giving
2. Western BBQ committee

Comments from Prior Contact Reports:

1. Appears from address to have money.
2. Annual gift renewed by phone last two years; has not been called on.
3. Ask Mary Moneybanks if she knows them and what their interests might be.

- -

Contact Report Summary

Date of meeting: _____ Time: _____

Place of meeting: _____

Comments on visit: _____

_____

Question areas: _____

Annual gift renewed? [ ] Yes Amount: $ _____   [ ] No

Upgrade requested? [ ] Yes Amount: $ _____   [ ] No

Overall assessment: [ ] Major gift candidate   [ ] Planned Gift candidate

Follow-up required: [ ] Yes   [ ] No

Exhibit 8.3 Sample Prospect Assignment Card and Contact Report Summary

a role-playing exercise will help volunteers to remember details. Speakers might stress only two or three key points for volunteers to remember and use in their conversations with donors. Each speaker must be carefully prepared on the topic, project a positive and optimistic attitude about soliciting, and convey enthusiasm about what the money raised will accomplish. Other information volunteers may find useful should be placed in their information kit (see Exhibit 8.4). Each document should be reviewed briefly to explain what it contains and how to make use of it.

Volunteers will be anxious to learn how they should ask for money. There are two parts of this section of the meeting: (1) assignments from the donor list and (2) training on how to ask for a gift. Volunteers should have an opportunity to review the list of donors prior to the orientation and training session. For example, a volunteer who has agreed to serve should be sent the list of qualified donors and requested to return it by a set date—after they have identified all the names (not just five) of donors they would be willing to accept as their solicitation assignments. Confirmation of their actual assignments, made by campaign leadership and staff, will be completed prior to the date of the orientation and training session. This open session is not the place or the time to air everyone's assignment preferences. Assignments can be changed, but if each volunteer is assigned a few of the names requested, he or she is more likely to call on those prospects first, then see other donors who were not requested. Volunteers who ask for substitutes should be willing to accept the next donor(s) assigned to them; if they don't, there can be doubt whether they want to solicit anyone. Each donor who is returned or

Left Side	Right Side
1. Table of contents	1. Table of contents
2. Project fact sheet/Key points	2. Giving history and brief personal profile for each assigned prospect
3. Question/Answer sheet	3. Supply of contact/visit report forms
4. Basic fact sheet on the nonprofit organization	4. Organization chart of annual giving campaign committee
5. Most recent annual report	5. Roster of annual giving committee members
6. Supply of stationery and envelopes	6. Supply of postage-paid reply envelopes

Exhibit 8.4 Contents of a Volunteer Solicitor's Information Kit

exchanged for reassignment to another volunteer should be reassigned as soon as possible.

Training in how to solicit prior donors is the last topic on the agenda. This "moment of truth" can be a stumbling block for many volunteer solicitors. They need to know how to guide the discussion, what approach to use when asking for a gift, and what vocabulary is acceptable. They must be told that every solicitation will be unique; people are different, and there is no "one way" that will work every time. How they approach each donor and what they say can be the same; how to read each donor's response is hard to teach. Here are some basic facts to stress with volunteers at the outset:

1. Each person they will see is already a donor, just as they are;
2. Whether the donor knows the volunteer or not, both have positive feelings about the organization they are supporting;
3. The face-to-face meeting is essential for success;
4. Each donor has thoughts and opinions; invite comments to be shared with the organization;
5. There is no "easy way" to get this job done; other ways are never as successful as face-to-face meetings;
6. The organization cannot hope to call on all of its donors; only volunteers can complete this important contact each year.

Each volunteer also should be instructed on how important each prior donor is to the organization. Meeting with them is important, but continuous support is the true objective. Donors are investors; like clients or customers, they deserve to be treated well, which includes taking the time to meet with them at least once a year. If these annual visits are held faithfully, there can be every expectation that financial support will follow.

Donors are always interested in learning what the organizations they support are doing and planning. They will look forward to talking with someone who knows the plans firsthand and will be quite receptive to a chance to meet. Volunteers should take a moment to think about how they will make their initial approach to each donor. Among the options they should be encouraged to consider are: (1) call to ask for an appointment, (2) write a brief note to introduce themselves and say they will be calling for an appointment, or (3) try to intercept the donor in public to ask for an appointment. None of these options should be used for actual solicitation unless it is impossible to make the desired arrangement and meet with the donor. After the appointment has been made, here are some basic suggestions for how to prepare for the meeting with each donor:

1. Be yourself;
2. Remember that this is a social call and is voluntary by both parties;
3. Keep the appointment; donors deserve respect;
4. Select a time and place comfortable to the donor, not the solicitor;
5. Give the donor the choice of where and when to meet (safe at home, or in public);
6. Give the donor the deference due a host, but pick up the tab;
7. Prepare for the meeting; study the donor's giving history in particular;
8. Concentrate on requesting a repeat of prior support;
9. Begin by thanking the donor for the meeting and for his or her previous support;
10. Allow time to get acquainted, catch up on other topics, develop a comfort level;
11. Discuss key points about the organization and the targeted project; be informative, not boring;
12. Do not rush into the "pitch";
13. Explain your own interest; explain (briefly) your involvement and why you believe the cause is worth your time and money;
14. Explain that your assignment is to meet with other donors, to share information, and to answer questions;
15. Welcome any questions; try to answer those you know, and promise to get any answers you do not know (always a good follow-up opportunity);
16. Explain the project succinctly; again, invite questions; share campaign materials if there is interest in having them;
17. If asked, tell how much you have given;
18. Ask whether the donor is willing to consider continuing his or her important level of support again this year;
19. Explain the separate giving levels offered and the donor recognition benefits and privileges;
20. If the donor is willing to give again, extend warm thanks;
21. Depending on the context of the answer, ask whether the donor might consider adding "something extra" to the prior gift amount;

explain why a little more is needed and how it will make a difference;

22. If the donor is not ready to give, accept the indecision and allow
    time for further consideration; try to set a date for a call-back to
    receive the decision;

23. Thank the donor for his or her commitment and generosity and
    for the time spent with you;

24. Report the donor's decision to the fund development office; if a
    gift was made, deliver it as soon as possible; pass along any re-
    quests for follow-up action;

25. If it is your personal practice and style, send a brief, handwrit-
    ten note within a few days to thank the donor for the gift deci-
    sion and for the meeting.

The list of things "not to do" is brief and easy to remember:

1. Don't push;
2. Never hustle;
3. Don't overstate the need;
4. Never promise something you can't deliver;
5. Don't think any donor is easy;
6. Never meet with a donor unprepared;
7. Don't forget to say thank you.

Are there magic words to use? Because solicitation is a request, it can
be put in the form of a question: "It is possible you will be able to support
us again this year?" or "Can you consider a gift of $1,000 at this time?" or
"Can you see your way clear to join us with your gift again this year?"
Phrases that assume a gift is forthcoming or that imply a bit of pressure
(such as "Can we count on your again this year?" or "I hope you will
agree to support us") can work against a favorable gift decision. Donors
must decide whether they want to give again; nothing should be assumed. Here are some guidelines for reacting to their answer:

If they reply with the same gift as last year (and upgrading was mentioned), accept their decision.

If they decide to increase their gift, thank them twice: (1) for giving
again and (2) for giving more than before!

If upgrading was not mentioned, ask about it now.

If they decide on a smaller gift, thank them.

Donors may have a reason for reducing their support; more than likely, the reason will be revealed during the discussion. If the reason relates to any unhappiness or dissatisfaction with the organization, the project, or how they have been solicited or treated since giving their prior gift, these facts should come out during the discussion. If no reason has been mentioned and there is no evidence of hardship, the donors might be asked gently if they want to share any comments with the organization. Note taking may be necessary, and all the details should be reported to the team captain or office staff.

CAMPAIGN LEADERSHIP: THE KEY TO SUCCESS

Leadership is absolutely critical to a volunteer-led, personal solicitation annual giving campaign. Leadership adds legitimacy and brings credibility to the campaign; exhibits passion and a caring attitude about the organization and those who benefit from its programs and services; inspires volunteers to join and to perform; sets the tone and creates the spirit for the campaign; insists on deadlines being met, sets the performance levels expected, and fully accepts being accountable for the results. Leaders actively participate in decisions on campaign purposes, design, and goal setting. Leaders conduct the identification, recruitment, and training of volunteers, and provide personal direction from start to finish. If the individuals chosen to provide leadership also possess some of the following capabilities—visibility, respectability, clout, wealth, and a willingness to take responsibility for the work of others—and are fearless when it comes time to ask for money, the volunteer-led, personal solicitation campaign can be assured of success [3].

The role of volunteer leaders, their identification, recruitment, and training, and other operating details have already been discussed (see Chapters Two, Six, and Seven). The focus here will be on their role in organizing and managing volunteers who agree to be part of a personal solicitation campaign. The basic leadership talents needed include knowing how to conduct meetings, preserve order, keep to deadlines, be conscientious about the budget, delegate authority, create teamwork, and motivate others. There will be times when a problem may arise or something may not be going well. Corrective action must be taken, or a volunteer or donor may require a bit of "extra attention." Leaders must be willing to address these issues and sensitivities.

The most effective way to manage a volunteer-led, personal solicitation campaign is with a committee (see Exhibit 8.5). Experienced fundraising executives know how to direct a program through a committee, and volunteers understand how to perform as members of a committee.

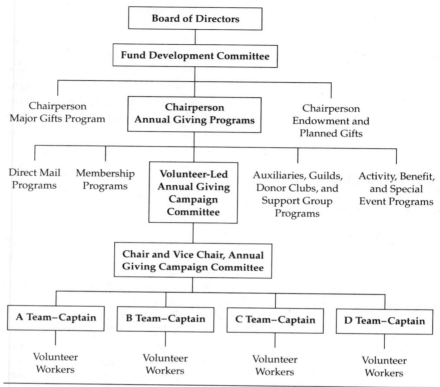

Exhibit 8.5   Organization Chart for Volunteer-Led Annual Giving Campaign Committee

There is a degree of comfort in the formal structure and procedural style that committees observe and in the ready access to others for help when needed. Committees spread the work around fairly and equitably; no one person is asked to bear too great a responsibility for the overall campaign. The duties for each of the various tasks, like job descriptions, can be explained so that each participant knows what to do, what others are doing, and where everyone's assignment fits into the overall committee design. Annual giving committees need only a minimal structure to support their assignment of solicitations of prior donors.

The organization must not be cumbersome or get in the way of the goal. It should be streamlined, utilizing just the forces needed for a successful program and no more. An overlarge organization requires a lot of care and feeding and does not ensure success. A compact group of compatible, effective, involved leaders representing the community or the organizational power structure can perform miracles. [4]

Each committee layer represents a rung on a ladder that volunteers can use to advance to greater responsibility. Because annual giving campaigns must be repeated every year, committees represent a training ground and a promotion sequence for those who choose to move up and share other areas of responsibility. A committee is the superior method to implement a leadership development program. In its simplest form, each layer should be required to have a chairperson and a vice chair. The chairperson is in charge this year and maybe next year too; the vice chair is assisting the chairperson as required and is in training to take over next year or the year after. Training volunteers to be successful as leaders of other volunteers is a significant step in the growth to maturity of every nonprofit organization.

Volunteer-led, personal solicitation annual giving campaigns will require several areas of management. The board of directors and the nonprofit organization depend on the annual giving campaign as a major source of operating revenue. Leaders who take responsibility to organize the campaign and direct the volunteers to produce these funds are also managers of the friend-raising and relationship building inherent in this process. Most of the volunteer solicitors will not be involved in campaign details such as decisions about appointment letters, agenda planning, budgets, notices, printed materials, orientation and training sessions, speaking appearances, thank-you letters, and donor and volunteer recognition and reward. Added to the responsibilities of campaign leaders are executive committee meetings, expense approvals, contract and liability requirements, progress reports to higher authority, and similar tasks. These levels of responsibility are significant and require some prior experience with previous campaigns. The fund development staff will support the campaign leaders in all of these activities, but will not make these decisions.

Shared responsibility is a key part of committee design and operation. The annual giving campaign chairperson who delegates authority along with responsibility is giving volunteers a larger role to play in the entire process and a greater stake in its success. Volunteers will then develop a better sense of how important their assignment is to the success of the overall campaign. As an example, team captains have to (1) be sure their volunteer workers attend orientation and training sessions, complete as many of their assignments with personal visits as possible, and report back on their experiences with their assigned donors; (2) evaluate the volunteers' and their own performance; and (3) identify likely candidates for added responsibility next year. The postcampaign critique session will invite everyone to offer suggestions for improvements. Capturing these suggestions and passing them along to the campaign leadership will be the final entry on the team captains' job description.

The assignments accepted by a volunteer solicitor are important to the overall campaign and to each volunteer's experience because they concentrate on meetings with prior donors. Nearly every other annual giving activity concentrates on acquiring new, first-time donors and then securing their second and third annual gift. The volunteer-led, personal solicitation campaign is designed to invite and train volunteers to meet with only selected prior donors. The annual contributions of these donors often represent as much as 60 to 80 percent of actual cash income received in each year. This campaign and its performance receive major attention from the nonprofit organization's board of directors and management.

Several performance areas will be monitored during and after the campaign. Each of these evaluations and their criteria will be defined in positive terms. Routine gift reports will provide basic details such as the number of donors who have made gifts to date, their gift amounts, and the average gift size. These results should be compared with prior campaigns at the same point in time. Much more data will be needed before the performance of a volunteer-led, personal solicitation campaign can be evaluated. How many prior donors qualified to be seen at the start of the campaign? How many of these donors were assigned to volunteer solicitors, how many were seen, and what gift decisions resulted? To understand the total campaign, this performance evaluation should also provide details on the number who were *not* assigned and *were not* seen, and the value of their prior gifts *not received* as a result. The form shown in Exhibit 8.6 will provide a comprehensive analysis and will help to illustrate what the personal solicitation campaign was able to accomplish. It is not reasonable to expect volunteers to be able to see every donor within a short campaign period, and there is no value in trying to assess what the no-visit problem may have been. Volunteers should believe they succeeded in their assignment if they met with each of their assigned donor prospects or *made every effort* to do so. The overall campaign evaluation should address the positive opportunity that remains: How, when, and where can these faithful donors be asked to give again? The answer is to try again, perhaps later in the year during a second volunteer-led, personal solicitation campaign. If a second campaign is not possible, alternate solicitation methods can be used. The same volunteer or team captain can try to call the donor in a few months. If that fails, a personal letter can be sent. The final objective is to be sure that every prior donor receives an invitation to continue to make his or her annual gift sometime within each year.

1. Number of qualified prospects and volunteers available	Prospects	=	_____
	Volunteers	=	_____
2. Number and percent of prospects assigned to volunteers	Number	=	_____
	Percent	=	_____%
3. Number of calls made, number of gifts received, and ratio (percent) of calls to gifts	Calls made	=	_____
	Gifts made	=	_____
	Percent	=	_____%
4. Average gift size for all prior donors and average gift size for all new donors	Average gift (prior)	=	$_____
	Average gift (new)	=	$_____
5. Number of upgraded gifts received, percent of donors who upgraded, and average gift size	Number	=	_____
	Percent	=	_____%
	Average gift	=	$_____
6. Number of prior donors assigned who did *not* make a gift, percentage, and value of their lost gifts (total made in prior year)	Number	=	_____
	Percent	=	_____%
	Value	=	$_____
7. Number of prior donors who were *not* assigned and did make an FY 93 annual gift, percentage, and average gift size	Number	=	_____
	Percent	=	_____%
	Average gift	=	$_____
8. Number of prior donors who were *not* assigned and did *not* make an FY 93 annual gift, percentage, and value of gifts *not* received	Number	=	_____
	Percent	=	_____%
	Value	=	$_____

Exhibit 8.6 Evaluation Form for Volunteer-Led, Personal Solicitation Annual Giving Campaign Performance

MANAGEMENT OF THE ANNUAL GIVING CAMPAIGN

The annual giving campaign will require a lot of attention from everyone who is part of it. The overall campaign schedule (see Exhibit 8.7) illustrates the extent to which planning and attention to detail must be provided by the fund development staff. Campaign leadership must stay on top of each deadline as the schedule progresses. The vice chair and team captains must be in touch with volunteer workers throughout their period of training and actual solicitation. Once the campaign is begun, volunteers will be contacting their donor prospects to set up face-to-face meetings. Each gift they secure will require a proper thank-you letter,

April 15	Begin analysis of last year's effort.
May 15	Hold budget meetings; set goals and objectives for the campaign. Begin identification and recruitment of campaign leadership.
June 15	Complete leadership appointments; draft text and design for all campaign documents.
July 15	Complete recruitment and appointment of leadership team; hold first meeting to plan campaign. Resolve campaign dates, including kickoff function date and site; reserve facility for kickoff event.
August 15	Complete approval of all campaign plans and support documents. Begin volunteer identification and recruitment, beginning with team captains. Schedule orientation and training sessions; resolve contents of volunteers' information kits.
September 15	Complete recruitment and appointment of team captains, followed by recruitment and appointment of volunteer solicitors. Prepare donor prospect cards; circulate to entire committee to select preferred assignments. Complete preparation of orientation and training sessions. Expect delivery of all campaign documents for volunteers' information kits.
October 1	Begin campaign promotion and publicity. Complete assignments to all volunteers. Conduct volunteer orientation and training sessions before October 15.
October 15	Conduct campaign kickoff event. Begin all solicitations.
November 1	Conduct first report meeting for all volunteer solicitors. Report gift results. Recognize those who have completed their assignments.
November 15	Conduct second report meeting. Report gift results. Recognize those who have completed their assignments.
November 30	Conduct third report meeting. Conclude active solicitation campaign. Report all campaign results, including overall volunteer performance. Recognize those who have completed their assignments.
January 15	Complete preparation of all reports for gifts received as of December 31. Complete donor recognition. Conduct victory celebration and reward leaders and volunteers.
January 30	Complete thank-you letters to all volunteers. Publish results. Prepare final accounting report. Conduct critique meeting with campaign leadership. Prepare and submit critique report with all performance details to board of directors. Include nominations for next campaign's leadership.

Exhibit 8.7 Staff Schedule (Time Line) for Annual Giving Campaign

a personal text to be drafted, approved, prepared, and signed. A lot of follow-up is needed to keep everything moving and to complete everything by the established deadlines. A four- to eight-week campaign covers a brief period of time that passes all too swiftly.

Campaign report meetings are the best medium for maintaining momentum and keeping the campaign on schedule. Report meetings motivate volunteers to complete their assignments, to share their progress and their success, and to alert leaders and staff of any problems they have encountered. The meetings also offer opportunities to recognize and reward those volunteers who have completed their assignments: seen all of their assigned prospects and secured an annual gift from each one. Scores can be posted for each of these "100 Percent Club" performers; their example is for everyone to imitate. Additional scoreboards can keep track of other volunteer and team performance details, the number of donors who increase their gifts, the total gifts achieved compared to prior years, and other encouraging information. When a spirit of competition enters the annual campaign, it can spark enthusiasm and help to motivate volunteers to finish their assignments. Team captains and their team members will work together to achieve 100 Percent Club status for their percentage of calls completed, total dollars raised, highest average gifts, and other categories (see Exhibit 8.8). There can be a danger, however, in too much focus on team competition in annual giving campaigns. Some volunteers may forget that the purpose of their assignment is to meet with prior donors who have sincere commitments to the organization and the cause; campaign goals and team competitions are of little or no interest to donors (they may even be offended by the concept's application to the cause) and should not be discussed when meeting with donors to ask for their annual gift.

Campaign details that need leadership attention include the action steps to be taken if any deadline is missed, personal attention to prompt thank-you letters for each gift, separate meetings or telephone calls with other campaign leaders, and early planning on how to thank volunteers for their good efforts. Campaign leaders should talk one-on-one with any reluctant volunteers who need encouragement or a verbal "boot in the tail" to complete their calls on time. Leaders may be asked to join a volunteer and form a dual-visitor team for an important solicitation. Leaders themselves are often assigned to visit important prior donors, usually those with higher giving levels. Campaign leaders should screen for important gifts as they come in. They offer opportunities for a phone call to thank a special donor, a personal note to thank someone who has upgraded a prior gift, praise for a volunteer's performance or persistence, or a personal note attached to each progress report that is sent to all volunteer workers. Campaign gift reports with

Team	Volunteer Number	Donors Assigned	Donors Seen	Percent of Response	Value of Gifts	Average Gift Size
A	1	5	4	80%	$ 325	$ 81
	2	4	4	100	450	112
	3	5	5	100	500	100
	4	5	5	100	525	105
		19	18	95%	$1,800	$100
B	5	5	5	100	$ 235	$ 47
	6	5	5	100	750	150
	7	5	5	100	315	63
		15	15	100%	$1,300	$ 87
C	8	5	4	80	$ 425	$106
	9	5	5	100	550	110
	10	5	4	80	450	112
		15	13	86%	$1,425	$110
D	11	5	3	60	$ 325	$108
	12	5	5	100	450	90
	13	5	5	100	575	115
	14	5	5	100	450	90
	15	5	5	100	500	100
		25	23	92%	$2,300	$100
Team Summary:						
A	4	19	18	95	$1,800	$100
B	3	15	15	100	1,300	87
C	3	15	13	86	1,425	110
D	5	25	23	92	2,300	100
Total/Average	15	74	69	93%	$6,825	$ 99

Exhibit 8.8   Tracking System for Volunteer Solicitation Teams

details on volunteer performance (see Exhibit 8.9) are presented to the board committee on development and perhaps to the board of directors. As the campaign moves into its final scheduled days, campaign leaders will need to be in touch with team captains and volunteers to encourage them to make their final calls by the campaign deadline. Once the campaign is over, they will give their attention to the victory celebration and then the critique session. These final meetings must be well prepared so that everyone who participates can contribute to all areas in the performance evaluation, including a review of all campaign

Team	Number of Volunteers	This Time Last Year			Results This Year		
		Donors	Amount	Average	Donors	Amount	Average
A	4	14	$ 1,350	$ 96	18	$ 1,800	$100
B	3	14	1,075	77	15	1,300	87
C	3	12	1,320	110	13	1,425	110
D	5	18	1,740	97	23	2,300	100
	15	58	$ 5,485	$ 95	69	$ 6,825	$ 99
E	5	22	$ 2,350	$107	24	$ 2,550	$106
F	4	18	1,850	103	18	1,900	106
G	5	21	2,000	95	22	2,050	93
H	4	19	1,700	90	21	1,900	91
I	5	21	2,200	105	23	2,450	107
	23	101	$10,100	$100	108	$10,850	$101
J	4	18	$ 1,500	$ 83	18	$ 1,600	$ 89
K	4	15	1,250	83	16	1,300	81
L	5	22	2,300	105	24	2,800	117
M	4	17	1,800	106	18	2,150	119
N	5	21	2,350	112	22	2,550	116
	22	93	$ 9,200	$100	98	$10,400	$106
O	5	22	$ 2,450	$111	24	$ 2,650	$110
P	4	22	2,200	100	24	2,400	100
Q	5	18	2,150	119	20	2,450	123
R	4	17	1,550	91	16	1,400	88
	18	79	$ 8,350	$106	84	$ 8,900	$106
S	4	18	$ 1,500	$ 83	18	$ 1,400	$ 78
T	4	16	1,300	81	18	1,450	81
U	3	13	2,350	181	14	2,550	182
V	4	12	1,200	100	13	1,000	77
W	3	15	1,800	120	15	1,800	120
	18	74	$ 8,150	$110	78	$ 8,200	$105

Summary; Last Year vs. This Year

23	96	405	$41,285	$102	437	$45,175	$103

Improvement in Results This Year   +32   +$ 3,890   +$122

Exhibit 8.9 Sample Gift Report for Solicitation Teams in Personal Solicitation Annual Giving Campaign

support activities by fund development staff. A personal solicitation campaign is a personal "contact sport" from start to finish.

Evaluating the performance of a volunteer-led, personal solicitation campaign will require detailed analysis. A summary report on overall performance—what worked well, who performed well, who should be considered for leadership positions, what areas need attention next year—should be prepared and delivered to the board of directors. The board and management should join in assessing how the campaign fulfilled several objectives besides raising funds. Because this campaign is the only time during the year when the organization's best donors are actually seen, feedback on these meetings will be of critical interest to the board of directors, the campaign leadership, and the fund development staff. What do these donors think about the organization in general or about its direction, its progress, its problems, its fund-raising style? Suppose these donors' gifts were to decline. Unless they had made it a priority to ask for and to read visit reports from volunteers as part of the overall campaign performance evaluation, the board and management would have no clue to explain the cutback.

Considerable effort is invested in planning and executing the volunteer-led, personal solicitation annual giving campaign. Each volunteer will give an average of 15 to 25 hours to the campaign during its four to eight weeks of intensity. Campaign leadership will give twice that number of hours and will work a minimum of four to six months on the project. If 50 to 100 volunteers are involved in the campaign, their overall commitment represents a huge investment in the nonprofit organization. The board of directors and management can acknowledge this commitment by attending and participating in the victory celebration. The postcampaign celebration is an essential part of the overall campaign plan and the strategy to develop experienced and committed volunteers. The victory celebration is the final campaign report meeting; its primary purposes are: to report all the results, to honor volunteers and teams who achieved 100 percent Club status, and to thank the staff and volunteers for their hard work. After the campaign is over, a celebration of these good efforts is valuable to each volunteer's self-confidence. Everyone involved should feel good about what was accomplished by working with others on behalf of the nonprofit organization. Asking people for money was not an easy assignment for most volunteers. Taking the time to recognize and reward each volunteer for his or her contributions of time and effort is just as important as thanking each donor for a gift of money during the campaign. On a more pragmatic level, these are the volunteers who will be invited to serve again next year.

The campaign critique session is the final campaign activity. Volunteer solicitors may also be invited, but the campaign leaders need to perform this evaluation session for their own purposes. The role of professional and support staff throughout any campaign is to do everything possible to enable the volunteers to carry out their assignments. Staff efforts should be reviewed by all campaign volunteers and leaders, and their critique comments on staff support should be included in the summary report to the board. What ideas will volunteers have that would make their job more successful? The purpose of each critique session is to review and study what happened; its goal is to learn from experience and to improve next year's performance, not to find fault or point fingers at anyone or anything. If errors were committed, they should be noted alongside suggestions on how they can be prevented next time. The critique meeting will concentrate on volunteer and donor performance (using data from Exhibit 8.6), but should also examine all other areas of operations, perhaps separated into subgroups as follows:

1. Preparations (goals, leadership recruitment, documents);
2. Recruitment (identification, appointment letters);
3. Orientation and training (time, place, agenda, speakers, workers' kit contents);
4. Volunteer support (donor profiles, team captains);
5. Campaign operations (budget, gift reports, report meetings);
6. Donor relations (contact reports, thank-you letters);
7. Staff support (to leaders, volunteers, and donors);
8. Recognition and reward (donors and volunteers, victory celebration).

RECOGNITION AND REWARD

During the campaign and immediately afterward are the best times for recognition and reward. As soon as possible after receipt of a gift, the donor should receive a proper acknowledgment letter. Internal Revenue Service rules, following Congress's 1993 tax law changes, require nonprofit organizations to provide "substantiation" for each gift of $250 or more; a canceled check is no longer adequate evidence that the gift was made. Sending a substantiation letter creates an opportunity to initiate a series of positive experiences for a donor. There is more to gift acknowledgment than simply writing a letter of substantiation. Another factor is speed of delivery. If today is Friday and a donor mails a gift today, Monday will be the earliest the U.S. Postal Service will deliver it to the fund development office. If routine gift processing executes a

48-hour turnaround for all acknowledgment letters, a thank-you letter will be in the mail by Tuesday afternoon and received by Thursday, a full seven days after the gift was made. This sequence is about as quick a turnaround as is possible. The 48 hours may be shortened to 24 hours by saving one day in-house but the fact remains that a week will pass from the day the donor sends a gift and the day a thank-you letter is received in acknowledgment. Can this performance be improved?

A number of thank-you letters are possible. Personal solicitation campaigns offer different options and allow a variety of personal alternatives. Here are the thank-you possibilities:

1. The volunteer receives the check during the solicitation meeting and acknowledges the donor's generosity the next day, in a personal note.

2. The volunteer calls in the gift decision to the team captain, who may call or write the donor to express the organization's appreciation.

3. The donor receives a formal acknowledgment letter from the nonprofit organization one week later.

4. The donor's standing, or the size of the gift, warrants a second acknowledgment letter sent from the campaign chair, a board member, or the President/CEO.

5. If the gift size qualifies the donor for donor club status (see Chapter 5), another letter announces the donor's eligibility for the benefits and privileges of the donor club.

Are there other opportunities? Yes. Is there a need for more? Yes, if these good practices can be consistently applied to all donors who qualify because of the amount of their annual gifts. Some organizations send multiple letters to express their appreciation for gifts of $100, or $1,000; others reserve their enthusiasm for higher amounts. Whatever the practice, a number of thank-you opportunities are available and should be used when justified. The Internal Revenue Service may question the material value of "give backs" to donors when they receive umbrellas, tote bags, and coffee mugs, but no questions are raised over the number of thank-you letters a donor may receive.

Formal recognition policies and procedures are linked to giving levels and to cumulative giving histories (see Exhibits 4.4 and 6.3). These same guidelines should be used to support each method of annual giving that an organization uses. Additional features can be applied to the volunteer-led, personal solicitation campaign, beyond the thank-you notes sent to acknowledge the gift. They may pay off later when these same donors are invited to give again. Formal recognition practices provide opportunities for continued attention to *all* qualified donors, regardless of which annual giving program(s) developed their contribution. As an example, the benefits and privileges of donor club standing might be extended to every qualified donor in the personal solicitation campaign. To qualify for the full range of benefits and privileges provided to all donor club members, the only requirement would be the size of the gift ($100, $500, or $1,000). This recognition program maintains communications with donors through newsletters, annual reports, and other written documents, and sends courtesy invitations for a variety of activities, benefits, and special events held by the nonprofit organization. Some of these communications may arrive with a roster of major donors enclosed; people appreciate being thanked in public as well as privately. By tracking cumulative giving throughout each year (from any annual giving program to which donors respond), additional donors may qualify for donor club benefits. A complete program of honors and recognition should be made available to every donor, especially those whose gift size and history of support are largest, longest, and strongest. [5]

Some nonprofit organizations, in their effort to do right by their most faithful and generous donors, may overlook recognition and reward for their volunteers. Opportunities to acknowledge the extra efforts of each annual giving campaign volunteer arise during the campaign, at report meetings, and at the victory celebration. Because campaigns are repeated year after year, recognition procedures should be *consistent* from year to year. If there are a hundred ways to say thank you to volunteers, each one should be considered. Most volunteers will have already received several types of recognition in their career of service. Outstanding volunteers might share in some of the benefits and privileges reserved for donors. Finding novel ways to recognize volunteers year after year is a challenge, but good volunteers are worth this extra effort. Some unique and special reward should be reserved just for them, to add stature to what they do for the organization and to mark their special standing in the community. Plaques, certificates, and other objects are adequate, but a personal gift such as a watch, a clock, or an attractive paperweight will more accurately represent the appreciation and respect they are due. If the gift selected has space for engraving, the person's name and year of service can be inscribed. Each gift should be nicely wrapped, an inexpensive touch. How and where these symbols of recognition and reward are presented, and by whom, may offer the best way to show appreciation to volunteers. Thoughtfulness is what counts the most.

The final opportunity for recognition is to nominate donors *and* volunteers for honors and award programs sponsored by other organizations. Being nominated is a special form of recognition in itself, regardless of whether the nomination wins an award. For example, annual National

Philanthropy Day celebration programs are held across America, and donors and volunteers are honored by their communities for service to nonprofit organizations. Major donors and campaign leaders are logical candidates to nominate for these awards and are richly deserving of such public recognition. A nonprofit organization does not have to depend on others to define its donor and volunteer recognition program. Each annual meeting is a splendid and highly visible "family" occasion at which to confer awards, honors, and other forms of recognition to those donors *and* volunteers whose generosity and service have distinguished them above all others during the year.

FOCUS: CCUA Clean Up Cleveland Chapter

A week after the combination first annual meeting and first gala benefit evening, Karen Anderson called Mary Moneybanks and asked her to invite Iris Radiant and Trafalgar ("Telly") Temple to lunch at the Union Club. The purposes of this meeting were to be: a private celebration of the successful affair; a consensus critique, and a pooling of all the "lessons learned" from this first experience. Anderson added, "This evaluation will be crucial, especially because it was a first-time event; the decision to repeat it again next year depends on our critique report to the board of directors." Moneybanks agreed, and the date was set two weeks away—time enough for Anderson to collect and pay all the bills and to complete her financial analysis.

During lunch, everyone was still "high" on the success they had achieved. A lively discussion of all the details resulted. In appreciation of their leadership, Anderson presented each of the others with a small album of photographs taken during the gala evening.

Their critique began with agreement on the outcomes of their five primary goals and objectives:

1. Of the 700 tickets printed, 680 tickets were sold, and 668 people attended.

2. Net proceeds were 56 percent of gross revenue ($56,775 of $101,500), slightly below the 57 percent projected ($59,490 from $104,500) in the approved budget.

3. News coverage was adequate before the event, but it did not help ticket sales as much as had been expected. Postevent coverage was better, chiefly because of media coverage of the variety show performances by the professional athletes.

4. The report on fund-raising success was warmly received, but all were surprised when Harvey Clout's announcement of a $1.5 million federal grant toward the energy conversion plant received a standing ovation.

5. The event was clearly successful in heightening public awareness about the Clean Up Cleveland Campaign.

The group completed discussion of all aspects of the benefit. Anderson was asked to summarize their comments in a critique report to be presented at the next board of directors meeting (see Exhibit 8.10). All agreed to recommend that the combined annual meeting and gala benefit evening (and variety show) be continued next year, with a goal of $65,000 in net proceeds.

Anderson's next task was to prepare, for the next board meeting, a summary gift report on all fund-raising results to date. She also wanted to report her plans and recommendations for the fall fund-raising season. The spring mailings had again performed well, no doubt because of the gala and its media coverage. The final charter membership offer of two gala tickets for a gift of $100 appeared to work well. Considerable progress had been made over the past two years: 19,137 gifts had been received for a total of $714,118 (see Exhibit 8.11). Following the 75/25 split of all receipts, the construction fund for the new energy conversion plant had achieved $535,589; operating funds for marketing and fund-raising purposes were $278,529. Adding the $1.5 million grant from the federal government, the overall goal of $3.5 million for the plant was now 58.2 percent complete, with $2,035,589 in the bank.

While these figures represented considerable progress, Anderson expected the board to press for completion of all funding. Membership in The Circle of Champions now exceeded 288 individuals. There would be a growing need to personalize the renewal solicitation of these $100-plus annual donors; letters and telephone calls would not be enough to hold most of them for another year. Anderson planned to recommend that the coming fall campaign season would be an ideal time to initiate the first volunteer-led annual giving campaign. She estimated that between 35 and 50 Circle of Champions members would volunteer if asked. If each volunteer called on five prior donors, between 175 and 250 personal contacts could be made. Anderson prepared a complete plan. It began with recommendations on candidates for a campaign chairperson, a vice chair, and five team captains. Anderson also defined plans to prepare: donor lists with giving histories, orientation and training meetings, volunteer information kits, a budget for printed materials and meetings, and other campaign details. With the addition of personal solicitation to the overall annual giving plan, Anderson believed that the chapter's fund development program was now in place. She intended to expand her use of direct mail for acquisition and renewal and to continue to market memberships in The Circle of Champions as a combined membership association and donor club package. The annual gala would be offered as the major benefit event each year. With this balanced fund-raising program in place, Anderson believed that the Clean Up

Cleveland Chapter of The Campaign to Clean Up America would continue to make steady progress toward fulfilling its mission.

Clout called Anderson the next week, after returning from The Campaign to Clean Up America's national board meeting. He realized that it was time for the board to begin to address the chapter's plans following completion of the energy conversion plant's construction. The first phase in the overall strategy of The Campaign to Clean Up America would end with the completion of a visible project that had major economic as well as environmental impact. Phase two was scheduled to begin before the plant was completed and producing new electricity; it was to address one of three issues: (1) air, (2) land, or (3) water pollution. "Thanks to the ecology of Lake Erie and the decline of smokestack industries in the area, air quality around Cleveland is much improved," Cloud said. "Even Lake Erie water is making a comeback, but the water level is rising and causing erosion of the shore line. Perhaps land should be our next project, especially if we can begin to reclaim land sites where industrial waste burial jeopardizes the value and use of the property. We had best begin to study our options," added Clout. "Karen, can you call some of the other chapters and learn where they are with planning phase two? I'll also think about whom to appoint to a planning committee to begin work on our next project. Many thanks." To Anderson, there seemed to be several purposes for the chapter to continue with its mission for years to come.

First Annual Meeting and Gala Benefit Evening Critique Report

1. *Summary/Recommendations:* As a first-time effort, 668 people attended, $56,775 were the net proceeds (56%), entertainment was enjoyable and received good coverage, and public awareness of chapter mission was advanced. The combined annual meeting and gala benefit evening is recommended for continuation.

2. *Leadership/Volunteers/Staff:* The "triumvirate" (Moneybanks, Radiant, Temple) embodied enthusiasm, optimism and commitment to a quality program; they also divided responsibility, recruited volunteers, delegated duties, and supervised details. Need to add volunteer training and to develop future leaders for all areas.

3. *Invitations/Print Materials/Promotion/Publicity:* With more time next year, all printed and collateral materials will benefit from single graphic design (logo). Better coordination with media should improve pre-event coverage.

Exhibit 8.10   Gala Benefit Evening Critique Report

4. *Sponsorship/Ticket Sales:* Charter membership offer will have expired but offer of two seats for $100 Circle of Champions membership should continue. Gold/Silver/Bronze medalist sponsors can be improved and will help profits.

5. *Registration/Facilities/Arrangements/Decorations:* Need more volunteers at all entrances and in aisles to aid seating. Add staffed displays on project, membership booth, information desk, seating charts in lobby area. Postevent booths worked well; increase lighting and heating; larger signs for food vendors; add 10 tables/100 chairs to seat guests. Add valet parking as option for all guests.

6. *Program/Agenda/Entertainment:* Need to start on time (more volunteers to aid seating will help). Crisp business meeting was a blessing. Hard to repeat Clout's $1.5-million surprise announcement. Presentation of certificates took too much time; may not be necessary again as charter memberships are concluded. Competition between teams unnecessary; drop judging. Encourage more athletes to remain after and join in postevent reception.

7. *Food/Beverage/Service:* Preevent refreshments can be limited to light beverages at theater concession stands; no food. Postevent reception can be promoted better; concentrate menu on desserts and "finger food" tastings of vendors' wares. Wine and beer bar only. Keep everything "free."

8. *Added Fund-Raising Events/Prizes:* While revenue was solid, raffle ticket sales and drawings took time. Consider silent auction only; open theater lobby 90 minutes ahead of program to facilitate bidding; close 10 minutes before program to move crowd into theater. Winners posted on signs at entrance to postevent reception where prizes are paid for and picked up.

9. *Acknowledgment/Recognition:* Tickets costly and unnecessary. Thank-you letter can verify reservation and assigned seats; volunteers and ushers can assist entry and seating. Printed program is ideal for sponsor/underwriter recognition. Brief mention during meeting of lists, if large posters listing all medalist groups are displayed in lobby and at postevent reception. Can we link medalists with food vendors as partners?

10. *Budget Management:* Superb efforts by leadership and volunteers provided medalists' gifts plus in-kind gifts and donated services for many expense areas, which aided profits; may be hard to duplicate next year. Auction prizes can be fewer but of better quality. Solid staff work kept other expenses in line.

Exhibit 8.10 *(Continued)*

Letter	Program	Number Mailed	Replies Number	Replies Percent	Gift Income
Acquisition Phase (Chapters 2 and 3)					
A & B	July test mailing	30,000	348	1.16%	$ 8,527
B	Fall: Full test mailing	80,575	1,156	1.43	35,758
B	Spring 1—"Roll out"	200,000	1,831	0.91	56,936
C	Spring 2—Follow-up	194,476	1,822	0.94	59,975
	Subtotal	506,546	5,157	1.02%	$161,196
Donor Renewal Phase (Chapter 3)					
D	Spring renewal: Introduce charter membership	1,504	914	66.77%	$ 31,064
Year 1	Cumulative totals	506,546	6,071	1.20%	$192,260
Acquisition and Renewal Plus Donor Club Offer (Chapters 3–5)					
E	Fall: Second acquisition mailing plus charter membership offer	192,116	2,216	1.15%	$ 54,276
E	Fall: Follow-up letter	191,012	1,976	1.03	52,120
	Subtotal	383,128	4,192	1.09%	$106,396
F	Renewal 2 plus charter membership offer	6,661	1,864	27.98%	$ 81,872
F	Renewal 2 follow-up	3,797	1,519	40.00	44,664
	Subtotal	10,458	4,383	41.91%	$126,536
Circle of Champions: Renewal (Letter and Phone Follow-up)					
	Fall renewal	160	138	86.25%	$ 16,836
	Fall totals	393,746	8,713	2.12%	$249,768
	Cumulative totals	900,292	14,784	1.64%	$442,028
Spring Campaign: Acquisition, Renewal and First Gala (Chapter 7)					
G	Spring acquisition mailings (2) plus gala	187,334	1,835	0.97%	$ 97,665
G	Spring renewal mailings (2) plus gala	6,339	1,838	28.99%	$117,650
	Subtotal	193,673	3,673	1.90%	$215,315

Exhibit 8.11   Two-Year Totals and Cumulative Gift Summary

Letter	Program	Number Mailed	Replies Number	Replies Percent	Gift Income
	(A total of 128 additional charter memberships were received from the four spring mailings, bringing total membership count to 288)				
	Gala results	3,800	680	17.90%	$ 56,775
	Total spring results	197,473	4,353	2.20%	$272,090
	Year Two results	591,219	13,066	2.21%	$521,858
	Two years' cumulative totals	1,097,765	19,137	1.74%	$714,118

Distribution:	Public education (25%)	=	$ 278,529
	Energy plant (75%)	=	$ 535,589
	Federal grant	=	$1,500,000
			$2,035,589
	Plant construction cost	=	$3,500,000
	Percent of goal raised	=	58.2%

Exhibit 8.11 *(Continued)*

CHAPTER NINE

Other Ways to Raise Money Every Year

Nonprofit organizations invest their annual fund-raising budget in a variety of mailings and memberships; auxiliaries, guilds, donor clubs, and support groups; activities, benefits, and events; and volunteer solicitation programs. Their aim is to be able to raise friends and build relationships with a constituency of donors on whom they can depend for reliable annual support and, when necessary, for major and estate gifts as well. To establish and operate a comprehensive annual giving program requires (1) a major investment of time and money and (2) professional management to achieve maximum efficiency and profitability. Among the benefits to be realized are committed donors, volunteers, and leaders who will provide reliable gift support to meet the priority needs of the nonprofit organization.

If money-raising were the *only* objective for annual giving, most of the fund-raising programs described in this book would not be worth the time, cost, or trouble that must be invested in them. Money-raising is *not* concerned with friend-raising, relationship building, donor renewal, volunteer and leadership development, donor recognition, and all the rest; it is focused only on cash. Many nonprofit organizations may begin their fund-raising programs with a need for cash (starting at the bottom of the pyramid in Exhibit 1.2), but they must grow beyond a mercenary use of fund-raising methods if they hope to realize the potential that a comprehensive annual giving program can deliver. To grow beyond money-raising and to build a reliable base of support requires using the annual giving programs described in this book to attain several other objectives as well as reliable sources of cash (see Chapter Three). Fund development is a strategic plan for managing every fund-raising method toward achievement of a nonprofit organization's mission over multiple years. All of these programs are coordinated in a complex process toward the larger objective of enabling the institution to advance according to its own plans to provide services to the public at the highest level of quality possible. Money-raising alone can never fulfill these larger requirements.

The objectives of annual giving programs should be designed to *Acquire* donors, *Renew* donors, and *Maximize* donors' relationship with the organization. To fully *ARM* a nonprofit organization, each annual giving method of fund-raising should be selected not just to produce cash but because of its ability to fulfill most of the following objectives every year:

1. Develop the image linked to the mission;
2. Obtain friends to support the mission;
3. Identify and acquire new donors;
4. Continue to renew most prior donors;
5. Build relationships with donors;
6. Identify and involve volunteers;
7. Develop and train future leaders;
8. Raise money in a cost-effective manner;
9. Communicate and inform donors;
10. Recognize and reward donors;
11. Develop major and estate donors for the future;
12. Build confidence and trust in the organization.

As with a script for any stage play, the organization must first set the stage for why annual giving is necessary (its mission). "Star" players are selected from among the most experienced and successful performers (the annual giving techniques presented in Chapters Two through Eight). To complete casting and crew assignments, legitimate roles for the supporting cast and tasks for the stage hands are identified (other ways to raise money every year). The completed production team is then rehearsed in their roles to present a great story (the case for support). A successful production will attract an audience who will provide, night after night and year after year, the funds needed to continue and to expand.

The fund-raising techniques described in this chapter are the legitimate roles reserved for the supporting cast and the tasks assigned to the stage hands. Many of these methods might function well enough alone and be offered to the public year after year, but their potential is more likely to be realized when offered in concert with a comprehensive annual giving program. These programs are best used as "extras," especially when they can fulfill only one or a few of the 12 primary objectives listed above. Acting alone, they are less reliable for producing faithful donors, developing volunteers and leaders, and (most important) building confidence and trust in the organization. There may be times when these alternative fund-raising methods will be chosen because of competition for donors and dollars, or a lack of resources and volunteers to raise the money needed. Competition alone may not justify choosing what many donors and prospects will consider a less than professional or even a questionable fund-raising method, just to get money. Properly used as options and enhancements to ongoing annual giving programs, other ways to raise money every year can spark enthusiasm, capture attention, and add variety and spice. None is able to carry the full load of providing all the funds a nonprofit organization needs each year. In alphabetical order, these legitimate other ways to raise money every year are:

1. Advertising and coupons;
2. Commemorative and tribute giving;
3. Commercial sales, cause-related marketing, and affinity cards;
4. Door-to-door and on-street solicitation;
5. Federated campaigns;
6. Gambling and games of chance;
7. Multimedia options;
8. Premiums;
9. Telephone and telemarketing solicitation;
10. Television and telethon solicitation;
11. Various other annual giving ideas of merit.

ADVERTISING AND COUPONS

Among the media options for solicitation messages are newspapers and magazines, billboards and bus-backs, radio and television. Within these outlets are opportunities that may include news and feature articles, paid advertisements, and coupon cards. Achieving news coverage in the papers, in magazines, or on radio or television is quite difficult for nonprofit organizations. When a story does appear, it can increase public awareness and foster public confidence and trust— valued and coveted tangible results. Given these communications avenues, "good news" stories could be delivered daily, but they are not.

Media executives believe routine good works, "people helping people," are not newsworthy material most of the time. It is true that good works are soft news that cannot compete with crime, disasters, and politics, but stories about people helping people are valid news stories. Media readers, listeners, and viewers *are* people who volunteer at and give money to organizations that help people. To succeed in the news market, an organization must treat media representatives in the same manner as prospects or donors, and bring them only story ideas that they can use. They need to hear what nonprofit organizations are doing to combat hunger and poverty, illness and disease, abuse and cruelty, homelessness and illiteracy—all newsworthy topics. They will appreciate how the human spirit can be crushed, how polluting the environment affects everyone, why access to culture and the arts has value, what the rewards of volunteerism are, and how nonprofit organizations can make a difference. There are plenty of news ideas; they just have to be communicated more effectively.

Paid advertisements that will deliver the message are available to every nonprofit organization. If the primary goal is to communicate a message to a large number of people, to market a program or service, or to increase public awareness, advertising can be bought. However, it is budgeted as an expense. As a fund-raising method, advertising has never worked well to produce numbers of donors or substantial income. Commercial advertisements with clip-out product discount coupons work for retail stores and food markets because the customers are buying products, not giving their money away to store owners. The expense of advertising can be a double barrier: (1) because of its cost and (2) because the public's reaction may be, "If they can pay for advertisements in the papers and on television, they obviously don't need my money." Whether this conclusion is true or not, nonprofit organizations must remain conservative by nature and sensitive to public criticism.

The expense-of-advertising question requires further analysis. If a quarter-page newspaper advertisement for one week costs $5,000 and is circulated to 100,000 people, how does that expense compare to the postage required to mail a letter to the same 100,000 people? The third-class, presort bulk rate will be $0.08 × 100,000 = $8,000. Added costs are for rental of the mailing list, printing of the letter and envelope, and mailing house charges to affix the labels, sort, tie, and bag the letters, and deliver the entire shipment to the U.S. Postal Service. The lower cost makes paid advertising appear to be the clear winner, but advertisements alone do not raise money. When used together with a direct mail program or benefit event, they can boost the number of mail responses and ticket sales. The bottom line reads: The use of paid advertising increases the cost of fund-raising. Placements of paid advertising should be measured just as carefully as direct mail and event results, to verify whether an adequate increase in responses was realized, and whether the dollars raised exceeded their added expense.

The alternative to paid advertising is a public service announcement (PSA) for radio and television use. The Federal Communications Commission (FCC) used to require, as part of its licensing procedures, that stations reserve a portion of their on-air time for public service programs and announcements. This requirement was discontinued for radio in 1981 and for television in 1984. Each station has the option to air as much public service programming as it chooses. Two steps are recommended: (1) Meet with station representatives to learn their preferences, community relations objectives, and on-air styles, and (2) prepare and submit PSAs in 15- and 30-second segments (audiotaped or videotaped) for their use. In practice, 15-second tapes are likely to be played more often.

Exceptions to any rule are always possible. News stories and advertisements asking for gifts to aid victims of fires, floods, hurricanes, or earthquakes will achieve impressive results. A need is clear, people want to know how they can help, and the media provide the names and mailing addresses for responses. Nonprofit organizations cannot expect misfortune to be the source of motivation for their annual gifts. Those organizations whose mission is to support victims of emergencies will be prepared in advance to get their message to the media immediately. Because of the pace of news and the number of disasters reported almost daily, there is little time for the other means of annual solicitation to be communicated to the public in as timely a manner as the news.

News stories, magazine articles, advertisements, coupons, and PSAs can all be used by nonprofit organizations to enhance their annual giving programs, but they should not hope to meet all of their annual cash requirements through these media alone. Their best use is in combination with traditional methods, as part of a "multimedia" program plan. Two key decisions are needed to achieve maximum effect with multimedia messages: (1) control of timing and (2) choice of medium. The ability to control when a soft news story will be used is next to impossible to achieve. By contrast, paid advertisements and PSA on local radio and television (cable or commercial) can be scheduled to run during a week when mailings, invitations, or telephone solicitations are delivered. Multimedia messages will help to improve public awareness of the need, which, in turn, will help increase responses. There are no limits to the use of advertisements and coupons in the newsletters, magazines, and annual reports produced by nonprofit organizations. Each of these communications outlets should be used at all times to reinforce the message that annual gift support is requested and welcome at any time.

COMMEMORATIVE AND TRIBUTE GIVING

Several nonprofit organizations receive a regular number of commemorative and tribute gifts each year. Each gift may be reasonably modest ($10 to $25), but their volume can produce an impressive sum of money each year. Commemorative and tribute gifts are used most often to recognize special occasions—birthdays, anniversaries, promotions, graduations, confirmations, and weddings. They are also used to honor individuals by making a gift to charity in their name, as a tribute. Through the gift, the donor expresses both respect and generosity. There are many positive occasions for such donations, but most commemorative gifts to nonprofit organizations are made in memory of an individual after his or her death. These memorial gifts express sympathy to the surviving family and a desire to perpetuate the memory of the deceased. Families often designate a beneficiary of memorial donations, usually a nonprofit organization that the deceased or other family members have actively supported. Many obituary notices announce family preferences for a gift to a named charity in lieu of flowers.

A nonprofit organization's proper response to commemorative and tribute gifts consists of two acknowledgments: (1) a thank-you letter, receipt, or card sent to the donor, and (2) a notice forwarded to the honoree or family to announce that a gift has been made in an individual's name. The name and address of the donor (*never* the gift amount) are added to the second notice, for convenience, in case the honoree (or his or her family) wishes to send a personal acknowledgment.

Some of the donors who use commemorative and tribute gifts will be new to the nonprofit organization. Few of these people are likely to become candidates for other annual giving programs, including donor renewal solicitations, because their motive in making their first gift was to show respect for the person honored, not to support the designated organization. They probably will not give again, even if asked. The best hope for converting these donors into annual givers begins with properly acknowledging each donation, regardless of its size. A postage-paid reply envelope, to be used for a future commemorative or tribute gift, should be enclosed with the acknowledgment. This form of solicitation cannot be pushed on people; it must be treated as a special service offered to donors who choose to use it. An exception will be the prior donor who designated the organization to receive the memorial gifts and regularly makes commemorative and tribute donations. Supplying commemorative gift forms and postage-paid envelopes is a considerate and supportive service that will encourage repeat gifts. The cumulative gift history of these donors should reflect each additional contribution, especially when counting up the total for annual giving recognition purposes.

Every nonprofit organization can receive a commemorative or tribute gift and should be prepared to respond with the dual acknowledgments. National health agencies and healthcare organizations tend to receive memorial gifts; colleges and universities, museums, and arts organizations receive commemorative and tribute gifts. Organizations that are frequent recipients encourage this practice by preparing packets with multi-use forms and reply envelopes. The packet, usually a combination "turnaround" envelope that has detailed information printed on the preaddressed return envelope's back and flap, can be contained in a 3" × 9" brochure describing the many forms of commemorative and tribute gifts. The brochure may also describe the optional uses made of such gifts, illustrate the reply cards and quote their messages, and provide a supply of reply envelopes in a pocket flap. Displaying these brochures in lobbies and waiting rooms and near donor recognition walls will draw public attention to this gift option. Administrative details to support this program include hand-addressed envelopes and cards, records of all gifts received, separate accounting for each fund, communication of donors' names and addresses to the honored individual's family, assignment of the funds received, and special recognition. Most gifts received are retained within a special fund established in the honoree's name; each new gift received in that name is added to the special fund account. After the gifts are declared to be concluded, the funds are released to the purpose or project identified with the honoree or by the family. If significant funds ($2,500 or more), are involved, they may require additional consideration as to their use. They might be invested and preserved as an endowed fund for named scholarships or assigned to a priority purpose of the organization.

Recognition of commemorative gifts should be part of the nonprofit organization's honors and recognition policy (see Exhibit 4.4). The policy's guidelines may specify a minimum amount of funds needed to qualify for a named fund or for display within the donor recognition system (for example, $2,500 for inscription on the donor wall or on a plaque). Commemorative or tribute funds raised to establish an endowment fund—often to honor a retiring professor at a college or university—are likely to include several recognition components. The named endowment fund will carry the individual's name forward whenever the fund or the recipient is mentioned. Its complete title will appear in faculty rosters, catalogs, and publications. If a scholar-recipient publishes a research paper, the notation "Supported in part by the XYZ Research Endowment Fund" will be carried as a credit [1]. Prior to any announcement of the establishment of this form of recognition, commemorative and tribute gifts of considerable magnitude must be received by the nonprofit organization, and the naming and recognition must be approved and granted by the board of directors.

The names of honorees, the purposes of the funds, and the roster of participating donors may be published in institutional newsletters, magazines, and annual reports and may help to promote additional commemorative and tribute gifts. Apart from the visibility these named projects will enjoy, the name of each honoree and an updated list of those who have recently made gifts to the named fund should be a regular feature in the organization's newsletters, annual reports, and other publications.

Nonprofit organizations must be willing to invest the time and overhead needed to handle commemorative and tribute gifts properly. The effort and costs involved are minimal and will be repaid, but these gifts are not a predictable source of annual giving dollars. When a commemorative or tribute fund account is first established, a rush of giving usually follows; after a few weeks, the intensity often dwindles. Family members and honorees who expected more donors and larger gifts may be disappointed with these results. The reality is that most commemorative and tribute gifts are expressions of courtesy and respect, not investment decisions. The solicitation methods available are direct mail or obituary notices in the newspaper, certainly not the most effective ways to ask for gifts. In practice, commemorative gifts tend to have a short life; the period of intense giving lasts only several weeks at most. These gifts are also unpredictable for their ability to attract either a volume of donors or large donations, but each gift must be handled with care. Estimates of the annual results of commemorative and tribute gifts should always be conservative.

COMMERCIAL SALES, CAUSE-RELATED MARKETING, AND AFFINITY CARDS

These methods of raising money are unpredictable options. To understand what they are and what they can or cannot accomplish, some definitions are given here in alphabetical order:

Affinity cards. [Programs] in which an exempt organization is paid a portion of the revenues derived from the use of the cards by the consumers who make up the affinity group. The position of the IRS [Internal Revenue Service] is that the revenues from affinity card programs are taxable because they arise from the exploitation of mailing lists, and that the special exception for these lists is not available because the lists are provided to noncharitable organizations. [2]

Cause-related marketing. Fund-raising techniques used to generate nongift revenues, involving related and/or unrelated activities; the term usually includes charitable sales promotions and other forms of commercial co-ventures. [3]

Commercial co-venture. An arrangement between a for-profit organization and a charitable organization (sometimes more than one), whereby the for-profit entity agrees to make a contribution to the charitable entity, with the amount of the contribution determined by the volume of sales of products or services by the for-profit organization during a particular time period. [4]

The application of these options introduces three entirely new and complex questions that the board of directors and CEO must weigh at the outset:

1. May a commercial business be allowed to use the name of this nonprofit organization in advertising and selling its products?
2. What negotiations are required to resolve the amount to be received, or to verify the accounting for the sales of products or services that will provide income to this nonprofit organization?
3. Will this transaction qualify the nonprofit organization as carrying on an unrelated trade or business, for which it will be subjected to income tax on the revenue received?

The answer to the first question is: "Yes, but only after this gift horse has had a total body examination." Any nonprofit organization may enter into a written contract with a commercial business for sales and/or marketing purposes. State and local regulations, where applicable, will specify the details to be contained in the contract, the filing of copies with state and local authorities (which makes the details public knowledge), the financial reports due within a stated time following the campaign, and much more. All of these details demand additional investigation and complete observance. The contract should be signed by at least one officer of both parties.

Particular attention should be paid to (1) the methodology used to resolve the amount of money due to the nonprofit organization and (2) the specification of who is obligated for any expenses incurred.

The third question could be answered "Yes" or "No," depending on the product sold and the extent to which the nonprofit organization is involved in the product prior to and after a "sale" is made. One such marketing effort, a charitable life insurance program offered to members of the American Bar Endowment, lost its court case:

> Despite the findings of the lower courts, the U.S. Supreme Court held that the provision of group insurance policies, underwritten by major insurance companies, by the American Bar Endowment, a charitable organization, to its members constitutes the carrying on of an unrelated trade or business. The Court noted that the organization negotiates premium rates with insurers, selects the insurers that provide the coverage, solicits its membership, collects the premiums, transmits the premiums to the insurer, maintains files on each policyholder, answers members' questions concerning insurance policies, and screens claims for benefits. [5]

To some board members and CEOs of nonprofit organizations, commercial sales, cause-related marketing, and affinity cards may appear to be ways to produce "easy money with little effort on their part." (Those words telegraph a warning; beware!) These methods are not reliable sources of annual gifts, for two reasons:

1. When sales fail to meet expectations, the company withdraws from the program;
2. No record of the buyer/donor is captured; there is no opportunity to renew the gift.

An understanding of why these programs appeal to companies might come from standing in their shoes. They want to trade on the public image and reputation of a nonprofit organization to sell their products; they believe the public will be more inclined to purchase from them because they are donating a portion of the sales price for a well-known and respected charitable purpose. What's on the line for the company? Sales volume and profits. What's on the line for the nonprofit organization? Image and reputation! If a nonprofit organization wants to build a strong and lasting relationship with any local business, corporation, or firm, it should do so for reasons other than a windfall "easy money" gift opportunity.

Affinity cards are perhaps the most recent arrival among creative products used for annual giving. A common example is a bank credit card offered by a nonprofit organization to its donors. The organization enters into a joint venture with a bank and negotiates a competitive interest rate to offer donors for Mastercard or Visa credit card privileges. Most donors may already use more than one bank credit card at any one time, but they probably will not yet own one with their favorite nonprofit organization's name and logo on the face. The special added offer is that a percentage of the value of items purchased via card use will be returned to the organization as a "contribution." Affinity cards appear to overcome many of the objections lined up against other ways to raise money every year, as discussed at the beginning of this chapter. They build relationships with donors, encourage annual giving, raise money in a cost-effective manner, recognize and reward donors, and build confidence and trust in the organization. Of concern are the issues raised regarding commercial sales and cause-related marketing, including unrelated business income tax (UBIT) on the revenue delivered to the nonprofit organization.

Can commercial sales, cause-related marketing, and affinity cards be used by nonprofit organizations in their annual giving programs? Yes; but only after due diligence and full disclosure by both parties of their dual objectives and their ability to meet IRS and state regulations without potential damage to the nonprofit organization [6].

DOOR-TO-DOOR AND ON-STREET SOLICITATION

Friend-raising and relationship building can seldom be achieved using these "cold-call" approaches. As methods of annual giving, both have diminished in use by all but a few nonprofit organizations over the past decade. The reasons for this decline may include:

1. Loss of volunteer workers who would solicit;
2. Distaste for the confrontational style required;
3. Public resistance and suspicion;
4. City and state regulations; police enforcement;
5. Poor results; raising only "what's in my pocket at the time";
6. Too much of a money-raising-only tactic; no time or opportunity to present the case or consider the merits of the cause;
7. Names and addresses not retained for renewal requests;
8. Lack of an adequate public response;
9. Concern for the safety of volunteer workers.

Only a few successful practitioners of door-to-door and on-street solicitation remain. The best known are the annual cookie sale by the Girl Scouts of America and The Salvation Army and Volunteers of America holiday appeals, which feature musicians, singers, bell ringers, and "kettles and red pots." Many of America's national health foundations conducted door-to-door solicitations in the past but most of these have been absorbed into other causes or have adopted other media. The charity coin canisters that continue to be displayed, for example, in McDonald's restaurants, for Ronald McDonald houses, are usually linked with a corporate sponsor that accepts the responsibility to monitor the money and channel it properly. One national firm, Taco Bell Corp., collects about $1 million annually for the Muscular Dystrophy Association using "Jerry's Kids" canisters. Young people are obliged to use door-to-door and on-street solicitations as fund-raising methods for their school or camp projects. Offers of magazine subscriptions, specialty candy products, and car washes, which are actually commercial sales disguised as fund-raising opportunities, are common. Homeowners have developed sales resistance to door-to-door cold-calling solicitations. Telephone callers may be the last to pursue the strategy of cold calls to homeowners (see the section on telemarketing below), whose resistance to this method is growing as well. It seems fair to state that most door-to-door and on-street solicitations have become quite commercial in nature. The public has become confused about whether they are buying products or making gifts for charitable purposes. The media have given better than usual coverage to scams and con artists whose fraudulent and abusive practices originated from door-to-door and on-street charitable solicitations that defrauded the public. These criminals have hurt the overall image of nonprofit organizations, reduced volunteer effectiveness, increased public resistance, and damaged the public's underlying confidence and trust in making gifts when invited to do so, whether at their home or business, or on the street. Perhaps it is better for everyone that door-to-door and on-street solicitation is diminishing.

FEDERATED CAMPAIGNS

The annual operating budgets of many nonprofit organizations depend on being an approved institution or agency in a federated campaign. This style of annual solicitation is a combined or joint appeal held in the workplace once a year on behalf of all the members in the federation, who share in the results. Two of the most famous of these, United Way of America and the Combined Federal Campaign, have developed the workplace solicitation, payroll deduction, and corporate annual gift to a high degree of success. Because of the success of United Way of America and the Combined Federal Campaign, many nonprofit organizations that were not members of either group (and are denied access to the participating companies and their employees during campaign periods) have petitioned successfully to be allowed into the workplace at other times to solicit. Corporations and their employees are a proven source of reliable annual gifts, but the designated charities will not receive all of their annual gift support from workplace campaigns. Dependence on any single source of funds can become a liability when that source falters. Following the William Aramony scandal at United Way of America headquarters in 1992, contributions declined dramatically, including allocations from member United Way chapters across the country. The member organizations affiliated with these chapters received between 20 and 30 percent less money as their allocation, a large amount to make up in one year through other annual giving methods.

Federated campaigns appear to have established "turf" ownership of the corporation, its employees, and, to a degree, the Fall campaign period. For member organizations, any other corporate solicitation and employee solicitation at home is "off limits" throughout this period. Nonmember organizations are completely free to solicit both groups, but the competition is keen and the phrase "I gave at the office" is a frequently heard response. I am unaware of any major study that has demonstrated whether public giving has been diminished for nonmember organizations as a consequence of this practice. The Fall months remain the prime period for every nonprofit organization to conduct its annual giving campaigns. The results seem to suggest that the public also prefers to make most of its gifts during this time period.

GAMBLING AND GAMES OF CHANCE

Gambling is a strong word but it is accurate to describe a select group of fund-raising activities when they are used for annual giving purposes by nonprofit organizations. In alphabetical order, gambling activities include auctions, bingo, Las Vegas or Monte Carlo nights, lotteries, raffles, and sweepstakes. At issue here is not whether they can raise money; they do. The fact is that they are forms of gambling as defined by law in most states as well as in county and city jurisdictions, and may not be charitable giving opportunities at all. At best, they can be used only occasionally by nonprofit organizations to raise money for charitable purposes. Greg Gattuso [7] reports: "Lawmakers in a number of states are considering legislation that would ban charitable gambling. . . . A bill in the Rhode Island state legislature proposes a ban on all poker, slot machines, and other casino games in the state. . . . Recently, the state of Arizona banned all casino gambling, including all fund-raising gaming." Gambling has a limited ability to develop faithful annual donors; what it appears to develop is faithful gamblers. Advocates espouse the philosophy that gambling is OK because they will "clean the tainted money by its good works." Gambling in any of its forms is a risky business for any nonprofit organization to use for fund-raising purposes. Most states limit its use and a few outlaw it altogether. When and where permitted, gambling and games of chance may operate only under strict supervision and are limited as to their frequency. Several cities and counties have enacted additional local ordinances in an attempt to regulate and supervise most of the forms of gambling and games of chance, including bingo, within their jurisdiction. Exhibit 9.1 lists charitable gambling's games [8]. They can be a serious problem, especially for the uninitiated, unaware, and unthinking.

Auctions and raffles are included in these regulations because money is exchanged for goods bid on and purchased. Auctions may be the most benign of gambling forms; raffles can easily run afoul of state lottery laws. Even U.S. Postal Service regulations are involved, if raffle tickets are sold through the mail. Volunteers who espouse these methods often cite the fact that they have never heard of a nonprofit organization being prosecuted for holding an auction or raffle—yet. How much comfort should the board of directors and CEO take from that fact? Very little, according to Hopkius [9]:

> Players were charged a fixed amount for the use of bingo cards, the games were held on three nights each week, and the receipts from and expenses of the games were substantial. The IRS concluded that "the bingo games constitute a trade or business with the general public, the conduct of which is not substantially related to the exercise or the performance by the organization of the purposes for which it was organized other than the use it makes of the profits derived from the games." [The organization was unable to utilize the exemption from unrelated income taxation afforded by IRC § 513(f) because, under the law of the state in which it is organized (Texas), the bingo games constituted, at that time, an illegal lottery.]

All but four states allow one or more of the forms of charitable gambling. Permits for nonprofit organizations to hold a Las Vegas or Monte Carlo night, the most obvious form of gambling, as a fund-raising activity may be obtained (usually from city or county police departments), but they contain restrictions on the types of games allowed and the hours of operation, and they require strict financial controls (no "real money" is permitted; only scrip or chips). Local authorities will require at least one uniformed police officer to be present at all times (at the organization's expense), usually stationed at the "cage" where chips and scrip are exchanged for cash. No patron can win any money; winnings must be converted into prizes, which can be purchased, auctioned, or raffled off. A complete financial report must be filed following the event, and the city or county may exact an excise tax on the proceeds.

Bingo: Players buy cards printed with a grid containing letters or numbers, and cover the symbols that match those selected at random and announced to people in the bingo hall. The first player to cover all symbols arrayed in a certain fashion, usually in a row, wins a prize.

Calcuttas: Players bet on which participant in a sports event (a rodeo or golf tournament, for example) will be victorious. The size of the wager varies according to each participant's perceived skill—for example, a golfer's handicap. The bets are pooled, then divided based on the outcome of the event.

Casino Nights: Also called Las Vegas nights, Nevada nights, Monte Carlo nights, or millionaire parties, these are temporary mock casinos, featuring games like blackjack, craps, and roulette. In some states, players wager play money after paying an entrance fee; in others they buy chips as in regular casinos.

Charity Game Tickets: Available in hundreds of versions, known variously as pull-tabs, jar tickets, break-opens, pickle tabs, paper roulette, criss crosses, etc. Players buy a sealed bit of paper and unfold it, lift up the perforated tabs on a card, or otherwise reveal hidden numbers or symbols—like those on a slot machine. If the numbers of symbols disclosed match the winning array, they win a prize. The tickets are often sold at bingo games, in taverns or restaurants, or even in the offices of some charities.

Keno: Players bet on combinations of numbers. Those whose picks come closest to the ones drawn at random win a prize. Often played during casino nights.

Paddlewheels: Players bet on which number, color, or symbol will be selected when a large vertical wheel stops spinning.

Punchboards: Players punch a hole through a face sheet of a cardboard playing board to obtain a folded bit of paper. If the number or symbol on the paper matches the winning combination displayed on the board, the player wins a prize.

Raffles: Players buy numbered tickets, each of which represents a chance to win a prize of cash or merchandise. From the pool of all entrants, a number is selected at random, and the holder of the matching ticket wins the prize.

Tipboards: Players buy and remove game tickets affixed to a board and see if the number printed on the ticket matches a number printed on the board. If players have a match, they put their names on the board next to their number. When all the tickets have been purchased, a seal on the board is opened and an underlying number is disclosed. The player whose number matches the winning one takes the prize, which can be cash or merchandise.

Other Games: Games permitted in some states include video versions of bingo or poker; fish ponds, crane games, and other activities where the object is to capture a particular prize; sports pools, in which players bet on professional sports contests; and simulcast horse racing (or off-track betting). Alaska has spawned unusual variants like dog-mushing contests or fish derbies, in which players bet on whose dog sled will finish first along a certain course or on who will catch the first or the largest fish.

Exhibit 9.1 From Bingo to Tipboards: Common Charitable-Gambling Games [8]. Reprinted with permission of *The Chronicle of Philanthropy*.

Where they are allowed, they are closely regulated, involve high fixed costs for equipment rental and operator fees, and require fees of from 5% to 10% of income to city or county authorities, along with filing of a full financial statement of all income and expenses. They incur all the overhead costs of any special and benefit event and are hard to manage for a minimum goal of 50% net profit to the charity. If their only real benefit seems to be appeasement of those few volunteers and donors who just want to gamble, an organization must evaluate whether gambling is the type of activity it should be known for in the community. [10]

The amount of money involved in charitable gambling is staggering. In a report compiled by the National Association of Fundraising Ticket Manufacturers, more than $5.9 billion was wagered in 26 states during 1991, the latest year for which information is available. The figure is nearly double the $3.05 billion reported by 23 states in 1989. The amounts delivered to charity were not this total sum; the highest was 35 percent of gross revenue (in only two states). Most proceeds were in the 10 percent to mid-20 percent range, and five were below 10 percent. The final figure of note was the amount provided to the 26 states in 1991 in tax revenue: over $200 million [11].

The board of directors and CEO should exercise their stewardship responsibilities and be certain that whatever type of gambling or games of chance are offered, they will be conducted fully within the law. Volunteers may fail to recognize, in their well-intentioned enthusiasm to raise money for charity, that much more is at stake than staging a bingo party or a Las Vegas night, or that adding an auction or raffle to a black-tie dinner dance actually adds many complications. The tax-exempt status of the nonprofit organization may be put on the line.

Can any of the forms of gambling be used in an annual giving program, perhaps as a feature of a benefit? Yes, because the activity is held only once or twice a year by the sponsoring nonprofit organization. If the event were held weekly, the purpose would clearly change: gambling would become the chief reason for holding the event. Local regulations governing auctions, raffles, bingo, and Las Vegas or Monte Carlo nights, when followed meticulously and without deviation, can be used to enhance traditional annual giving methods—chiefly, activities, benefits, and special events. Lotteries and sweepstakes, where allowed, are in a different class because they use the mails; the U.S. Postal Service and the Treasury Department (income taxes are due on money raised from gambling) join state and local authorities as interested parties to these activities.

The United Cancer Council (which was one of the charities involved as a recipient of Watson & Hughey sweepstakes) had its tax exemption status pulled by the IRS, which said that the charity operated for the nonexempt purpose of operating sweepstakes games through its fund raiser (Watson & Hughey) to which it paid 93 percent of its total gross income in 1986 and 1987. [12]

Lotteries and sweepstakes are not recommended unless careful prior analysis of every layer of law and regulation is completed first. With so much at risk and with more efficient and profitable annual giving methods available to every nonprofit organization, the board of directors is well-advised to avoid gambling and games of chance as a "regularly carried on" portion of their annual giving programs.

MULTIMEDIA OPTIONS

Today's technology allows instant and effective communications with nearly everyone. Consequently, the public is deluged with instant worldwide information on every subject imaginable, visually, audially, and in writing. The challenges to nonprofit organizations are:

1. What is their message; what is it about their cause and appeal that will be heard?
2. Whom should they be trying to reach?
3. What media must they use to reach those whose help they seek?

For most nonprofit organizations, broadcast, telecast, or other mass communications will not be necessary in order to carry out their annual giving programs. A selection of national and international agencies (for example, UNICEF and World Vision) will engage in massive multimedia forms of communications because of their mission. A few other nonprofit organizations, using "televangelist" messages or "infomercials," will be able to deliver their programs and services directly into the home using live telecasts via satellite and telephone line. In advance of a telecast, an information packet and videotaped message promoting the program are received by mail, possibly followed-up by a telephone call to encourage watching the telecast. The telecast makes the case and invites contributions. A solicitation letter arrives within days to secure the gift. Such a level of "high touch" using multimedia "high tech" is available to only a few among even the largest and best funded of nonprofit organizations [13].

Being able to talk with or write to prospects and donors requires effective communication within an available segment of the total market. Market segmentation is the essential first step, as it is in direct mail solicitation, when the lists to be used for acquisition must be selected carefully to build a constituency (see Chapters Two and Three).

The key to success with nonprofit organizations is in keeping close to donors and prospects.

> Our focus must become one of understanding our donors, their needs, beliefs and attitudes. We need to get close to donors to aid their trust in our organizations and our programs. To succeed, we must master computers and the art of talking in the style of one-on-one dialogue with everybody. [14]

The five means available for audio and visual communications, each of which can be used with one or more annual giving fund-raising methods, are: advertising, radio, television (including cable channels and video cassettes), the computer, and the telephone. Budget will remain the single largest constraint on how much each of these (or more than one) will be put to use by nonprofit organizations. Creativity can overcome many fiscal constraints. Computer access to the "technology highway" offers multiple ways of using alternate forms of multimedia techniques in support of annual giving communications. For those who do find a way to access the airwaves, improved results will likely occur.

PREMIUMS

A premium is a gift returned to a donor in exchange for the gift amount requested. The quality of the premium and its uniqueness or distinctive nature are advertised to encourage the gift. Premium objects appear to be "for-sale" items, except that the value of the premium is well below the amount of the gift required to qualify for or "purchase" the premium. If any object or "gift" is given back to a donor as a token of appreciation or as a recognition award after the contribution is received, it may not be a premium because it was not a condition for a gift; the exchange or "sale" of the object was not advertised or known to the donor prior to the gift decision. The types of objects often used as premiums range from bumper stickers, decals, calendars, and coffee mugs to caps, tote bags, and umbrellas, all bearing the nonprofit organization's logo and message. The theory behind the practice of offering premiums is that the object is a desirable commodity, or the promise of a "give back" is enticement enough for the donor to make the gift.

Premiums and donor recognition "presents" work quite well when the product can somehow be related to the exempt mission and purpose of the nonprofit organization. For example, public radio and television stations offer tapes of popular programs already aired; they are known to be of high quality and are not available in stores or from any other source. Likewise, museums offer reprints and art books picturing their special collections; colleges offer graduation rings; the U.S. Olympic Committee offers patches and pins; environmental groups offer bumper stickers, decals, and wildlife stamps; veterans groups send key chains and return address labels; the list is endless. Other nonprofit organizations may not have (as of yet) objects to match their purposes. Soup kitchens, for example, probably could not sell their soup even if markets gave them counter space. For these organizations, an alternative is to purchase objects they can offer as premiums or "gifts" for donors. Some donors look forward to receipt of the premium product they purchased, if that was their motive in giving. Many other donors are less interested in what is offered in exchange for their gift. If premium objects are considered trinkets or the type of "stuff" people already possess in excessive supply (how many bumper stickers will one car hold? how many coffee mugs will fit on one shelf?), the incentive has less effect. More favorable results may be attained from premiums or "give backs" offered as incentives for donor renewal rather than for acquisition of first-time donors, especially when they represent a reward for upgrading to higher annual gift levels. Considerable creativity is required to find the right object, one that is appealing and has a low unit cost. Once premiums and "gifts" are introduced to annual donors, objects of equal attractiveness and appeal must be found *every year*. Many donors do not react well when the annual "extra" is discontinued.

For guidance when considering the use of premiums, the advice of the Disabled American Veterans, which has been using premiums since 1942, is valid:

1. Use premiums which have a logical tie-in with your organization. . . .
2. Use premiums with the highest perceived value at the lowest cost. . . .
3. Feature premium offer in copy. . . .
4. Use premiums which require periodic replacement. . . .
5. Provide quality premiums. . . .
6. Use premiums only when cost-effective. [15]

Premium objects provided in advance, at the time of solicitation, are called *unsolicited merchandise* and are used only occasionally today. The intent behind this practice is to engender guilt in the recipient, who may feel that the object should not be kept and used without making a gift to the organization that sent it. The cost of such objects must be added to the already high mailing expense; with rising postage and materials costs, this practice may soon disappear altogether. Veterans groups and a few others continue shipping return address labels and decorator stamps as part of their direct mail solicitations; environmental groups offer holiday greeting cards (printed with soy ink on recycled paper). Most recipients use the cards and address labels without making a gift, and they decorate their personal and business mail with the wildlife and Easter seal stamps (insinuating to recipients that the sender supports these nonprofit organizations). For the sake of those who *are* faithful donors, sending out unsolicited merchandise *after* a gift is made would seem a fairer (or more honest) protocol to follow.

Donor recognition gifts are part of the donor relations and donor communications program. Donors are worth extra attention and even a "gift" now and then to acknowledge the importance of their support. Guidelines for donor recognition gifts should be well-defined and tied to the amount(s) of the annual gift, the cumulative gifts made throughout the year (see Exhibit 5.5), and the cumulative giving history (see Exhibit 6.4). As an example, the names of donors who gave $1,000 within one year might be displayed on a special plaque throughout the following year. They also might receive a certificate attesting to their status as members of the "Millenium Club." Donors who achieve higher levels, such as $10,000, $25,000, or $100,000, either with a single gift in one year or from cumulative gifts after many years, may receive a donor recognition "gift" of a glass paperweight or quartz clock displaying the logo of the nonprofit organization. The IRS will be interested in the actual value of these objects if they exceed 2 percent of the original gift value. Most organizations buy these objects in bulk to keep the unit price down, but there is potential for an IRS challenge to the amount a donor may claim as a charitable contribution deduction. If the premium or "give-back" object exceeds the 2 percent test amount, the material value of the object will reduce the value of the original contribution.

Donor recognition is an important part of annual giving, especially in renewal communications. Caution should be exercised when offering recognition that may more accurately be defined as customer relations or benefits purchased in exchange for premiums, "gift" objects, and services. Will a donor "switch" products (and nonprofit organizations) if a nicer premium or a lower interest rate is offered? The "commerciality test" is a valid measurement of whether premiums, "gift" objects, and services are more accurately benefits and privileges extended to donors in recognition of their generosity, or commercial products and services in exchange for gift amounts. The variety and value of donor recognition programs, benefits, and privileges seem to outweigh the commercial exchange, especially when building with donors relationships that need to last for many years.

TELEPHONE AND TELEMARKETING SOLICITATION

Technology offers wonderful tools for organizations to use in annual gift fund-raising. A telephone conversation is "the next best thing to being there." (In-person, eyeball-to-eyeball contact remains number-one.) The telephone is an important instrument for raising friends and building relationships with prospects, donors, and volunteers because it allows discussion and encourages comments and questions. Information can be exchanged in a few moments, and conversation allows emotion and enthusiasm to be added. The multiple uses of telephone solicitation for annual giving purposes, in ascending order of effectiveness, include:

1. Cold calls, to acquire a first-time donor;
2. Thank-you calls, to thank a donor for a gift that has just arrived;
3. Lapsed donor calls, to try to recapture prior donors;
4. Ticket sales calls, to follow-up on invitations to activities, benefits, and special events and encourage attendance;
5. Membership calls, to invite and renew annual memberships;
6. Club, guild, or group calls, to retain interest and participation;
7. Upgrade calls, to invite a larger gift than last time;
8. Renewal calls, to request another, perhaps ungraded gift;
9. Recruiting calls, to invite someone to volunteer time and talent;
10. Recognition calls, to thank someone for service or to announce an award;
11. Donor relations calls, to maintain close contact with donors.

The telephone can assist each annual giving fund-raising program in improving its effectiveness and efficiency. In certain situations, telephone solicitation may be able to stand alone as an independent annual giving technique. Computer access to communications networks over telephone lines has opened both the information database and the technology highway to use for annual giving purposes. Up-and-down links to networks and databases that include telephone numbers and demographic details allow nonprofit organizations (or their telephone consultants and vendors) to access and retrieve volumes of suspect names (and telephone numbers) anywhere in the world. Computers can analyze these data as easily as they sort direct mail prospects and discover candidates who are likely to be well-matched to the mission of the nonprofit organization. The next steps, representing a leap in technology, will begin with automatic dialing (using power dialing and predictive dialing) to place a call for a volunteer or paid caller, who will use a computer screen instead of a paper script during conversation with the prospect or donor. A facsimile message might initiate this contact and follow-up with automatic dialing within minutes. The discussion will be supplemented with added information received by FAX in response—instantaneously—to questions. After the gift decision, the pledge form will be received and returned by FAX, or, better yet, the gift will be made immediately by electronic funds transfer (EFT). Only minutes will elapse from dialing to gift deposit, and the entire transaction will be done over telephone lines. The telephone has already demonstrated its effectiveness in today's world, and the level of cost-effectiveness appears to be equally promising. With widespread accessibility to such "high tech" potential for efficient and effective fund-raising just over the horizon, nonprofit organizations need to be concerned with preserving as much "high touch" with their prospects and donors as they can, for as long as possible.

Because the telephone can be an organization's golden goose, attention should be given to its care and feeding. Public resentment and resistance are increasing in response to the intrusive volume of commercial and nonprofit calling. As discussed earlier in this chapter, the use of commercial methods by nonprofit organizations can cloud the public's ability to distinguish between a call for help from a needy nonprofit and a call for a commission from a product sales rep or service organization. Proposed legislation to limit telemarketing's persistent use of telephone lines has been introduced in several states and at the federal level. Controls may be imposed to limit calling hours and to allow telephone owners to "block" automatic dialing calls, which will curtail the efficiencies now becoming available. Technology produces wonderful tools; appropriate use will be the test of their flowering or demise. The most natural control, cost, will slow nonprofit organizations from immediate access to some predicted advances in telephone technology. Cost also will be the measuring factor as organizations try to resolve whether direct mail, an increasingly expensive medium because of rising postal and materials costs, can remain effective in acquiring and retaining donors. The answer may lie in linkage rather than choice; the telephone and the letter can complement each other in a multimedia effort to achieve positive results.

Within a nonprofit organization, the fund development office should lead the way in utilizing telephone skill and technology. Annual giving is a people business dedicated to friend-raising and relationship building among large numbers of people. For many organizations, especially those with limited resources, organizing and training volunteers to make telephone calls to donors and prospects will be an effective addition to their existing annual giving solicitation program. Office telephones will remain a constant and personal link to prospects, donors, and volunteers.

Fund-raising consulting and telemarketing firms can provide considerable skill and expertise in telephone use for all forms of annual giving solicitation. Many organizations prefer (or can only afford) volunteer callers, but outside firms can be hired to train volunteers and staff on how to conduct calls. They can also guide the organization in prospect identification, data preparations, follow-up procedures, and pledge notices. There is some debate over whether volunteer callers, who cost less, are better than paid callers, who are supposed to get better results (even after higher costs). Each nonprofit organization must evaluate where telephone solicitation best fits into its overall annual giving program, and the role it can play to aid in friend-raising, relationship building, and donor renewal. Experience to date suggests that *initial use* of phonathon and telemarketing techniques boosts the number of donors participating and their gift size. The nonprofit organization must measure (1) whether other annual giving methods decline in performance as a result of telephone use, and (2) how well telephone solicitation continues to perform over several years, in the level of pledges made and collected. The track record of traditional annual giving methods is well established for comparative purposes. The telephone is powerful, but its joint use in conjunction with other, ongoing annual giving programs appears to be its best application at the present time.

> Adding a mail component to telemarketing takes the process a giant step forward. A letter or series of letters from key [hospital] staff, physicians, or volunteers can most effectively present the case for support and present it with a request for specific level of support. Especially when personalized letters are signed (with a signature machine) and sent using live stamps, an impression of one-to-one solicitation is created. Since people have time to read the letter, they can also think about the dollar request made. The call, when it comes, is not a cold call but the culmination of a careful cultivation process. The caller can more easily establish a rapport with the prospect, aiming not at a quick yes or no response but a decision. [16]

All the results should be measured to learn how much of a difference telephone use has made to the total annual giving program. When use of the telephone is considered separately as a stand-alone fund-raising method (perhaps as an economic decision, just to raise money), the results should be compared with the start-up costs and first three years' performance of other annual giving programs. If telephone use can prove its ability to raise friends and build relationships that last over many years, it will become a true partner in the annual giving process.

Potential problem areas also surround telephone use. Con artists are always current with technology and with public weaknesses. Scams, fraud, and abuses do occur, but legitimate nonprofit organizations can easily stay within the law and avoid problems. Caution is important when considering a decision to hire a firm or an individual to make calls or to engage in commercial sales or cause-related marketing projects in the name of the organization. Detailed contracts with professional solicitors will protect the contracting parties, the prospects and donors, and the organization's image and reputation. To paraphrase another well-known admonition, *Don't* leave the calling to them. One of the newer problems involves fraudulent use of 900 numbers as a pay-per-call medium for ordering merchandise and for other services. Fraud has also appeared in multimedia form: television or radio appeals announce 800 or 900 numbers to call for premiums and services that ask for credit card numbers, with predictable results. The FCC and several state attorneys general have begun to place restrictions on use of 900 numbers. Robert Abrams, New York's Attorney General, has warned: "While many of the 900 numbers are legitimate—offering such services as stock prices, used-car tips and sports scores—a growing number are run by con artists who have taken advantage of the industry's enormous power and regulatory loopholes to perpetrate fraud after fraud upon unsuspecting customers" [17]. As with other problem areas, the trust the public places in the use of alternate fund-raising methods by nonprofit organizations raises more hard questions and provides few good answers.

The next leap in telephone technology is untested for annual giving purposes: the use of "E-mail" and the videophone. Both are beginning to be available. E-mail allows instant access to enormous numbers of people and, coupled with EFT, will challenge all mailing forms as the preferred mass communications strategy. After videophone installations become commonplace, the telephone will likely become as effective as face-to-face meetings for fund-raising purposes. A visual–voice medium is the strongest communications combination possible.

TELEVISION AND TELETHON SOLICITATION

Much of the information and advice that applies to telephone use to enhance annual giving also applies to television as a medium for sales and solicitation, except that television costs more. Several nonprofit organizations are already using television, notably churches and "televangelists," a word coined out of their preference for this most personal of mediums. Other well-known users are public television stations, for their pledge campaigns; the Children's Miracle Network (a consortium of children's healthcare causes); and the Muscular Dystrophy Association, for its traditional Labor Day telethon starring Jerry Lewis and "Jerry's Kids." There are other, mostly local users, and they have proportionately similar results. How strong is television as a fund-raising medium? Each of the national appeals raises millions each time it goes on the air. These productions are maximum efforts, but they yield maximum returns. A telethon is a major benefit, a membership drive, and a personal appeal—all rolled into one powerful communications channel. Telethons have larger followings than most hit TV series. Cable systems and transmission via satellite offer an increasing array of access channels as alternate outlets for television use. With FCC regulations endorsing every radio station and television (including cable) channel to offer some hours of PSAs each week, an array of prepared programs, "infomercials," and PSAs can be effective for nonprofit use. If "the medium is the message," then fund-raising has begun to build a home in television.

Only a few nonprofit organizations currently have access to television or can afford to purchase air time, but the other use of this visual medium is becoming widespread—video cassettes. They are no more expensive than newsletters, magazines, or annual reports, and they are far more able to "make the case" eloquently and succinctly and stir a donor to action. With over 80 million video cassette recorders (VCRs) sold in the past decade, nearly every homeowner can play a cassette received in the mail and may be moved to reply. The proper name, mailing address, and telephone number of the charity should be provided in the mailing packet and repeated frequently on the screen. Again, multimedia strategies appear to work best.

The problems with television use are not as great as those with telephone use. By controlling transmission, the medium thwarts most fraudulent schemes, although a few scams and con-artist schemes do occur, usually in the form of copyright infringements on pirated videos. One problem area for annual giving programs is in building a constituency that cares about the mission of the nonprofit organization as much as the "show" that sparked the gift. The exception here appears to be religious organizations' telecasts; donor renewal is pursued vigorously, and the programs are on the air constantly. For other organizations, donor renewal rates can be improved with better donor relations and communications between broadcasts, but these represent added expenses. Television reaches hundreds of thousands, even millions of people instantly. The frequency with which TV donors will move into other annual giving categories and upgrade their annual gifts is about the same as for any other fund-raising method. A special problem is TV pledge collections: defaults may run as high as 20 to 25 percent, the highest in fund-raising practice.

VARIOUS OTHER ANNUAL GIVING IDEAS OF MERIT

The best use of all these other ways to raise money every year is in partnership with ongoing annual giving programs. When they are offered alone, they may perform well only once or twice. Usually, their performance peaks at the beginning because they offer something new to the constituency; they may fade when they are seen as just another way to ask for money each year. Using them intermittently and coordinating them with ongoing programs will help to keep them fresh. The same criteria used to measure the annual giving methods described in Chapters 2 through 8 should be applied: How well can they raise new friends, build new relationships, and renew annual gifts from prior donors? There are some higher tests to pass: Do they enhance the image and reputation of the nonprofit organization? Do they inspire greater public confidence and trust in its mission and purposes as well as its ability to use their money well? Some of these other forms to raise money every year may not meet these final standards. If not, that is reason enough to give them a second look or to divert their investment of time and budget to already proven annual giving programs.

In what other ways can an organization raise money every year? Art shows, bake sales, sports tournaments, travel tours, and other fund-raising ideas are conducted as activities, benefits, and special events (see Exhibit 7.9 for a list). No doubt there are quite a few others. The other ways to raise money discussed in this chapter may find a good home in one or more of the broad-based annual giving programs of mailings, memberships, clubs, and volunteer solicitors. Some may be usable in combinations, emerging as creative fund-raising concepts for annual giving purposes. The final assessment is whether any other ways can pass the CARE test:

1. Comfort for the donor in the cause, the solicitation method used, and how the approach is made;
2. Anticipation of the request and preparedness with adequate information that encourages a decision to give;
3. Readiness to give because of a conviction that the money will be well used for charitable purposes that serve the public good;
4. Enjoyment in the act of giving and a welcome to the invitation to give again.

SCAMS AND CON ARTIST'S FRAUD AND ABUSE

Unfortunately, ours is not a perfect world. There are a few people who would use all of the annual giving fund-raising methods presented in this book (and the other ways to raise money every year described in this chapter) to defraud the public and put the money raised to personal use. The public is not easily able to distinguish between a legitimate nonprofit organization that is soliciting via mail or telephone, or offering a coupon or premium, from another that acts, looks, and sounds exactly alike, but is not legitimate. Public confusion is increased when "look-alike" and "sound-alike" names are given to bogus organizations. The American Cancer Society is the official name of the largest public health agency in America, and its name is well-known to most people. Dozens of other legitimate cancer support organizations use the word "cancer" in their title but are not as well known. A name for a fictional organization may include "Cancer" and add, at the beginning or end, "American," "National," "Coalition," "Friends," "Association," "Institute" or other imaginative choices. Why do scams, run by con artists, engage in fraud, and abuse the public's good intentions in giving to charity? To keep the money for themselves. Harvey Dale [18] described the effect on the independent sector:

> [A]buses hurt the sector. In the wake of the televangelist scandals, donations to almost *all* television ministries fell dramatically. When Father Ritter came under criticism, Covenant House was severely and adversely impacted. Although government can raise funds by forced exaction, and business can tempt investors with profits, the nonprofit sector has nothing to offer except its good image, good purposes, and good activities. We should be vigilant to seek out and eliminate undesirable conduct before it corrodes and tarnishes the luster of our activities. We should be concerned, then, when an inadequate level of supervision and scrutiny leaves an enlarged scope for undetected abuses.

The role of government is to protect the public from fraud and abuse. Because it is difficult and expensive to do so, problems arise. State governments have the police powers to provide consumer protection services and to enforce antifraud activities. David Ormstedt [19] warns:

> There will always be fraud and other misuse of charitable assets. There is fraud and abusive conduct in every segment of society. Government cannot eradicate it. The best government can hope for, and the most the public should expect of government, is that efficient regulation will keep problems reasonably under control.

Government's limited resources to pursue illegal activities have hindered its effectiveness. A locked door or safe can be picked, but at least entry is delayed. A door that is open just a crack offers no protection at all. When criminals choose to use annual giving and other recognizable fund-raising methods to defraud the public of money in the name of charity, nonprofit organizations and their donors have cause for concern. Ormstedt [20] gives this summation:

To maintain a strong charitable sector and to foster confidence in charitable institutions, fraud in the name of charity must be minimized. The public needs reasonable assurance that their donations and the donations of others, as well as their tax dollars that are, in effect, used to subsidize charities, are being used in a manner consistent with their expectations. Thus, government needs to be able and prepared to ensure the due application of charitable funds. This means not only prosecuting fraud. It also means ensuring that restricted donations are used for the restricted purpose. A person who donates money in response to an appeal for money for financial assistance to victims of a disease has every right to expect that the donation will be used for that purpose and not some other purpose, even if the alternate purpose serves a charitable objective.

One of the most difficult challenges to prospects and donors, to nonprofit organizations, and to state and local regulators, is the use of annual giving fund-raising methods by professional solicitors. Many of these "paid" or "commercial" solicitors operate within the law, but some do not and others appear to teeter at the very edge of legality and legitimacy. Anyone is entitled to conduct a business and to provide qualified professional solicitation services to nonprofit organizations. Some nonprofit organizations, however, hire paid solicitors because they believe they cannot raise money (or they do not want to), and they will accept the offer of a sizable gift in return for "no-effort-on-your-part" services (warning!). Some commercial solicitors have been allowed considerable freedom in the use of organizations' names and in the methods chosen for public solicitation. The organizations appear to be willing to look the other way in order to receive the money promised.

The solicitation practices that have caused much public criticism and regulatory pursuit include telephone requests from a police or firefighter "widows and orphans fund." The caller, implying that he or she is a police officer or firefighter, appeals to the public's concern for the families of deceased public servants, and offer to come to the home or business within a few hours to pick up the money. (Legitimate appeals of this origin remind the prospect, on the telephone, to ask for the solicitor's identification and to accept a receipt and perhaps a window sticker that carries the organization's seal. Checks made out to the organization are requested rather than cash.) Another scam is a ticket sales campaign to take hospitalized or handicapped children to a circus or sports event, again using a "runner" to come and get the money. A third example is a request for advertising in a program book for a special veterans benefit, to which the caller is also selling tickets. Each of these appeals may actually exist (or the event may have been recently held). The caller may be operating in its wake and pocketing the funds collected. The "runner" may even arrive wearing a uniform but is not a police officer or firefighter. A few circus tickets may be delivered, but the circus may never come to town. The program book never gets printed and the benefit event to honor veterans is never held. Each contact was a deception to defraud the public of money. Additional clues to fraudulent behavior include: the caller has no literature to send out, pledges cannot be paid later, and the organization has no mailing address. The excuse will be that by not incurring these expenses, more money can be delivered to the charity. A "tax ID number" will be volunteered as a supposed verification of legitimacy (the number can be fictitious). Another clue to fraud is an offer to take care of all money matters, including deposits and payment of expenses, and bring the nonprofit organization the net proceeds. These con artists will open a bank account and gain complete check-writing authority, and will indeed pay all the bills plus their own salaries, commissions, and marketing and promotion fees. Is it any wonder that little money is left for the charity when all this is over? All too often, scams and con artists operate for one or two weeks, collect a surprising amount of money from an unsuspecting public, and leave town before authorities can respond. To prevent or at least reduce fund-raising traps, how should nonprofit organizations proceed? By drafting a comprehensive, well-considered, properly worded agreement and not allowing any involvement with the outside agent until it is signed and the agent's credentials are verified. A contract can be the best protection, says Errol Copilevitz [21], provided each of the following elements is dealt with effectively:

1. When an organization is working with a direct-marketing company or a telemarketing company, a competitive bidding process should be utilized;
2. There should be a clear description of the relationship of the parties and the functions that each will perform;
3. Provisions dealing with donor file ownership and use should be clear and in accordance with industry standards;
4. The use of the nonprofit postal rate should be addressed in accordance with the standards of the U.S. Postal Service;
5. The receipt, control, and distribution of proceeds should be set forth with specificity and in accordance with various state laws;
6. The issue of state registration should be addressed and compliance assured, where applicable;
7. An addendum to comply with the various state laws should be a part of the contract;
8. The provisions dealing with the fees to be paid should be clear and concise;
9. The responsibility for project expenses must be unequivocal;

10. The organization should have direction and control over creative and program service material used; and

11. The activity, where applicable, should make a distinction between donor acquisition and donor renewal fund-raising with appropriate provisions dealing with contacts, content, and costs.

Responsible nonprofit organizations and regulatory authorities are frustrated in their efforts to reduce scams and con artists' fraud and abuse. Especially harmed are the legitimate police, firefighter, and veterans groups that seek public gift support. Constant efforts are made to educate the public about "wise giving" throughout the year and especially during the end-of-the-year holiday season. The news media do give coverage to fraudulent and deceptive solicitation techniques such as "fake" Santas and phony religious impersonators, and will describe how the scam was operated or the con was perpetrated. However, the effect is limited. The public has some responsibility to ensure that any solicitation given a response is legitimate and that the donation will actually be delivered to a nonprofit organization for charitable purposes. Victims must do more than complain loudly when they have been hoodwinked.

The problem of scams and con artists' fraud and abuse is complicated by misconceptions and overreaction by legislators. In Colorado, when a legislative regulation was proposed, the situation was described by Hopkins [22] as follows:

[F]raudulent charitable solicitations are a widespread practice in this state which results in millions of dollars of losses to contributors and legitimate charities each year. Legitimate charities are harmed by such fraud because the money available for contributions continually is being siphoned off by fraudulent charities, and the goodwill and confidence of contributors continually is being undermined by the practices of unscrupulous solicitors. [The law enacted is] necessary to protect the public's interest in making informed choices as to which charitable causes should be supported.

The final area to discuss here is the abuse of funds raised. Donors who restrict the use of their gift to any purpose are asking the nonprofit organization to use their money only for that specific purpose. In most solicitations, the purpose is a project or priority identified by the nonprofit organization; the funds are requested for exactly this use. Once the money is received, it may be used only in fulfillment of that purpose. If a donor makes a gift for a purpose that is unacceptable or cannot be fulfilled, the nonprofit organization has the right to refuse the gift. Once a gift is accepted, the organization is bound by law to retain the money until the purpose can be fulfilled. Among the problems that can occur within nonprofit organizations regarding the use of restricted funds are: a lack of proper accounting for all restricted funds received and spent, a lack of knowledge and appreciation (even by board members and managers) of correct accounting procedures, and legal complications associated with changing donor restrictions or using funds raised for purposes other than those intended by donors.

A recent, highly publicized example of improper use of funds raised was the fraud perpetrated by James and Tammy Fay Bakker and their colleagues on donors to the PTL Ministries. The trial of James Bakker revealed several fraudulent practices. One area of activity was overselling the accommodations promised to the PTL's "lifetime partners" (a number of free days and nights at the PTL Grand Hotel, Towers Hotel, Bunkhouse, and 1100 Club in exchange for gifts of $1,000). These offers, by mail and during PTL television programs, raised in excess of $158 million. Many of the partners could not get a reservation as promised; portions of the facilities were never completed although more than enough money had been raised for their construction. A second area of fraud was in the use of PTL "construction" money to purchase expensive homes for the Bakkers. Third, numerous (and quite generous) bonuses were paid to both James and Tammy Fay Bakker as well as to David Taggart. Bonus payments paid to James Bakker, which the court found to be excessive and qualified as "private inurement," were in amounts from $10,000 to $300,000. In the final days of PTL Ministries, between June 1986 and March 1987 (just prior to bankruptcy), the Bakkers, David Taggart, and Richard Dortch together received more than $2 million in bonus payments [23]. Bonus payments in *any* amount were not the intent of the donors; construction of the named facilities was the restriction that was abused.

Scams and con artists' fraud and abuse are major problems, especially when they occur within nonprofit organizations and involve contribution dollars. Good and sufficient laws are in place to protect the public from most of these practices. Despite the best efforts of public servants, however, illicit activity continues. Scandals will occur from time to time, and they are especially harmful to the public's willingness to continue to place confidence and trust in nonprofit organizations, in charitable giving, and in the many board members, volunteers, and employees who work on behalf of nonprofit organizations for charitable purposes.

CHAPTER TEN

Managing the Comprehensive Annual Giving Program

nnual giving programs are an organization's building blocks. Each annual giving method is like a cut stone: it has shape and size, color and weight, presence and function, stability and supportive strength even when it is standing alone. When several of these stones are assembled together with skill, they can form the foundation, the most important part, of a structure. The quality of the stones selected for the foundation is all-important because the entire structure will rest on them.

In the pyramid of giving (Exhibit 1.2), the entire structure of the giving process has been presented graphically. When the process is successful, donors will move from annual giving to major gifts and then to estate or planned giving, but only if the foundation of the pyramid is firmly in place, well-aligned, and able to carry the added weight placed on it. A nonprofit organization builds upward as it prepares for its future. Annual giving programs, an important element of the organization's foundation, are needed to make that upward structuring possible.

The primary and continuing objectives of every annual giving program are:

1. Identify and recruit new friends and donors;
2. Build lasting relationships through gift renewal and volunteerism;
3. Raise the money needed each year for priority projects;
4. Expand the relationship between community and organization;
5. Improve public understanding of the mission;
6. Increase public confidence and trust in the organization;

335

7. Fulfill the promise to make maximum use of gifts received by rendering quality services for public benefit;

8. Provide honors and recognition to faithful donors and volunteers.

A comprehensive annual giving program will make several contributions to the image and reputation of the nonprofit organization. By marketing and promoting the organization's programs and services and by communicating its vision far and wide, the comprehensive annual giving program will attract and keep donors and will provide opportunities for any person who chooses to become an active participant in its accomplishments.

No organization is complete and no charitable purpose is fulfilled while unmet needs remain. A generous, caring public is prepared to assist to the extent that personal means allow. Such charitable motives are reinforced by government's advocacy of giving and its granting of privileges of tax-deductibility for qualified donors. Public needs are many; resources are inadequate. Annual giving programs invite the public to join a cause and participate to the extent that time, talent, and treasure will permit. Society's unmet needs are mirrored in the mission statements of nonprofit organizations whose purposes are to respond to the best of their ability. A nonprofit organization's ability to meet public needs depends on its acquiring the public's support. This entire process begins with, is sustained by, and is dependent on the comprehensive annual giving program.

BALANCED PARTICIPATION: A KEY TO SUCCESS

This final chapter will discuss the support features necessary to the management of annual giving programs. The several fund-raising methods and techniques described in this book provide the means to accomplish the annual priorities identified by the organization's board of directors and CEO. Responsibility for fund-raising is shared among the board of directors, management, volunteers, donors, and staff. Fund-raising guidance and direction, training and materials, and management of all the internal support details required are the responsibilities of the fund development staff. When leaders lead and volunteers carry out their assignments, and when plans are solid and supplies are adequate, there can be every expectation that the annual goals and objectives of a nonprofit organization will be achieved with reliability. Facilitating that success is another responsibility of the fund development staff.

The annual giving process might be compared to an election campaign; comprehensive plans are made; options are examined and counter-plans are resolved; the district is studied to identify areas of opportunity and strategic value; campaign workers are recruited and trained for assigned missions; supplies are acquired, timetables are coordinated, and a campaign launch date is set. The campaign begins on schedule, progress reports communicate results, reactions, and any problems encountered. When the campaign is over, a critique is performed to communicate the lessons learned and to prepare for the next campaign. The role of the fund development staff is to enable each of the parts of the annual giving campaign to succeed, year after year. Every campaign begins with leadership, is carried out by volunteer workers, and is sustained throughout by the rear guard, the fund development staff. When it is over, the leaders, volunteers and donors share the glory.

The Role of Leadership

All leaders are volunteers, and volunteerism *is* philanthropy. Robert Payton calls philanthropy "voluntary action for the public good" [1]; volunteerism is action where "people helping people" "brings out the best in all of us." Volunteerism is a powerful concept; it continues to be a vital part of developing America as a unique nation. Alexis de Tocqueville [2], commenting on the use of public associations in America, wrote in 1835:

> I met with several kinds of associations in America of which I confess I had no previous notion; and I have often admired the extreme skill with which the inhabitants of the United States succeed in proposing a common object for the exertions of a great many men and in inducing them voluntarily to pursue it.

Leadership brings people together, builds on their skills and talents, and motivates them to address the needs of others. The spirit of "people helping people" exists everywhere in the world and, most recently, has begun to flower again among the people of the former Union of Soviet Socialist Republics. Leadership sets the example that others follow. When leadership addresses basic human needs, people everywhere follow.

Leadership in annual giving begins with the board of directors and the CEO. Their vision of the mission, purposes, goals, and objectives of a nonprofit organization is the source of inspiration and motivation for annual giving's leaders and volunteers, prospects and donors. Together, the board and CEO interpret the vision and formulate a statement of the organization's annual priorities of need. They serve as stewards of all of the organization's resources—employees, finances, and facilities—and supervise the delivery of its programs and services to the public. Visionary leaders and top executives will guide their craft through calm and

stormy waters to safe harbors of quality programs and improved benefits to all whom they serve.

> When annual contributions from regular supporters are the life-blood of
> an organization, the appeal deserves the full attention of board members. Re-
> member that annual giving is not the same as mass mailings to unknown
> prospects; rather, it is the solicitation each year of a first or repeated donation
> from preselected individuals who already know, or know about, the organiza-
> tion. But annual giving must be more than mere reminders to members that
> their dues are due. Annual giving solicitations are carried out primarily by
> mail, although churches in their "every member canvas" try to have all
> parishioners asked in person for donations to match or increase their previ-
> ous year's contributions. Three cardinal elements count heavily in annual gift
> solicitations: the *mailing list,* the *appeal letter,* and the *personalized approach.* [3]

Nonprofit organizations with strong and effective leadership will be
able to attract and maintain the levels of public support they need each
year. Others, especially those whose vision appears to be concentrated
on financial survival or job security, are not as likely to realize such an
ill-defined mission nor will they succeed in delivering quality services
to those in need; they will, moreover, be forever begging for whatever
public gift support they can find.

The Value of Volunteers

Volunteerism is next in importance to leadership, if nonprofit organizations are to achieve their vision, mission, annual purposes, and goals.
Volunteers must be identified and recruited, oriented and trained, encouraged and rewarded each year. Volunteers are the "arms and legs" of
annual giving and the force that enables each of the methods and techniques described in this book to blossom to its potential. Without the active involvement of volunteers at all levels of annual giving, nonprofit
organizations will not make as many friends, will be limited to fewer
people for quality relationships, and will spend more of the money
raised to hire staff to do what volunteers could do better and for free.

The best way to build a base of committed and loyal volunteers is to
imitate the steps for building a base of committed and loyal annual
donors. To develop volunteers in numbers and to utilize their time and
energy productively each year requires a commitment of time and budget by the nonprofit organization. Each volunteer has the opportunity
to enjoy a lifetime relationship with several nonprofit organizations.
Along the way, the volunteer will need preparation, training, experience, promotion, and recognition, all of which are begun in the comprehensive annual giving program (see Exhibit 10.1). The organization

Year 1 Invited by mail to make first annual gift; sends $25.
Invited by friend to public function (free); attends with spouse.
Invited to visit facilities; visits East Wing.
Receives two newsletters, one annual report.
Asked to renew (and upgrade) annual gift; sends $35.

Year 2 Invited to join the membership association; sends $100.
Invited to membership "mixer" to meet others; no charge. Attends
with spouse.
Invited to serve on a committee; selects membership. Attends
orientation and training session. Renews own membership at
$100 and brings in two new members at $100 each.
Invited to a public activity, one benefit, and a special event (annual
meeting). Attends the activity and buys two tickets to benefit at
$100/couple.
Takes second tour of facility (Main Wing); spouse joins tour.
Receives two newsletters, one annual report with name on
membership roster.
Asked to renew (and upgrade) annual gift; sends $50.

Year 3 Invited to work on membership committee again; accepts and
attends orientation and training session. Renews own
membership at $100 and brings in five new members (three from
office) at $100 each.
Invited to a public activity, one benefit, and a special event (annual
meeting). Attends the activity; buys two tickets to benefit and
invites two new members and spouses who attend.
Attends annual meeting.
Becomes tour leader after two training sessions.
Receives two newsletters, one annual report.
Asked to renew (and upgrade) annual gift; continues at $50.

Year 4 Invited to serve as vice chair of new-member drive; on membership
committee; helps plan orientation and training sessions; on
agenda to report on successful solicitation techniques. Recruits
five more new members.
Invited to serve on benefit planning committee; accepts. Attends
orientation and training session. Agrees to serve on ticket sales
committee. Invites four couples, to sell table of ten; calls members
recruited to encourage them to join as well.
Accepts appointment as vice chair of tours program; defines two
new tour areas.
Attends annual meeting; is recognized for new-member recruiting
services.
Asked to renew (and upgrade) annual gift; sends $100 and joins
Century Club.

Exhibit 10.1 Beginning Service Cycle of a Volunteer: Preparation, Training,
Experience, Promotion, and Recognition

Year 5   Invited to serve as chairperson of new-member campaign.
           Invited to serve on benefit ticket sales committee.
           Serves one-year term as chair, tours program. Recruits five new
              guides.
           Receives two newsletters, one annual report.
           Attends annual meeting; is recognized for leadership in voluntary
              service.
           Renews annual gift at $100 again (has not been asked for larger gift).

Exhibit 10.1 *(Continued)*

that invests in its volunteers will achieve their life-long commitment
and loyalty, plus their willingness to continue to give of their time, talent, and treasure. Some nonprofit organizations favor hiring employees
to do the fund-raising work of volunteers, believing that, although they
cause extra expense, employees are more reliable, can be told what to
do, and can be held more accountable for their performance. Where volunteers are full partners with "their" nonprofit organization, they will
remain while employees will come and go. Volunteers, who should
never be treated as employees, are an invaluable "extra" resource that
allows an organization to achieve quality relations with people. Volunteers are also willing and able to add a wide variety of extra benefits
and can raise *and give* more money than employees ever will. Volunteers
exemplify the following attributes:

1. Participate publicly in the life of the organization;
2. Act as committed and loyal ambassadors and spokespersons;
3. Represent with pride "their" organization to friends and neighbors,
   co-workers and business contacts, family and relatives;
4. Give of their time, talent, and treasure annually;
5. Lead prospects and donors into giving;
6. Lead other volunteers into service;
7. Enhance the image and reputation of the nonprofit organization
   by their visible association;
8. Prepare to become future leaders as well as future donors.

The Role of Fund Development Staff

Vision and mission are translated by staff into a "case statement" for
all to hear and read. Communicating the case is carried out jointly by

the external relations team of employees in the planning, marketing, public relations, and fund development offices:

Planning documents the vision and mission and describes its annual components in terms of product lines (programs and services);

Marketing identifies to whom the case is addressed (target markets) and prepares a strategy that will bring the organization and the markets together;

Public relations creates the image and describes the availability and quality of the programs and services for those who need them;

Fund development, because of the good advance work done, is positioned to raise the friends and funds to carry out the programs and services that fulfill the mission.

In order for each of these objectives to be realized, employees who do the planning, marketing, public relations, and fund development work must come together in a spirit of *cooperation, coordination,* and *communication.* By joint scheduling of all their activities (*calendar control*) they can achieve a *comprehensive* effort that will be *competitive* with others. *Collaboration* is the road to success for everyone involved.

The public, to whom the care is addressed and for whom the programs and services are intended, is often the same people—community residents living near the organization. Given the volume of messages to deliver and the diversity of audiences who receive them, a high degree of *cooperation* and *coordination* is needed among the external relations team. Each *communication* should improve and expand public understanding and respect in order to reinforce confidence and trust in the organization. *Calendar control* helps to guide internal decisions (and budgets) on when each message is to be sent, to whom it will be addressed, what purpose it intends, and how its effectiveness will be measured. Without calendar control, messages can rain down on people, causing them to wonder "How well-managed is this organization?" and "Is this how they spend my money?" To be maximally effective in public communications requires a *comprehensive* effort by all parties working together. *Competition* for leaders and volunteers, for prospects and donors, and for clients will intensify; organizations will not survive if they fail to gain the public's acceptance and gift support. There will be new opportunities for *collaboration* among organizations in the community. Joint efforts will become more desirable than unnecessary duplication and expensive competition. The continued success of the organization and its annual giving program depends on the successful implementation of these concepts of integrated management.

MANAGING ANNUAL GIVING PROGRAMS

When competent professional and support staff are matched with solid plans and effective and efficient communications systems, they will be able to meet the needs of leaders and volunteers, prospects and donors, and success in annual giving. Continuing success will build everyone's confidence in the nonprofit organization and in each of its annual giving programs. Thomas Broce [4] described the delicate balance that is involved:

> Much of the success of the annual campaign depends on good staff work, including the professional, clerical, and record-keeping staffs. The professional staff members should do everything possible to set the pace, maintain momentum, and create the sense of urgency and excitement that is vital to the campaign. Each meeting and special event must be planned with precision and conducted in good taste. A poor meeting will ensure a low turnout for the next one. The staff members must maintain pressure on volunteers without offending them. The visibility of the professional staff is higher in annual fund campaigns than in any other kind of fund raising.

The variety of functions performed by the fund development office is a daily challenge, a joy of association, and a source of affirmation to those of us who work there. Development work is never done; there are too many people to talk with and listen to, too many details to be resolved, and too many deadlines. Conflicting directions do arise because of too many "bosses" and too many priorities. Expectations set by others not closely involved with annual giving performance (and without consultation with more active and informed leaders and volunteers) can add unproductive stress.

> Organizations and their volunteer boards have high expectations, sometimes too high for the individual charged with meeting them, or fail to support an effort themselves, or are impatient with the time required for results. Fund development is not a quick fix; it is a life-long process that, with time and attention, can grow each year. [5]

Unrealized expectations are not thoughtful statements of multiyear goals and objectives for annual giving programs; they are short-term measurements of cash-only results. They also are a frequent cause of the rapid turnover in fund development staff. One of the duties that should be written into the job description of every fund-raising professional is to educate the organization in how fund-raising works. This book provides a structured and logical presentation of what steps to take and in what order to take them to realize the potential that annual giving offers. Each method contributes to the maximum efficiency and effectiveness of the others. Too often, the board of directors and CEO, who have defined the vision and mission after extensive studies, will, without much reflection, assign annual giving goals to achieve these purposes. Fund-raising professionals who cannot explain what they do, cannot educate others on how annual giving performs, and cannot communicate what the expected results from the budgets invested will be, may soon be in another line of work. Fund development staff are assumed to possess these articulation abilities; they are hired because of their knowledge and experience and should be able to explain annual giving concepts to board members and volunteers, prospects and donors. They are also expected to provide guidance and direction in how to use these proven, reliable, tested annual giving methods to achieve success.

Annual giving, like every other fund development program, does not operate in a vacuum. The letters mailed today may not get a quick response; but the second letter, or a telephone call, or the next event invitation may stimulate a reply. When donors and prospects receive other communications about the organization, whether they are promotions for services, news stories about results, or advertisements of coming events, these communications will help keep the organization in the public eye.

The primary duties of the annual giving program remain:

Acquisition (identify and recruit friends);

Renewal (build relationships);

Maximization (involve as many people as possible in the life of the organization).

Because similar messages are being sent by the same organization to the same people, annual giving programs, through their own added communications, will contribute to the objectives that advertising, marketing, promotion, and publicity are trying to achieve for the organization. Annual giving performance will be measured against separate objectives, including how many people responded to each solicitation and how much money was received from them. Success should be measured by the overall rate of *growth in giving* (see Exhibit 10.2) that the comprehensive annual giving program is achieving. Other questions to use in measuring annual giving performance are:

1. By how much did each program increase the number and percentage of prior donors renewed compared to last year and two years ago?

	Two Years Ago	Last Year	Annual Rate of Growth (%)	This Year	Annual Rate of Growth (%)	Cumulative Rate of Growth (%)
Number of donors						
Number of volunteers						
Number of dollars:						
By source						
By purpose						
By annual giving program						
Average gift size						
Average cost per gift						
Overall "bottom line" cost percentage						

Exhibit 10.2   Rate of Growth in Giving

2. How many different solicitations were offered to prior donors and how many acquisition efforts were made to prospects in the past 12 months?

3. Did the total number of donors and the value of all their gifts increase this year?

4. How many volunteers were recruited and trained and how did they perform compared to last year's volunteers?

5. Have volunteers identified any ideas about how to increase public participation and gift support?

6. How many volunteers and donors were identified as having leadership ability that the organization can look to for direction in the future?

Evaluations of these results and of other areas will verify whether a comprehensive annual giving program has been achieved. To accomplish many of the program's potential objectives, the fund development staff will be required to carry out several functions beyond solicitation. Ten support areas will be necessary to complete their management responsibility:

1. Board, CEO, and employee relations;
2. Management of changing annual priorities;
3. Gift reports;
4. Budget preparation and management;
5. Cost–benefit standards and guidelines;
6. Program performance measurement;
7. Office functions, operating procedures, and computer support;
8. Training for all staff members;
9. Financial accounting and reporting;
10. Donor relations.

BOARD, CEO, AND EMPLOYEE RELATIONS

Members of the fund development office enjoy a unique association with the board of directors and the senior management staff. They must be able to develop a working relationship with them and enjoy their confidence and trust. The CEO and other senior management staff may have concerns about the extent of the fund development office's personal contact with the board. The purposes and results of this contact must be communicated to the CEO and senior management, not just to allay their fears but to keep them fully informed of plans and proposals arrived at in all of the discussions at which they were not present. Few other employees other than the CEO rely on board members' direct participation to carry out their work. The job descriptions to fund development staff are quite unlike those of other employees in many areas, just as the programs and services provided to the public by the fund development staff are quite different from those delivered by other employees. No CEO would permit his or her employees to ask board members for money!

Fund development staff are involved almost exclusively *outside* the organization; their business is different from that of the employees *inside* the organization. Fund development staff are seldom involved in program and service delivery—a separation of function that can cause misunderstanding and even tension from time to time, when other employees see the fund development staff spending their time in activities that do not appear to be "work." It is the responsibility of the fund development staff to go to their fellow-employees and explain what their job is and how they do it, to bridge the gap between perception and reality. My own experience has been that, after other employees learn more about fund development tasks, they confess that they would never want to ask people for money. Fund development employees must integrate themselves into the culture and life-style of their organization and not hold themselves apart, as though they were different (or better). We are employees too, just like everyone else; only our jobs are different.

MANAGEMENT OF CHANGING ANNUAL PRIORITIES

By nature, annual giving depends on the annual operating needs of the nonprofit organization. These needs change at least annually, and sometimes within the same operating year. The messages in each annual appeal are designed to achieve public understanding of these needs and encourage a decision to support the project. Each new project requires time and effort to establish the level of public understanding needed for a decision to participate as a donor or a volunteer. Annual giving communications are necessary and may be sent as often as two dozen times a year (see Exhibit 4.2). These messages are most effective when the projects "for sale" are part of a well-defined, multiyear plan that has been explained many times before; the basic story has not changed, only the details of how it will be continued in this year's projects are different. The projects promoted each year are the next steps in the overall plan. Previous projects completed (with donors' help) have been fitted into the plan like pieces of a mosaic. The next priority is explained as the next component to the picture; with donors' help again, the plan will keep moving forward on schedule. Consistency is critical in annual giving communications, especially when the message must be repeated many times to the same audience. In their messages, some organizations express their plans only in terms of the annual operating budget; their objective is financial survival for another year. Which organization will donors want to give their money to today, and for the next five years?

GIFT REPORTS

The results of annual giving are of interest to everyone involved in this yearly effort. Donors want to know that their money was received and has been spent as they were promised. Volunteers want to know whether all their hard work paid off and the level of their success. The board and CEO want to know how much money has arrived so they may proceed with their programs and plans. Regular gift reports are recommended to convey information in three basic areas: (1) sources of gifts, (2) purposes or uses of funds raised, and (3) annual giving methods used to raise the money (see Exhibits 1.4, 1.5, and 1.6). Frequent reports will help maintain momentum for each annual giving program, and will give incentive to donors and volunteers alike. Another benefit of gift reports is that they help everyone to understand how annual giving works, how the separate methods are performed, and what can be expected based on previous performance. Gift reports take the guesswork out of annual giving and allow volunteers and staff to begin to feel comfortable in forecasting how each of these methods will continue to perform. Each method will possess flexibility for adjustment and room for improvement; these can be enlisted next time, to achieve the results that are needed. These recommendations should be presented when the next year's budgets are prepared and when reliable gift revenues are being forecast.

BUDGET PREPARATION AND MANAGEMENT

A nonprofit organization should expect a reliable level of annual gift support from a reasonable investment of its operating budget. The amounts for both should be based on performance during the past three years, not just the past year. The results seldom are dramatically different from year to year, but steady growth can be expected unless new methods are introduced or new performance levels are established. The several methods of annual giving described in this book perform at different levels of net income and operating costs. It stands to reason that if it cost $100,000 to raise $250,000, the organization should not expect to be able to reduce the budget by $10,000 and increase the results by $25,000 unless dramatic and detailed information is on hand to justify these expectations. The relationship between fund-raising cost and results is linked to each method used, the maturity of each program, and its previous performance. If the same or slightly increased results are needed, the investment must total the same amount or a bit more, not less. When needs are increased substantially, the most profitable annual giving method should get most of the added budget. Most annual giving programs are not limited by a lack of prospects and donors, but by a lack of enough volunteers and enough resources to carry out the most efficient methods of asking that are required. Performance measurements conducted for each annual giving method will provide reliable details for assessing the quality of the method's performance and estimating its future revenues and the budget to be invested to achieve them. Using only "bottom line" figures of total revenue and total budget from the previous year can be a misleading and an inaccurate way to forecast future results. To develop accurate projections and to study productivity and efficiency, the following five measurements should be applied to *each* annual giving method in use:

1. Percentage rate of return;
2. Average gift size;
3. Average cost per gift;
4. Program cost percentage and return on investment (ROI);
5. Overall "bottom line" cost percentage.

Percentage Rate of Return

Counting the number of donors who respond validates the quality of the prospect lists chosen, the effectiveness of the solicitation package, and the consensus about the needs (and the message) that prompted a reply. Each method of annual giving will perform with a different rate of return each time it is used, even when the method is the same. For example, the direct mail acquisition program seeks first-time donors; if it achieves a response rate of 1 percent after each mailing and from each list used, it should be judged as quite successful. In practice, each list does not often yield a 1 percent rate of return each time. By comparison, a donor renewal effort, which also uses the mail, should achieve a 50 to 60 percent response rate, because it is asking previous donors to repeat (and upgrade) their last gift.

> *Method:* Divide the number of responses received by the number of solicitations made; the result is the percentage rate of return. Using the CCUA Clean Up Cleveland Chapter as a familiar continuing example, 5,157 replies from a first mailing to 506,546 prospects = 1.02 percent; 914 replies from 1,504 prior donors = 60.77 percent. (See Exhibit 8.11 for other illustrations of annual giving performance.)

Average Gift Size

How much people give is a strong clue to their level of respect and confidence as well as their financial ability. Direct mail replies may average between $25 and $50. If the average falls below these levels, the mailing lists, package, message, and timing should be examined. When a variety of gift levels is offered, people tend to choose the minimum amount. The number of people who give at each level is an indicator of how carefully the list was segmented and how well the "case for support" is being received.

Method: Divide the total amount of contributions ($192,260) by the number of gifts received (6,071) = $31.67.

Average Cost per Gift

Cost–benefit ratios are the relationships between gross revenue received and net revenue available after expenses. Fund-raising costs are not well understood; reasonable cost levels to be used as generally accepted standards or guidelines are needed. For example, the net results achieved by the CCUA Clean Up Cleveland Chapter in its first series of "roll-out" mailings were 3,653 replies from 396,467 letters mailed (a 0.92 percent response rate), which produced $116,911 and an average gift size of $32 (see Exhibit 4.8). The average cost per gift was $27.10, and a "profit" of $4.90 per gift was achieved in the first year—a higher-than-average achievement. How else ought these results to be interpreted?

Method: Divide the total fund-raising costs ($99,000) by the number of gifts received (3,653) = $27.10.

Program Cost Percentage and Return on Investment (ROI)

Each of the several acquisition and renewal mailings conducted by the CCUA Clean Up Cleveland Chapter performed with slightly different results. Analysis of the mailings' individual performance levels helped the board and fund development officer decide how to proceed each time. Some acquisition lists performed better than others; donor renewal fluctuated in the Spring and Fall months. Introducing a $100 donor club, charter memberships, and tickets to a summer concert and a theater performance were effective in sparking a higher response from both lists. When the year was over, 7,713 gifts had been received yielding $249,678 (see Exhibit 8.11). Comparing these results with the first acquisition efforts, which produced 6,071 gifts and $192,260, there were 1,642 more gifts worth an added $57,508. The individual program cost percentage and return on investment (ROI) percentage for an acquisition and a renewal mailing must then be determined. (See Exhibits 4.8 and 4.9.)

Method: Divide first-year acquisition program total costs ($99,000) by total contributions received ($116,911) = $0.85; multiply by 100 for a program cost percentage of 84.67 percent, or $0.84 to raise $1 and 118 percent ROI. Divide the costs of the first renewal request

($1,827) by total contributions received ($31,064) = $0.058; multiply by 100 for a program percentage of 5.88 percent, or $0.58 to raise $1 and 1,700 percent ROI.

Overall "Bottom Line" Cost Percentage

This final evaluation looks at the results of the comprehensive annual giving program for overall profitability and productivity and for return on investment (ROI). "Bottom line" analysis is useful here because comparable data from prior years are available. These results can be misleading if they are not accompanied by the details (see above) of each solicitation method, which allow comparison with results in previous years. The CCUA Clean Up Cleveland Chapter received 6,071 gifts and $192,260 in its first year, a 1.20 percent rate of return, and a $31.67 average gift. In its second full year, with more prior donors to renew, more emphasis on charter memberships in The Circle of Champions, and additional net profits from its first gala benefit evening, the results increased to 13,066 gifts and $521,858, a 2.21 percent rate of return, and a $43.25 average gift. The increased performance came mainly from the four renewal mailings and the gala, not from the four acquisition mailings still looking for new, first-time donors. Both were necessary and successful, but their performance was markedly different.

> *Method:* Divide the total fund-raising costs for the first year of operation ($100,827) by the total gifts received ($192,260) = $0.52; multiply by 100 for the overall "bottom line" cost percentage of 52.44 percent or $0.52 to raise $1, and a 191 percent ROI.

COST–BENEFIT STANDARDS AND GUIDELINES

Efficiency and productivity in fund-raising results will require more analysis than percentage rate of return, average gift size, "bottom line," and return on investment percentages, valuable as they are. How well do these results compare with those of other nonprofit organizations of the same type and in the same community? National standards published by the Philanthropic Advisory Council of the Council of Better Business Bureaus and the National Charities Information Bureau, both of whom examine several management and operations performance areas, advocate a fund-raising cost–benefit ratio of 35 percent as a minimum guideline. No other guidelines are available at this time. It is generally accepted that comparative analysis should begin *after three years* of continuous annual giving operation, when each of these solicitation programs has begun to achieve a level of performance maturity. Again, *each* fund-raising method should be evaluated separately and completely. To do so requires that all direct expenses, plus indirect and overhead costs, be applied against gift results. This is the correct principle to advocate, but the fact remains that organizations do not count their results or tally their expenses using any available commonly accepted accounting procedure. This inadequacy has been raised several times in the past decade with the Financial Accounting Standards Board (FASB) [6] and the American Institute of Certified Public Accountants (AICPA). The reasonable cost guidelines suggested in Exhibit 10.3 can be applied for two purposes: (1) to measure cost-effectiveness of current programs and (2) to forecast future results based on continued budget investment [7]. Attempting to predict fund-raising results for annual giving methods from one year to the next is an uncertain exercise. There are too many variables that can influence results—economic conditions, volunteer and staff performance, and Murphy's law. The variables that can be controlled, such as list management (segmentation, merge-purge, letter copy, amounts requested, benefits offered, address corrections),

Direct mail acquisition	$1.00 to $1.25 per dollar raised
Direct mail renewal	$0.20 to $0.25 per dollar raised
Membership associations	$0.20 to $0.30 per dollar raised
Auxiliaries, guilds, donor clubs, and support groups	$0.20 to $0.30 per dollar raised
Activities, benefits, and special events	50 percent of gross proceeds*
Volunteer-led, personal solicitation	$0.10 to $0.20 per dollar raised

* Based on special and benefit event direct costs only.

Complete performance measurement must include assessments of added value received by the nonprofit organization in the following areas: marketing, media relations, community relations, major gift cultivation, donor relations, image building, and influence on other external affairs constituents (government and business officials, vendors, suppliers, and so on).

To calculate "bottom line" *net proceeds* from each benefit event, calculate an estimated value for the above items as revenue, then subtract those portions of internal and overhead costs (staff, time, budget, and so on) required for benefit support.

Exhibit 10.3 Reasonable Fund-Raising Cost Guidelines for Annual Giving Programs after Three Years of Continued Use

meeting deadlines for mailing dates, and others, require considerable discipline and some expense. To predict likely expectations, one must study prior results in detail.

PROGRAM PERFORMANCE MEASUREMENT

Performance measurement includes assessing the rate of growth in giving, evaluating the support systems, and testing options for alternate action. It is also necessary to evaluate and to score (using a range of opinions of low/medium/high) consistency of messages, personalization, and the effects of each method on community relations, volunteerism, and leadership development (see Exhibit 10.4). With more understanding, it is possible to define fund-raising potential and to gauge each method's capacity. There is a difference between potential and capacity in annual giving: Potential is raising as much money as is needed; capacity is raising as much money as can be raised. Performance measurement must begin with an internal analysis of how the following elements are performing individually and how well they interact:

People	**Systems**
Leadership	Prospect identification
Volunteers	Office systems/operations
Training	Donor relations
Performance	Budget management

	Score
1. Comparison with prior-year results	Low/Medium/High
2. Growth in donor universe	Low/Medium/High
3. Penetration of new markets	Low/Medium/High
4. Quality of effort	Low/Medium/High
5. Leadership development	Low/Medium/High
6. Consistency and personalization of messages	Low/Medium/High
7. Regular reports and analysis of the results	Low/Medium/High
8. Staff training and development	Low/Medium/High
9. Matching institutional needs (dollars delivered on schedule)	Low/Medium/High
10. Forecasting future income and each program's performance	Low/Medium/High

Exhibit 10.4   Areas for Annual Giving Program Assessment

Annual giving program managers must be willing to consider options to their current practices. Neither change nor risk is a popular concept in fund-raising management. There are many opportunities to test alternate ideas, to experiment with different packages, and to use multimedia and other creative techniques. Any change to annual giving practice should first be tested (see Chapter Two); the results will be known immediately. The following roster of options to current practices should be considered; some of them might be exercised each year:

1. Keep using what is working, especially if it is effective and efficient;

2. Study all the performance data to learn where improvements may lie;

3. Report current results to others and explain what they mean;

4. Define options for improvements based on results, not speculation;

5. Define a business plan each year for every annual giving activity, and review the results at quarterly intervals;

6. Propose changes based on performance plus improvements, and be willing to forecast likely results;

7. Forecast a three-year plan for each activity, stating the performance standards to be achieved; integrate these plans into the overall annual giving program;

8. Ask for more budget to implement the total program of annual giving activities, including improvements; base the requested amount on the forecast of increased net revenue that will result.

OFFICE FUNCTIONS, OPERATING PROCEDURES, AND COMPUTER SUPPORT

Many activities are conducted in the fund development office and, like any group of office procedures, they are largely taken for granted. A review of a few of the orientation instructions provided to new clerical assistants who have no prior experience with fund-raising operations will reveal the details involved. They may include the following:

1. How telephones are answered (the preferred wording of the greeting);

2. The names of board members, volunteers, and important donors;

3. The assigned duties and how they relate to what others are doing;

4. How to handle mail, especially when checks are enclosed;

5. How every gift received must be recorded, deposited, added to the donor's records and files, and thanked;

6. The capabilities of the computers and the preferred (or required) format of reports;

7. How to process reservations for all activities, benefits, and special events;

8. How address changes are entered and communicated.

There are many subjects to learn and procedures to master. Quality office operations are reflected in gift results, effective volunteers, and satisfied donors. Annual giving involves large numbers of people every year. They will call to report their address changes, ask for information, offer suggestions, and make complaints. Membership associations require priority attention to member services. Volunteer solicitors, who are worth their weight in gold, also require priority attention to help them succeed with their assignments. These duties require the personal attention of everyone in the fund development office. Friendships and close working relationships will develop among the donors and volunteers and everyone who works in the office. Taking the time to have meetings, to visit with people over the phone, and to exchange personal notes in the mail may, to some observers, seem unnecessary or unproductive if they believe staff should only be asking for money! A study of donor renewal behavior often proves the value of personal attention. Those who are actively in touch with office staff are usually the most frequent and generous donors and the most reliable and effective volunteers.

Management of annual giving methods has been a recurring topic throughout the book, and some details have been given on the basic office functions that support each program. Exhibit 10.5 illustrates common office activities and staffing assignments for a three-person and a 13-person department. Teamwork is essential; so are telephone coverage and etiquette, cross-training, a discipline regarding accuracy, and a respect for confidential information. Office procedures grow up over time and can become fixed in stone; they should be broken open at least every two years to examine whether all the steps being followed remain necessary. To increase office efficiency and improve morale, the people who work in the office should be asked what improvements are needed.

Computers have added greatly to the efficiency of annual giving operations; it is hard to imagine how the fund development office ever functioned without them. They maintain infallible records on everything,

General Duties	Office Staff Assignments	
	Three-Person Office	Thirteen-Person Office
Leadership and direction	Fund-raiser	Fund-raiser/leader
Fund-raising solicitations	Fund-raiser	Fund-raisers (3)
Office supervision; budget and personnel management	Secretary	Office manager
Secretarial tasks	Secretary	Secretaries (3)
Gift processing, donor records, pledge billing, gift reports	Gift records clerk	Gift records clerks (2)
Thank-you letters and cards for all gifts received	Gift records clerk	Gift records clerk
Research and files control	Gift records clerk	Research clerk
Computer records, data input, and data control	Gift records clerk	EDP coordinator
Mail, phone, visitors	Secretary	Receptionist
Supplies, equipment, storage	Secretary	Office manager
Mail-list preparation, changes, maintenance, control	Secretary	EDP coordinator
Personnel training and skill development	Secretary	Office manager
Fund development training	Fund-raiser	Fund-raiser
Activities, benefits, and special events	Everybody	Everybody
Plaques, awards, honors, and donor recognition	Fund-raiser	Fund-raiser and Secretary
Donor clubs and membership associations	Fund-raiser	Fund-raiser and Secretary
Volunteer-led, personal solicitation committees	Fund-raiser	Fund-raiser and Secretary

Exhibit 10.5   Basic Functions of the Fund Development Office

which is a major asset when the numbers of prospects, donors, and volunteers keep growing. Although accurate historical records are valuable, the sophistication of present-day software is able to provide data management functions relating to annual giving programs. As an example, assuming the information has been entered correctly into the database, the computer can sort and print out (on envelopes or mailing labels) a list of all the donors who gave $50, $75, and $100 as of a certain date, match them to a letter text, and produce personally addressed individual letters with prior-gift and suggested upgrading amounts inserted in the text—all within a few hours. To attempt such a task for hundreds or thousands of donors without a computer would be excessively expensive today, and the gift results would be the same. Computers also assist with budgeting and cost–benefit ratio analysis, gift reports, accounting and management of funds raised, investment management, donor recognition, and almost every other routine office procedure. They also provide a host of word-processing tasks, and, with laser and jet-ink printers, they produce a high-quality product. To make the best use of computers and data management, three things are required: (1) modern equipment, (2) current software, and (3) well-trained employees who are genuinely interested in using their machines for time-saving tasks that will increase productivity.

TRAINING FOR ALL STAFF MEMBERS

Professional staff employees in for-profit companies usually have academic degrees in fields that relate to their job descriptions. People may assume that professional staff in the fund development office of a nonprofit organization have been equally prepared. Few people realize that fund-raising is not available as an academic discipline except in a few colleges and universities. Most staff have earned a bachelor's or master's degree, but not in fund-raising. The primary training comes from on-the-job experience, and national trade associations provide most of the instructional opportunities. Training programs are offered at local, regional, and national conferences and workshops; through journals, newsletters, and special reports; in an increasing number of books; and by networking. Nonprofit organizations should not hesitate to budget the modest amounts needed for memberships and attendance at one or two professional fund-raising association conferences each year. Accreditation and certification programs are also offered; they will help both employers and fund-raising professionals to validate their knowledge and experience. Fund development remains an experience-driven field and, with patience and investment in training, employers and employees will benefit. Training should not stop at the professional level. The information gained should be shared with volunteers in the form of improved orientation and training programs. The entire office staff will not attend conferences, but those who do should conduct minisessions after they return, to pass on to others what they have learned. Local meetings and workshops are also learning opportunities for support staff, who should be encouraged to attend when possible. Improving the entire staff's knowledge of how fund-raising works will increase the efficiency and productivity of the entire fund development program.

FINANCIAL ACCOUNTING AND REPORTING

Because annual giving raises money, exemplary financial accounting and reporting procedures are required. Internal accounting procedures for receipt, deposit, and use of annual gifts require meticulous recordkeeping and reports prepared for internal and external use (see Exhibit 4.2). Internal summaries should contain details such as cost–benefit ratio analysis and performance measurements, to illustrate efficiency as well as effectiveness. External reports should fulfill the accountability due to donors on the use of their money, especially where restricted gifts are involved. Reports of annual giving results must be correct for each program in operation; they should present details clearly and in a form that is easy to read and understand. When annual giving results are success stories, they will serve to motivate volunteers and donors. They will also help everyone to appreciate how results were achieved and how improvements can be made. Withholding the "bad news" about a program that was not able to make its goal is unwise, for two reasons:

1. Several volunteers were involved and many donors gave as requested; all these personal efforts remain worthwhile;
2. Failure may bring to light a method or technique that is not working well for volunteers and staff; by finding and correcting it, the expectations for next year may be secured.

DONOR RELATIONS

Investing time and budget dollars in donor communications, recognition, and reward is as valuable as investing in donor acquisition and renewal. Everyone agrees that "donors are the best prospects," but not everyone pays as much attention to keeping existing donors as they do to acquiring new ones. As long as the focus of annual giving is on raising money and not donors, donor relations will suffer. Donors are the source of most of an organization's income, and maximum efficiency is realized by working toward their giving again. The second-year results of the CCUA Clean Up Cleveland Chapter annual giving program, when there were donors to renew, showed 3,383 prior donors giving $126,536 in the

Fall, and 1,838 prior donors giving $117,650 in the Spring; a total of 5,221 donors renewed and gave $244,186 (see Exhibit 8.11). By comparison, the results from acquisition mailings in the same time periods were 4,192 gifts and $106,396, and 1,835 and $97,665 respectively, for a total of 6,027 new donors and $204,061. Both groups used only direct mail solicitation. There will be better results from continued attention to current donors, although acquisition efforts should not stop.

An important statement is worth repeating one more time: Donor relations begins with the first gift. The cost required to achieve a first gift is high (between $1.00 and $1.25 per dollar raised). When such an investment has already been made, it is certainly worth a bit more expense to maximize continued giving. Follow-up begins with personalized acknowledgment letters. The fund development office is responsible for processing each gift and sending a thank you. Donors also can be offered honors and recognition. These benefits are usually reflected in increased communications from the organization, which will keep them informed in an effort to stimulate their interest and will invite their involvement again. Donors want to know (1) whether their gift was received safely, (2) how it will be used, and (3) whether it made a difference. If satisfied on all three concerns (and if they hear again from the organization), they are more likely to repeat their gift when asked. Repeat contributions can become a habit pattern among donors. The annual giving methods described in this book permit many ways to ask a donor to participate and to give more than once a year; repeat gifts create an opportunity to begin building relationships with donors. A friendship can start on the first day a donor calls and is addressed by name before he or she has said who is calling.

Wise nonprofit organizations establish and announce guidelines for how donors who make substantial contributions, especially those who make major gifts, will be rewarded. Donors of $1,000 should receive more attention than donors of $100, but everyone who gives $1,000 should be treated equally. A cumulative donor records system linked (via computer) to a donor recognition program will allow donors who are faithful givers to qualify in time for some level of recognition. Written guidelines help everyone to understand how much is required for the promised benefits and privileges (see Exhibits 4.4 and 6.4). Uniformity of treatment is a major factor in an honors and recognition policy.

Rewards to donors, including the privileges and benefits of donor clubs, are part of donor relations. Material objects reflecting the organization's appreciation for a donor's dedication and generosity can be added as tokens. As stated before, the object given is treasured far less than the recognition—the ceremonial occasion when the gift was presented, who was present, and the compliments paid. Donors deserve sincere attention; they are more than their gifts reflect, and donor relations is more than a gesture [8].

ISSUES AND CHALLENGES FOR THE FUTURE OF ANNUAL GIVING

This book concludes with a look at the issues and challenges anticipated to affect philanthropic practice in general and annual giving in particular. Annual giving is quite sensitive to change because of its instant response style. Changes occur rapidly in society today; keeping pace with those that affect philanthropy and annual giving is no small challenge. Each time the U.S. Postal Service increases the rates for third-class, bulk-rate mailings to cut its revenue losses, it increases the costs for nonprofit organizations to communicate with their constituencies. Lists and mailing schedules have to be revised and decisions made on where to cut back. As a consequence, gift income may be reduced (which happens immediately), and some public programs and services may have to be scaled back.

Most of the issues and challenges that affect nonprofit organizations are beyond their control. Awareness of these issues and of their possible influence on annual giving programs will be helpful. Any changes within the control of the nonprofit organization need to be anticipated, if possible, so that alternative fund-raising plans can be made early enough to reduce the negative effects on programs and services. Alternate fiscal sources have to be developed, which takes time. The option to increase the number of donors and the amount of contributions from annual giving programs also will take time to organize and implement from one year to the next. The list (in alphabetical order) of issues and challenges in Exhibit 10.6 can change how nonprofit organizations and their annual giving programs will perform in the future. Each of these topics is described in the following sections.

Accounting Standards	IRS Special Emphasis Program
Charitable-Purpose Tests	Mergers and Multi-Institutional Systems
Donor Bill of Rights	Nonprofit Compensation and Salaries
Effectiveness and Efficiency	Prospect Research and Rights of Privacy
Ethics in Fund-Raising	State and Local Fund-Raising Regulations
Government Deficits	Total Quality Management
"High Tech, High Touch"	

Exhibit 10.6 Annual Giving: Issues and Challenges

Accounting Standards

The Financial Accounting Standards Board (FASB) has been engaged in an effort to define uniform standards of accounting for use by all non-profit organizations. Four separate audit and accounting guidelines, issued by the American Institute of Certified Public Accountants (AICPA), already exist. They are guides for (1) colleges and universities, (2) providers of healthcare services, and (3) social and welfare organizations, and (4) a general-purpose guideline for all others (Statement of Position 78-10). Several accounting issues associated with philanthropic practice need clarification, and some of these are being addressed. The two statements issued by the FASB in June 1993, on standards for contributions and standards for financial statements of nonprofit organizations [9], will result in uniform procedures in these two broad areas. The intent is twofold: to enhance "the relevance, understandability, and comparability of financial statements" issued by charities; and to bring nonprofit accounting practices closer to those used by for-profit companies [10]. New rules were introduced in the following areas: how pledges ("conditional promise(s) to give") and donated services by volunteers will be counted, three display forms for financial statements, and increased segregation and reporting of restricted gifts. One challenge (an expense) is in revising internal accounting procedures. The issue will be to explain these changes to board members, volunteers and donors, government agencies, and the general public. The language used in financial statements that will display these details is also a concern. For example, because pledges and donated services are counted as income in the year they occur, the organization may appear to have more resources than actually are in hand. Will such an interpretation discourage annual donors from making contributions? Probably not; few people will seriously consider withdrawing their gifts based on this information. Whether it will affect major gifts or planned giving and estate planning is harder to predict. On the plus side, more information will be reported about contributions received and how these funds are spent, which can aid discussions with donors at all levels. Similar information was not available or was not easily presented previously. Audits and financial statements are complex documents that are not easily understood. New formats and changed rules increase the potential for confusion. A separate concern is the desire to make nonprofit organizations appear more like for-profit organizations.

Charitable-Purpose Tests

For a nonprofit organization to retain its privileges as a pure public charity under Section 501(c)(3) of the Internal Revenue Code, it must be careful not to engage in activities that might alter its status. The issues here are private inurement rules, commerciality, and community benefits tests. Must nonprofit organizations pass a test to retain their exempt status? As will be discussed shortly, government deficits have caused even normally safe "sacred cows" such as tax-exempt status to be challenged in the quest for tax revenue. No part of the net earnings of a charitable organization can result in private gain for any individual; the organization exists to serve only public interests, *not* private interests. The law has always been such; some individuals have ignored it, to their detriment and the detriment of their nonprofit organization. Commerciality, an even more complex issue, arises when for-profit business interests (or the Small Business Administration) believe that nonprofit organizations are offering services identical to their own but at competitively lower prices (because of tax-exempt privileges) than the for-profit businesses can achieve, which they claim is an unfair advantage. A community benefits test documents the charitable purposes for benefit of the public that are being carried out by a nonprofit organization [11]. Each of these issues is cause for concern to nonprofit organizations because tax-exempt status or parts of it are at risk. Government may choose to leave the bigger issue of exempt status alone if enough money can be collected in tax payments from nonprofit organizations. The exemption from sales tax has already disappeared in many state jurisdictions. Some state, county, and city governments have gone to court and won cases to remove exemption from property taxes, a previous privilege of nonprofit hospitals in Utah and Pennsylvania, among other states. Utah now administers a procedure whereby the exemption can be retained if the level of charitable purposes is high enough [12]. This issue impacts annual giving because the money to pay taxes will have to come from the operating budget. The challenge will be in convincing donors to continue giving even when a portion of their annual gifts may be used to pay these taxes.

Donor Bill of Rights

Fund-raising executives are responsible for seeing that, out of respect for their generosity, donors are treated fairly and equitably. The issue of a donor bill of rights arose, in part, from fraudulent and abusive fund-raising practices. The challenge has been to define practice standards that espouse positive entitlement and to have appropriate authorities proclaim it rather than to try to use it to counter illicit behavior. Among the contents are the donor's right to receive a list of board members, to review the latest financial statement, to know how gifts will be used, to receive appropriate recognition, to be treated with dignity, and to ask questions and expect to receive answers promptly. Widespread use of a donor bill of rights will help to retain donor confidence and trust for nonprofit organizations that adopt these tenets of professional conduct. Two such documents are now available. The first was prepared by the Department of Social Services, City of Los Angeles—the office charged with enforcement of fund-raising solicitation practices. The second and most recent text is a product of the "Consortium," an informal group of volunteer chairpersons and chief executive officers of professional societies concerned with fund-raising practice. Members include the American Association of Fund Raising Counsel (AAFRC), Association for Healthcare Philanthropy (AHP), Council for Advancement and Support of Education (CASE), and National Society of Fund Raising Executives (NSFRE). See Exhibit 10.7 for the text of the new Donor Bill of Rights. The implications for annual giving are positive. Official endorsement of a donor bill of rights by the board of directors of the nonprofit organizations is the first step. Notice should be sent to all volunteers so they know their organization has adopted a donor bill of rights and will adhere to its precepts on behalf of donors at all times. Copies should be sent to all donors, and all routine means of communications from the organization should publish this text.

Effectiveness and Efficiency

There is increased interest in fund-raising performance, beyond how much money is raised each year. Board members, management staff, volunteers, donors, and government officials are asking for more details on gift results along with financial and program performance by nonprofit organizations. Fund-raising activity is only one of many measurable areas of a nonprofit organization's performance, but its high visibility attracts attention. Media attention to public scandals, fraud, abuse, and illicit fund-raising practices has fueled these requests. Accountability is the issue here; the challenge is in learning how to use measurement tools and how to explain their results. Productivity analysis is quite helpful in measuring the relationship among the sources of giving, the methods used to secure gifts, and the budget needed to achieve the money raised. Fund development executives should be able to present the results of their annual giving programs in detail so that their performance can be understood, appreciated, and continued. To do so, these executives will need to improve their understanding of assessment methods and learn how to improve their effectiveness (doing the right things) and efficiency (doing the right thing better). Volunteers and donors are quite interested in the value of their investment and in the net amount delivered for charitable purposes. Performance

A Donor Bill of Rights

PHILANTHROPY is based on voluntary action for the common good. It is a tradition of giving and sharing that is primary to the quality of life. To assure that philanthropy merits the respect and trust of the general public, and that donors and prospective donors can have full confidence in the not-for-profit organizations and causes they are asked to support, we declare that all donors have these rights:

I.

To be informed of the organization's mission, of the way the organization intends to use donated resources, and of its capacity to use donations effectively for their intended purposes.

II.

To be informed of the identity of those serving on the organization's governing board, and to expect the board to exercise prudent judgment in its stewardship responsibilities.

III.

To have access to the organization's most recent financial statements.

IV.

To be assured their gifts will be used for the purposes for which they were given.

V.

To receive appropriate acknowledgment and recognition.

VI.

To be assured that information about their donations is handled with respect and with confidentiality to the extent provided by law.

VII.

To expect that all relationships with individuals representing organizations of interest to the donor will be professional in nature.

VIII.

To be informed whether those seeking donations are volunteers, employees of the organization or hired solicitors.

IX.

To have the opportunity for their names to be deleted from mailing lists that an organization may intend to share.

X.

To feel free to ask questions when making a donation and to receive prompt, truthful and forthright answers.

DEVELOPED BY
AMERICAN ASSOCIATION OF FUND RAISING COUNSEL (AAFRC)
ASSOCIATION FOR HEALTHCARE PHILANTHROPY (AHP)
COUNCIL FOR ADVANCEMENT AND SUPPORT OF EDUCATION (CASE)
NATIONAL SOCIETY OF FUND RAISING EXECUTIVES (NSFRE)

ENDORSED BY
(IN FORMATION)
INDEPENDENT SECTOR
NATIONAL CATHOLIC DEVELOPMENT CONFERENCE (NCDC)
NATIONAL COMMITTEE ON PLANNED GIVING (NCPG)
NATIONAL COUNCIL FOR RESOURCE DEVELOPMENT (NCRD)
UNITED WAY OF AMERICA

Design: Lipman Hearne/Chicago

Please help us distribute this widely.

Exhibit 10.7   A Donor Bill of Rights

measurement should reaffirm their wisdom in choosing to support an organization that is well-managed and their assessment of the quality of its annual giving programs. There is every reason to believe that annual giving programs should be "profitable." The net gain to the nonprofit organization will be more funds available and better stewardship of budgets invested in annual giving.

Ethics in Fund-Raising

Misconduct by fund-raising professionals is damaging to all of philanthropic practice. So too are incidents of misconduct by others associated with charitable giving. Examples are: fraudulent behavior by an attorney in directing the assets of elderly clients into his or her personal control; self-appropriation for personal gain or for purposes other than those intended by the donor of contributions received by nonprofit organizations; or deceitful solicitations that misrepresent the appeal and deliver little actual cash for the charitable purpose intended. Most people know to avoid unprofessional and unethical conduct. Those who do not— thankfully, only a few people—are a source of embarrassment and of general erosion of public confidence and trust. Government regulation in this area is difficult; consumer protection and fraud are complex legal issues, and lawsuits brought against illegal acts take years to resolve. In the meantime, the media give these incidents wide coverage, and public confidence and trust are further damaged. At issue also is the ethical conduct of nonprofit organizations. Areas deserving attention include governance, organizational integrity, finances, fund-raising and public relations, management practice and human resources, program services, and public policy. One such statement of ethical conduct has been adopted by InterAction, a coalition of 132 international relief organizations whose members have to abide by the standards [13]. Their leadership may soon be followed by other groups of nonprofit organizations as well as individual institutions and agencies. Nonprofit organizations and their boards of directors, volunteers, and fund development executives must avoid shortcuts and quick fixes that promise easy money. They should remain committed to the proven, tested, and highly successful annual giving methods described in Chapters Two through Eight. Some of the other ways to raise money every year discussed in Chapter Nine (particularly gambling) might well be avoided if they cause suspicion as a potentially undesirable way to raise money. Adequate regulations originate from the IRS, the U.S. Postal Service, and state and local authorities. Those who are not well-informed on current regulations are advised to become so informed, before being forced to do so in response to legal action [14]. The basic moral values associated with nonprofit organizations and fund development, as identified by Michael Josephson [15] of the Josephson Institute for the Advancement of Ethics, include honesty, integrity, promise keeping, fidelity, loyalty, and fairness. Josephson warns against "slippage" in the form of creative accounting, misleading results, over-statement of case, marketing hype, deceptions to influence others, con-cealment of bad news, or false credit for others' work. Professional fund-raising societies have adopted statements of ethical principles and standards of professional practice, and have added enforcement proce-dures to address ethical issues raised by their members or involving members and nonmembers. These "codes of conduct" are notable ad-vances, but they will not prevent illicit activity, especially among non-members.

Government Deficits

Government deficit spending of the past decade has crippled the econ-omy of the nation and remains the chief cause for limited government support to basic human services. The issue before nonprofit organiza-tions is how they can meet these needs when government funds with-drawn in their entirety cannot be replaced. Because of politics, the deficit is difficult to contain and even harder to reduce. It is the prime motive behind government challenges to tax-exempt privileges, as men-tioned earlier under charitable-purpose tests, because of a belief that im-portant amounts of new revenue are to be found here. The deficit will remain the prevailing economic force affecting the management deci-sions of nonprofit organizations for many years. The challenge to annual giving programs will be whether they can be expected always to in-crease public support, year after year. Overburdened nonprofit man-agers are hard-pressed to invest more budget dollars in annual giving programs when faced with cuts in public programs and services.

"High Tech, High Touch"

At issue here is the degree of impersonalization resulting from the use of modern technology for mass communications with volunteers, donors, prospects, and the general public. Challenges include competing for public attention with commercial messages from businesses that have larger advertising and communications budgets; access to every media area (especially television); saturation of the airwaves; and increasing public resistance to mass communication forms. Because annual giving remains a social exchange using a personal communications style, non-profit organizations must modify how they think about paid advertising in newspapers, magazines, billboards, and bus-backs; on radio; and on cable and commercial television. The public is attuned to noticing and responding to these messages. Personal messages can be delivered effectively and efficiently using direct mail communications for the same cost as (or less than) advertising and with improved "high touch." Video cassette tapes also hold much promise for some methods of annual giving, especially when accompanied by mail and telephone communications, because of the opportunities they offer to personalize the message. The proper use of telemarketing is more difficult to fathom because of increased public resistance to its invasion into home and office. The same reaction may be ahead for the use of FAX machines and computer networks. Despite all these technological advances, most annual giving methods presently in use are likely to continue to be successful because of personal interactions of donors and prospects with volunteers and staff. Fund-raising will remain a "contact sport."

IRS Special Emphasis Program

The IRS has two objectives for this program. Its first purpose is to ensure that donors' claims about gifts made to nonprofit organizations are verified; organizations are required to document their transaction with a receipt sent to the donor. Gift verification affects annual giving in the area of activities, benefits, and special events where admission is sold. Those attending received "material benefits" (food and drink) in exchange for their gift, and the value involved may not be claimed as a charitable deduction. Donors must be notified *at the point of solicitation* (on the invitation) what amount of the admission price is not allowed as a deduction. The 1993 tax law added the requirement that every donor of $250 or more must receive a receipt. Most organizations already acknowledge gifts of this size, but administrative burdens increase operating costs and provide little or no benefits to nonprofit organizations.

The IRS's second issue is to investigate business practices of nonprofit organizations in order to collect unrelated business income tax (UBIT). The IRS believes that charities owe more tax on their for-profit business enterprises than they are paying. Inspections are under way at several nonprofit organizations (chiefly, hospitals, colleges, and universities) to resolve the quest. A related issue is the degree to which nonprofit organizations are engaged in commercial activities as an alternate revenue source. The IRS is scrutinizing corporate sponsorships of benefits, monitoring gambling activities, examining larger organizations affiliated with complex systems of subsidiaries, and reviewing organizations engaged in political activities. The latest IRS Form 990 requires more of these business details to be reported. The challenge to annual giving programs related to these areas of IRS activity is a concern whether any change in giving patterns has resulted; with an economic recession in full force for several years now, it is hard to know for certain. Paying taxes on the income received is a minor consequence compared with loss of tax-exempt status because of commercial activity. Audits by IRS agents will focus on how IRS Form 990 report data are calculated, the use of commercial or "paid" solicitors, and other internal and external financial transactions [16].

Mergers and Multi-Institutional Systems

Some nonprofit organizations are large, multi-institutional systems that have operating units around the country. National agencies and their affiliated chapters number in the hundreds. Many colleges and universities have multicampus sites. Hospitals have become affiliated with others, have been acquired, or have merged together to form regionally integrated, multipurpose healthcare delivery systems with satellite outpatient offices and surgical centers, nursing and retirement homes, rehabilitation centers, and even for-profit subsidiaries. After any of these multi-institutional systems survive antitrust and IRS reviews, they offer special issues and challenges to annual giving programs. Ownership and name changes confuse the public about where their gift dollars go, who controls them, and where they will be spent. Preserving loyalties with local donors when an organization is now under outside control will be a unique challenge to annual giving. Many of the units in these systems, hospitals in particular, have set up separate 501(c)(3) foundations as subsidiaries or related organizations. In one plan to preserve community support, local community members are elected to the foundation board and manage local fund-raising activities and the use of funds raised. Additional mergers and even collaborative programs involving several organizations may result in other variations to preserve local identity and support.

Nonprofit Compensation and Salaries

One of the ancient myths about nonprofit organizations is that they employ people who cannot succeed in the regular business world. A related myth says that salary and benefit programs should be inferior to those for for-profit employment positions. Recent public opinion on compensation has crystallized around William Aramony's dismissal at United Way of America. Some people are concerned about stories of $100,000-plus salaries and retirement packages paid to top executives at nationally respected, nonprofit organizations. Some people believe that no one in the nonprofit world should earn more than $100,000 in salary, and that donors will not be pleased to learn about salaries higher than this arbitrary figure [17]. Larger nonprofit organizations are complex enterprises with multimillion-dollar annual operating budgets nearly equivalent to Fortune 1000 companies. Their public responsibilities in areas such as higher education, health and human services, social welfare, and emergency relief are essential to the nation and require the same advanced degrees from business schools as do for-profit corporations. Similar levels of compensation for competent management are not unreasonable. Public wariness and media confusion are often fueled by reports of nonprofit organizations that generate a "profit" (excess of revenue over expense) on the operating budget through good management. Profits are a sign of success everywhere. In addition, any excess revenue may be used only for programs and services, and not for the private gain of any board member or employee. Legitimate concerns have been raised over some nonprofit organizations' decisions to provide low-interest loans to top executives, to pay board members for voluntary service, to use contributions, government grant money, and other revenue for housing, cars, club memberships, travel, and the like. These practices have been called questionable or abusive by some people. Congressman J.J. Pickle has initiated House Ways and Means Committee subcommittee hearings on many of these issues and has suggested limits on what charities can pay their executives. Prior to current attention directed toward Aramony and Pickle, the compensation debate was focused on how fund-raising professionals were paid and the ethics of commission and percentage payment programs. Professional trade associations (AAFRC, AHP, CASE, NSFRE, and others) have announced their opposition to commission and percentage payment, but a few nonprofit organizations choose to employ fund-raising staff on this basis. Their board members and senior management believe that fund-raising staff will work harder if motivated by personal gain [18]. Public debate calling attention to compensation, "profits," perks, and other financial transactions can affect annual giving because donors will be concerned their gift dollars might be involved. The challenge to every nonprofit organization is to be forthright about its management practices, including how gift dollars are spent; open and full disclosure can only help to preserve public confidence and trust.

Prospect Research and Rights of Privacy

Fund development offices have always accumulated personal information on their donors and prospects. Details such as age, education, business career and current position, marital and family status, and so on, were needed to develop a relationship with donors and preserve their annual support. These and other details about donors' financial resources are gathered from public sources available in any library. However, when coupled with donor giving histories, the information becomes a comprehensive personal profile to be treated with confidentiality. What is sensitive about these data is how they are gathered and used today. Fund development is a competitive endeavor and information is valuable. Increased computer technology and the "information highway" offer access to more personal and financial data than ever before. The issue is how much information is needed and at what point does its accumulation begin to trespass on individual rights of privacy. Professional research associations advocate standards of professional practice to all who use prospect information. Related to these issues is public access to this information, especially to donor records. Public record laws permit access to records *at public institutions,* which has been interpreted recently to include donor records and files in the fund development offices of public colleges and universities. Court cases in South Carolina, Michigan, West Virginia, and, most recently, Ohio have handed down decisions on opening donor records to the public [19]. These actions are in sharp contrast with IRS regulations. Nonprofit organizations are required to submit the names, addresses, and value of gifts of $5,000 or more with their IRS Form 990 each year, but these details are prohibited from public access. The separate issue of privacy rights offers another contrasting argument to public access. If resolved by court decision in favor of disclosure, such actions may challenge personal rights of privacy guaranteed in the U.S. Constitution. The challenge to every nonprofit organization will be to preserve the willingness f its donors to continue to make annual gifts, even if the details m.., 'ecome public knowledge. Releasing the names of donors is an entire different, even benign requirement compared to public access to personal details contained in office records and files. Most nonprofit organizations already publish their roster of donors in their newsletters and annual reports as part of a donor recognition program and a way of thanking them again for their generosity.

State and Local Fund-Raising Regulations

Several of the issues discussed here, notably accounting standards, charitable-purpose tests, the IRS special emphasis program, compensation, prospect research, and privacy, appear to be headed for a collision with state and local fund-raising regulations aimed at controlling fundraising practices. Local authorities receive complaints from community residents about fraud, abuse, scandals, and scams perpetrated on them in the name of charitable activity. Illicit fund-raising behavior is a growing issue. Joseph Mixer [20] observes: "Concerns by the general public and legislators over fraud, excessive costs, commercial ventures, tax avoidance, improper accounting practices, and further abuses of charitable purposes have stimulated this trend. More than two-thirds of states have laws regulating solicitations." State and local authorities have had difficulty in regulating fraudulent fund-raising practices. They are largely limited to requiring annual registration and reporting requirements from every nonprofit organization. Three U.S. Supreme Court decisions have limited state and local authority further in the use of administrative procedures as a means of enforcement. This trend may be reversed—or should be, in Harvey Dale's [21] opinion:

> Like it or not, the independent sector will be more scrutinized and more regulated. It is not only futile but, as I have argued, perverse to struggle unduly against this trend. Our country has always honored diversity, and has always been distrustful of unchecked power, authority, and privilege. As the size of the nonprofit sector grows, it seems inevitable that regulation of it will grow. Because it has been perhaps the least regulated portion of our society, the rate of regulatory growth may well be even more swift than the growth of the sector itself.

Public disclosure about nonprofit organizations' fund-raising performance has had limited success to date. The challenge is extensive public education about how to make more careful and informed gift decisions. Donors should investigate persons to whom they make gifts. Illicit behavior can be limited by donors who take the time to "check out" a request rather than give money to anyone who asks for it in the name of charity. The additional challenge to annual giving programs will be to willingly disclose details about the organization's financial affairs, including details on how the money raised will be used and on the fund-raising cost–benefit ratio analysis. If the public agrees that the money donated is being used well and that the cost of fund-raising programs is reasonable, public support is likely to continue. When state and local fund-raising regulations honor such disclosure and join in public education programs, the giving public will be better served.

Total Quality Management

Nonprofit management in many sectors has begun to embrace total quality management (TQM) and its partner, continuous quality improvement (CQI), to move organizations to higher levels of annual operating performance. TQM and CQI encourage employees to work together as a team rather than separately, to be customer-driven, and to concentrate on quality indicators and continual evaluations to monitor improvements of nearly every function within the organization.

What are the benefits of TQM for nonprofit organizations?

Constantly improved quality of services and products (which contributes
  directly to our national quality of life);
Happy patrons and motivated volunteers;
Greater productivity—more payoff per hour of effort;
More services for less money;
High staff morale. [22]

TQM and CQI concepts can be implemented in the fund development program quite easily; making donors feel like valued customers is
important. So too are teamwork and performance assessment. The issue behind TQM and CQI is their ability to effect cultural changes
within nonprofit organizations because they influence the mission,
values, and style of employees at every level. TQM and CQI concentrate
on the "process" of how things are done and encourage employees to be
alert to and rewarded for improvements. The challenge that TQM and
CQI offer to annual giving is to examine, *from the customer's point of
view,* how each of the current fund-raising methods is conducted, and
to focus on *the donor as a customer.* Annual giving is caught up in its constant quest for more donors and dollars, and in the need to meet goals
and objectives and to deliver cash for priority needs within each operating year. Diane Cox [23] warns: "Too many times we direct our full
attention to what the organization wants and needs with little or no attention to what the donor wants and needs. We crank out thousands of
personal letters on the word processor without knowing our customer." Personalized, "high touch" communications are the preferred
style of customer relations. In addition to measuring their performance, fund development departments should measure donor satisfaction on the annual giving programs offered to them. What do donors
think about the number of mailings they receive, the types of benefits
and special events they are invited to attend, how their gifts are handled, and how soon they receive a thank-you letter or receipt? Who has
ever asked for their opinion about the organization, about its programs
and services? Market research and focus groups, questionnaires and
surveys, and other data-gathering tools on public attitudes can provide
this information and help to improve both solicitation performance and
donor satisfaction. If friend-raising and relationship building are the
primary purposes in annual giving, an organization should not be
afraid to ask these friends for their opinion of the other party to the
relationship. Quality should be the constant goal for every annual giving program in use each year. Donor relations, to take one example, can
achieve quality improvement with a 48-hour turnaround procedure to
thank donors for their gifts. Coupled with improved forms of personal

solicitation next time, increased results (larger numbers and higher amounts of repeat gifts) can be achieved. The challenge is not to find activities that can be improved, but to change attitudes from just soliciting money to relating better to donors as people.

CONCLUDING THOUGHTS

Among the many tested precepts of fund-raising is one that has special meaning for annual giving.

After you have completed an entire year of successful annual giving programs, celebrate! Tomorrow, you get to do it all over again.

Take heart and be encouraged by these final thoughts:

> There are no secrets to success. It is the result of preparation, hard work, and learning from failure.
>
> Colin L. Powell

> The vineyards of philanthropy are pleasant places, and I would hope good men and women will be drawn there . . . if these vineyards are to thrive and bear their best fruit, they must always have first-class attention.
>
> Harold J. Seymour

APPENDIX A

Operating Rules and Procedures for a Support Group Organization

WHEREAS, the [name of parent nonprofit organization] is a corporation organized under the [state name and title of state code identified for nonprofit public benefit corporation law];

WHEREAS, the Board of Directors of [name of parent] is authorized under the [state name and title of state code] to establish committees and support groups that do not exercise the authority of the Board of Directors of the [name of parent];

WHEREAS, the Board of Directors of [name of parent] has established a support group to solicit property to be received, administered and disbursed by the [name of parent] and to carry on other related tax-exempt purposes in accordance with the [name of parent]'s articles of incorporation; and

WHEREAS, the Board of Directors of [name of parent] has adopted the following Operating Rules and Procedures for the government of the following support group.

ARTICLE I.   Name.

The name of this support group of the [name of parent] shall be
_____.

ARTICLE II.   Affiliations and Operations.

Section 1.   Affiliation:

The _____, sometimes referred to herein as the
"_____," shall be a support group of the [name of parent], but shall not be a committee of the Board of Directors of [name of parent] and shall not exercise the authority of such Board. The activities and affairs of the [name of parent] shall be managed and all corporate powers of the [name of parent] shall be exercised under the ultimate direction of the Board of Directors of the [name of parent].

Section 2. Title of Property:

Any and all property solicited by the "_____" shall be and shall remain the property of the [name of parent].

ARTICLE III. Principal Office.

The principal office of the _____ shall be located at [full description of the location and mailing address of the support group].

ARTICLE IV. Purposes.

Section 1. General Purpose:

The "_____" seeks to build understanding, appreciation, and long-term commitment by individuals, corporations, and foundations of the work of the [name of parent].

Section 2. Specific Purposes:

1. The "_____" shall provide financial support for [name of parent] through membership dues, benefit events, and other fund raising activities;

2. Any such property so received shall be administered and disbursed by the [name of parent] in accordance with [name of parent]'s articles of incorporation. Property solicited by the "_____" and the income therefrom shall be disbursed by the [name of parent] solely to, or for the benefit of, the [name of parent] which is operated at [full mailing address]. Such disbursements by the [name of parent] shall be used at the [name of parent] for only the following purposes and no other purposes, mainly related to [cite specific restricted purposes, if funds are directed to one or more programs or services of the parent] in the form of (a) capital expenditures; (b)renovation of the buildings and facilities; (c) equipment purchases; (d) education; and (e) research;

3. The "_____" shall increase public awareness of the facts about [name of parent and specific restricted purposes, if any], through ongoing community education;

4. The "_____" shall seek to build public understanding of [cite restricted purposes, if any] through a publication program, including its newsletter and other communications;

5. The "_____" shall endeavor to stimulate personal involvement toward the common goal of promoting the highest quality of [cite parent's mission and restricted purposes, if any] in this region through [name of parent].

ARTICLE V. Members.

Section 1. Voting Member:

The only voting member of this organization as defined in [state name and code] shall be the [name of parent] which shall have sole voting control over the final election of the Board of Directors of "＿＿＿＿＿＿." There shall be only one class of voting membership.

Section 2. <u>Nonvoting Members</u>:

The nonvoting members of this organization shall be those persons who have applied for membership in the "＿＿＿＿＿＿," been approved by the Membership Committee, and have, from time to time, paid annual dues to the "＿＿＿＿＿＿."

There shall be four classes of membership, based solely on the amount of dues paid by the nonvoting members, as follows:

    (a) Life Members
    (b) Gold Members
    (c) Silver Members
    (d) Bronze Members

The amount of dues for each level of membership shall be determined, from time to time, by the Board of Directors of the "＿＿＿＿＿＿." All such nonvoting members shall have the same rights and privileges regardless of the amount of dues paid.

<u>Family Membership</u>: When a married individual becomes a member, his or her spouse shall automatically be deemed a member, be entitled to the same privileges as a nonvoting member, and be known as a Family Member. Each such couple shall be deemed to be (1) member on the records of the "＿＿＿＿＿＿." At "＿＿＿＿＿＿" membership events where admission is charged, <u>each</u> individual shall pay an admission charge except as modified by the Board of Directors.

<u>ARTICLE VI</u>. <u>Board of Directors</u>.

Section 1. <u>Number and Qualifications</u>:

The Board of Directors shall consist of ＿＿＿＿ (＿＿) elected directors.

Of that number, ＿＿＿＿ (＿＿) shall be members of the professional staff who are serving as employees of [name of parent] in the following capacities:

    (a) Director of the ＿＿＿＿＿＿.
    (b) Director of the ＿＿＿＿＿＿.
    (c) A delegate appointed by the ＿＿＿＿＿＿.

If Co-Directors of any of these professional services are acting, either or both such Co-Directors may attend the "＿＿＿＿＿＿'s" Board meetings and vote thereon but they shall have only one (1) vote between them.

The remaining directors shall be lay individuals selected from the community. Their minimum qualification shall be current membership standing of the "＿＿＿＿＿＿."

No more that 49 percent (49%) of the persons serving on the Board may be interested persons. An "interested person" is (a) any person compensated by the "＿＿＿＿＿＿," or by the [name of parent] for services rendered within the previous twelve (12) months, whether as a full-time or part-time employee, independent contractor, or otherwise, excluding any reasonable compensation paid to a director as a director; and (b) any brother, sister, ancestor, descendent, spouse, brother-in-law, sister-in-law, son-in-law, daughter-in-law, mother-in-law, or father-in-law of such person. However, any violation of the provisions of this paragraph shall not affect the validity or enforceability of any transaction entered into by the "_____" or its Board of Directors.

Section 2.   Terms of Office:

A total of _____ (____) lay directors shall be elected each year, each for a three (3)-year term. Lay directors may be re-elected for a second consecutive three (3)-year term but may not be re-elected thereafter until the expiration of at least one (1) year following the completion of his or her last term on the Board of Directors.

Professional staff members who, by reason of office, possess membership on the Board of Directors, shall serve during such time as they hold the staff position set forth in Section 1 above.

Section 3.   Election of the Board of Directors:

The lay members of the Board of Directors shall be nominated by the Nominations Committee at the regular meeting prior to the annual meeting.

The slate of candidates selected by the Nominations Committee shall be voted on by the Board of Directors at the annual meeting. Such slate, if approved by the Board of Directors, shall then be submitted to the [name of parent] for confirmation.

Any lay director may be removed at any time by the [name of parent] by vote of its Board of Directors.

The professional staff members of the Board of Directors shall be selected as provided in Section 1 of this Article.

Section 4.   Powers of the Board of Directors:

Subject to the provisions and limitations of [state name and code section] and any other applicable laws, as well as subject to the policies and procedures of the [name of parent], the "_____" activities and affairs shall be managed, and all powers shall be exercised, by and under the direction of its Board of Directors.

The Board of Directors shall:

(a) Perform any and all duties imposed on them collectively or individually by law, by the [name of parent], or by these Operating Rules and Procedures.

(b) Elect the officers of this organization.

(c) Approve all activity and event plans.

(d) Establish committees and ratify the appointment of committee members.

(e) Supervise all officers, committees, and volunteers of the organization to ensure that their duties are properly performed.

(f) Develop an activities plan for submission annually to the Board of Directors of [name of parent].

(g) Make recommendations periodically to the [name of parent] as to the application of funds raised by the "_____."

(h) Set membership dues for all levels of nonvoting members.

Section 5.　Vacancies:

Any vacancy as to a lay director on the Board of Directors shall be filled by election of a new director for the unexpired term in accordance with the provisions of Section 1 and 3 above.

Section 6.　Meetings of the Board of Directors:

(a)　Regular meetings of the Board of Directors shall be held at least quarterly at the time and place specified by the Board of Directors.

(b)　The annual meeting of the Board of Directors shall be held in the month of _____ each year.

(c)　Written notice of the time and place of meeting shall be delivered personally to each Director or sent to them by United States Mail, postage prepaid, at least seven (7) days prior to such meeting.

(d)　Special meetings of the Board of Directors may be called by the President, or, if he or she is absent or is unable or has refused to act, by the Vice President or by any two (2) Directors, and such meeting shall be held at the place designated by the person or persons calling the meeting.

(e)　One (1) more than half the number of directors then serving shall constitute a quorum of the Board of Directors for the transaction of business, except to adjourn.

(f)　The transactions of any meeting of the Board of Directors, however called and noticed or wherever held, are as valid as though the meeting had been duly held after proper call and notice, provided a quorum, as hereinabove defined, is present.

(g)　Every action taken or decision made by a majority of the Directors present at a duly held meeting at which a quorum is present shall be the act of the Board of Directors, subject to the more stringent provisions of the [state name and code section] including, without limitation, those provisions relating to (i) approval of transactions in which a director has been a direct or indirect material financial interest, (ii) approval of certain transactions between organizations having common directorships, (iii) creating of and appointments to committees of the Board of Directors, and (iv) indemnification of Directors.

(h)　A meeting at which a quorum is initially present may continue to transact business, despite the withdrawal of directors, if any action taken or decision made is approved by at least a majority of the required quorum for that meeting.

Section 7.　Action without a Meeting:

Any action that the Board of Directors is required or permitted to take may be taken without a meeting if all members of the Board consent in writing to the action, provided, however, that the consent of any Director who has a material financial interest in a transaction to which the organization is a party and who is an "interested Director" as defined in Section _____ of the [state name and code section] shall not be required for approval of that transaction.

Such action by written consent shall have the same force and effect as any other validly approved action of the Board. All such consents shall be filed with the minutes of the proceedings of the Board.

ARTICLE VII.   Officers.

Section 1.   Appointed Officers:

The officers of this organization shall be a President, a Vice President, a Secretary, a Treasurer, and an Immediate Past President. An officer of the "_____" shall not be an officer of the [name of parent] unless he or she has otherwise been appointed an officer of the [name of parent] in accordance with the Bylaws of the [name of parent].

Section 2.   Election of Officers:

The officers shall be nominated by the Nominations Committee at the regular meeting of the Board of Directors prior to its annual meeting. The officers shall be elected by the majority vote of the Board of Directors at its annual meeting.

Section 3.   Term of Office:

The officers shall serve a term of one (1) year, or until their successors have been elected and qualified or until removed by majority vote of the Directors.

Section 4.   Vacancies:

A vacancy occurring in any office shall be filled by election of a new officer for the unexpired term by majority vote of the Board of Directors.

Section 5.   Duties:

The duties of the officers shall be as follows:

(a) President:

The President shall be the executive officer of the organization and, subject to the control of the Board of Directors, shall have general supervision, direction, and control of the affairs of the organization. The President shall preside at all meetings of nonvoting members and at all meetings of the Board of Directors. The President shall appoint the committee chair of all standing committees (other than the Long-Range Planning Committee and the Nominating Committee) in accordance with these Operating Rules and Procedures, subject to the approval of the Board of Directors, and shall be an ex-officio member of all committees.

(b) Vice President:

The Vice President shall, in the absence or disability of the President, perform all of the duties of the President, and when so acting shall have all of the powers of, and be subject to the restrictions on, the President.

(c) Secretary:

The Secretary shall keep at the principal office of the organization a book of minutes of all meetings of the Board of Directors and of the nonvoting members prepared by the Secretary or by the support staff of the [name of parent]. The Secretary shall maintain a membership book showing the name and address of each nonvoting member. The Secretary shall serve as parliamentarian at all meetings of the Board of Directors and shall perform such other duties as may be designated by the Board of Directors.

(d) <u>Treasurer</u>:

By virtue of the relationship between this organization and the [name of parent], all funds generated by the "_____" are paid directly to the [name of parent], which shall furnish regular reports of income and expenses to the Treasurer for submission to the Board of Directors of this organization. The Treasurer shall, in conjunction with the Chair of each Events Committee and appropriate support staff of the [name of parent], review the budget for each event prior to submission of that budget to the Board of Directors.

(e) <u>Immediate Past President</u>:

The Immediate Past President, by reason of his or her prior experience, shall act as Chair of both the Nominations Committee and the Long-Range Planning Committee.

ARTICLE VIII.   <u>Committees</u>.

Section 1.   <u>Executive Committee</u>:

The Executive Committee shall include the five (5) elected officers who shall conduct such day-to-day affairs of the Board of Directors as may be required in the absence of meetings or between regularly scheduled meetings of the Board of Directors. Actions taken by the Executive Committee shall be presented to the Board of Directors at their next meeting for approval.

Section 2.   <u>Other Standing Committees</u>:

The following committees shall be considered standing committees of the Board of Directors. The Chairperson of each standing committee shall be appointed annually by the President and ratified by the Board of Directors. The Chairperson shall be invited to attend meetings of the Board of Directors. All committee members asked to serve shall be nonvoting members of the "_____" and their appointment shall be approved by the Board of Directors annually.

The other standing committees are:

(a) <u>Membership Committee</u>:

The Membership Committee shall be responsible for recruitment and renewal of nonvoting members annually at all dues levels. Activities of this committee shall include membership recruitment and renewal activities including the solicitation of friends of present nonvoting members and their friends, and all orientation events for new members.

(b) Event Committees:

Each event committee shall be responsible for definition and operation of its designated benefit event held, and shall observe the [name of parent]'s budget guidelines to achieve a goal of at least fifty percent (50%) net profit for each event held. Each event committee shall also advise and assist, where appropriate, those other activities that will support annual membership solicitations, other benefit events, and such additional fund-raising activities as may be defined as the priority of the [name of parent].

(c) Long-Range Planning Committee:

The Long-Range Planning Committee shall monitor implementation of the existing long-range plan and shall conduct any continuing or new long-range planning process at the request of the Board of Directors.

(d) Communications, Public Relations, and Marketing Committee:

The Communications, Public Relations, and Marketing Committee shall be responsible for assisting [name of parent] in the plans for and the use of the "_____" publications, invitations, membership directory, membership brochure, and other materials for public consumption and for use of the roster of members of the "_____."

(e) Fund-Raising Committee:

The Fund-Raising Committee shall be responsible for such special projects and campaigns among the members where the "_____" can be of special help to the [name of parent] in meeting its identified needs. The Chairman shall also be invited to participate in any campaign committee of the [name of parent] where the goal includes projects of benefit to the [restricted purposes of the "_____"] so that maximum coordination in fund-raising activities will occur between the "_____" and the [name of parent].

(f) Policy and Procedures Committee:

The Policy and Procedures Committee shall be responsible for periodic review of these Operating Rules and Procedures so that they remain current and correct regarding the operating policy of the [name of parent] as well as federal and state law and regulation. In addition, the Committee shall conduct such reviews of its policy and procedures as requested by the Board of Directors and develop recommendations for action by the Board of Directors.

(g) President's Circle:

The President's Circle shall be composed of all previous Presidents of the "_____," who shall be responsible for preparation and conduct of the annual meeting and for the nomination of candidates for any awards program of the "_____" or [name of parent]. The President's Circle shall make itself available to periodically advise the Board of Directors and the Officers of this organization.

(h) Nominations Committee:

The Nominations Committee shall be chaired by the Immediate Past President. Members shall also include the current President and two members selected and appointed by the President from the President's Circle. The Nominations Committee shall perform their duties as defined in Article VI, Section 3, and Article VII, Section 2, of these Operating Rules and Procedures.

Section 3. Other Committees:

The President, with approval of the Board of Directors, shall appoint and define the duties of such special committees and advisory groups as may be necessary from time to time to achieve the objectives of this organization and which shall serve ad hoc at the pleasure of the Board of Directors.

ARTICLE VIII. Rules of Order:

Robert's Rules of Order, Revised, shall govern the deliberations of this organization and all procedures not expressly covered in these Operating Rules and Procedures.

ARTICLE IX. Limitation on Political Activities.

None of the activities of this organization shall consist of the carrying on of propaganda, or otherwise attempting to influence legislation, nor shall this organization participate in or intervene in (including the publishing or distributing of statements) any political campaign on behalf of any candidate for public office.

ARTICLE X. Insignia:

The Board of Directors may adopt, use, alter, or cancel an insignia for the "_____" and by rule shall prescribe the time, manner, and place in which such insignia may be worn or used.

ARTICLE XI. Amendments:

These Operating Rules and Procedures may be amended at any time by written approval of the Board of Directors of the "_____." These Operating Rules and Procedures, and any amendments thereto, shall not become effective until their being adopted by the Board of Directors of the [name of parent].

RESOLUTIONS. Adoption:

We, the undersigned, being the directors of the "_____" of [name of parent] as well as the directors of the [name of parent] hereby consent to and do, adopt the foregoing Operating Rules and Procedures as the Operating Rules and Procedures of the "_____."

Dated: _____, 19XX

Board of Directors
of "_____"

Board of Directors
of [name of parent]

_____
(name of Director)

_____
(name of Director)

_____
(name of Director)

_____
(name of Director)

_____
(name of Director)

_____
(name of Director)

_____
(name of Director)

_____
(name of Director)

etc.
etc.
etc.

etc.
etc.
etc.

Certificate of the Secretary:

    I certify that I am duly elected and acting Secretary of the "_____,"
that the above Operating Rules and Procedures, consisting of _____ (___)
pages, are the Operating Rules and Procedures of this organization as adopted
by the Board of Directors of the [name of parent] on _____, 19XX, and that
they have not been amended or modified since that date.

    EXECUTED, this _____ day of _____, 19XX, at [name of city and
state].

_____
[name of Secretary]

Master Checklist for Activities, Benefits, and Special Events

[Author's Note: Each activity, benefit, or special event will require preparation of a separate master checklist to aid leadership, volunteers, and staff to schedule and monitor progress of all the details required to execute the function without error or serious mishap. There is no single checklist or master schedule complete enough to fit every conceivable form of activity, benefit, or special event; the following roster of details represents one guide. There is no order to the list of details needed to help plan a function, assign responsible parties, establish costs and expenses, and monitor progress to meet established deadlines, as illustrated below. This same document can be used to guide the postevent critique evaluation and as a preplanning tool for the next activity, benefit, or special event.]

Function Name or Title: _____

Name of Sponsor: _____

Location or Site: _____

Day, Date, and Time(s): _____

Requirements: [ ] New Function   [ ] Existing Function
                                              (Prior Critique Report attached)

                [ ] Activities, Goals, and Objectives form submitted

                [ ] Proposed Budget (revenue and expenses) submitted

Part A: Approvals

1. Sponsor: _____

   Name: _____ Date: _____
                    (Signature)

2. Fund Development Officer: _____   Date: _____
                                   (Signature)

3. Fund Development Committee: [ ] Yes   [ ] No   Date: _____

4. Board of Directors: [ ] Yes   [ ] No   Date: _____

Part B: Prefunction Planning Details

1. Leadership and Volunteer Committee Status

                                                  Date/Deadline

[ ]   Chairperson or co-chairs recruited and accepted on   _____

[ ]   Leadership orientation conducted on   _____
      by _____

[ ]   Leadership approval of function plan, committees and
      subcommittee structure, and master schedule on   _____

[ ]   Leadership approved master schedule/time line on   _____

[ ]   Committees and subcommittees identified with
      leadership candidates   _____

[ ]   All committee leadership recruited by   _____

[ ]   Leadership orientation conducted on   _____
      by _____

[ ]   Honorary chair/co-chairs identified on   _____

[ ]   Convene first general meeting by   _____

[ ]   General meeting schedule established by   _____

[ ]   Volunteers recruited and appointed to all
      committees and subcommittees on   _____

[ ]   Volunteer orientation conducted on   _____
      by _____

[ ]   Committees and Subcommittees began planning and
      preparations for their duties and responsibilities on   _____

[ ]

2. Program Plan, Agenda, Principal Speakers, and Entertainment

[ ]   Master of ceremonies accepted on   _____

[ ]   Required/courtesy speakers accepted on   _____

[ ]   Date and time confirmed with each speaker on   _____

Date/Deadline

[ ] Speaker biographic data/photos required by   —————

[ ] Main speaker or entertainment confirmed on   —————

   [ ] Speaker references checked on   —————

   [ ] Talent interviewed/auditioned on   —————

   [ ] Recording/taping requirements agreed to on   —————

   [ ] Verified site can provide stage support on   —————

   [ ] Contract negotiated and signed on   —————

   [ ] Advance to be paid on   —————

   [ ] Balance of fee is due on/by   —————

   [ ] Escorts/local transportation resolved by   —————

[ ] Auction/raffle/door prize plan approved on   —————

[ ] Committee for auction/raffle prizes appointed on   —————

[ ] Program or "ad book" decision approved on   —————

[ ] Sales committee leadership appointed on   —————

[ ] Volunteer sales force recruited and trained by   —————

[ ] Other honoraria/travel/accommodations set by   —————

[ ]

3. Mailing Lists and Invitations

   [ ] Mailing lists resolved and total count by   —————

   [ ] Graphics designer/printer selected by   —————

   [ ] Save-the-date notice/card to be mailed by   —————

   [ ] Invitation graphics design package approved by   —————

   [ ] Donors' contribution deduction resolved by   —————

   [ ] Invitation/ticket texts approved by   —————

   [ ] Invitations to be addressed by   —————

   [ ] Invitations to be mailed by   —————

   [ ] Reservation/acknowledgment system ready by   —————

   [ ] Second invitation to be addressed/mailed by   —————

   [ ]

Date/Deadline

4. Facilities

[ ] Location/room inspection conducted on _____

[ ] Parking (access, valet, number of spaces) verified on _____

[ ] Special needs/modifications identified on _____

[ ] Speaker/entertainer audiovisual needs resolved on _____

[ ] Audiovisual requirements resolved on _____

[ ] Notification of authorities completed on _____

[ ] All required permits received on _____

[ ] Medical and security needs resolved on _____

[ ] Concessions and other service needs resolved on _____

[ ] Catering or food service decision on _____

[ ]

5. Food/Beverage Requirements (Reception, Function, Postfunction Party)

[ ] Preliminary budget estimate to determine deduction value and to set ticket prices resolved by _____

[ ] Facility/function seating capacity resolved on _____

[ ] Equipment rentals identified and resolved by _____

[ ] Menu plan complete and tasting performed by _____

[ ] Full beverage plan completed by _____

[ ] Linen, tableware, service resolved by _____

[ ] Budget for decorations approved by _____

[ ] Centerpieces resolved by _____

[ ] Preliminary floor plan approved by _____

[ ] Favors or special gifts approved by _____

[ ]

6. Collateral Printing and Official Program

[ ] Graphics designer and printer resolved by _____

[ ] Sponsor/underwriter materials needed by _____

[ ] Stationery, envelopes needed by _____

Date/Deadline

[ ]   Print advertisements/posters needed by   ———————

[ ]   Advance banners/flags/signs needed by   ———————

[ ]   Official program design approved by   ———————

[ ]   All copy for program text needed by   ———————

[ ]   Program delivery required by (time and date)   ———————

[ ]   Tickets, place cards, drawing tickets due by   ———————

[ ]   On-site banners, signs, posters, displays due by   ———————

[ ]   Badges, identification ribbons due by   ———————

[ ]

7. Advertisement, Promotion, and Publicity

[ ]   News conference decision needed by   ———————

[ ]   Promotion and publicity plan approved by   ———————

[ ]   Press release texts approved by   ———————

[ ]   Media release mailing list completed by   ———————

[ ]   PSA/Advertising materials completed by   ———————

[ ]   Media invitation list completed by   ———————

[ ]   Press kit prepared for advance promotion by   ———————

[ ]   Press kit prepared for function needed by   ———————

[ ]   Press room/equipment/materials resolved by   ———————

[ ]   Photographer(s) and assignments resolved by   ———————

[ ]

8. Support Details at the Function

[ ]   Extra invitations, RSVP forms, tickets due by   ———————

[ ]   Event site ticket sales/will-call desk resolved by   ———————

[ ]   Cash box/credit card machine/receipts needed by   ———————

[ ]   Raffle ticket sales/trained salespersons resolved by   ———————

[ ]   Raffle ticket bin for drawing needed by   ———————

[ ]   Display tables for auction prizes needed by   ———————

[ ]   Ushers, table hosts appointed and trained by   ———————

Date/Deadline

[ ] Reservation lists/table seating charts needed by _____

[ ] Name tags prepared with table numbers needed by _____

[ ] Parking validation stamp/ink pad needed by _____

[ ] Adequate staff and trained volunteers resolved by _____

[ ] Volunteers as official greeters at all doors resolved by _____

[ ] American and state flags visible to all guests due by _____

9. Final Function Checklist: What Not to Forget

[ ] Phone numbers for critical personnel needed by _____

[ ] Extra supply of invitations and programs due by _____

[ ] Copies of all speakers' scripts due by _____

[ ] Adding machine, hand calculator needed by _____

[ ] Supplies (pens, markers, name tags, easels, tape, poster board, etc.) needed by _____

[ ] Informational literature about organization due by _____

[ ] Locations for restrooms and public phones needed by _____

[ ] Appointment of clean-up committee due by _____

[ ] Foul weather and disaster plan resolved by _____

[ ]

10. Critique Meeting and Performance Evaluation

[ ] Invitation lists and performance; analysis

[ ] Advertising and promotion results; analysis

[ ] On-site coverage; press requirements

[ ] Postfunction coverage evaluation

[ ] Sponsor and underwriting sales results; analysis

[ ] Attendance (how many, who, guests' names, seating)

[ ] Table placement, seating plan evaluation

[ ] Program evaluation (speakers/A-V/timing, etc.)

[ ] Facilities and staff evaluation

[ ] Food and beverages evaluation

[ ]   Service and courtesy evaluation

[ ]   Arrival (greeters, ushers, table hosts)

[ ]   Registration table (name tags, guests lists, ticket sales)

[ ]   Parking; access and egress evaluation

[ ]   Print materials, deadlines, and use

[ ]   Collateral materials, deadlines, and use

[ ]   Raffle and auction performance

[ ]   Quality of prizes, awards, auction items

[ ]   Budget review and final approval on all bills

[ ]   Thank-you letters prepared for all volunteers

[ ]   Complete master file of all materials

[ ]   Critique report prepared and delivered to Board

[ ]

Notes

Notes to Chapter One

1. Henry A. Rosso, *Achieving Excellence in Fund Raising* (San Francisco: Jossey-Bass Publishers, Inc., 1991), 4.

2. Robert L. Payton, *Philanthropy: Voluntary Action for the Common Good* (New York: Macmillan Publishing Co., 1988).

3. Brian O'Connell, *America's Voluntary Spirit: A Book of Readings* (New York: The Foundation Center, 1983), xx.

4. Bruce R. Hopkins, *A Legal Guide to Starting and Managing a Nonprofit Organization,* 2nd ed. (New York: John Wiley & Sons, Inc., 1993), 38. Details on formation and operation of nonprofit organizations will be found in this readable text. Complete legal details are contained in Hopkins's basis textbook, *The Law of Tax-Exempt Organizations,* 6th ed. (New York: John Wiley & Sons, Inc., 1993).

5. Hopkins, *A Legal Guide,* 3.

6. John Gardner, as quoted in Hopkins, *A Legal Guide,* 4.

7. Gardner, as quoted in O'Connell, *America's Voluntary Spirit,* xv.

8. John D. Rockefeller 3rd, "America's Threatened Third Sector," *Across the Board,* The Conference Board (March 1978), as reprinted in *Reader's Digest,* (April 1978).

9. Payton, *Philanthropy,* 40.

10. Robert L. Payton, Henry A. Rosso, and Eugene R. Tempel, "Toward a Philosophy of Fund Raising," in *Taking Fund-Raising Seriously,* Dwight F. Burlingame and Lamont J. Hulse, Editors (San Francisco: Jossey-Bass Publishers, Inc., 1991), 11 and 41.

11. Harold J. Seymour, *Designs for Fund Raising: Principles, Patterns, Techniques* (New York: McGraw-Hill, 1966), 43. (A second edition of this exemplary text was reissued in 1988 in paperback by The Fund Raising Institute, Ambler, PA.)

12. "Giving in America: Toward a Stronger Voluntary Sector," Report of the Commission on Private Philanthropy and Public Needs, John H. Filer, Chairman, 1975.

13. Harvey P. Dale, "Tax-Exempt Organizations: Winds of Change," Distinguished Norman A. Sugerman Memorial Lecture sponsored by the Mandel Center for Nonprofit Organizations at Case Western Reserve University, Cleveland, OH, May 20, 1991.

14. *The Chronicle of Philanthropy* (July 17, 1993), 34.

15. Payton, Rosso, and Tempel, "Toward a Philosophy of Fund Raising," 7.

16. Jon van Til & Associates, *Critical Issues in American Philanthropy* (San Francisco: Jossey-Bass Publishers, Inc., 1990), 226–227. Reprinted with permission.

17. Seymour, *Designs for Fund Raising*, 115.

18. Payton, Rosso, and Tempel, "Toward a Philosophy of Fund Raising," 16.

19. Peter F. Drucker, *Managing the Nonprofit Organization: Practices and Principles* (New York: HarperCollins Publishers, 1990), 56.

20. Hopkins, *A Legal Guide*, 102–103.

21. Payton, Rosso, and Tempel, "Toward a Philosophy of Fund Raising," 4.

22. *Id.*, 7.

23. Financial Accounting Standards Board, *Statement of Financial Accounting Standards No. 116: Accounting for Contributions Received and Contributions Made* (Norwalk, CT: FASB, June 1993), 7–8 (pars. 22–26), and 30–38 (interpretations, pars. 87–117).

24. *Id.*, 3 (pars. 9 and 10); 38–40 (pars. 118–124).

25. Thomas E. Broce, *Fund Raising: A Guide to Raising Money from Private Sources*, 2nd ed. (Norman: University of Oklahoma Press, 1986), 17–25.

26. William K. Grasty and Kenneth G. Sheinkopf, *Successful Fund Raising: A Handbook of Proven Strategies and Techniques* (New York: Charles Scribner's Sons, 1983), 61.

Notes to Chapter Two

1. A survey by The Gallup Organization, Inc., commissioned by Independent Sector, reported in 1990 that households gave more if a volunteer was present. See *Giving and Volunteering in the United States* (Washington, DC: Independent Sector, 1990), 38, (Table 1.14). (Hodgkinson, Weitzman, and The Gallup Organization, Inc. Copyright and Published by Independent Sector, Washington, DC, 1990, as cited in *Nonprofit Almanac 1992–1993* (Washington, DC: Independent Sector, 1992), 74, (Table 2.15).)

2. Robert L. Torre and Mary Ann Bendixen, *Direct Mail Fund Raising: Letters That Work* (New York: Plenum Press, 1988), 1.

3. *Id.*, 1–3.

4. Mal Warwick, *You Don't Always Get What You Ask For: Using Direct Mail Tests to Raise More Money for Your Organization* (Berkeley, CA: Strathmoor Press, 1992), 25.

5. Kay Partney Lautman and Henry Goldstein, *Dear Friend: Mastering the Art of Direct Mail Fund Raising*, 2nd ed. (Rockville, MD: Fund Raising Institute, 1991), 292.

6. Warwick, *You Don't Always Get What You Ask For*, 32.

7. David J. Harr, James T. Godfrey, and Robert H. Frank, *Common Costs and Fund-Raising Appeals: A Guide to Joint Cost Allocation in Not-for-Profit Organizations*, (Pittsburgh, PA: Frank & Company, p.c., 1991). This book was published in conjunction with the Nonprofit Mailers Federation.

8. Lautman and Goldstein, *Dear Friend*, 288.

9. Arthur Franzreb, personal communication.

10. Jerry Huntsinger, *Fund Raising Letters: A Comprehensive Study Guide to Raising Money by Direct Response Marketing*, 3rd. ed. (Richmond, VA: Emerson Publishers, 1989).

11. See note 5.

12. Huntsinger, *Fund Raising Letters*, 11.

13. Lautman and Goldstein, *Dear Friend*, 10.

14. *Id.*, 141–171.

15. *Id.*, 10–11.

16. Huntsinger, *Fund Raising Letters*, 23-3–23-5.

17. *Id.*, 23-11.

18. The Campaign to Clean Up America was invented by Bruce R. Hopkins to illustrate principles contained in his text, *A Legal Guide to Starting and Managing a Nonprofit Organization*, 2nd ed. (New York: John Wiley & Sons, 1993). Permission to link the examples in this book to his fictional organization is greatly appreciated.

Notes to Chapter Three

1. Edith H. Falk, "The All-Important Annual Campaign," in *Getting Started: A Guide to Fund Raising Fundamentals* (Chicago: The National Society of Fund Raising Executives, Chicago Chapter, 1988), 45–46.

2. Kay Partney Lautman and Henry Goldstein, *Dear Friend: Mastering the Art of Direct Mail Fund Raising*, 2nd ed. (Rockville, MD: Fund Raising Institute, 1991), 5–7.

3. Thomas E. Broce, *Fund Raising: A Guide to Raising Money from Private Sources*, 2nd ed. (Norman: University of Oklahoma Press, 1986), 86–88.

4. Roger M. Craver, "The Power of Mail to Acquire, Renew, and Upgrade the Gift," in Henry A. Rosso and Associates, *Achieving Excellence in Fund Raising* (San Francisco: Jossey-Bass Publishers, 1991), 65.

5. William K. Grasty and Kenneth G. Sheinkopf, *Successful Fundraising: A Handbook of Proven Strategies and Techniques* (New York: Charles Scribner's Sons, 1982), 130–133.

6. Robert L. Torre and Mary Anne Bendixen, *Direct Mail Fund Raising: Letters That Work*, 2nd ed. (New York: Plenum Press, 1990), 267.

7. Lautman and Goldstein, *Dear Friend*, 3–4.

8. Jerry Huntsinger, *Fund Raising Letters: A Comprehensive Study Guide to Raising Money by Direct Response Marketing*, 3rd ed. (Richmond, VA: Emerson Publishers, 1989), 47-9.

9. *Id.*, 35-1.

10. Mary Lou Roberts and Paul D. Berger, *Direct Marketing Management* (Englewood Cliffs, NJ: Prentice-Hall, Inc., 1989), 2.

Note to Chapter Four

1. William K. Grasty and Kenneth G. Sheinkopf, *Successful Fundraising: A Handbook of Proven Strategies and Techniques* (New York: Charles Scribner's Sons, 1982), 48–49.

Notes to Chapter Five

1. Constance Clark, "Membership Development," in Tracy Daniel Connors, Editor, *Nonprofit Management Handbook: Operating Policies and Procedures* (New York: John Wiley & Sons, Inc., 1993), 486.

2. Bruce R. Hopkins, *A Legal Guide to Starting and Managing a Nonprofit Organization*, 2nd ed. (New York: John Wiley & Sons, Inc., 1993), 37–38.

3. *Id.*, ix.

4. Cliff Underwood, "Building Donor Relationships Strengthens Zoo's Membership," *Fund Raising Management* (January 1984), 36.

5. Clark, "Membership Development," 489.

6. NSFRE membership invitation details are provided courtesy of the National Society of Fund Raising Executives. For full information, write to NSFRE at 1101 King Street, Suite 700, Alexandria, VA 22314, or call (703) 684-0410 during normal business hours.

7. James A. Brandt, "Five Rules for Getting Started on a Membership-Development Campaign," *Non-Profit Times* (March 1991), 23.

8. Patricia Gaby and Daniel Gaby, *Nonprofit Organization Handbook* (Englewood Cliffs, NJ: Prentice-Hall, 1979), 53.

9. Richard P. Trenbeth, *The Membership Mystique: How to Create Income and Influence with Membership Programs*, (Rockville, MD: Fund Raising Institute, The Taft Group, 1986), 200.

10. *Id.*, 264.

11. Gaby and Gaby, *Nonprofit Organization Handbook*, 34.

12. *Id.*, 55.

13. Arch McGhee, "Why Members Volunteer. . . . and . . . Work Harder," *Association Management* (August 1971), 85, as quoted in Tracy Daniel Connors, Editor, *The Nonprofit Management Handbook*, 2nd ed. (New York: McGraw-Hill, 1988), 21.4.

14. Tracy Daniel Connors, "Membership," in Tracy Daniel Connors, Editor, *The Nonprofit Management Handbook*, 2nd ed. (New York: McGraw-Hill, 1988), 21.9–21.11.

15. Gaby and Gaby, *Nonprofit Organization Handbook*, 35.

16. *Id.*, 38–39.

17. *Id.*, 44–45.

18. Mike Mueller, as quoted in Sean Mehegan, "Keeping Members: The New Priority," *Nonprofit Times Special Report* (April 1993), 21.

19. Mehegan, "Keeping Members," 21.

20. Maurice Gurin, *What Volunteers Should Know for Successful Fund Raising* (New York: Stein & Day, 1981), 71.

21. Joan Jeffri, *Arts Money* (Minneapolis: University of Minnesota Press, 1983), 187.

22. Trenbeth, *The Membership Mystique*, 268–278.

Notes to Chapter Six

1. Marlene Cassini, "The Craig Hospital Auxiliary—Making a Personal Difference in the Lives of the Disabled," article in brochure produced by Craig Hospital, Englewood, Colorado, 1989.

2. James M. Greenfield, *Fund-Raising: Evaluating and Managing the Fund Development Process* (New York: John Wiley & Sons, Inc., 1991), 83.

3. Thomas E. Broce, *Fund Raising: A Guide to Raising Money from Private Sources*, 2nd ed. (Norman: University of Oklahoma Press, 1986), 92.

4. *Id.*, 91.

5. William K. Grasty and Kenneth G. Sheinkopf, *Successful Fundraising: A Handbook of Proven Strategies and Techniques* (New York: Charles Scribner's Sons, 1982), 76–77.

6. *Id.*, 76.

7. Harold J. Seymour, *Designs for Fund-Raising: Principles, Patterns and Techniques*, 2nd ed. (Ambler, PA: Fund-Raising Institute, 1988), 145.

8. Greenfield, *Fund-Raising*, 207.

9. *Id.*, 206–210.

10. Internal Revenue Service, *Deductibility of Payments Made to Charities Conducting Fund-Raising Events*, Revenue Ruling 67-246 (June 1988), Publication 1392.

Notes to Chapter Seven

1. Virginia A. Hodgkinson and Murray S. Weitzman, *Giving and Volunteering in the United States: Findings from a National Survey* (Washington, D.C.: Independent Sector, 1992), 2. (See also pp. 21–33 for complete details on volunteerism and charitable giving statistics.)

2. Sara H. Skolnick, "Special Appeals," in Tracy Daniel Connors, Editor, *The Nonprofit Management Handbook: Operating Policies and Procedures* (New York: John Wiley & Sons, Inc., 1993), 590.

3. William K. Grasty and Kenneth G. Sheinkopf, *Successful Fund Raising: A Handbook of Proven Strategies and Techniques* (New York: Charles Scribner's Sons, 1983), 165.

4. Marilyn E. Brentlinger and Judith M. Weiss, *The Ultimate Benefit Book: How to Raise $50,000-Plus for Your Organization* (Cleveland, OH: Octavia Press, 1987), 20.

5. Grasty and Sheinkopf, *Successful Fund Raising*, 160.

6. Lee Katz, "Vital Ways and Means in Planning a Major Benefit," *Fund Raising Management* (December 1988), 52.

7. Ralph Brody and Marcie Goodman, *Fund-Raising Events: Strategies and Programs for Success* (New York: Human Sciences Press, Inc., 1988), 64.

8. Internal Revenue Service, *Deductibility of Payments Made to Charities Conducting Fund-Raising Events*, Revenue Ruling 67-246 (June 1988), Publication 1392.

9. Office of the Attorney General of Connecticut, special report, as reprinted in *The Chronicle of Philanthropy* (May 2, 1989), 25.

10. Philanthropic Advisory Service, Council of Better Business Bureaus, New York, 1982, as reported in *The Chronicle of Philanthropy* (June 1, 1993), 29.

11. For additional information on cause-related marketing and commercial sales, see James M. Greenfield, *Fund-Raising: Evaluating and Managing the Fund Development Process* (New York: John Wiley & Sons, Inc., 1991), 142–146, 212, 237–239.

12. *Id.*, 79.

13. Grasty and Sheinkopf, *Successful Fund Raising*, 163.

Notes to Chapter Eight

1. James M. Greenfield, *Fund-Raising: Evaluating and Managing the Fund Development Process* (New York: John Wiley & Sons, Inc., 1991), 85.

2. Thomas E. Broce, *Fund Raising: The Guide to Raising Money from Private Sources*, 2nd ed. (Norman: University of Oklahoma Press, 1986), 87.

3. Irving R. Warner, *The Art of Fund Raising* (New York: Harper & Row, 1975), 24–25. For additional leadership characteristics, see Sara H. Skolnick, "Special Appeals," in Tracy Daniel Connors, Editor, *The Nonprofit Management Handbook: Operating Policies and Procedures* (New York: John Wiley & Sons, Inc., 1993), 590

4. Broce, *Fund Raising*, 86.

5. Greenfield, *Fund-Raising*, 231–236 (Policy on Honors and Recognition).

Notes to Chapter Nine

1. James M. Greenfield, *Fund-Raising: Evaluating and Managing the Fund Development Process* (New York: John Wiley & Sons, Inc., 1991), 231–236 (Appendix A, "Policy on Honors and Recognition"). See also James M. Greenfield, "Fund-Raising Overview," in Tracy Daniel Connors, Editor, *Nonprofit Management Handbook: Operating Policies and Procedures* (New York: John Wiley & Sons, Inc., 1993), 460–462.

2. Bruce R. Hopkins, *The Law of Fund-Raising* (New York: John Wiley & Sons, Inc., 1991), 414.

3. Bruce R. Hopkins, *A Legal Guide to Starting and Managing a Nonprofit Organization*, 2nd ed. (New York: John Wiley & Sons, Inc., 1993), 282.

4. *Id.*, 284.

5. *United States v. American Bar Endowment*, 106. S. Ct. 2426 (1986), as quoted in Hopkins, *The Law of Fund-Raising*, 414.

6. This debate has proponents too; see Jay L. Vestal, "Hitch Your Wagon: Cause-Related Marketing Works," *NAHD Journal* (Spring 1986), 35–38. The author's opposition can be found in Greenfield, *Fund-Raising*, 142–146, 212, 237–239.

7. Greg Gattuso, "Charity Gambling on the Way Out?" *Fund-Raising Management* (May 1993), 8.

8. Stephen G. Greene and Grant Williams, "Charities' Big Gamble," *The Chronicle of Philanthropy* (May 18, 1993), 27.

9. Hopkins, *The Law of Fund-Raising*, 402.

10. Greenfield, *Fund-Raising*, 98.

11. Greene and Williams, "Charities' Big Gamble," 28.

12. Robert L. Krit, "Sweepstakes—A Benefit for Whom?" *Fund-Raising Management* (August 1991), 35. See also Carol M. Gibbons, "The Sweepstakes Appeal: Friend or Foe?," *Fund-Raising Management* (July 1988), 48–49.

13. For additional discussion on multimedia options, see Greenfield, *Fund-Raising*, 70–73.

14. John R. Groman, "Fund-Raising in the 90's: Five Key Changes to Make or Break Success," address to Breakfast Plenary Session, NSFRE Orange County Chapter Conference, Anaheim, CA, October 16, 1989.

15. Max L. Hart, "How Premiums Can Help Your Organization," *Fund-Raising Management* (July 1988), 32–38.

16. Diane Carlson, "A Partnership for the 1990s," *NAHD Journal* (Fall 1988), 17–22.

17. Robert Abrams, as quoted in *Fund Raising Management* (May 1991), 10. This same issue carried two additional articles on telephone use: Curt Herwers, "Getting Pledges by Phone," 28, and Hayes Fletcher, "Telephone Etiquette for the Development Office," 40.

18. Harvey P. Dale, "Tax-Exempt Organizations: Winds of Change," Distinguished Norman A. Sugerman Memorial Lecture sponsored by the Mandel

Center for Nonprofit Organizations at Case Western Reserve University, Cleveland, OH, May 20, 1991.

19. David E. Ormstedt, "Government Regulation of Fund Raising: A Struggle for Efficacy," in James M. Greenfield, Editor, *Financial Practices for Effective Fund Raising* (San Francisco: Jossey-Bass, Inc., in press).

20. *Id.*

21. Errol Copilevitz, "Avoiding Fund-Raising Traps," *Fund Raising Management* (June 1993), 39.

22. Bruce R. Hopkins, "Charitable Solicitation Acts and Fund Raising: Part Two," *Fund Raising Management* (September 1990), 70.

23. For a detailed account of the documents and court proceedings in the James Bakker trial, see Gary Tidwell, *Anatomy of a Fraud: Inside the Finances of the PTL Ministries* (New York: John Wiley & Sons, Inc., 1993). For the bonuses paid, see this source's Exhibit 5.2.

Notes to Chapter Ten

1. Robert L. Payton, *Philanthropy: Voluntary Action for the Public Good* (New York: Macmillan Publishing Co., 1988).

2. Alexis de Tocqueville, "Democracy in America," in Brian O'Connell, Editor, *America's Voluntary Spirit: A Book of Readings* (New York: The Foundation Center, 1983), 54.

3. Fisher Howe, *The Board Member's Guide to Fund Raising* (San Francisco: Jossey-Bass, Inc., 1991), 27.

4. Thomas E. Broce, *Fund Raising: The Guide to Raising Money from Private Sources*, 2nd. ed. (Norman: University of Oklahoma Press, 1986), 96.

5. James M. Greenfield, *Fund-Raising: Evaluating and Managing the Fund Development Process* (New York: John Wiley & Sons, Inc., 1991), 193.

6. In June 1993, the Financial Accounting Standards Board (FASB) released two new statements that address these concerns: Statement of Financial Accounting Standards No. 116, *Accounting for Contributions Received and Contributions Made,* and Statement of Financial Accounting Standards No. 117, *Financial Statements of Not-for-Profit Organizations* (Norwalk, CT: Financial Accounting Standards Board, 1993).

7. There are only limited cost guidelines based on empirical research. Generally accepted performance standards allow a range of 20 to 25 percent as the "bottom line" cost–benefit ratio for broad-based and mature fund development programs (three years' continuous experience) and up to 35 to 50 percent for annual giving programs collectively. America's colleges and universities reported (*Chronicle of Philanthropy*, September 4, 1990) a 16 percent cost–effectiveness ratio (a 525 percent return on investment), while hospital studies revealed a 12 percent performance factor in the same year. For details on how these data were developed, see Council for the Advancement and Support of Education, *Expenditures in Fund Raising,*

Alumni Relations, and Other Constituent (Public) Relations, (1990), and Association for Healthcare Philanthropy, *USA Report on Giving, FY 1990.*

8. A sample policy on donor recognition is found in Greenfield, *Fund-Raising,* 227–230.

9. Financial Accounting Standards Board, *op. cit.*

10. Grant Williams, "Sweeping Changes in Accounting Rules," *The Chronicle of Philanthropy* (June 29, 1993), 31–36. See also Bruce Miller, "Charity Officials Say Proposed Accounting Rules Don't Add Up," *The Chronicle of Philanthropy* (May 21, 1993), 32.

11. For additional details on the legal standards involved in being legally nonprofit, see Bruce R. Hopkins, *A Legal Guide to Starting and Managing a Nonprofit Organization,* 2nd ed. (New York: John Wiley & Sons, Inc., 1993), 37–67.

12. *Country Board of Equalization of Utah County v. Intermountain Health Care, Inc.,* 709 P.2d 265 (Sup. Ct. Utah 1985). See also Kristin A. Goss and Grant Williams, "Will Charities Have to Prove They are Charitable?", *The Chronicle of Philanthropy* (May 21, 1991), 1, 34–35.

13. The text of the standards and guidelines adopted by InterAction may be requested from any international relief organization. A copy appeared in *The Chronicle of Philanthropy* (May 21, 1991), 30.

14. Errol Copilevitz, "Avoiding Fund-Raising Traps," *Fund Raising Management* (June 1993), 36–39.

15. Michael Josephson, "Major Donors: Ethical Issues and Solutions. Principled and Practical Decision Making in the Trenches," presentation at NSFRE International Conference, March 15, 1988, Nashville, TN.

16. Grant Williams, "IRS to Step Up Its Scrutiny of Non-Profit Groups; Unrelated Business Activities Are a Key Target," *The Chronicle of Philanthropy* (May 21, 1991), 29.

17. Stephen G. Greene and Jennifer Moore, "Interest Still High in Charity Salaries," *The Chronicle of Philanthropy* (April 6, 1993), 1.

18. The thesis for compensation by salary and fee only is presented in James M. Greenfield, "Professional Compensation," *NSFRE Journal* (Spring 1990), 35–39.

19. Bruce Miller, "When Donor Records Are No Longer Private," *The Chronicle of Philanthropy* (July 27, 1993), 23.

20. Joseph R. Mixer, *Principles of Professional Fundraising* (San Francisco: Jossey-Bass Publishers, Inc., 1993), 249.

21. Harvey P. Dale, "Tax-Exempt Organizations: Winds of Change," Distinguished Normal A. Sugerman Memorial Lecture, Mandel Center for Nonprofit Organizations at Case Western Reserve University, Cleveland, Ohio, May 20, 1991.

22. Ellen Earle Chaffee and Lawrence A. Sherr, "Total Quality Management," in Tracy Daniel Connors, Editor, *The Nonprofit Management Handbook: Operating Policies and Procedures* (New York: John Wiley & Sons, Inc., 1993), 4.

23. Diane S. Cox, "TQM: A Primer," *AHP Journal* (Spring 1993), 21–24.

Selected References

Philanthropic Concepts

*Brakeley, George A., Jr. *Tested Ways to Successful Fund Raising.* New York: AMACOM, 1980.

Bremner, Robert H. *American Philanthropy,* 2nd ed. Chicago: The University of Chicago Press, 1988.

Burlingame, Dwight F., ed. *The Responsibilities of Wealth.* Bloomington: Indiana University Press, 1992.

Cutlip, Scott M. *Fund-Raising in the United States: Its Role in American Philanthropy.* New Brunswick, NJ: Rutgers University Press, 1990 (reprint of a 1965 work).

Hodgkinson, Virginia A. and Associates. *The Nonprofit Almanac 1992–1993: Dimensions of the Independent Sector.* Washington, DC: Independent Sector, 1992.

Hodgkinson, Virginia A., and Murray S. Weitzman. *Giving and Volunteering in the United States: Findings from a National Survey.* Washington, DC: Independent Sector, 1992.

*Hodgkinson, Virginia A., and Richard W. Lyman and Associates. *The Future of the Nonprofit Sector: Challenges, Changes and Policy Considerations.* San Francisco: Jossey-Bass Publishers, Inc., 1989.

Howe, Fisher. *The Board Member's Guide to Fund Raising.* San Francisco: Jossey-Bass Publishers, Inc., 1991.

Joseph, James A. *The Charitable Impulse.* New York: The Foundation Center, 1989.

Magat, Richard A. *Philanthropic Giving.* New York: Oxford University Press, 1989.

Marts, Armaud C. *Philanthropy's Role in Civilization: Its Contributions to Human Freedom.* New Brunswick, NJ: Transaction, 1991 (reprint of a 1953 work).

Nichols, Judith. *Changing Demographics: Fundraising in the 1990s.* Chicago: Precept Press, 1990.

*O'Connell, Brian. *American's Voluntary Spirit: A Book of Readings.* New York: The Foundation Center, 1983.

*————.*Philanthropy in Action.* Washington, DC: Independent Sector, 1987.

* The Heritage Collection of the National Society of Fund Raising Executives (NSFRE) Library.

*O'Neill, Michael. *The Third America: The Emergence of the Nonprofit Sector in the United States.* San Francisco: Jossey-Bass Publishers, Inc., 1989.

Payton, Robert L. *Philanthropy: Voluntary Action for the Public Good.* New York: Macmillan Publishing Company, 1988.

Salamon, Lester M. *America's Nonprofit Sector: A Primer.* New York: The Foundation Center, 1992.

Van Til, Jon, and Associates. *Critical Issues in American Philanthropy.* San Francisco: Jossey-Bass Publishers, Inc., 1990.

Annual Giving: General

*Broce, Thomas E. *Fund Raising: The Guide to Raising Money from Private Sources,* 2nd ed. Norman: University of Oklahoma Press, 1986.

Burlingame, Dwight F., and Lamont J. Hulse, eds. *Taking Fund Raising Seriously.* San Francisco: Jossey-Bass Publishers, Inc., 1991.

*Flanagan, Joan. *The Grass Roots Fundraising Book.* Chicago: Contemporary Books, Inc., 1982.

Glossary of Fund Raising Terms. Alexandria, VA: National Society of Fund Raising Executives, 1986.

*Grasty, William K., and Kenneth G. Sheinkopf. *Successful Fund Raising: A Handbook of Proven Strategies and Techniques.* New York: Charles Scribner's Sons, 1983.

*Gurin, Maurice G. *Confessions of a Fund Raiser: Lessons of an Instructive Career.* Washington, DC: The Taft Corporation, 1985.

Lord, James Gregory. *The Raising of Money.* Cleveland, OH: Third Sector Press, 1987.

*Rosso, Henry A., and Associates. *Achieving Excellence in Fund Raising.* San Francisco: Jossey-Bass Publishers, Inc., 1991.

Rowland, A. Westley. *Handbook of Institutional Advancement,* 2nd ed. San Francisco: Jossey-Bass Publishers, Inc., 1986.

Seltzer, Michael. *Securing Your Organization's Future: A Complete Guide to Fundraising Strategies.* New York: The Foundation Center, 1987.

*Seymour, Harold J. "Designs for Fund-Raising." New York: McGraw-Hill, 1966. (Paperback edition: Ambler, PA: The Fund Raising Institute, 1988.)

Taylor, Bernard P. *Guide to Successful Fund Raising for Authentic Charitable Purposes.* South Plainfield, NJ: Groupwork Today, Inc., 1976.

*Warner, Irving R. *The Art of Fund Raising.* New York: Harper & Row, 1975.

Williams, M. Jane. *The FRI Annual Giving Book.* Rockville, MD: Fund Raising Institute (a division of The Taft Group), 1981.

Direct Mail

Bendixen, Mary Anne, and Robert L. Torre. *Direct Mail Fund Raising: Letters That Work.* New York: Plenum Press, 1988.

*Huntsinger, Jerry. *Fund Raising Letters: A Comprehensive Study Guide to Raising Money by Direct Response Marketing.* Richmond, VA: Emerson Publishers, 1985.

*Lautman, Kay, and Henry Goldstein. *Dear Friend: Mastering the Art of Direct Mail Fund Raising,* 2nd ed. Englewood Cliffs, NJ: Prentice-Hall, Inc., 1991.

Roberts, Mary Lou, and Paul D. Berger. *Direct Marketing Management.* Englewood Cliffs, NJ: Prentice-Hall, Inc., 1989.

*Warwick, Mal. *Revolution in the Mailbox.* Rockville, MD: Fund Raising Institute (a division of The Taft Group), 1990.

———. *You Don't Always Get What You Ask For: Using Direct Mail Tests to Raise More Money for Your Organization.* Berkeley, CA: Strathmoor Press, 1992.

Membership Associations

Gaby, Patricia, and Daniel Gaby. *Nonprofit Organization Handbook.* Englewood Cliffs, NJ: Prentice-Hall, Inc., 1979.

Trenbeth, Richard P. *The Membership Mystique.* Ambler, PA: Fund Raising Institute (a division of The Taft Group), 1986.

Activities, Benefits, and Special Events

Brentlinger, Marilyn E. *The Ultimate Benefit Book: How to Raise $50,000-Plus for Your Organization.* Cleveland, OH: Octavia, 1987.

Brody, Ralph, and Marcie Goodman. *Fund-Raising Events.* New York: Human Sciences Press, Inc., 1988.

Freedman, Harry A., and Karen F. Smith. *Black Tie Optional: The Ultimate Guide to Planning and Producing Successful Special Events.* Rockville, MD: Fund Raising Institute (a division of The Taft Group), 1991.

Harris, April L. *Raising Money and Cultivating Donors through Special Events.* Washington, DC: Council for Advancement and Support of Education, 1991.

*Whitcomb, Nick B. *Money-Makers, A Systematic Approach to Special Events Fund Raising.* Charles E. Alberti, George E. Macko, and Mike B. Whitcomb, 1983.

Volunteer-Led Personal Solicitation

*Gurin, Maurice G. *What Volunteers Should Know for Successful Fund Raising.* New York: Stein & Day, 1981.

Other Ways to Raise Money Each Year

*Balthaser, William F. *Call for Help: How to Raise Philanthropic Funds with Phonothons.* Rockville, MD: Fund Raising Institute (a division of The Taft Group), 1983.

Blimes, Michael E., and Ron Sproat. *More Dialing, More Dollars.* New York: American Council for the Arts, 1985.

Schultz, Louis A. *Telepledge: The Complete Guide to Mail-Phone Fund Raising.* Rockville, MD: Fund Raising Institute (a division of The Taft Group), 1987.

Management of Annual Giving Programs

Accounting and Financial Reporting: A Guide for United Ways and Not-for-Profit Human-Service Organizations, rev. 2nd ed. Alexandria, VA: United Way of America, 1989.

*Arthur Andersen & Company. *Tax Economics of Charitable Giving*, 11th ed. Chicago: 1991.

*Barendt, Robert, and J. Richard Taft. *How to Rate Your Development Department*. Washington, DC: The Taft Group, 1984.

Connors, Tracy Daniel. *Nonprofit Organization Management: Policies and Procedures*. New York: John Wiley & Sons, Inc., 1993.

*Dannelley, Paul. *Fund Raising and Public Relations: A Critical Guide to Literature and Resources*. Norman: University of Oklahoma Press, 1986.

Giving USA: The Annual Report of Philanthropy. New York: American Association of Fund Raising Counsel, Trust for Philanthropy (an annual publication).

*Greenfield, James M. *Fund-Raising: Evaluating and Managing the Fund Development Process*. New York: John Wiley & Sons, Inc., 1991.

*Gross, Malvern J., William Warshauer, and Richard F. Larkin. *Financial and Accounting Guide for Not-for-Profit Organizations*, 4th ed. New York: John Wiley & Sons, Inc., 1991.

*Hopkins, Bruce R. *The Law of Charitable Giving*. New York: John Wiley & Sons, Inc., 1993.

———. *The Law of Fund Raising*. New York: John Wiley & Sons, Inc., 1991.

———. *The Law of Tax-Exempt Organizations*, 6th ed. New York: John Wiley & Sons, Inc., 1991.

———. *A Legal Guide to Starting and Managing a Nonprofit Organization*, 2nd ed. New York: John Wiley & Sons, Inc., 1993.

*Jenkins, Jeanne B., and Marilyn Lucas. *How to Find Philanthropic Prospects*. Ambler, PA: The Fund Raising Institute, 1986.

*Kotler, Philip, and Alan R. Andreasen. *Strategic Marketing for Nonprofit Organizations*, 3rd ed. Englewood Cliffs, NJ: Prentice-Hall, Inc., 1987.

Lindahl, Wesley E. *Strategic Planning for Fund Raising*. San Francisco: Jossey-Bass Publishers, Inc., 1992.

Murray, Dennis J. *The Guaranteed Fund-Raising System: A Systems Approach to Planning and Controlling Fund Raising*. Boston: American Institute of Management, 1987.

New, Anne L., and Wilson C. Levis. *Raise More Money for Your Nonprofit Organization: A Guide to Evaluating and Improving Your Fundraising*. New York: The Foundation Center, 1991.

*Schneiter, Paul H. *The Art of Asking: A Handbook for Successful Fund Raising*. New York: Walker and Company, 1978.

Index

403